ENCOUNTERS WITH
BIBLICAL THEOLOGY

ENCOUNTERS WITH
BIBLICAL THEOLOGY

John J. Collins

FORTRESS PRESS

MINNEAPOLIS

ENCOUNTERS WITH BIBLICAL THEOLOGY

Pages 231–32 serve as an extension of this page, containing acknowledgments to prior publishers of various articles contained in this book.

Cover image: "The Dream of Nebuchadnezzar: The Tree." Mozarabic Bible, folio 319. © Bridgeman-Giraudon / Art Resource, NY.
Cover and book design: James Korsmo

ISBN 0-8006-3780-1 (hc)
      0-8006-3769-0 (pb)

The paper used in this publication meets the minimum requirements of American National Standard for Information Sciences — Permanence of Paper for Printed Library Materials, ANSI Z329.48-1984.

Manufactured in the U.S.A.

09   08   07   06   05   1   2   3   4   5   6   7   8   9   10

CONTENTS

Abbreviations   vii

Introduction   1

PART ONE **THEORETICAL ISSUES**

1. Is a Critical Biblical Theology Possible?   11

2. Biblical Theology and the History of Israelite Religion   24

3. The Politics of Biblical Interpretation   34

PART TWO **TOPICS IN THE PENTATEUCH**

4. Faith without Works: Biblical Ethics and the Sacrifice of Isaac   47

5. The Development of the Exodus Tradition   59

6. The Exodus and Biblical Theology   67

7. The Biblical Vision of the Common Good   78

PART THREE **WISDOM AND BIBLICAL THEOLOGY**

8. The Biblical Precedent for Natural Theology   91

9. Proverbial Wisdom and the Yahwist Vision   105

10. Natural Theology and Biblical Tradition: The Case
    of Hellenistic Judaism   117

PART FOUR **APOCALYPTIC LITERATURE**

11. Temporality and Politics in Jewish Apocalyptic Literature   129

12. The Book of Truth: Daniel as Reliable Witness
    to Past and Future in the United States of America   142

13. The Legacy of Apocalypticism   155

PART FIVE CHRISTIAN ADAPTATIONS OF JEWISH
         TRADITIONS

14. Jesus and the Messiahs of Israel   169

15. Jewish Monotheism and Christian Theology   179

Notes   191

Acknowledgments   231

Index of Modern Authors   233

Index of Ancient Literature   238

ABBREVIATIONS

ANCIENT SOURCES

Ant.	*Jewish Antiquities* (Josephus)
b.	Babylonian Talmud
B. Bat.	*Baba Batra*
Bib. Ant.	*Liber antiquitatum biblicarum*
CD	Cairo Genizah copy of the *Damascus Document*
Decal.	*De decalogo* (Philo)
Gen. Rab.	*Genesis Rabbah*
J.W.	*Jewish War* (Josephus)
Mos.	*De vita Mosis* (Philo)
Opif.	*De opificio mundi* (Philo)
Q	Qumran, preceded by the number of the cave of discovery and followed by short title or ms. number
Qu. In Exod.	*Quaestiones et solutiones in Exodum* (Philo)
Qu. In Gen.	*Quaestiones et solutiones in Genesin* (Philo)
Sanh.	*Sanhedrin*
Sib. Or.	*Sibylline Oracles*
Spec.	*De specialibus legibus* (Philo)
y.	Jerusalem Talmud

MODERN SOURCES

AB	Anchor Bible
ABD	*Anchor Bible Dictionary*
AJA	*American Journal of Archaeology*
AnBib	Analecta biblica
ANET	*Ancient Near Eastern Texts Relating to the Old Testament*
ANRW	*Aufstieg und Niedergang der römischen Welt: Geschichte und Kultur Roms im Spiegel der neueren Forschung*
BA	*Biblical Archaeologist*
BAR	*Biblical Archaeology Review*
BBB	Bonner biblische Beiträge
BETL	Bibliotheca ephemeridum theologicarum lovaniensium
BHT	Beiträge zur historischen Theologie
Bib	*Biblica*
BibS(N)	Biblische Studien (Neukirchen, 1951–)
BJS	Brown Judaic Studies
BTB	*Biblical Theology Bulletin*
BZ	*Biblische Zeitschrift*
BZAW	Beihefte zur Zeitschrift für die alttestamentliche Wissenschaft

CBQ	*Catholic Biblical Quarterly*
CBQMS	Catholic Biblical Quarterly Monograph Series
CH	*Church History*
ChrCent	*Christian Century*
CP	*Classical Philology*
CRBR	*Critical Review of Books in Religion*
DJD	Discoveries in the Judaean Desert
DSD	*Dead Sea Discoveries*
EBib	*Etudes bibliques*
ErIsr	*Eretz-Israel*
EvT	*Evangelische Theologie*
ExAud	*Ex auditu*
FOTL	Forms of the Old Testament Literature
HBT	*Horizons in Biblical Theology*
HR	*History of Religions*
HTR	*Harvard Theological Review*
HTS	Harvard Theological Studies
ICC	International Critical Commentary
IDB	*The Interpreter's Dictionary of the Bible*
Int	*Interpretation*
JAAR	*Journal of the American Academy of Religion*
JAARSup	Journal of the American Academy of Religion Supplement Series
JANES	*Journal of the Ancient Near Eastern Society*
JAOS	*Journal of the American Oriental Society*
JBL	*Journal of Biblical Literature*
JJS	*Journal of Jewish Studies*
JNES	*Journal of Near Eastern Studies*
JR	*Journal of Religion*
JSJSup	Journal for the Study of Judaism in the Persian, Hellenistic, and Roman Periods: Supplement Series
JSOT	*Journal for the Study of the Old Testament*
JSOTSup	Journal for the Study of the Old Testament: Supplement Series
JSPSup	Journal for the Study of the Pseudepigrapha: Supplement Series
LCL	Loeb Classical Library
NIB	*The New Interpreter's Bible*
NovT	*Novum Testamentum*
NovTSup	Supplements to *Novum Testamentum*
NT	New Testament
NTS	*New Testament Studies*
OT	Old Testament
PTMS	Pittsburgh Theological Monograph Series
RB	*Revue biblique*
REA	*Revue des études anciennes*
RevQ	*Revue de Qumran*

RelSRev	*Religious Studies Review*
SAK	*Studien zur Altägyptischen Kultur*
SBL	Society of Biblical Literature
SBLMS	Society of Biblical Literature Monograph Series
SBLSymS	Society of Biblical Literature Symposium Series
SBS	Stuttgarter Bibelstudien
SBT	Studies in Biblical Theology
SHANE	Studies in the History of the Ancient Near East
SJOT	*Scandinavian Journal of the Old Testament*
SJT	*Scottish Journal of Theology*
SPB	*Studie Post-Biblica*
SPhilo	*Studia philonica*
STAR	Studies in Theology and Religion
SVF	*Stoicorum veterum fragmenta*
TSAJ	Text und Studien zum antiken Judentum
TDNT	*Theological Dictionary of the New Testament*
TDOT	*Theological Dictionary of the Old Testament*
TD	*Theology Digest*
TS	*Theological Studies*
UF	*Ugarit-Forschungen*
VT	*Vetus Testamentum*
VTSup	Supplements to *Vetus Testamentum*
WBC	Word Biblical Commentary
WMANT	Wissenschaftliche Monographien zum Alten und Neuen Testament
WO	*Die Welt des Orients*
ZAW	*Zeitschrift für die alttestamentliche Wissenschaft*
ZBAT	Zürcher Bibelkommentare. Altes Testament
ZTK	*Zeitschrift für Theologie und Kirche*

INTRODUCTION

The essays collected in this volume were published over three decades. Approximately one third of them appeared in the last five years. Another third dates from the 1990s and one third from the 1980s. (Chapter 8, "The Biblical Precedent for Natural Theology," appeared in 1977.) All represent encounters with biblical theology, but the encounters are of different kinds. A few address theoretical issues. Some deal with historical issues that have important implications for biblical theology (the development of the Exodus tradition, the relation of Jesus to Jewish messianic expectation). Several of the essays are descriptive accounts of the theology of segments of the biblical tradition (wisdom, the apocalyptic literature). A few raise critical questions about the implications of biblical texts for the modern world, especially in the area of ethics (see especially chapter 4 on the sacrifice of Isaac and chapter 13 on the legacy of apocalypticism). Taken together, they have the character of probes and soundings. They are in no way comprehensive or systematic and do not reflect all the topics that I would regard as important for biblical theology. (The most obvious lacuna is in the area of the prophetic corpus.)

The essays are reproduced here as originally printed. In some cases, important treatments of the topics have appeared in the interim. (This is especially true in the case of the older essays on the wisdom literature).[1] I do not believe that the content of the essays has been rendered obsolete, but I would like to put the more theoretical discussion of biblical theology, especially as formulated in the first essay, in the context of the ongoing discussion.

What these essays have in common is the attempt to address biblical theology consistently from the perspective of historical criticism, broadly conceived. On the one hand, they reject a view of historical criticism, and of biblical scholarship in general, that brackets out all questions of the significance of the text for the modern

1

world. On the other hand, they also reject a view of biblical theology as a confessional enterprise, exempt from the demands of argumentation that characterize the discipline as a whole. The project is complicated, however, by the fact that both historical criticism and biblical theology are contested concepts that are understood by different people in different ways, and that are all too frequently subjected to polemical distortion.

HISTORICAL CRITICISM

By historical criticism I mean any method or approach that attempts to interpret the biblical text first of all in its historical context, in light of the literary and cultural conventions of its time. As James Barr has insisted, historical criticism so understood is not strictly a method, but a loose collection of methods (source criticism, redaction criticism, sociological criticism, etc.) that are sometimes conceived as being in conflict with each other.[2] Historical criticism so understood strives for objectivity by assessing the plausibility of any interpretation in light of historical and literary context, including historical philology, or the range of meanings that may be assigned to a given word in a particular context. The objectivity in question is never absolute. It is one of the principles of historical criticism that any conclusion is open to revision in light of new evidence or argumentation.[3] It is rather a matter of making an argument by appeal to assumptions and knowledge shared by the participants in a particular conversation. Historical criticism sets limits to that conversation by limiting the range of what a text may mean in a particular context. Contrary to what is often asserted, this does not mean that a text has only one valid meaning. Many texts are ambiguous or multivalent, and texts can acquire new meanings in new contexts. Historical criticism, properly understood, does not (or at least should not) claim that the original historical context exhausts the meaning of a text. Neither can it, nor need it, claim to be the only valid method, regardless of circumstances. In contrast to some (not all) postmodernists, historical criticism does try to set limits to the meaning of a text, so that it cannot mean just anything at all. But, in practice, historical criticism over the last century or two has been in constant flux, as the consensus of one generation yields to the revisionism of the next. What is essential to the approach is not positivism but the insistence that any position is open to discussion in light of relevant evidence. Even the range of evidence that can be deemed relevant is subject to constant negotiation. It is precisely this open-ended character of historical criticism that has often been considered incompatible with, or hostile to, biblical theology.

BIBLICAL THEOLOGY

But biblical theology, too, is a contested concept. Although some scholars argue that it can only be done from a specific confessional perspective, in light of a faith commitment, this view is not universally accepted.[4] For some scholars, it is primarily a descriptive discipline, concerned primarily with "what it meant" and only secondarily with "what it means," in the famous distinction of Krister Stendahl.[5] Most scholars, I think, would agree with Rudolf Bultmann that in biblical theology historical reconstruction stands in the service of the interpretation of the biblical writings "under the presupposition that they have something to say to the present."[6] Biblical theology in this sense can be undertaken in the service of the church, but it can also be conceived as an academic discipline, a subject for public discussion regardless of faith commitments. It is concerned with the truth-claims and ethical values presented by the biblical text, and in any critical biblical theology these claims and values are open to question. Whether or not one can conceive of a biblical theology grounded in historical criticism obviously depends on whether one insists on a faith commitment that exempts some positions from criticism, or whether one is willing to regard biblical theology as an extension of the critical enterprise that deals with truth-claims and values in an open-ended engagement with the text.

LEVENSON'S CRITIQUE

The proposal for a critical biblical theology outlined in the first essay in this collection was subjected to a critique by Jon Levenson in an essay published in 1993.[7] Levenson seizes upon my statement that historical criticism "too is a tradition, with its own values and assumptions, derived in large part from the Enlightenment and Western humanism."[8] He claims that this statement undercuts any claims based on historical criticism in the area of biblical theology: "When the legacy of the Enlightenment becomes just another *tradition*, it inevitably suffers the same deflation that Marxism suffers when it becomes another ideology. We are left with the discomforting question: Why this tradition and not another?"[9] But not all traditions are alike. While historical criticism is itself a tradition, it is a tradition of a very different order from religious orthodoxy, as it does not require the a priori acceptance of any particular conclusions. It is neither committed nor opposed in principle to any particular reconstruction of the history of Israel, or to the unity or divine origin of the Bible. Any position can be defended, so long as evidence is adduced and arguments are made. A confessional approach, such as that advocated by Levenson and many others, wants to privilege certain positions and exempt them from the requirement of supporting arguments, thus in effect taking biblical theology out of the public discussion.

Levenson insists on "the inability of a self-consciously universalistic and rationalistic method to serve as the vehicle of any particularistic religious confession."[10] Implicit in this formulation is the assumption that biblical theology should serve as the vehicle of a particularistic religious confession. Consequently he argues that although Jews and Christians can work together on the more limited literary and historical contexts of a passage, "when we come to 'the final literary setting' and even more so to 'the context of the canon' we must part company, for there is no non-particularistic access to these larger contexts, and no decision on these issues, even when made for secular purposes, can be neutral between Judaism and Christianity."[11]

Elsewhere, he grants that historical criticism makes possible a meeting of Jews and Christians on neutral ground, but insists that "neutral" is not "common" as it requires both Jews and Gentiles to bracket their religious identities.[12]

At issue here is the nature of the conversation in which we wish to participate. One of the great strengths of historical criticism has been that it has created an arena where people with different faith commitments can work together. The bracketing of religious identities and faith commitments has allowed dispassionate assessment of historical and literary questions, even when this might seem subversive to the religious identities in question. Levenson has participated actively and fruitfully in such conversation on many issues, but he wishes to draw the line when theological issues are at stake, presumably so that religious identity may not be threatened. This seems to me to be an unfortunate limitation of the academic study of the Bible. In fact, distinctive articles of faith, such as the question of a divine role in history, cannot ultimately be decided by historical-critical discussion in any case, but there is much that can be discussed about them from a neutral perspective nonetheless.

NONFOUNDATIONALISM

Levenson's rejection of a historical-critical approach to biblical theology, like the canonical approach of Brevard Childs, for which he expresses admiration, can be seen in part as a reaction against an earlier phase of biblical theology, which proceeded as if Christian beliefs could be established by "objective" scholarship. On the one hand, this led to a naïve use of history as if the affirmation of acts of God could be supported by archaeology.[13] On the other hand, the presumed objectivity of Christian faith often carried very negative implications for Judaism.[14] It is better to recognize that faith in supernatural beings or events can never be confirmed by historical or literary research. Recognition of this fact has gone hand in hand with the rise of nonfoundationalism, in both philosophy and theology, which argues that the quest for foundations, in the sense of unassailably certain beliefs, is misguided. Philosophical nonfoundationalism holds that truth is not the correlation of mind and reality, but a matter of coherence within a set of shared beliefs. There is no neutral ground from which to evaluate competing claims. For a philosophical nonfoundationalist such as Richard Rorty, this means that nothing is certain, everything is negotiable.[15] Theological nonfoundationalists, in contrast, tend to make an exception for Christian faith, which is taken to provide its own certainty.[16]

It is true that the putative foundations of biblical theology in a previous era have crumbled in the last quarter of the twentieth century. The collapse is most obvious in the case of history, where many of the crucial "salvific" events, such as the Exodus and Conquest, are now widely viewed as unhistorical.[17] Gerhard von Rad was already troubled by the gap between the biblical "history of salvation" and the history reconstructed by modern scholarship.[18] Brevard Childs noted the problem, but offered no solution.[19] Appeals to faith are of little help here, as it is difficult to see the virtue in continuing to affirm on a theological level what has been shown to be erroneous on the historical.

BRUEGGEMANN

By far the most sweeping attempt to formulate a nonfoundational approach to biblical theology, and the most impressive new approach to the subject in recent years, is that of Walter Brueggemann.[20] Brueggemann argues rightly that "in every period of the discipline, the questions, methods, and possibilities in which study is cast arise from the sociointellectual climate in which the work must be done."[21] In the current, postmodern situation, "the great new fact is that we live in a pluralistic context, in which many different interpreters in many different specific contexts representing many different interests are at work on textual (theological) interpretation. . . . The great interpretive reality is that there is no court of appeal behind these many different readings. There is no court of appeal beyond the text itself. . . . The postmodern situation is signified precisely by the disappearance of any common universal assumption at the outset of reading."[22] Since there is no foundation outside the text, Brueggemann holds that "speech constitutes reality, and who God turns out to be in Israel depends on the utterance of the Israelites, or, derivatively, the utterance of the text."[23]

There is much to admire in Brueggemann's bold constructive proposals. One admirable feature is the recognition that the Bible includes not only "testimony" but also "counter-testimony"—that is, it contains different perspectives, which may sometimes be contradictory. He argues that both the testimony and the counter-testimony must be held in tension: "Lived faith in this tradition consists in the capacity to move back and forth between these two postures of faith."[24] From my perspective, however, the metaphor of testimony, which is currently fashionable with many theologians besides Brueggemann, is problematic.[25] As Brueggemann recognizes, "In any serious courtroom trial, testimony is challenged by other, competing testimony. In any serious trial, no unchallenged testimony can expect to carry the day easily."[26] But the only competing testimony that Brueggemann allows is the countertestimony found in the text itself. It is obviously unsatisfactory to say that "what 'happened' (whatever that may mean) depends on testimony and tradition that will not submit to any other warrant."[27] There is, after all, the testimony of archaeology, which is often at odds with the biblical account of early Israelite history. The testimony about the conquest of Canaan by divine command runs afoul of modern sensibilities about the morality of genocide. No one in modern pluralist society can live in a world that is shaped only by the Bible. We are all heirs to other traditions as well, including the Enlightenment and several other intellectual movements. We may agree that none of these provides secure foundations from which to judge the others, but they cannot be ignored, and the Bible alone does not provide a secure foundation either. Herein, it seems to me, lies the fundamental weakness of any nonfoundational approach that would exempt the Bible from criticism based on external traditions and sources.

The most startling proposal in Brueggemann's book is surely his contention that "speech constitutes reality." "Yahweh," he writes, "lives in, with, and under this speech, and in the end depends on Israel's testimony for an access point to the world."[28] He rejects "the ancient Hellenistic lust for Being, for establishing ontological reference behind the text."[29] Yet he qualifies this rejection in a footnote: "It is not my intention to be anti-ontological. It is rather to insist that whatever might be claimed for ontology in the purview of Israel's speech can be claimed only in and through testimonial utterance. That is, once the testimony of Israel is accepted as true—once one believes what it claims—one has ontology, one has the reality of Yahweh. But to have the reality of God apart from the testimony of Israel is sure to yield some God other than the Yahweh of Israel."[30]

Here again Brueggemann's exclusive reliance on biblical testimony seems to me problematic, even by biblical standards. Two of the essays in the present collection are devoted to the wisdom literature as natural theology, which draws not only on Israelite tradition but on what it perceives as common human experience.[31] I do not wish to suggest that natural theology, either in its biblical or in any other formation, is without its own problems. "Common human experience" often turns out to be less than universal, and to depend on the cultural assumptions of a particular time and place. But it is important to recognize that within the Bible itself there is considerable "testimony" that suggests that God can be known apart from the distinctive testimony of Israel. This testimony is most explicit in the wisdom literature, but it is found throughout the biblical corpus, as James Barr has shown.[32]

It is also problematic to suggest that one can move directly from the testimony of the biblical text to claims about ontological reality. Brueggemann is quite right that the Bible contains little if anything by way of ontological argument. It consists of writings in various genres that make claims about God that defy any process of verification. But then, if we want to discuss biblical theology in the public realm, or in an academic setting, we must bracket our ontological claims. Whereof we cannot speak, thereof we must be silent, however important we may think it is. It is not the case that historical criticism, or any other kind of biblical criticism, disproves the reality of the God of Israel, or of anything attributed to God in the Bible. But it does not have the means to affirm it either. Responsible academic criticism of the Bible, of whatever persuasion, does not have the resources to assess metaphysical claims made in the text.

BIBLICAL TEXTS AND MODERN ETHICS

What does lie within the competence of biblical theologians, and what should engage us much more than it has traditionally, is the pragmatic study of the effects of biblical texts, and the metaphysical affirmations contained in them, on human behavior and society. The point may be illustrated by consideration of the apocalyptic literature, which is the focus of chapters 11–13 and is also discussed in chapter 2. There is little to be gained by arguing about the reliability of predictions of the end of the world. The nonfulfillment of apocalyptic predictions over more than two thousand years strongly suggests that they should be taken as symbolic in any case. What we can evaluate are the kinds of actions that have been inspired by such beliefs, both within the biblical record and in the history of its reception.[33] A similar approach may be applied fruitfully to more "history-like" areas of the Bible, such as the disputed history of Exodus and Conquest. Here again it would be highly problematic simply to accept the testimony of the biblical text. Think, for example, of Abraham's willingness to sacrifice his son, depicted as a heroic act of faith,[34] of the command to slaughter the Canaanites,[35] the laws about slavery, or the treatment of women. The first responsibility of the historical critic is always to ensure that a law or story is understood as fully as possible, by thick description of the historical and social contexts, insofar as these are available. But there is also an obligation to reflect on the implications that biblical texts may have for those who regard them as scripture in the modern world.

The Bible was written long ago and in another culture, vastly different from our own. Any attempt to apply it to a modern situation, or to deduce ethical principles from it, must be approached with caution. But it remains a powerful book in modern society, and its power is not restricted to the church or synagogue. The theological dimension of this literature, broadly understood as to what it has to say to the modern world, is too important to ignore. It is also too dangerous to be removed from public discussion and relegated to the realm of unquestioned belief and acceptance.

PART ONE

THEORETICAL ISSUES

CHAPTER I

IS A CRITICAL BIBLICAL THEOLOGY POSSIBLE?

Biblical theology is a subject in decline. The evidence of this decline is not so much the permanent state of crisis in which it seems to have settled or the lack of a new consensus to replace the great works of Eichrodt or von Rad. Rather, the decline is evident in the fact that an increasing number of scholars no longer regard theology as the ultimate focus of biblical studies, or even as a necessary dimension of those studies at all. The cutting edges of contemporary biblical scholarship are in literary criticism on the one hand and sociological criticism on the other. Not only is theology no longer queen of the sciences in general, its place even among the biblical sciences is in doubt.

The reasons for the decline of biblical theology are manifold, but one of the most deep-rooted is the perennial tension between biblical theology and the historical-critical method, with which its history has been closely intertwined. The distinction of biblical theology as an independent discipline is usually ascribed to the inaugural address of Johann Philipp Gabler at the University of Altdorf in 1787. His subject was "The Proper Distinction between Biblical and Dogmatic Theology and the Specific Objectives of Each."[1] The main thrust of this address was to establish the necessity of making this distinction. Biblical theology was conceived as a descriptive, historical discipline, in contrast to dogmatic theology, which derived its knowledge not only from Scripture but also from other sources such as philosophy. The theological character of this enterprise was not a problem for Gabler, since he was convinced that the Bible contained "pure notions which divine providence wished to be characteristic of all times and places" as well as ideas that were historically relative.[2] Biblical theology in the stricter sense was constituted by the collection and arrangement of these universal ideas. Nonetheless, Gabler's insistence on the historical, descriptive nature of the discipline contained from the outset the seeds of later tension between biblical theology and the history of Israelite and early Christian religion.

THE PRINCIPLES OF HISTORICAL CRITICISM

The difficulty of conceiving biblical theology as a descriptive historical discipline became evident in the work of the "history of religions" school approximately one hundred years later. Critical historiography, as it developed in the nineteenth century, had its own principles, without deference to the expectations of theologians. Among theologians these principles received their classic formulation from Ernst Troeltsch in 1898. Troeltsch set out three principles:[3] (1) The principle of criticism or method-ological doubt: since any conclusion is subject to revision, historical inquiry can never attain absolute certainty but only relative degrees of probability. (2) The principle of analogy: historical knowledge is possible because all events are similar in principle. We must assume that the laws of nature in biblical times were the same as now. Troeltsch referred to this as "the almighty power of analogy." (3) The principle of correlation: the phenomena of history are interrelated and interdependent and no event can be isolated from the sequence of historical cause and effect. To these should be added the principle of autonomy, which is indispensable for any critical study. Neither church nor state can prescribe for the scholar which conclusions should be reached.[4]

The problem posed by these principles for biblical theology was most sharply formulated by Wilhelm Wrede in his essay, "The Task and Methods of New Testa-ment Theology." Wrede found that, in theory, most people would grant that biblical theology is a historical discipline. In practice, however, it was still subordinated to dogmatics so that biblical material was pressed for answers to dogmatic questions and distorted to fit dogmatic categories. Consequently, unorthodox biblical ideas were suppressed, and the Bible was not heard in its own right. For Wrede,

> Biblical Theology has to investigate something from given documents. . . . It tries to grasp it as objectively, correctly, and sharply as possible. That is all. How the systematic theologian gets on with its results and deals with them—that is his own affair. Like every other real science, New Testament theology has its goal simply in itself and is totally indifferent to all dogma and systematic theology. What could dogmatics offer it? Could dogmatics teach New Testament theology to see the facts correctly? At most, it could color them. Could it correct the facts that were found? To correct facts is absurd. Could it legitimize them? Facts need no legitimation.[5]

Wrede's confidence that historical criticism could establish "the facts" sounds naïve, even arrogant, a century later, but he had correctly perceived a fundamental opposi-tion between historical method and dogmatics. Criticism cannot offer assured facts, but it offers degrees of probability, based on evidence. The evidence, whatever its strength or weakness, cannot be cast aside or overruled for dogmatic, a priori reasons.

Wrede's view of biblical theology was, in effect, indistinguishable from the his-tory of religion. He made no apology for that fact: "But in what should the specifically theological type of treatment consist? . . . Can a specifically theological understanding of the discipline guarantee some kind of knowledge that goes beyond the knowledge of the historical fact that such and such was taught and believed?"[6]

The "specifically theological understanding" against which Wrede polemicized consisted of a faith perspective derived from dogmatic theology. This entailed the profession that the biblical writings were inspired or revealed and should be regarded as normative. Invariably, it also implied agreement between the Bible and the postulates of dogmatic theology. Wrede's basic complaint was that dogmatic concerns led to historical distortions. He was not, however, only calling for a separation of the historical and dogmatic tasks, as Gabler had done. In his view, historical criticism undercut some of the postulates of traditional theology. So, "for logical thinking there can be no middle position between inspired writings and historical documents."[7] Equally, "it is impossible to continue to maintain the dogmatic conception of the canon," since canonical status is not intrinsic to the biblical writings but only represents the judgment of the church fathers.[8] The tension here is not a matter of specific doctrines or conclusions, but, as Van Harvey has put it,[9] is a clash between two conflicting moralities, one of which celebrated faith and belief as virtues and regarded doubt as sin, whereas the other celebrated methodological skepticism and was distrustful of prior commitments.

THE NEO-ORTHODOX PHASE

The revival of biblical theology in the decades after World War I corroborated Wrede's judgment that theological commitment lends itself to historical distortion. The dominant neo-orthodox theology sought to reconcile historical criticism with dogmatic views of the Bible as an inspired document. Walter Eichrodt conceded that "OT theology presupposes the history of Israel" and that one should "have the historical principle operating side by side with the systematic in a complementary role."[10] He also declared his rejection of "any arrangement of the whole body of the material which derives not from the laws of its own nature but from some dogmatic scheme"[11] and professed his intention to "avoid all schemes which derive from Christian dogmatics."[12] Yet he conceived his task as "to understand the realm of OT belief in its structural unity and . . . by examining on the one hand its religious environment and on the other its essential coherence with the NT, to illuminate its profoundest meaning."[13] The view that the profoundest meaning of the Hebrew Bible is disclosed by its relation to the New Testament is, however, plainly a matter of Christian dogmatics and was accompanied by a highly distorted view of Judaism, as Jon Levenson has pointed out.[14] The discovery of structural unity in a tradition that spans a millennium has also proven endlessly problematic from a historical point of view and, here again, Eichrodt was more dependent on dogmatic considerations than he seems to have realized.

Again, the internal contradictions of the so-called Biblical Theology Movement in America have often been rehearsed.[15] G. E. Wright insisted that biblical theology must start from the descriptive work of the historian. Yet he saw its task as the "recital" of the acts of God, which were not simply the results of historical research but "history interpreted by faith"[16] that involves a "projection of faith into facts that is then considered as the true meaning of the facts."[17] In typical neo-orthodox fashion Wright was attempting to combine the contradictory moralities of modern scientific method and traditional, confessional faith. Even apart from the question as to whether Wright's reconstruction of the history was unduly colored by his conviction that "in Biblical faith everything depends on whether the central events actually occurred,"[18] it is clear that his understanding of these events depended on dogmatic rather than strictly historical considerations.[19] Even Gerhard von Rad, who tried harder than most to respect the historical variety of the Hebrew Bible, argued that any attempt to interpret the Old Testament without reference to the New Testament must "turn out to be fictitious from a Christian point of view."[20] His critics may be pardoned for suspecting that this conviction colored his detection of a tension between law and gospel already in the pentateuchal traditions. More fundamentally, von Rad's position was undermined by the tension between his view that the theologian's task was to testify to the biblical salvation history and his acceptance, as a historian, of the quite different reconstruction of that history by critical scholarship.[21] Biblical theology, then, in the second and third quarters of the twentieth century, has been vulnerable to the charge of inconsistency—of allowing dogmatic convictions to undercut its avowedly historical method. The problem is not that the theologians brought presuppositions to the text, since this is also true of even the most "objective" historians, but that their theological presuppositions were inconsistent with the historical method on which they otherwise relied. This was true even of the most radical of biblical theologians, Rudolf Bultmann, in his insistence on the unique significance of Jesus Christ.[22]

Throughout the neo-orthodox period of biblical theology, the theological component was seen as confessional faith, which was understood to require some measure of a priori belief and conviction. The specific requirements might vary greatly in scope, from the historicity of the "acts of God" to the nature of the relation between the Testaments or the uniqueness of Israel or of Christ, but they affirmed some certainty that was independent of historical research and was more specific than a general commitment of loyalty to a religious tradition. There does, in fact, seem to be an inherent contradiction between theology so conceived and historical criticism, as understood by Wrede and Troeltsch. One of the basic principles formulated by Troeltsch was the principle of criticism, by which any conclusion or conviction must be subject to revision in the light of new evidence. Historical criticism, unlike traditional faith, does not provide for certainty but only for relative degrees of probability. Many of the convictions most dearly cherished by biblical theologians were challenged by historical criticism: the historicity of crucial events, the unity of the Old Testament, the uniqueness of Israel (or some conceptions thereof), or the view that the Old Testament is best understood as a process leading to Christ. A biblical theology that takes historical criticism seriously will have to forego any claim of certainty on these matters.

If, then, there is an inherent contradiction between historical criticism and theology conceived as confessional faith in the neo-orthodox manner, biblical theology can only proceed in one or the other of two ways: by abandoning historical criticism, at least in theological matters, or by reconceiving the theological aspects of the discipline. The issue is no longer the quest for a unifying center within the Old Testament or the Bible, but the context within which biblical theology should be pursued and the nature of the pursuit itself.

CHILDS'S APPROACH

There have always been attempts by religious conservatives to evade the consequences of historical criticism for biblical theology. In recent years, however, a more substantial challenge has been mounted by Brevard Childs, in his "canonical approach" to biblical theology.[23] Childs does not reject historical criticism or dispute its results, but he grants it no theological importance. For theological purposes the text is not to be read in its historical context but can confront the reader directly as the word of God. Childs rightly objects to the label "canon criticism," since his view of the Bible is not a criticism at all.[24] He explicitly rejects the principle of analogy between biblical and modern situations, which has been a cornerstone of critical method since Troeltsch.[25] He also resolutely distinguishes his theological approach from literary and hermeneutical methods with which it has some affinities, but which construe the text as a human product.[26]

Childs's work has been widely reviewed and the main criticisms are by now well known.[27] His explicitly confessional approach cannot be faulted for consistency, but it has grave liabilities, nonetheless. Chief of these is the apodictic way in which the approach is presented. For Childs, "the status of canonicity is not an objectively demonstrable claim but a statement of Christian belief."[28] It is not clear, however, that Childs's view of the canon has ever been normative, even in Protestant Christianity, not to mention in Catholicism or Judaism. Childs fails to give reasons why anyone should adopt this approach to the text unless they happen to share his view of Christian faith. The canonical approach then fails to provide a context for dialogue with anyone who does not accept it as a matter of faith.

A further liability of Childs's approach is its lack of explanatory power. We are repeatedly told that the Scripture shapes and enlivens the church or mediates the revelation of God, but we are not told *how*. Childs is convinced, as Bultmann was, that the text has something to say to the present, but he has no hermeneutic, as Bultmann had, that might provide the common ground necessary for intelligibility. Again, his rejection of sociological approaches excludes a potentially fruitful source of analogies that might permit us to relate the biblical situations to our own. Some of the most suggestive biblical scholarship in recent years has been in the areas of sociology and feminism, and its power has lain in the perception that biblical texts, like any other, serve and legitimate specific human interests. Childs's refusal to reckon with the ideological aspects of biblical texts as human products seems naïve and superficial and weakens the credibility of his ideological affirmations.

The effect of Childs's proposal is to isolate biblical theology from much of what is vital and interesting in biblical studies today. Such a strategy, it seems to me, must ultimately be self-defeating. If biblical theology is to retain a place in serious scholarship, it must be able to accommodate the best insights of other branches of biblical scholarship and must be conceived broadly enough to provide a context for debate among different viewpoints. Otherwise it is likely to become a sectarian reservation, of interest only to those who hold certain confessional tenets that are not shared by the discipline at large. Childs's dogmatic conception of the canon provides no basis for advancing dialogue. In my opinion historical criticism still provides the most satisfactory framework for discussion.

CRITIQUES OF HISTORICAL CRITICISM

Historical criticism has often come under attack in recent years, not always for valid reasons. The most telling of these critiques have been directed against the pretense of value-free objectivity. Philosophers such as H. G. Gadamer and Paul Ricoeur[29] have repeatedly made the point that there is no strictly autonomous reason. Without a tradition (a "text" in Ricoeur's terms) no understanding is possible. George Lindbeck has recently made the same point in somewhat different terms:

> It seems, as the case of Helen Keller and of supposed wolf children vividly illustrate, that unless we acquire language of some kind we cannot actualize our specifically human capacities for thought, action and feeling. Similarly, so the argument goes, to become religious involves becoming skilled in the language, the symbol system of a given religion.[30]

The critical ideal of autonomy, then, must be severely qualified. We can no longer claim with Wrede that historical criticism gives us objective facts. It too is a tradition, with its own values and presuppositions, derived in large part from the Enlightenment and Western humanism.

If there is no interpretation without presuppositions, and if the presuppositions of critical scholarship differ from those of traditional Christianity, then some biblical theologians suggest that we should refashion the presuppositions of scholarly method and replace the "hermeneutic of suspicion" with a "hermeneutic of consent" that would be "open to transcendence."[31] However, the inevitability of presuppositions should not be taken as an invitation to excel in bias.[32] Some presuppositions are better or more adequate than others. One criterion for the adequacy of presuppositions is the degree to which they allow dialogue between differing viewpoints and accommodate new insights. The great strength of historical criticism lies in Troeltsch's principle of criticism. All conclusions are subject to revision in the light of new evidence and arguments. This openness to revision is the trademark that distinguishes critical method from dogmatism of any sort. Consequently, historical criticism has proven itself highly adaptable in accommodating the new insights of form criticism, redaction criticism, etc. Even the recent sociological and feminist critics, who are highly critical of the claims of objectivity,[33] have nonetheless relied on the standard critical methods to argue for their revisionist reconstructions. Perhaps the outstanding achievement of historical criticism in this century is that it has provided a framework within which scholars of different prejudices and commitments have been able to debate in a constructive manner.

Where the principle of criticism is consistently applied, there is no basis for the common objection that the principle of analogy dogmatically disallows real novelty in history.[34] No possibility is excluded in principle, but the critic endorses the Enlightenment ideal that the assurance with which we entertain a proposition be proportional to the evidence that supports it.[35] The demand for evidence and reasoned calculation of probability is precisely what enables the critical method to serve as a forum for dialogue between people of different views. So while historical criticism does not enjoy the degree of autonomy or of objectivity that has often been claimed for it, it still has many advantages to commend it.

The modification of the claim of autonomy is significant for biblical theology. Critical method is incompatible with confessional faith insofar as the latter requires us to accept specific conclusions on dogmatic grounds. It does not, and cannot, preclude a commitment to working within specific traditions, and biblical theology is inevitably confessional in this looser sense. For biblical theology, the biblical tradition is a given and it is assumed to be meaningful and to have continuing value, although the meaning and value can be subject to critical examination.[36] Parenthetically, the biblical theologian inevitably works with some canon of Scripture (contrary to Wrede), although this does not necessarily imply a qualitative difference over against ancient literature but only a recognition of the historical importance of these texts within the tradition.

The modern theologian, however, is heir to more than one tradition. We are shaped by the rational humanism that underlies our technological culture and political institutions, no less than by the Bible (usually far more so). It is possible to have critical dialogue between our modern worldview and the Bible, but we cannot simply abandon our modern context for the ancient world. Rather than a "hermeneutic of consent," then, we need a model of theology that provides for critical correlation among the various traditions in which we stand. It has been said that "the heart of any hermeneutical position is the recognition that all interpretation is a mediation of past and present."[37] It cannot be a mere recital of sacred history or submission to a canonical text. The point here is not just that the theologians *should* be informed by sources other than the Bible or the Christian tradition, but that they cannot avoid it. Biblical fundamentalism is influenced by nineteenth-century rationalism.[38] Biblical archaism, as advocated by Wright and others, is a product of twentieth-century positivism.[39] Childs's focus on the canonical shape of the text has affinities with the twentieth-century literary theory of "new criticism," which cannot be dismissed as coincidental, whether he acknowledges them or not.[40]

THE TASK OF A CRITICAL THEOLOGY

The principles of critical method identified by Troeltsch are deeply ingrained in modern consciousness, and their relevance is not confined to purely historical criticism. The new developments of literary and sociological criticism are often critical of the more antiquarian kind of historical research, with its obsession with sources, but they too abide by the principles of analogy and criticism. As Troeltsch already observed, "The historical method, once it is applied to biblical science . . . is a leaven which transforms everything and finally explodes the whole form of theological methods."[41] The crucial methodological shift is a matter of epistemology. Traditional theology started, so to speak, from the side of God and relied on the postulate of revelation to guarantee theological truth. Historical method starts from the human side and insists on the epistemological questions: How do we control our evidence, and what warrants do we have for the assertions we make? Obviously these questions become acute when we are dealing with assertions about God.

If biblical theology is to be based on critical methodology, then its task is the critical evaluation of biblical speech about God. It is an area of historical theology, and as such is one source among others for contemporary theology.[42] It necessarily overlaps with the history of religion. It is the specialization of that discipline that deals with the portrayal of God in one specific corpus of texts. Biblical theology should not, however, be reduced to "the historical fact that such and such was thought and believed"[43] but should clarify the meaning and truth-claims of what was thought and believed from a modern critical perspective. (I have attempted to do this in various writings on apocalypticism; see my essay "Apocalyptic Eschatology as the Transcendence of Death."[44])

THE QUESTION OF GENRE

The primary contribution of historical criticism to biblical theology, in my opinion, lies in its clarification of the various genres in the biblical text and the different expectations appropriate to them. The basic point is simple and obvious. The truth-claims that can be made for a biblical passage vary according to the kind of writing involved.[45] The point was raised forcefully in Gunkel's classic discussion of the legends of Genesis, where he made a sweeping distinction between history and legend: "History, which claims to inform us of what actually happened, is in its very nature prose, while legend is by nature poetry, its aim being to please, to elevate, to inspire and to move."[46] This statement would certainly have to be reformulated now, perhaps in terms of a contrast between referential, informative language and expressive, evocative language,[47] but Gunkel's work marked an important shift away from the attempt to interpret the text as a record of objective reality, toward an appreciation of it as a medium of human expression.

The implications of Gunkel's linguistic turn for biblical theology were largely obscured in the heyday of the Biblical Theology Movement, at least in North America. In recent years the issue has again come to the fore in the much-heralded paradigm shift from history to "story" in biblical theology.[48] James Barr was among the first to proclaim this shift: "The long narrative corpus of the Old Testament seems to me, as a body of literature, to merit the title of story rather than that of history. Or, to put it another way it seems to merit entirely the title of story but only in part the title history."[49] Elsewhere Barr has distinguished two sorts of writing: "The first is intended as information; its value can be assessed from the accuracy of its reports about entities ('reference,' thing referred to) in the outside world. The second has a different kind of meaning and value. Its meaning lies rather in the structure and shape of the story, and in the images used within it. It is valued as literature, aesthetically, rather than as information."[50] He adds that "much of literature, to put it bluntly, is fiction." Barr's reformulation of biblical theology parallels the proposal of literary critic Robert Alter that biblical "sacred history" should be read as "prose fiction."[51]

This shift, of course, has not gone unchallenged. Meir Sternberg accuses Alter and his admirers of "a category mistake of the first order,"[52] mixing "truth value and truth claim, source (the nature of the materials) and discourse (their working in context), standards of literariness, especially literary excellence, and marks of fictionality."[53] His point is well taken. The genre of a text is determined by its intention, or truth-claim, rather than by its success or value. However, Sternberg's objection does not obviously affect the paradigm shift in biblical theology. For Sternberg, "history-writing is not a record of fact—'of what really happened'—but a discourse that claims to be a record of fact. Nor is fiction-writing a tissue of the inventions but a discourse that claims freedom of invention."[54] History-writing too is a form of human expression, of *poiesis*, of imagination, and that is the main point at issue in the introduction of the category story in biblical theology.

Moreover, the truth-claims of the biblical narratives are more complex than Sternberg allows. Ancient writers did not distinguish fact and fiction as sharply as we do. The biblical narratives include enough discrepancies and make enough use of folklore and mythic themes to qualify the common assumption that "their religious intent involves an absolute claim to historical truth."[55] Moreover, the teleology of a text like Exodus is not exhausted by one intention. We may grant that the story in Exodus 1–15 was assumed, in ancient Israel, to be historically reliable. Nonetheless, it also served, and was intended to serve, other functions. It served as the basis for the covenantal law and as the motivation for ethical conduct. It also served as a paradigm by which later historical events could be interpreted, notably the Babylonian exile in Second Isaiah (Isa 40:3-5; 51:9-11). Ultimately, it served as a formulation of Jewish identity in the festival of the Passover, so that everyone must think of themselves as having been slaves in the land of Egypt.[56] In all of these functions the historicity of the Exodus is scarcely a consideration—indeed, in Second Isaiah the crossing of the sea is mentioned in parallelism with the mythical piercing of the dragon. The value of the story, then, cannot be adequately assessed if it is judged only as historiography.

It may well be an objection that the real problem here is that biblical theology has worked with a deficient notion of history and historiography. In effect, both terms have been understood primarily as "a factually reliable account of the past," and it is this oversimplified understanding that has been undermined in the recent discussion. If history is understood more adequately, with due allowance for the blend of fact and fiction that it necessarily entails, it may well be the better genre designation for much of biblical narrative. In the context of biblical theology, however, the shift in terminology from history to story has served a useful purpose, in making the point that the biblical narratives are imaginative constructs and not necessarily factual. They do, of course, provide valuable historical information, but they do not provide the bedrock of certainty that theologians have often sought. Their value for theology lies in their functions as myth or story rather than in their historical accuracy.

The significance of the paradigm shift from history to story is that it abandons the last claim of biblical theology to certain knowledge of objective reality. A story is a work of the human imagination, drawing on the ingredients of human experience. It does not lay claim to logical necessity in the manner of a philosophical system—a point already emphasized in the Biblical Theology Movement. Neither does it rely on the factual verifiability of historical records. We recognize stories as "true" or as valid expressions of reality insofar as they fit our experience, although the fit cannot be scientifically verified and the view of reality is necessarily partial and perspectival. Stories can also be read as proposals that open up new ways of viewing life—though again, there is no guarantee of their value or validity. They may provide insight or inspiration but not the reassuring certainty that has so often been sought by biblical theologians.

The same point can be made with reference to other biblical genres besides narrative—the poetic genres of prophecy and psalms or the inductive, pragmatic formulations of wisdom. Biblical theology is not only narrative theology, but more broadly it is an experiential, symbolic theology, which can find expression in several genres.

It seems to me, then, that Paul Ricoeur has correctly identified the first step in a critical biblical theology when he speaks of "a return to the origin of theological discourse"[57] by analyzing the various genres of biblical speech. He invites us "to place the originary expressions of biblical faith under the sign of the poetic function of language,"[58] which addresses our imagination rather than our obedience.[59]

This way of viewing the biblical text also seems, in principle, compatible with a process hermeneutic that "regards Biblical texts precisely in their function as *proposed* ways of understanding (aspects of) objective reality," with the provision that "the truth of a text's proposal, however, cannot be taken for granted."[60]

THE PORTRAYAL OF GOD

The polemical thrust of Barr's distinction between story and history was directed against biblical theologians such as G. E. Wright, who read the Bible as a source of historical information from which the nature and attributes of God can be inferred. The paradigm shift, however, is no less damaging to some other biblical theologians who are ostensibly more attuned to the literary character of the text. David Kelsey contrasted Wright with Karl Barth's construal of Scripture as "rendering an agent." In Barth's usage, "Narrative is taken to be the authoritative aspect of scripture"; it "is taken to have the logical force of stories that render a character, that offer an identity description of an agent"; and it is "like the patterns in a realistic novel or short story to which a literary critic might draw attention when he tries to analyze characterization. Indeed it is as though Barth took Scripture to be one vast loosely-structured, non-fictional novel—at least, Barth takes it to be non-fiction."[61] Therein, of course, lies the rub, for a nonfictional novel is a contradiction in terms. Many Christians of conservative leanings have welcomed the category "story" as a means of evading the possibility of disconfirmation to which history is subject. The freedom from disconfirmation, however, is bought at a price, since it necessarily excludes the possibility of confirmation, too.

If we recognize that much biblical "history" is fiction, in the sense of Ricoeur's poetic language, then we must also recognize that statements about God must be interpreted in the context of that fiction. Sternberg objects that, "were the narrative written or read as fiction, then God would turn from the lord of history into a creature of the imagination, with the most disastrous results."[62] The modern reader, however, who can no longer accept the historical truth value of Genesis or Exodus, can only choose between inaccurate historiography and imaginative fiction. It is not clear why fiction should appear the more disastrous of these alternatives, if we free ourselves of the prejudice that equates fiction with falsehood and accept it as a fundamental way of apprehending reality.

If we regard biblical texts as fictions, or proposals whose truth or adequacy remains to be assessed, we must admit the possibility of a distinction between God the character in a biblical story and "the living god" or the power that moves the universe.[63] This distinction is not especially novel: virtually all strands of biblical theology have emphasized the transcendence of God in the Hebrew Bible and the inadequacy of any portrayal, iconic or verbal. Ricoeur, for example, refers to "God's trace in the event" and goes on to insist that the God who reveals himself is still a hidden God.[64] A consistent critical approach, however, goes further. God the character must be understood in terms of his function within the story and of the human experiences and concerns from which it arises. Biblical assertions about God are not necessarily always pointers to transcendence but can also serve various functions of a more mundane nature.

The radical implications of historical criticism for biblical theology can be seen most clearly in recent sociological and feminist scholarship. Norman Gottwald's thesis that Yahweh was the symbol for the social idea of early, tribal Israel is a case in point.[65] Whether or not we regard such a definition as reductionistic, there is no doubt that religious language often functions to legitimate social power structures.[66] When we are told that the conquest of Canaan was justified by divine command or that God gave his unconditional support to the king, we may suspect that we are dealing with ideological rhetoric rather than theological truth, however tentative. God-language is no less ideological when it is used in more "liberal" causes, to authorize the Sinai covenant or to support prophetic preaching of social justice.

Historical criticism lends itself most readily to a view of biblical religion as a functional system where myth and cult are supporting devices to regulate the conduct that is at the heart of the religion. We can understand how the accounts of creation fostered respect for humanity as the image of God or led to the subordination of women, or how the expectations of reward after death strengthened the Maccabean martyrs. We cannot establish whether those beliefs were well founded.

Consequently, assertions about God or the supernatural are most easily explained as rhetorical devices to motivate behavior. Such an analysis of biblical God-language is in itself a theological exercise, since it clarifies our use of theological language. It also has some warrant in the Hebrew Bible, where *miṣwôt* are the end of history[67] and ethical performance is more important than belief.

A biblical theology that ignores the ideological uses of God-language must appear naïve in the modern culture, which is permeated with the hermeneutic of suspicion. Nonetheless, a biblical theology that adverts *only* to sociological and historical functions is reductionistic. The biblical texts must also be recognized as proposals about metaphysical truth, as attempts to explain the workings of reality. This aspect of the Bible is perhaps most obvious in the Wisdom literature but is also a factor throughout the Bible, from the creation stories to the apocalypse. The proposals are diverse. The God of Job is appreciably different from the God of the Deuteronomist, and either from the God of Daniel. The question here is whether any of these biblical accounts can now be accorded any explanatory value—whether any of the biblical worldviews can be said to be true as well as useful. The problem is that we lack any acceptable yardstick by which to assess metaphysical truth. It is possible to compare and contrast biblical worldviews with a modern system, such as process philosophy, but philosophical systems too are traditions of discourse and there is no consensus on their validity in contemporary culture. It is not within the competence of biblical theologians as such to adjudicate the relative adequacy of metaphysical systems. Their task is to clarify what claims are being made, the basis on which they are made, and the various functions they serve.

CONCLUSION

We return, finally, to our initial questions as to whether a critical biblical theology is possible. The answer evidently depends on the model of theology we are willing to accept. Historical criticism, consistently understood, is not compatible with a confessional theology that is committed to specific doctrines on the basis of faith. It is, however, quite compatible with theology, understood as an open-ended and critical inquiry into the meaning and function of God-language. Biblical theology on this model is not a self-sufficient discipline but is a subdiscipline that has a contribution to make to the broader subject of theology. The main contribution of the biblical theologian is to clarify the genre of the biblical material in the broad sense of the way in which it should be read and the expectations that are appropriate to it.

Despite the critiques to which it has been subject, historical criticism remains the most satisfactory context for biblical theology. Some of the claims for the objectivity of that method are now recognized to be exaggerated. It has its presuppositions. Nonetheless, it still commands the allegiance of the great majority of biblical scholars, including most of those who work in biblical theology, and with good reason, since it provides a broad framework for scholarly dialogue. My purpose here has been to explore the implications of accepting historical criticism as a basis for biblical theology. It is my thesis that there is a legitimate enterprise that goes beyond the simple description of what was thought and believed (à la Wrede), while stopping short of the "projection of faith into facts" that was characteristic of neo-orthodoxy. Theological language is an integral part of the biblical material and should not be simply bypassed in the interests of secular interpretation. We can only ask that the methods we endorse in historical and literary research be applied consistently also to the theological problems.

CHAPTER 2

BIBLICAL THEOLOGY AND THE HISTORY OF ISRAELITE RELIGION

One of the primary ways in which teachers influence their students is by the questions to which they direct their attention. One such question, often posed by the late Dr. Dermot Ryan,[1] is a classic dilemma of biblical studies: Is it possible to write a theology of the Old Testament, as distinct from a history of the religion of Israel? In the 1960s this question arose especially in the context of the debate occasioned by Gerhard von Rad's *Old Testament Theology*,[2] a work which in Dr. Ryan's view was really an exercise in the history of the religion. In his view, Biblical Theology could not be an independent discipline but only a subsidiary part of a dogmatic theology.[3] This position was at odds with the prevailing wisdom of the time, both in the American "Biblical Theology Movement" and in the great European theologies of Eichrodt and von Rad. Indeed the whole history of Biblical Theology was founded on its separation as a discipline from Dogmatic Theology,[4] and in the 1960s the possibility of basing Biblical Theology on historical-critical method was generally taken for granted.

THE INFLUENCE OF DOGMATICS

Some decades later, however, the scene has changed considerably. It is now widely acknowledged that the independence from dogmatic principles, which Biblical Theology professed, was largely illusory. J. P. Gabler's foundational essay of 1787, which called for the distinction of Biblical from Dogmatic Theology, nonetheless saw the role of the former as laying a firm foundation for Dogmatics.[5] When historical criticism developed its independence from Dogmatic Theology in the nineteenth century, Biblical Theology was generally abandoned in favor of the History of the Religion.

"Could dogmatics teach New Testament theology to see the facts correctly," asked Wilhelm Wrede in 1897. "At most it could colour them."[6] The revival of Biblical Theology after 1920, however, was marked by the reintroduction of dogmatic principles, despite professions to the contrary. Walther Eichrodt was typical. He announced his intention to "avoid all schemes which derive from Christian dogmatics," yet he held that the "profoundest meaning" of the Old Testament could only be perceived in the light of its "essential coherence with the NT."[7] G. E. Wright based his theology on critical historiography and archaeology, yet saw theology as a "recital" that involved "a projection of faith into facts."[8] In the more recent words of Brevard Childs, "The presence of Christian assumptions is implicit in virtually every modern Old Testament theology and even in the allegedly objective histories of the religion of Israel."[9]

The tension between these Christian assumptions and historical criticism was pointed out by a number of critics in the 1960s, notably by Langdon Gilkey and James Barr.[10] The criticisms were drawn together by Childs in 1970 in a manifesto that marked a watershed in modern Biblical Theology.[11] The problems went beyond the shortcomings of individual theologians and concerned the compatibility of historical criticism with dogmatic theological presuppositions. It is not that historical criticism is free of presuppositions or is purely objective,[12] but that one of its principles is methodical doubt, which holds that any conclusion can in principle be questioned in the light of new evidence or arguments.[13] It therefore disallows the possibility of dogmatic certainty. This aspect of historical criticism was especially problematic for any attempt to base Biblical Theology on historical fact,[14] but it also undermined the certainty of other theological convictions, such as the essential coherence of the Old Testament with the New.

Much of the criticism of the so-called Biblical Theology Movement of 1920–1970 has come from within theological circles. There is also increasing criticism of theological interpretation of the Bible as such. A major criticism here is that biblical theologians engage in unnecessary mystification, by "explanation by reference to the inexplicable."[15] So we find proposals that biblical sociology should replace Biblical Theology,[16] or that scholars should devote themselves to literary study without feeling a need to pursue theological questions.

The proposal of Childs, that the context of the canon play a normative role, opted for one horn of the dilemma that the Biblical Theology Movement had tried to straddle, by taking an explicitly confessional starting point. As his critics have pointed out, the idea of canon is extrinsic to the biblical texts.[17] It is a dogmatic construct, imposed on the Bible from without. Quite apart from the specific problems associated with Childs's notion of canon,[18] the very appeal to dogmatic principles cuts off the possibility of dialogue with those who do not share those principles. Moreover, Childs is certainly vulnerable to the charge of mystification. In his view, "understanding derives ultimately from the illumination of the Spirit. . . . There is no one hermeneutical key for unlocking the biblical message, but the canon provides the arena in which the struggle for understanding takes place."[19] Hence he is deliberately vague on the procedure of interpretation, apart from the fact that one is to focus on the canon. Without denying the limits of human understanding, most scholars find it possible to give a much fuller account of the process of interpretation without resorting to such "explanation by the inexplicable." Childs has rendered a considerable service to Biblical Theology, however, by clarifying the antithesis between the critical study of religion and biblical theology based on dogmatic presuppositions. Not all practitioners of Biblical Theology have perceived the tension between historical criticism and dogmatic theology as sharply as this, or conceded the force of the criticisms, but intermediate positions have been undermined nonetheless.[20]

AN ALTERNATIVE PROPOSAL

The contemporary biblical scholar then is often confronted with a choice between the explicit appeal to dogmatic considerations, à la Childs, on the one hand, and the Bible without theology, à la Gottwald and Oden, on the other. I would like to suggest, however, that there may be another alternative. Biblical Theology need not be conceived as a normative discipline, but instead as an area of Historical Theology, which is one source among others for contemporary Dogmatic or Systematic Theology.[21] As an area of Historical Theology it necessarily overlaps with the history of religion. Within the history of the religion, it focuses on the portrayal of God in one group of texts, the Bible.[22] While the material to be explained is canonical, the context of interpretation is not restricted, as it is in Childs's canonical approach. Biblical Theology can make full use of historical, sociological, and literary research, and so can be integrated fully into the mainstream of biblical research.

Any attempt to construct a biblical theology on this basis must evidently guard against the problems that beset the Biblical Theology Movement. Confessional statements about God's activity in, and purpose for, history go beyond the bounds of such historical analysis.[23] We can only say that a community construed God's activity or purpose in a particular way, and consider why. Again, sociohistorical criticism does not permit us to draw conclusions about the divine nature. We can only say how various groups in Israel imagined God, and how their belief shaped their life.[24] From this perspective we can discuss how Christianity adapted the Hebrew Bible as its Old Testament, but we are not justified in making claims about the essential or necessary unity of the Testaments.

This model of Biblical Theology has clear advantages insofar as it facilitates dialogue with other areas of biblical study and provides a context for discussing the basis of theological beliefs. Properly followed, it is not open to the charge of mystification. Two objections, however, require consideration. On the one hand, can such an enterprise be really considered theological? And on the other, is there a need for Biblical Theology and does it really add anything to the nontheological study of religion advocated by Gottwald and Oden?

What counts as "theological" depends, of course, on the model of theology we are willing to accept. Anyone who regards theology as essentially confessional, or who sees the role of the theologian as "awaiting in anticipation a fresh illumination of God's Spirit,"[25] can hardly be expected to accept the approach proposed here. On the other hand, anyone who regards theology as an academic discipline, which is analytical rather than confessional, must surely accept the analysis of biblical God-language as a valid contribution. This model is designed for the academy rather than for the church, but its practical value should not be underestimated. J. A. Sanders has argued that Scripture ("canon" in his parlance) "functions, for the most part, to provide indications of the identity as well as the life-style of the ongoing community which reads it."[26] It is "adaptable for life" and has in fact been adapted in a great variety of ways, beginning already in ancient Israel. The sociohistorical approach to Biblical Theology lends itself well to rendering the Scriptures adaptable for life. The typical historical-critical procedure is to reconstruct the situation in which a text was composed. Such reconstructions are necessarily hypothetical, but they provide ways of imagining how a text might have made sense in a real-life situation. They thereby provide analogies for ways in which it might be appropriated in the present. The primary goal of Biblical Theology as proposed here is understanding rather than praxis, but it can also enhance, and certainly does not lessen, the applicability of a text.

The need for Biblical Theology arises from the fact that theological language is an important part of the text and is of crucial importance for most readers of the Bible. The very fact that this language is often taken uncritically ensures the need for a critical Biblical Theology. Its contribution to the history of religion is to ensure that the theological aspects of the texts are adequately explained, and neither glossed over as irrelevant nor too hastily translated into the categories of whatever discipline is of primary interest to the historian (cf. Gottwald's sociological reduction of Yahwism). This model of Biblical Theology, then, tries to guard on the one side against the mystification and apologetics of which the discipline has often been rightly accused and, on the other, against the disinterest of secular critics in an important dimension of the text. Our concern here is to distinguish this critical approach to Biblical Theology from the confessional-dogmatic approach, most clearly represented by Childs. The value of this approach for the history of religion can best be judged by the light it sheds on the text.

THE CASE OF DANIEL

The theoretical issues confronting Biblical Theology may be illustrated by consideration of some aspects of the book of Daniel. This book is usually relegated to the periphery of Biblical Theology, and in many ways it is atypical of the Hebrew Bible. For that very reason it allows us to focus on some problems that are often glossed over in treatments of Biblical Theology that focus on the more central texts of the Torah or Prophets.

The primary difference between the canonical approach of Childs and the sociohistorical approach advocated here lies in the choice of context in which the book is viewed. For Childs, the context is the canon of Scripture itself. For a sociohistorical approach, the literary context is provided by the other writings of the time, especially the emerging genre of apocalypses,[27] while the historical context (for the complete Hebrew-Aramaic book) is the persecution of Antiochus Epiphanes and the

Maccabean revolt. We will consider the significance of these different contexts for three problems: the pseudepigraphic attribution of the book, the portrayal of God, and the hope for resurrection.

Pseudepigraphy

For anyone who accepts the results of historical criticism, the first problem posed by the book of Daniel is that of pseudepigraphy. Few would now pose this problem in such extreme terms as the nineteenth-century conservative Pusey: "It admits of no half-measures. It is either Divine or an imposture. . . . The writer, were he not Daniel, must have lied on a most frightful scale."[28] It is now generally recognized that pseude-pigraphy cannot be simply equated with deception. Yet, as Childs observes, "the issue continues to trouble the average lay reader,"[29] and some biblical theologians too. Childs proposes to solve the problem by arguing "that the author of chs. 7–12 understood his role as one of filling in the details of the early visions of Daniel through the study of scripture and thus confirming Daniel's prophecies in the light of the events of contemporary history."[30] According to Childs, the author "had no new prophetic word directly from God. Rather he understood the sacred writings of the past as the medium through which God continued to make contemporary his divine revelation. His own identity had no theological significance and therefore he concealed it. It is basically to misunderstand the work of the Maccabean author to characterize it as a ruse by which to gain authority for himself, nor was it a conscious literary device. Rather, it arose from a profoundly theological sense of the function of prophecy, which was continually illuminated through the continuing reinterpretation of scripture."[31]

This attempt to resolve the problem of pseudepigraphy has two aspects that require comment, one exegetical, the other theological. The exegetical claim is that chapters 7–12 are an amplification of the early visions of Daniel through the study of Scripture. The evidence offered in support of this claim is slight indeed. The strongest case involves the parallelism of chapters 2 and 7. In Childs's view, chapter 7 attests to the truth of the four kingdom schema with reference to the new circumstances of the Maccabean period. This statement is true enough as far as it goes, but it does scant justice to chapter 7, which is presented as a vision in its own right, not as an interpretation. (Contrast Daniel 9 in this respect.) The motif of the four kingdoms is overlain with the new imagery of beasts rising from the sea and a heavenly judgment scene. This imagery is not derived from Daniel 2 and can be only partially explained from older Scripture. Childs's inner biblical exegesis leaves unexplained the contrast between the turbulent sea and the manlike figure who comes on the clouds, a contrast best understood against the background of ancient myth.[32] Chapter 2 provides one of the building blocks for chapter 7, but the latter is a new and independent vision. Even in chapter 9, where Daniel draws explicitly on older Scripture, the interpretation is not inhibited by the plain sense of the text (seventy years become seventy weeks of years) and so can scarcely be said to be bound by Scripture at all. The primary purpose of Daniel 7–12 is to interpret the crisis of the Maccabean period. The interpretation of older Scripture is one means to that end.

The theological issue that Childs addresses here is the scandal of pseudepigraphy, with its implications of deception. It is not clear that his solution really alleviates that problem by construing the visions as elaborations of Daniel 2. While the dream and interpretation in that chapter are surely older than chapters 7–12, their association with Nebuchadnezzar and Daniel is nonetheless fictional (at least according to the critical consensus that Childs appears to accept). In short, the problem of fictional attribution arises already in the oldest stratum of the Daniel tradition. It is not clear why a pseudepigraphic elaboration of an older, legendary oracle should be less problematic than a new pseudepigraphic vision.

A sociohistorical approach to the problem of pseudepigraphy places it in the wider context of the ancient, and especially the Hellenistic, world. It was a widespread phenomenon, and its motivations were diverse.[33] The notion of forgery was certainly known and condemned in antiquity, but not all false attributions were made with the intention of deceiving. The composition of speeches in the name of famous individuals was an accepted convention of Greek historiography. Speeches in the name and style of great orators were composed as rhetorical exercises. The motivations associated with pseudepigraphy could differ from genre to genre. The case of an apocalypse attributed to Daniel or Enoch may be different from that of a letter attributed to a recent historical personality like Paul. There has been much speculation on the psychology of apocalyptic pseudepigraphy. It has been suggested that the authors saw themselves as heirs to traditions stretching back to Daniel or Enoch, and that their work was attributed to the source of the tradition by a concept of corporate personality[34] or that the visionary's alter ego is identified with a famous visionary of the past because of the nature of the experience.[35] There is ultimately no way to verify such theories, but at least they show that Childs's theory is not the only one that allows that the authors may have acted in good faith.

The effects of apocalyptic pseudepigraphy are more accessible than its motives. There can be no doubt that attribution to a famous ancient visionary enhanced the authority of the message and indeed was necessary to permit the presentation of past history in the guise of prophecy. We must suppose that the common people accepted the attribution, or the message would lose much of its effect. On the other hand, the immediate circle of the authors must have been aware of the manner in which the works were actually produced. In view of the urgency of the message, we may assume that the authors and their immediate circles considered the literary fiction justified and that it did not detract from the religious value of the revelation. There is no self-conscious reflection on the need for a "noble lie" such as we find in Plato.[36] Yet, however we understand the psychology of the apocalyptic writers, the phenomenon of pseudepigraphy helps underline the fact that their works are fictions, works of imagination, whose truth is of the same order as that of Plato's myths.[37]

There is no inherent reason why designating Daniel as fiction should pose a problem for Biblical Theology.[38] The fact that Daniel contains so much historical material, both garbled (chapters 1–6) and accurate (chapter 11) confuses the reader's generic expectations. A sociohistorical approach frankly recognizes the fictional, imaginative character of the book and denies that its theological value is thereby prejudiced. That value must be assessed in terms of the substantive content of the book rather than of the literary form in which it is presented, although appreciation of the literary form is crucial for our understanding of the theological content.

Portrayal of God

Childs makes a valid point when he insists that "the witness of the book is theocentric" and adds that "neither the faith of Daniel nor that of a Maccabean author can be made the object of the biblical witness when it is divorced from the hope which evoked the obedient response."[39] It is somewhat surprising, then, that he has little to say about the portrayal of God in Daniel and contents himself with general statements about "the purpose of God" to allow Israel to languish for a time and to bring in the kingdom, suddenly, by divine intervention.

There is, naturally, much more to be said about the God of Daniel.[40] The main lines of the portrayal are in accordance with other Old Testament books: God is the universal judge, who is sovereign over the kingdoms of the earth. There are also some distinctive aspects. God appears more remote from humanity than in the older books because of the increased prominence of angelic mediators, and God's purpose has taken on a deterministic character. While older prophecy frequently allowed the possibility that God would "repent" (e.g., Amos 7, Hosea 11), this possibility is no longer envisaged.[41] Biblical theologians who seek to extract a consistent picture of God from the Old Testament often disregard these aspects of Daniel's God as atypical. Childs speaks vaguely of "theological tension"[42] and seems to leave its resolution to the Spirit.

For a sociohistorical approach, the issue is not whether there really is an irrevocable divine plan for history, but why the author of Daniel portrayed God in this way. This question must be viewed in the context of the cosmological views current in the Hellenistic age. Many scholars have posited influence of Babylonian determinism on apocalyptic literature and on Daniel in particular.[43] Deterministic cosmology, possibly influenced by Babylonian conceptions, was propagated in the Hellenistic world by the Stoics. Closer to Daniel, very similar views of God and history were developed in the early apocalypses of Enoch, some of which, at least, antedate Daniel. Daniel, in short, was a child of his time. The book's conception of God cannot be regarded simply as a projection inspired by the Maccabean crisis, but it was evidently found appropriate and meaningful in view of those circumstances.

The problem presented by the deterministic God of Daniel is essentially the same as that presented by the mythology and cosmology of the New Testament, so eloquently addressed by Bultmann.[44] The portrayal of God is embedded in a dated, time-conditioned view of the world that is no longer accepted. Bultmann proposed to interpret the theocentric myths in terms of an anthropocentric understanding of human existence. For all his insistence on the theocentric character of Daniel, Childs is not as far from this position as we might expect. Like Bultmann, he abstracts from most of the particulars of the biblical text and affirms only the general trustworthiness of God. The appropriate human response is faith and obedience,[45] but the precise object of these virtues is left vague and indeterminate.[46] There is, of course, a fundamental difference in attitude. Childs leaves the application of the text to the guidance of the Spirit. Bultmann, in contrast, sought to demystify theology and placed the emphasis on human decision. The point of analogy, however, is that both finally disregard the particularities of the biblical text.

Any theological approach that wants to appropriate the message of a biblical book must abstract to some degree from its particular circumstances. Childs is right that such a process of abstraction was entailed by the process of canonization, and Bultmann is right that apocalyptic cosmology is no longer accepted by anyone in the modern world. Yet the historical particularities retain more of their significance in a sociohistorical approach than they do for Childs or Bultmann. The book of Daniel provides a case study that is potentially "adaptable for life" (in Sanders's phrase). To apply it properly we must appreciate that it is not a general philosophy of life, but a reaction to specific circumstances. Daniel's obedience to the food laws in chapter 1 is located in a very specific situation: it enables him and his companions to preserve their identity in the Diaspora. The virtue of the act cannot be divorced from the circumstances in which it takes place. Again, the characterization of Gentile kingdoms differs noticeably between chapters 1–6 and 7–12. The portrayal in chapter 7 is specifically a response to the Antiochan persecution and is only justified in analogous situations. Not every Gentile kingdom is appropriately identified as a beast from the sea. The applicability of the visions requires an analogy between our situation and that of the author, and the specificity of the author's situation is therefore important.

The portrayal of God cannot be taken as revealed truth but is a way of construing the world, which led to a particular course of action. That portrayal must now be evaluated both in terms of its credibility in view of modern science and in terms of the values that it supported. In any case it provides a model for imagining God that must be adapted in the light of new circumstances. The fact that Daniel's portrayal of God is inconsistent with other biblical portrayals is no longer problematic if we look on the Bible as a store of models appropriate to different contexts rather than as a consistent whole.[47]

The Hope of Resurrection

Our final theological issue from the Book of Daniel concerns the belief in resurrection in chapter 12. As is well known, this is the only passage in the Hebrew Bible that speaks unambiguously of the resurrection of individuals for reward or punishment. Childs minimizes the novelty of the belief, claiming that "the Old Testament provided the grounds on which both later Jews and Christians developed their understanding of the afterlife."[48] This is an oversimplification. The Old Testament contains some significant precedents in the notion of the fullness of life in the presence of God, in the Psalms, and in prophetic passages that speak of the resurrection of the corporate people (Ezekiel 37; Isa 26:19), and these surely facilitated later adoption of the belief in resurrection.[49] Yet it remains true that the predominant witness of the Old Testament is to the expectation of mere survival of the shade in Sheol,[50] and

Ecclesiastes, one of the books closest in date to Daniel, bitterly disputes the notion that the lot of humanity is any different from that of the beasts (Eccl 3:19-22). There can be no suggestion that belief in resurrection was implicit in the Old Testament before Daniel.

It would be too simple to attribute the origin of the belief in Daniel simply to reflection on Scripture. Such reflection played a part, as can be seen from echoes of the terminology of Isaiah 26 and 66.[51] Yet it now appears that the idea of resurrection was first developed in Judaism in the Enoch tradition (*1 Enoch* 22), where it is presented in the context of mythical geography and is indebted to Babylonian and Greek traditions.[52] Daniel has a point of affinity with the Enoch tradition when it associates the risen sages with the stars (cf. *1 Enoch* 104). It is very probable that Daniel was influenced by the noncanonical Enoch material as well as by the texts in Isaiah. Moreover, the belief in Daniel cannot be divorced from the historical context of the Antiochan persecution, in which people suffered death for their faith. In view of the early development of the Enoch tradition, the belief in resurrection cannot be regarded simply as a reaction to the persecution, but the historical situation surely prompted Daniel's acceptance of the idea.

In the context of the book of Daniel itself, the belief in resurrection is not presented as a reflection on Scripture but as part of a revelation. The revelation poses its own theological problems. In part, it consists of prophecies after the fact (11:2-39), in part of erroneous predictions (11:40-45), and finally of the eschatological prophecy. The nonfulfillment of the concluding predictions did not discredit the book in antiquity, as Childs has rightly noted. The fact that the eschaton did not come as the author expected does not prove that it will not come at all. Like the use of pseudepigraphy, however, it should warn us not to take the predictions at face value. They are works of the imagination, attempts to make sense of historical experience. Whether they construe reality correctly, in their hope of justification after death, must await eschatological verification. For the present we can only discuss how the belief arose and how it functioned.

The function of afterlife is especially clear in the book of Daniel. It is the hope that empowers the martyrs to lay down their lives in the time of persecution.[53] In the context of the Maccabean crisis it offered one model of conduct. There were other models available, including that of the zealot Phinehas from Numbers 25, cited in 1 Macc 2:26 as the paradigm of the Maccabees. There is no guarantee as to which model is the right one in any given situation. What Daniel offers is a way of looking at the world in which nonviolence and martyrdom make sense. The attractiveness of that vision is not necessarily undermined by the knowledge that it is a work of imagination rather than univocal fact, an object of hope rather than of knowledge.

CONCLUSION

If nothing else, our discussion has shown that the alternatives of Biblical Theology and History of Religion are a good deal more ambiguous than they appeared when

Dr. Ryan posed them to his students in the 1960s. There are various models of Biblical Theology, colored in different degrees by dogmatic presuppositions. It can be viewed as a normative discipline or as an area of Historical Theology. On the other hand, the History of Religion may or may not be construed so as to address theological questions. Childs may fairly claim to have overcome the inconsistency of the Biblical Theology Movement by making his dogmatic presuppositions fully explicit. In doing so, however, he has shut his Biblical Theology off from dialogue with other areas of biblical research, especially sociology, and thereby diminished his ability to explain the text. His work is also open to the charge of undue mystification. The proposal advanced here moves in the opposite direction from Childs and fully embraces historical criticism. The History of Religion approach, then, is not an alternative to be avoided but an ally to be utilized. While it may be difficult for any Christian to avoid dogmatic prejudices and apologetics in addressing theological questions, it is an ideal worthy of our aspirations. Such an approach will not satisfy those who see theology as an essentially confessional enterprise, but it does affirm the possibility of a Biblical Theology that is consistent with the regnant historical-critical method.

CHAPTER 3

THE POLITICS OF BIBLICAL
INTERPRETATION

In 1996, an English scholar named Keith Whitelam published a book with the provocative title *The Invention of Ancient Israel.* The subtitle was even more provocative: *The Silencing of Palestinian History.*[1] Needless to say, it caused a storm of controversy, which no doubt is what the publisher, and probably also the author, hoped for. In the modern English-speaking world, biblical scholarship is normally a pretty tame affair. But Whitelam suggested that it is neither as inconsequential nor as innocent as is usually supposed. On the contrary, he claimed, it is implicated in lending a cloak of legitimacy to one side in one of the most contentious political disputes on the planet, while pretending to engage in objective, disinterested scholarship.

Many scholars reacted angrily to Whitelam's book, especially in North America and in Israel, and dismissed it as ideologically motivated or even anti-Semitic. But while Whitelam is exceptional among biblical scholars in his apparent endorsement of Palestinian rights, he is very much in line with recent trends in other respects. On the one hand, he is part of a much-publicized group of revisionist historians who have earned the label "minimalist" by their extreme skepticism toward the biblical account of Israelite history, and who claim that both the biblical account and the supposedly critical reconstruction of Israelite history in modern scholarship are "inventions" that are more fiction than fact.[2] On the other hand, he allies himself with the broad trend in academic circles known as postmodernism, which denies that there is any such thing as disinterested, objective scholarship, or that it is possible to give any single, unambiguously valid account of the past.[3] The implications of Whitelam's argument for the legitimacy of modern Israel are limited, since the support of biblical scholarship is hardly of vital importance for the Jewish state, even if it is useful on occasion. The more significant implications of his book concern the legitimacy and credibility of biblical scholarship as it has been practiced in modern times.

HISTORICAL-CRITICAL SCHOLARSHIP

Biblical scholarship as it has developed over the last few centuries has been dominated by the approach that is loosely called historical criticism. As James Barr has insisted, historical criticism is not strictly a method but a loose umbrella that covers a range of methods (source criticism, form criticism, sociological criticism, etc.) that may sometimes be at odds with each other.[4] But underlying these various methods are certain common assumptions. The most fundamental of these is that texts should be interpreted in their historical contexts, in light of the literary and cultural conventions of their time. Time is of the essence, and anachronism is a deadly sin. Beyond that assumption, biblical scholarship has usually been short on theory. The most influential attempt to articulate the presuppositions of historical criticism has been that of the German theologian and sociologist of religion Ernst Troeltsch, whose views were later reformulated in the American context by Van Harvey.[5] Three of the principles identified by Troeltsch and Harvey are of immediate relevance to the current discussion.

First is the principle of autonomy. This principle is associated with the Enlightenment and especially with Immanuel Kant, although he certainly was not the first to conceive of it.[6] As Harvey has aptly described it, it represented a change in what may be called the morality of knowledge. Where medieval culture had celebrated belief as a virtue and regarded doubt as sin, the modern critical mentality regards doubt as a necessary step in the testing of knowledge and the will to believe as a threat to rational thought. In the context of biblical studies, autonomy meant first of all freedom from ecclesiastical authorities and heresy trials. In that narrow sense, the need for autonomy can hardly be questioned. But it also represented an ideal of judgment. In the words of the historian R. G. Collingwood,[7] "so far from relying on an authority other than himself, to whose statements his thought must conform, the historian is his own authority." In this sense, autonomy is opposed not only to ecclesiastical interference but also to undue deference to received opinion. Biblical scholarship has not always been characterized by autonomy in the latter sense!

The idea of autonomy, more broadly defined as freedom from tradition, has become quite controversial in modern times, with some justification.[8] No interpreter is independent of all tradition, and all interpretation is influenced by its context.[9] No one is autonomous in an absolute sense. As we shall see, one of the themes of Whitelam's book is the degree to which supposedly objective scholarship is colored by ideological agendas. Pretty much everyone in the contemporary debate complains about the tyranny of unexamined presuppositions and professes the need for awareness of one's presuppositions. It makes a difference, however, whether it is sufficient to declare one's faith perspective or traditional allegiance, or whether one regards all presuppositions as open to criticism.

A second principle of historical criticism that has been controversial is the principle of analogy.[10] To understand the ancient context of a text requires some sympathetic analogy between ancient and modern situations. Indeed, one of the assumptions of historical criticism is that texts are human products, and that human nature has not changed beyond recognition over the centuries. We can assess what is plausible in an ancient situation because we know what human beings are capable of. Biblical scholarship has often been accused of alienating the text from the modern reader and making it an object of antiquarian interest. No doubt the complaint is justified in some cases. But it is not, I think, justified with regard to historical criticism as a whole. On the contrary, one might argue that biblical scholarship is often distorted by the impulse to read the biblical text in light of modern situations.

The third principle of historical criticism to be noted here is "the principle of criticism."[11] Scholarship is an ongoing process; its results are always provisional and never final. This is perhaps especially obvious in historical scholarship where new evidence is constantly coming to light. The historian tries to establish the most likely account of the past, but absolute certainty is never available. Today's results may be overturned by tomorrow's excavation. This element of uncertainty in biblical scholarship has always been especially unsettling for church authorities and for traditional theologians, more so even than heretical conclusions, because it implies that church teachings too may not be founded on certainty after all.

I do not mean to suggest that all biblical scholars who regarded themselves as historical critics over the last century subscribed to Troeltsch's principles, or even that those who did subscribe to them abided by them in practice. Professors do not always appreciate either the autonomy of their students or the uncertainty of their own conclusions. So my account of historical criticism is somewhat idealized; it is a summary of what I would regard as historical criticism as it ought to be done, and sometimes has been, at least approximately. I am also, of course, speaking on a very general level, so as to construct an umbrella large enough to accommodate several groups of scholars who disagreed sharply with each other, even on methodological grounds. The great bulk of biblical scholarship in the twentieth century, at least down to the last two decades, has been historical-critical, insofar as it tried to interpret the biblical texts in their historical context and thereby to give these texts a certain objectivity over and against later tradition. And even allowing for the shortcomings of its practitioners, historical criticism has not, I think, been the kind of dogmatic system that some of its recent critics accuse it of being.[12]

POSTMODERNISM

At the beginning of the twenty-first century, however, the situation of biblical scholarship is very different from what it was a hundred years ago. If there is any one thing that is characteristic of academia at the beginning of the new millennium, it is diversity. Much biblical scholarship is still done with church or synagogue in view, and tensions still exist that are similar to those of a century ago. But many other biblical scholars operate in a university context, where church concerns are of little relevance and, indeed, are viewed with great suspicion. In this context, there is a new conflict of interpretations, arising from the left rather than from the right, often nowadays bearing the label of postmodernism. Postmodernism, it should be said, is even more of a mirage than historical criticism, and it encompasses a wide range of approaches and methods.[13] But like historical-critical approaches, postmodernist ones have a family resemblance, and their general, widely shared assumptions are such as to put those of historical criticism, and biblical scholarship as it has been practiced in the last century, in doubt.

Here I mention only a few of these assumptions that are of immediate relevance to the discussion of Whitelam's book. Perhaps the most widely shared assumption of postmodernist critics is that "objectivity" is no more than a pretense that masks the vested interests of the interpreter. This assumption is articulated very forcefully in Stanley Fish's book *The Trouble with Principle*.[14] If this is correct, and everyone has a power-seeking agenda, then it is better to have these agendas out in the open. The postmodernist rejects the dichotomy between subjective and objective, arguing that there is no disinterested knowledge.[15] Typically, postmodernists will also deny that they are claiming absolute truth for their own positions, although this claim is often difficult to reconcile with the vehemence of their rhetoric.[16] But in any case, the denial of objectivity poses a direct challenge to a basic aspiration of historical criticism.

Another common postmodernist assumption is that there is no univocal, unambiguous meaning. Any text is open to multiple interpretations. Biblical postmodernists often claim that this is antithetical to historical criticism, but this is not so obvious. There is no reason why historical critics should not appreciate ambiguity in texts. But historical critics often argue that one meaning is primary—either the author's intention or what the text would have meant in its original setting. Thoroughgoing postmodernists, in contrast, deny that there is any one primary meaning. In the words of A. K. M. Adam, they "suspect that any univocity is a product of an interpretive violence that suppresses ambiguity by a will to unity."[17]

A third assertion of at least some postmodernist critics is that time is not an essential consideration in meaning.[18] The fact that texts were composed long ago and in another place is not necessarily significant. Accordingly, they do not share the historical critic's dread of anachronism.

Postmodernists claim that they do not reject modernist interpretations (such as historical criticism) but only their claims to hegemony or primacy. According to the article on "Post-Modern Biblical Interpretation" in the *Dictionary of Biblical Interpretation,* postmodern critics are unfailingly modest: "Post-modern biblical interpretation does not surpass, improve, perfect, contravene, or undermine modern biblical interpretation—except when modern interpreters claim the exclusive prerogative to determine interpretive legitimacy on their own modern terms."[19] What remains unclear in this, however, is whether some interpretations are superior to others, and if so, by what criteria. At least some biblical postmodernists reserve the right to affirm one interpretation over another but on grounds that are strictly ad hoc and relevant only to the issue in question.[20]

THEORIES OF THE ORIGIN OF ISRAEL

The postmodernist turn in recent intellectual life provides the context of Whitelam's book, to which I now return. The subject of the origin of Israel has been a topic of heated debate for most of the past century. According to Whitelam, however, "this often fierce debate has profound political implications which have rarely surfaced. The reason for the heat of the recent debate is to do precisely with the political, cultural and religious implications of the construction of ancient Israel."[21] Historical criticism, as practiced over the last century, is regarded as "positivistic"—in the sense that it is possible to give one objective account of "what actually happened." The recent revisionist work of people like Thompson and Davies is said to undermine the search for such a "master story," or authoritative account of Israel's past. Whitelam intends to mount another such challenge, and to locate himself squarely in the discourse of postmodernism.

Albright

The most influential reconstruction of the origin of Israel in American scholarship in the twentieth century was developed under the influence of William Foxwell Albright, who was a dominant figure in the period between 1910 and 1960. Albright and his students basically accepted the biblical account of the Israelite conquest of Canaan and sought to confirm it by archaeological excavation.[22] Archaeology showed that several Canaanite cities had been destroyed at the end of the Late Bronze Age (around the thirteenth century B.C.E.) and replaced by poorer settlements. Albright saw this evidence as confirmation of the biblical account in the book of Joshua, that the Israelites had taken the land by force, even though some sites (like Jericho) that were mentioned in the Bible did not seem to have been destroyed at that time. In retrospect, many scholars would now say that Albright had a presumption in favor of the reliability of the ancient accounts, and that this led him to place great weight on evidence that supported them and to disregard evidence that did not. (It should be said, however, that this was not a matter of faith for Albright, and that he was perfectly willing to correct an ancient account if he felt the evidence so required.) Moreover, it is now generally appreciated that the destruction of the Canaanite cities was not necessarily due to Israelite invasion but may have been caused by Egyptian armies or invading sea peoples. Whitelam, however, finds another factor at work. Albright's account of the situation after the conquest, when the remaining Canaanites were gradually absorbed into Israel, is "remarkably reminiscent" of the situation in Palestine in the 1920s, after the Zionist influx into Palestine.[23] A much closer parallel to the situation in Palestine is found in the account of the German scholar, Albrecht Alt, who held that there was no violent invasion, only gradual infiltration.[24] Whitelam recognizes this,[25] but then one has to wonder how Alt and Albright produced such diametrically opposite accounts of the origin of Israel if both were influenced, even unconsciously, by events in Palestine in the 1920s.

Whitelam, however, points to another aspect of Albright's work that is more troubling.[26] To his credit, the archaeologist paused to consider the moral problem of the slaughter of the Canaanites. "Strictly speaking," he wrote, "this Semitic custom [of total slaughter, or *herem*] was no worse from the humanitarian point of view than the reciprocal massacres of Protestants and Catholics in the 17th century" or several other historical examples. "We Americans," Albright went on,

> have perhaps less right than most modern nations, in spite of our genuine humanitarianism, to sit in judgement on the Israelites of the thirteenth century B.C. since we have, intentionally or otherwise, exterminated scores of thousands of Indians in every corner of our great nation and have crowded the rest into great concentration camps. The fact that this was probably inevitable does not make it more edifying to the Americans of to-day.

So far, we might say, fair enough, but Albright continued: "From the impartial standpoint of a philosopher of history, it often seems necessary that a people of markedly inferior type should vanish before a people of superior potentialities, since there is a point beyond which racial mixture cannot go without disaster."[27] Here Albright is guided by a master narrative that sees the coming of Christianity as the climax of antiquity and the rise of Israel as an essential step toward that goal. In Whitelam's words, "Israel, as the taproot of Western civilization, represents the rational, while 'Canaan,' the indigenous Palestinian population, represents the irrational Other which must be replaced in the inexorable progress of divinely guided evolution."[28]

For Whitelam, the problem here is not just a matter of the philosophy of history. It shows the entanglement of biblical scholarship in modern politics. In the words of Neil Asher Silberman:

> there is something more to Albright's legacy than historical ideas. Can a scholar, who is also a product of a modern society, with a particular national, religious and economic position, really enter a strife torn society (like Palestine was in the 1920s) without participating, willingly or unknowingly, in the political struggle that is going on? Can he or she obtain rights to an archaeological site . . . and most of all present a version of the past that is susceptible to modern political interpretation, without contributing—again, knowingly or unconsciously—to the modern political debate?[29]

In fact, Albright contributed explicitly to the political debate. While he tried to maintain friendship with both Jews and Arabs, he became increasingly a supporter of Zionism. He invoked the historic right of the Jewish people to Palestine: "Palestine is the home of the patriarchs, poets, and prophets of Israel; Palestine is the workshop in which Jews forged three right instruments of Western culture; the Hebrew Bible, the New Testament, and the Second Law."[30] Moreover, the Jews would construct "a center of European civilization in the heart of the Near East," and this would ultimately be beneficial for the entire region. Evolutionary providence, that had seen to the overthrow of the Canaanites, was now on the side of the Jews in the struggle for Palestine. This teleological, or goal-oriented, view of history is a good example of what postmodernists call a master narrative. It leads people to construe historical facts in one way rather than another and even determines to a degree what facts are accepted in the first case.

Gottwald

Albright's view of the origin of Israel has not stood the test of time. Ironically, it was brought down primarily by the archaeological evidence, to which he had looked confidently for confirmation.[31] Archaeology has shown that many of the sites mentioned in the Bible, like Jericho, were not even occupied in the thirteenth century B.C.E., when the Israelites were supposed to have destroyed them. There was some upheaval in Canaan at that time. There was a great increase in village settlements in the central highlands of Palestine. These new settlers are generally assumed to be the early Israelites. But their material culture was essentially the same as that of the Canaanites. The archaeological evidence finds nothing to suggest that they had been wandering in the wilderness or had ever sojourned in Egypt.

A different model for understanding the origin of Israel was proposed by Albright's student, George Mendenhall, who postulated a peasant revolt in Canaan at the end of the Bronze Age.[32] This model was developed at length by Norman Gottwald, and it is on his presentation that I will focus here.[33] In this case, there is no problem at all in identifying a political agenda. (It should be said that this was not true of Mendenhall.) Gottwald dedicates his book to the memory of the first Israelites and follows this by citing an anonymous tribute to the people of Vietnam. He comments explicitly that

> two decades of involvement in civil rights struggles, in opposition to the war in Vietnam, in anti-imperialist efforts, in analysis of North American capitalism, and in the rough-and-tumble of ecclesial and educational politics have constituted an ever-informative "living laboratory" for discerning related social struggles in ancient Israel.[34]

In short, he uses his own experience of social struggle as a heuristic tool to understand the social struggles of the ancient world. In this, he is not exceptional, although few scholars are so forthright.

The revolt model allows that there was some influx of Israelites from Egypt:

> The advocates of the revolt model for Israelite origins picture these Israelite tribes as immediate allies of the Canaanite lower classes. The former slaves from Egypt, now autonomous, presented an immediate appeal to the restive serfs and peasants of Canaan. The attraction of Israelite Yahwism for these oppressed Canaanites may be readily located in the central feature of the religion of the entering tribes: Yahwism celebrated the actuality of deliverance from socio-political bondage, and it promised continuing deliverance whenever Yahweh's autonomous people were threatened.[35]

One would be hard pressed to find evidence in the Bible for the "restive serfs and peasants of Canaan" who rallied to the new religion of liberated Israel. In fact, insofar as the revolt theory rests on ancient evidence, that evidence is found in the Amarna letters, which date from about a century before the usual date of the Exodus. The letters show that there were indeed restive serfs and peasants in Canaan, and, intriguingly, they sometimes refer to them as Habiru.[36] Moreover, the revolt hypothesis is quite compatible with the archaeological evidence.[37] The new settlements in the central highlands around the thirteenth century B.C.E. could have been established by dissident Canaanites who had withdrawn their allegiance from the city-states. Whether this is more than a possibility remains an open question. The assumption that these people constituted early Israel depends primarily on the Bible (with a little support from the stele of Merneptah), and the Bible does not describe the development as a social revolution at all.

Neither Gottwald nor Mendenhall viewed early Israel as an ethnic unity. Rather, they were "astonishingly diverse ethnically and culturally, but they had in common social and political experiences,"[38] and they proceeded to develop, according to Gottwald, an egalitarian, nonhierarchical society, free from the tyranny of monarchy, in a way that was exceptional if not unique in the ancient world. All of this sounds suspiciously modern, even, perhaps, American. But Whitelam, to no one's surprise at this stage, sees a different analogy:

> What is interesting about this view is that it sounds remarkably like a description of early Zionism where Jews from many different European countries, or more recently from the influx of American, Russian, and Ethiopian Jews, among others, "diverse ethnically and culturally," have been welded together as a modern nation.[39]

Whether Gottwald would acknowledge this analogy is doubtful. It is true, however, that he never questions Israel's right to the land. This is less of a problem for him than it was for Albright, since his Israelites are largely made up of indigenous peasants, and he dismisses the accounts of mass slaughter as hyperbolic. And although he is an avowed liberationist, and is sympathetic to the Vietnamese, it is remarkable that he never mentions the modern Palestinians. The revolting peasants may be indigenous, but they only find their voice when they become Israelites. Very little is said about the Canaanites who did not rebel, or who were left behind in the cities.

Finkelstein

The most recent and currently influential account of Israelite origins arises from the work of the archaeologist Israel Finkelstein.[40] Finkelstein surveyed the settlements in the central highlands and found no evidence that the people there had come from a culture outside of Canaan. They were, then, presumably, Canaanites who had moved to this region for whatever reason—perhaps because of turmoil on the coastal plain due to the invasion of the sea peoples who became the Philistines. Ethnic markers for the new settlers are in short supply, although a possible intriguing marker is the absence of pig bones.[41] Finkelstein has been criticized, however, for assuming that these people were in fact Israelites or proto-Israelites, who eventually developed into the nation-states of Israel and Judah, and thereby using his findings to corroborate Israel's claim to the land. In the words of a reviewer, cited by Whitelam,[42]

> The immediate question raised here is not the use of biblical history to validate modern political stances, but rather the smuggling into "objective" historical inquiry of values configured by modern experience and expectation. Such values can never be eliminated, but surely can, and must, be understood as part of historical discourse, a part moreover that usually directly shapes the nature of questions asked and of answers presented.[43]

This does not strike me as a fair criticism of Finkelstein. His work may be colored by the debate about modern Israel, but it has tended to undermine the authority of claims based on biblical history rather than the reverse. One wonders at this point whether Whitelam regards any acknowledgment of ancient Israel as necessarily tainted by its potential use in the modern political debate.

Whitelam

There need be no doubt, of course, of Whitelam's own values. They are indicated repeatedly by his identification of the Canaanites of the Late Bronze Age as Palestinians. This identification is problematic in several respects. It is anachronistic, in the sense that the land was not called Palestine in the Late Bronze Age—the name in fact comes from the Philistines, who were invading the land at approximately the same time as the Israelites (if the Israelites were indeed invading).[44] The modern Arab Palestinians only emerged as the people of this land well into the Common Era. The ancient Canaanites are of no genetic relevance to the modern Palestinians; at most they provide a historical analogy. Just as the ancient Canaanites were displaced by the Israelites, according to the biblical account, so the modern Palestinians have been displaced by modern Israel. This analogy, of course, is of some significance. However little historical connection there may be between the Canaanites and the Palestinians, the depiction of the Canaanites in biblical scholarship is likely to rub off on the Palestinians among people who are influenced by that scholarship.[45]

It seems to me that Whitelam exaggerates his case and hurts his cause when he argues that biblical scholarship has silenced Palestinian history, or even Canaanite history. Biblical scholars, by definition, are primarily interested in the Bible, and the Bible is interested in Israel, and only incidentally in the Canaanites. I don't think any biblical scholar would object if someone were to write a book on the Canaanites; in fact, such books as we have on the Canaanites, and more particularly on the Canaanite literature from Ugarit, are largely the work of biblical scholars. Scholarship inevitably arises from, and depends on, modern interests, and in the modern West far more people are interested in ancient Israel than in ancient Canaan. This interest arises from the commitments of Christians and Jews. About twenty-five years ago there was a movement to replace "Biblical Archaeology" with the presumably more impartial discipline of Syro-Palestinian Archaeology, led by a prominent young archaeologist named William Dever. A decade or two later, Dever discovered to his dismay that Christian seminaries were no longer interested in hiring archaeologists.[46] But why should they be? What was the relevance of Syro-Palestinian archaeology for Christian seminarians? Dever has now become the champion of "the new biblical archaeology." It would, of course, be very interesting to get an account of ancient history from an Arab point of view, but one can hardly expect Jews, or European or American Christians, to produce it. Moreover, the regrettable fact is that we have very few resources for the history of peoples other than Israel in this area. Whitelam himself has complained at length about the neglect of "Palestinian history" but has not actually done anything to remedy the situation.

HISTORY AND OBJECTIVITY

All that said, it remains true that most (possibly all) depictions of the history of Israel and its neighbors in antiquity are one-sided and viewed from the Israelite perspective and consequently should not be mistaken for objective truth. The most interesting question raised by Whitelam's book is whether objective historical scholarship is possible at all. He makes the point loud and clear that supposedly objective scholars (Albright is the paradigm case) were in fact guided by their prejudices, or their implicit master narrative, to a great degree. But we hardly had to wait for postmodernism to discover that. More than a century ago Albert Schweitzer showed how most modern accounts of the life of Jesus produced a Jesus in the author's image and likeness.[47] The standard practice of historical criticism, as I have described it, has no problem in recognizing such prejudices. This is one reason why we have the principle of criticism, the constant need for revision. But can we do anything except replace one set of prejudices with another?

At the risk of appearing old-fashioned and out of touch with the latest trends in academia, I believe that we can. No one is free of prejudice, ideology, or political agendas, but it is possible nonetheless to recognize and acknowledge data that do not fit with our ideological presuppositions. This is essentially what happened in the case of Albright. As Whitelam admits, the edifice constructed by Albright crumbled, not because people were offended by his master narrative (most Americans are not), but because the archaeological evidence did not sustain his interpretation. The development of the debate on the origin of Israel fits quite nicely the theory of scientific discovery expounded by Thomas Kuhn in his book *The Structure of Scientific Revolutions*.[48] One starts out with a hypothesis that seems to explain most of the data. Some loose ends can be tolerated. But if the loose ends proliferate, eventually one is forced to abandon the original hypothesis and find a new one. As T. H. Huxley (father of Aldous) once allegedly remarked, "The tragedy of science is the slaying of a beautiful hypothesis by an ugly fact." Ideological commitments may produce beautiful hypotheses, but they fail if they cannot explain the evidence. Gottwald's model of the peasant revolt similarly failed in the end, not just because its ideological roots were transparent but because there was not enough evidence to sustain it. The new consensus, based on the work of Finkelstein, may not be final either, but at present it represents the best account of the available evidence. To be sure, it should not be taken as final objective truth. It is based, after all, on decisions to examine some sites and not others, and it is shaped by one master narrative and not by others. But the archaeological evidence available places limits on what a responsible historian can now hold. One can no longer expound the biblical account of violent conquest by outsiders as historical fact. There is, of course, room for further debate as to who those people were who occupied the central highlands at the end of the Bronze Age, but such debate is the lifeblood of historical criticism. If this issue is to be settled, it will not be because one solution fits an Israeli master narrative, but because someone finds ethnic markers that cannot be denied or provides arguments that explain the available data in a persuasive way. Moreover, this is an area where progress is clearly possible, not because new theories are necessarily superior to older ones, but because new data are made available.

I would argue, then, that there are some questions of fact that are, in principle, univocal, even though we may not always be able to answer them. Either there was a community called Israel in the central highland of Canaan in the twelfth century B.C.E., or there was not. Other questions are of necessity perspectival. If the Israelites did conquer Canaan in the thirteenth century B.C.E., this was not necessarily by divine providence, and it was not a good thing from everyone's point of view. A distinction can be made, in short, between questions of fact and questions of significance. There will still be debates as to what counts as fact, but these debates can be conducted on a different level of abstraction from the "master narratives" that guide the grand reconstructions of history.[49] Perceptions of fact are inevitably subject to distortion by prejudice, like everything else, but they admit of correction by debate between people who approach the issue with different points of view.

Nonetheless, I would like to conclude by emphasizing that there is something to be learned from Whitelam and his allies. There is always more than one point of view in history. The most important contribution of postmodernist interpretations, in my view, is their attention to voices from the margins, to the Others of history, who appear only as a foil in biblical and in other historical narratives. It is also salutary to be alerted to the prevalence of hidden agendas, conscious or not, in apparently objective scholarship. We should not, however, collapse into cynicism about the inevitability of prejudice. Even if absolute objectivity is an unattainable goal, the attainment of consensus remains a worthy objective if academic dialogue is not to collapse into partisan warfare.

PART TWO

TOPICS IN THE PENTATEUCH

FAITH WITHOUT WORKS
Biblical Ethics and the Sacrifice of Isaac

"Was not our ancestor Abraham justified by works when he offered his son Isaac on the altar? You see that faith was active along with his works, and faith was brought to completion by the works. Thus the scripture was fulfilled that says, 'Abraham believed God, and it was reckoned to him as righteousness'" (Jas 2:21-23).

The books of the Bible were written long ago and in a culture far removed from the modern world. With few exceptions they do not deal in generalities but are embedded in the particularities of ancient society. Yet millions of Jews and Christians in the modern world continue to regard these books as the Word of God and look to them for guidance in their lives. In many cases this demand for modern relevance is unproblematic. The call of a prophet like Amos for social justice, for all its historical specificity, finds ready analogies in the modern world. But in many cases the demand is problematic, and the possibility of a biblical theology linking past and present is rendered doubtful. The sacrifice of Isaac in Genesis 22 is such a story. The narrative does not fail to engage the reader; in fact, few stories in world literature are so absorbing. But how is a modern person to appropriate a story where God tells a human father to offer up his only son as a burnt offering?

THE LITERARY UNIT

"In the case of a narrative like this one," wrote Gerhard von Rad, "one must from the first renounce any attempt to discover one basic idea as *the* meaning of the whole. There are many layers of meaning."[1] The multilayered character of the story is reflected in the scholarly debates. The basic story in Gen 22:1-14, plus 19,[2] is generally ascribed to the Elohist source[3]; vv. 15-18 ("The angel of the lord called to Abraham a second time") are generally recognized as a secondary redaction.[4] There are problems with the source-critical attribution, since "the angel of YHWH" is mentioned in v. 11, and v. 14 explains the name Moriah by the phrase "YHWH will see" (or be seen). Hermann Gunkel supposed that the name YHWH has been inserted in place of El or Elohim at these points, but this approach requires the dubious reconstruction of the place-name as "Jeruel."[5] Henning Graf Reventlow suggested that an older narrative, containing the name YHWH, has been reworked by the Elohist.[6] Yet another suggestion is that the narrative comes from a late, postexilic date when the divine names were used interchangeably.[7] Such a late date seems to me implausible, but the attempt to distinguish precisely between J and E sources is increasingly admitted to be problematic.[8] The attribution of Gen 22:1-14 and 19 to the Elohist has the advantage of drawing attention to the affinities of the story with Genesis 21 (the sending away of Ishmael). The main redactional addition in vv. 15-19 serves to integrate the story into the Yahwistic theme of the promise, although these verses cannot be ascribed to the classic J source.[9] These observations help explain the plurality of emphases in the text and nuance our appreciation of what Brevard S. Childs would call the canonical shape.[10] Ultimately, all aspects of the text have something to offer to the interpreter.

Since the pioneering work of Gunkel, many scholars have argued that the story originated as a cult legend, which authorized the substitution of an animal for the human victim.[11] Recent commentators, however, are increasingly and correctly reluctant to reconstruct hypothetical source documents.[12] The text before us is not a free-standing legend, but a narrative that is well integrated into the unfolding history of the Patriarchs. Nonetheless, the text speaks to the issues of human sacrifice and substitution at some level, and these issues cannot be eliminated entirely.

STRUCTURE AND THEME

This text is exceptional among the narratives of Genesis in offering a very explicit key to interpretation in the opening sentence: "God tested Abraham." Claus Westermann takes the notion of testing as the key to the structure of the story, in its original Elohistic formulation: vv. 1-2 state the nature of the test; vv. 3-10 describe Abraham's attempt to carry it out; vv. 11-12 abort the original test and announce that Abraham has passed it. Verses 13 and 19 provide the conclusion of the narrative, culminating in Abraham's return home.[13] Westermann concludes that "it follows from this structure that the narrative is dealing with a test in all three parts; it is not dealing primarily with child sacrifice itself nor child sacrifice forestalled at the last moment."[14] But this is an extremely formalistic approach, which proceeds as if the content of the text, or the substance of the test, were of no account. Gerhard von Rad goes so far as to say that this was "a demand which God did not intend to take seriously," adding that what was deadly serious for Abraham was the divine command.[15] Here again there seems to be an attempt to evade the specificity of the demand. (Von Rad assures us that the apparent loss of the promise is "much more frightful than child sacrifice," a peculiarly theological sense of priorities.)[16] The Jewish scholar Nahum Sarna contends that "the reader is informed in advance that God is only testing Abraham and does not want the sacrifice for His own needs."[17] But the Hebrew verb *nissāh* carries no implication that the test should not be carried out, or that Isaac should not actually be sacrificed.[18] To say that God is *only* testing Abraham is to trivialize the test and distract attention from the awfulness both of the test proposed and of Abraham's response to it.[19]

The emphasis on testing lends itself readily to viewing the story as exemplary. In the words of George W. Coats: "The legend provides an edifying example of obedience for all subsequent devotees of Yahweh. Indeed, it emphasizes the importance of obedience for Israel by making the primary saint of obedience the father of Israel."[20] Claus Westermann demurs, on the grounds that the praise should not be given to Abraham, but to God.[21] But the text itself very clearly commends Abraham, both in the basic story (v. 12) and again in the redactional addition (vv. 16-18). His exemplary character cannot be denied and was recognized by both Jewish and Christian traditions from earliest times.[22]

Claus Westermann's understanding of the structure of the text has been criticized by Horst Seebass, who follows Gunkel's division of vv. 1-3, 4-8, 9-14.[23] In fact, the initial reference to testing is most probably an editorial comment, whether by the Elohist or someone else, and extrinsic to the basic story, although it should not be ignored for that reason.[24] On Seebass's reading, Abraham's response to Isaac ("God will provide a sheep," אלהים יראה לו השׂה) is the climax of the middle section. It points forward to the name Abraham gives to the mountain in v. 14: "YHWH will see/provide" (יהוה יראה). Hence the point of the story is that the Lord provides. But while Seebass gives the better account of the structure of the story, we should be mindful of von Rad's warning that the story has more than one point. The themes of testing and providence are both important aspects of the story.

Seebass's understanding of the structure accords well with the classic Christian interpretation in Heb 11:17-19: "By faith Abraham, when put to the test, offered up Isaac. . . . He considered the fact that God is able even to raise someone from the dead—and figuratively speaking, he did receive him back."[25] This is also the position of Martin Luther: "He did not give up his hope in the divine promise but, believing in the resurrection of the dead, he was comforted by his faith that God's promises must stand."[26] The faith in resurrection, of course, is anachronistic in the story of Abraham; there is no hint of such a faith in the Hebrew text. But the key element in this line of interpretation is the presumed trust of Abraham that Isaac would not be lost. Søren Kierkegaard, who imagined most vividly the horror of the situation, nonetheless affirmed that Abraham believed, "by virtue of the absurd, that God would not require Isaac of him"; "God could give him a new Isaac, could recall to life him who had been sacrificed."[27] It is not apparent from the Hebrew text, however, that Abraham had any such belief.[28] We are told nothing of his inner thoughts. His answer to Isaac "is on the surface an effort to dodge the frontal pain of a straightforward reply,"[29] although it turns out to be more prophetic than he knows. Von Rad speaks here of "a road out into Godforsakenness,"[30] since all indications have been that God would indeed require Isaac of him. At the end, Abraham is not commended for what he believed, but for fearing God; the story is concerned with obedience and fear rather than faith or belief. To retroject faith that Isaac would be delivered into this story is to fail to understand the total submission and surrender implied in "the fear of the Lord."

A third aspect of the story is highlighted by the redactional addition in vv. 15-18: what is at stake is not only the fate of Isaac but the fulfillment of the promises that God has made to Abraham. This passage does not seem to have been part of the original story, but its redactional character lends it special importance for the "canonical shape." So for Childs: "The theological issue at stake is that God's command to slay the heir stands in direct conflict with his promise of salvation through this very child, and therefore Abraham's relation to God is under attack. The Old Testament bears witness that God was faithful to his promise and confirmed his word by providing his own sacrifice instead of the child."[31] This too is a level of meaning of the text. But why should the concerns of the redactors ("canonical shapers") of the text be paramount, or override other themes such as the testing of Abraham? Again, we must heed von Rad's warning against the reduction of the text to a single meaning.

Each of the themes we have considered thus far, the testing of Abraham, the providence of God, the fulfillment of the promises, tends to draw attention away from the specificity of the initial command to sacrifice a child.[32] Yet the grip that this story has had on the popular imagination derives precisely from this point. The promise is endangered earlier in Genesis when Abraham and Sarah remain childless into old age, but this episode arouses none of the fear and trembling that we associate with Genesis 22. The reader is kept in suspense right up to the point where Abraham lifts the knife. If the promise is confirmed in vv. 15-18 it is not because of what Abraham believed but because he has not withheld his only son. Any interpretation that fails to come to grips with the problem of child sacrifice cannot begin to do justice to the story of Abraham and Isaac. Yet this aspect of the story is very often skirted by interpreters, especially those whose focus is theological.[33]

CHILD SACRIFICE IN ISRAEL

Scholars who have taken seriously the fact that the story is concerned with child sacrifice have usually assumed that this story serves as an etiology for the substitution of an animal for the human victim. Several parallels for such substitution can be found in the ancient Mediterranean world and the Near East.[34] This theory is not negated by evidence that animals were regarded as the normal sacrificial victims from the opening chapters of Genesis, and also by Isaac in Genesis 22.[35] The order of the biblical books is not the order of their composition, and we cannot assume a straight-line evolution from human to animal sacrifice in any case.[36] Yet it is unlikely that Genesis 22 was meant to serve such an etiological purpose. As Jon Levenson has argued, "It is passing strange to condemn child sacrifice through a narrative in which a father is richly rewarded for his willingness to carry out that very practice."[37] Not only does Genesis 22 not polemicize against child sacrifice; it does not condemn it at all. The command to Abraham is revoked, but this may be an exceptional case. The paradigmatic or exemplary aspect of the story lies in the obedience of Abraham, not in the substitution of the animal for the victim.

Nahum Sarna has argued that "the narrative is the product of a religious attitude that is already long conditioned to the notion that Israelite monotheism is incompatible with human sacrifice."[38] But this is far from true. Rather than taking for granted that one would recoil from such a sacrifice,[39] the story assumes that it was credibly a demand of the God of Israel.

In fact there is considerable evidence for the practice of child sacrifice in Israel and Judah, down to the time of the Babylonian exile. Most of the biblical references condemn the practice, and it is often assumed that the offerings are made to a deity other than YHWH. Jeremiah is most emphatic on this point:

> Because the people have forsaken me and have profaned this place by making offerings in it to other gods whom neither they nor their ancestors nor the kings of Judah have known; and because they have filled this place with the blood of the innocent and gone on building the high places of Baal to burn their children in the fire as burnt offerings to Baal, which I did not command or decree, nor did it enter my mind. Therefore the days are surely coming, says the Lord, when this place shall no more be called Topheth or the valley of the son of Hinnom, but the valley of Slaughter. (Jer 19:4-6)

The valley of the son of Hinnom (Gehinnom) was just south of Jerusalem. The Topheth was the installation where children were burned. Isaiah alludes to it, as a metaphor for the coming punishment of Assyria: "The Topheth has long been ready for him; he too is destined for Melech—his firepit has been made both wide and deep, with plenty of fire and firewood, and with the breath of the Lord burning in it like a stream of sulfur."[40] *Melech* or *Molech* is variously interpreted as a kind of sacrifice,[41] or, more usually, as the name of a Canaanite deity.[42] Deut 12:31 denounces the sacrifice of children as an abhorrent Canaanite custom. The offering of children to Molech is very explicitly prohibited in Lev 18:21 and 20:2-5. Deut 18:10 stipulates that "no one shall be found among you who makes a son or daughter pass through fire." Yet we are told that kings of Judah (Ahaz, 2 Kgs 16:3; Manasseh, 2 Kgs 21:6) made their sons "pass through fire."[43] Josiah is said to have "defiled Topheth, which is in the valley of Ben Hinnom, so that no one would make a son or a daughter pass through fire as an offering to Molech" (2 Kgs 23:10). Yet the Topheth was evidently in use a generation later in the time of Jeremiah, and Isa 57:5, written after the exile, condemns those who slaughter their children in the valleys under the clefts of the rocks.

There are moreover indications that such sacrifices were sometimes offered to YHWH. Otto Eissfeldt argued that the sacrifices in Gehinnom were offered to YHWH down until Josiah's reform, and that the word Molech, which originally designated a type of sacrifice, was only later taken as the name of a god.[44] Even if we dismiss that argument, however, there is other evidence of human sacrifice to YHWH. Mic 6:6-8 addresses a Yahwistic worshiper who wonders "with what shall I come before the Lord, and bow myself before God on high? Shall I come before him with burnt offerings, with calves a year old? . . . Shall I give my firstborn for my transgression, the fruit of my body for the sin of my soul?" Micah responds that God only requires that one do justice and kindness and walk humbly before God. But the question shows that worshipers of YHWH could contemplate human sacrifice in the eighth century B.C.E., and that human and animal sacrifices were contemporary options—the one had not superseded the other. Moreover, the text says nothing to indicate that if justice were practiced the sacrifice of an animal would be acceptable, while that of a child would not be. One might infer that either God repudiates all sacrifice, or human sacrifice is acceptable on the same conditions as other offerings.[45]

The most startling text on the subject of human sacrifice in the Hebrew Bible is undoubtedly Exod 22:28-29: "The firstborn of your sons you shall give to me. You shall do the same with your oxen and with your sheep: seven days it shall remain with its mother; on the eighth day you shall give it to me." Commentators are quick to harmonize this law with Exod 34:19-20, which likewise says that "all that first opens the womb is mine," but adds "all the firstborn of your sons you shall redeem."[46] But it is not quite accurate to say with Westermann that the command given in Exodus 22 is "simultaneously abolished."[47] Exodus 22 belongs to a distinct unit, the Book of the Covenant, and represents an earlier phase of Israelite religion than the other passages. We do not know how this law was interpreted, or how early the law of substitution was introduced. It is difficult to believe that the law of any society would require that all firstborn males be sacrificed.[48] Perhaps the law only expressed an ideal, as is sometimes claimed for other law codes from antiquity.[49] But it surely gives the lie to Jeremiah's assertion that the thought of child sacrifice had never entered YHWH's mind.

The demand for human sacrifice is also attributed to YHWH in Ezek 20:25-26: "Moreover I gave them statutes that were not good and ordinances by which they could not live. I defiled them through all their very gifts, in their offering up all their firstborn, in order that I might horrify them, so that they might know that I am the Lord." These "statutes that were not good" are given to the Israelites as a punishment for their failure to keep the commandments they had been given. This allegedly happened before the entry into the land, so there is no question of Canaanite influence.[50] Walther Zimmerli supposes that the reference here is to Exod 22:28. During peaceful times the law of substitution would have prevailed, but "there came into currency in the time of Ahaz and Manasseh, undoubtedly under various foreign influences, a literal interpretation of the command."[51] This theory seems unnecessarily speculative. Ezekiel is engaging in a polemical diatribe, which is a dubious source for historical reconstruction. Nonetheless, as Moshe Greenberg has observed, his comment on child sacrifice "was not spun out of thin air." The polemic against child sacrifice in Deuteronomy and Jeremiah "indicates that at least from the time of the last kings of Judah it was popularly believed that YHWH accepted, perhaps even commanded, it."[52] From the eighth century on, prophets and reformers raised their voices in protest, but a custom that was practiced by kings must have had official status, at least during the reigns of those kings.[53]

Hermann Gunkel reasoned that the absence of polemic against child sacrifice shows that the story is pre-prophetic. A century later, we know that Israelite religion did not evolve in a straight line. We can only say that the story shows an attitude to child sacrifice that is quite different from that of Jeremiah. Later, in the Hellenistic period, Judaism would be distinguished in the Gentile world for its protection of the lives of infants. "Raise your own offspring and do not kill it," the Sibyl warns the Greeks, "for the Most High is angry at whoever commits these sins."[54] But there were evidently different opinions on the subject within Yahwism in the period before the exile.

The biblical story with which the sacrifice of Isaac is most often compared and contrasted is that of Jephtah and his daughter. Jephtah famously vowed to offer up "whoever comes out of the doors of my house to meet me" if he was victorious in battle with the Ammonites (Judg 11:31). As George F. Moore saw clearly in his commentary on Judges, the language implies human sacrifice.[55] It would have been ridiculous to offer whatever animal came out of his house, whether fit for sacrifice or not. But Jephtah evidently did not expect that his daughter would be the one. He expresses more grief than Abraham, and no less steadfastness in fulfilling what he sees as his religious duty. This time there is no ram in the bushes. Commentators are quick to point out that Jephtah was not commanded by God to make the sacrifice, but initiated the tragedy by a rash vow.[56] The biblical text, however, does not pronounce the vow rash, and Jephtah is never condemned in the biblical tradition. The New Testament proclaims him, like Abraham, a hero of faith "who through faith conquered kingdoms" (Heb 11:32-34). Moreover, the Hebrew text would seem to imply that he was acting under the influence of the spirit of the Lord when he made his vow. (The spirit of the Lord fell on him in v. 29; he made the vow in v. 31).[57] His case, then, may not be so different from that of Abraham, as is often assumed.

THE MORAL PROBLEM

If the text fails to condemn Jephtah, it is very explicit in its commendation of Abraham: "Now I know that you fear God, since you have not withheld your son, your only son, from me." In the redactional addition in vv. 15-18, Abraham's action leads to a reconfirmation of the blessing and the multiplication of his descendants. Contrary to the Epistle of James, quoted at the beginning of this chapter, Abraham is not praised for his works, but for his willingness (faith?) and obedience. But herein lies the real problem of the text, for one cannot praise Abraham's willingness to perform a deed while condemning the deed itself. Abraham would be no less laudable if the angel of the lord had not intervened and he had killed his son, and indeed some midrashim envision exactly this possibility.[58] One may claim for Abraham the morality of the soldier who follows commands without question, especially when the future of his people is at stake.[59] But while such "morality" is appreciated by military authorities, it is no longer accepted as a justification of one's actions in the modern world, in the wake of Nuremberg and My Lai. Child sacrifice is abhorrent not only to the modern, enlightened West but also to Jewish and Christian tradition, dating back to the prophets and the Torah. As we have noted, Jeremiah was emphatic that such a demand never entered YHWH's mind. Jeremiah shows no awareness of the story of Genesis 22. He could hardly have held it up as an example of virtuous behavior.

While it is not "taken for granted that one would normally recoil from such an act as child sacrifice"[60] in the context of ancient Israel, it certainly is in modern Christianity and Judaism. How then can Abraham be justified? Only, as Kierkegaard saw, by a teleological suspension of the ethical; only, in short, if ethical considerations do not apply when a divine command is involved. So, for Sarna, "the Akedah has nothing in common with pagan human sacrifice, which was practiced in order to appease an angry or inattentive deity, as in 2 Kgs 3:21-27. In such cases, it is the worshiper who takes the initiative. In the case of Abraham, there is no emergency, no impending disaster to be warded off. *It is God Himself who makes the request.*"[61] Here we come to the heart of the matter. The justification of Abraham's act depends entirely on the authenticity of the revelation, on the confidence that the command is truly a command of God.

This confidence has not been universally shared. In the Book of Jubilees, written in the second century B.C.E., we find that the idea that Abraham should sacrifice Isaac originated not with God but with the prince of evil, Mastema (*Jub.* 17:16).[62] Mastema's role here is obviously modeled on that of Satan in the Book of Job, but, unlike the biblical Satan, Mastema is the leader of demonic spirits, whose role is to corrupt and lead astray. The command to Abraham still comes from God, but it is prompted by Mastema. When God and his angel intervene to abort the sacrifice, Mastema is put to shame. A fragmentary text from Qumran, 4Q225, similarly claims that Mastema initiated the trial by accusing Abraham before God regarding Isaac. It further depicts a scene in which the angels of holiness are initially weeping, while the angels of Mastema rejoice over the impending sacrifice of Isaac, but concludes that God blessed Isaac all the days of his life.[63] The idea that Satan prompted God to test Abraham persists in the Talmud (*b. Sanh.* 89b).[64]

Jewish tradition from an early date also tried to lessen the offense of Genesis 22 by claiming that Isaac was a willing victim. The antiquity of this idea is disputed. The majority view holds that it was pre-Christian,[65] but some have held that it only arose after 70 C.E.[66] According to the paraphrase of Genesis 22 in Targum Neofiti, Abraham tells Isaac openly that he may be sacrificed. When Abraham takes the knife, Isaac asks him to "bind me properly that I may not kick you and your offering be made unfit." The angels of heaven comment that these are the only two just men in the world: "The one slays, and the other is being slain. The slayer does not hesitate, and the one being slain stretches out his neck."[67] Similarly, in the *Biblical Antiquities* of Pseudo-Philo, Abraham tells Isaac openly that he is going to offer him as a sacrifice. Isaac responds: "Why should you be saying to me now, 'Come and inherit eternal life and time without measure'? Why if not that I was indeed born in this world in order to be offered as a sacrifice to Him who made me? Indeed this will be my

blessedness over other men—for no such thing will ever be—and in me the generations will be proclaimed and through me nations will understand how God made a
human soul worthy for sacrifice" (*Bib. Ant.* 32:2-3). It now appears that Isaac also
gives his consent to the sacrifice in 4Q225.[68] In frag. 2, col. ii, line 4, Isaac speaks to
his father a second time, after the answer to his question about the sacrificial animal.
Unfortunately, the content of his second utterance is broken off. The editors restore:
[יפה אותי כ]פות "bind me well," as in the Targum, but only the כ of the first word is
visible, and that only partially.[69] If this restoration is correct, the willingness of Isaac
firmly dates to pre-Christian times, but the issue will remain in dispute because of the
fragmentary nature of the text.

We need not enter here into the complex question of the relation of these traditions to the New Testament.[70] For our present purposes, their main significance is that
they show that ancient readers noticed a moral problem in the text and attempted to
address it. If Isaac was a willing victim, then Abraham is less vulnerable to the charge
of attempted murder; the episode is not so much a sacrifice as self-sacrifice. Books
like *Jubilees,* 4Q225, and Pseudo-Philo are examples of the quasi-genre "rewritten
Bible," a forerunner of haggadic midrash. The freedom they enjoy in reformulat-
ing the biblical text is similar to that of the modern novelist or dramatist. No such
freedom is granted to the exegete who wishes to find an authoritative meaning in the
text. But while these ancient authors alter the story very significantly, they only partially address the fundamental problem involved in recognizing the demand for child
sacrifice as a legitimate revelation of God. In *Jubilees,* the demand for the sacrifice
comes from Satan/Mastema, but it is still endorsed by God, with scant regard for his
faithful subject. Pseudo-Philo leaves unexplained why God should demand such a
sacrifice at all.

The notion of a divine command or revelation in defiance of human morality
was less problematic in antiquity than in the modern world, but the problem was
not unknown, even in the biblical tradition. We have noted Jeremiah's insistence
that it had never entered YHWH's mind to demand human sacrifice, despite powerful evidence to the contrary in Exodus 22. His contemporary Ezekiel deals with
the problem in a different way, by suggesting that the sacrifice of the firstborn was a
punishment for Israel's disobedience. What is remarkable is the prophets' reluctance
to say that the supposed divine command is really a human fabrication. We find a
similar reluctance in the story of Micaiah ben Imlah in 1 Kings 22. There the story
makes no secret of the fact that the prophets have conspired to prophesy the success
of the king. But while Micaiah knows this, he does not accuse them of conspiracy.
Rather he says that "the lord has put a lying spirit in the mouth of all these your
prophets" (1 Kgs 22:23), although such an idea hardly seems less problematic than
human fabrication of revelation. The reluctance of biblical authors to confront the
all-too-human origin of supposed revelations is understandable in the mythological
mind-set of antiquity, although Jeremiah's denunciations of the false prophets show
that it was not inevitable.[71] Such reluctance is less excusable in modern exegetes and
theologians.

THE EPISTEMOLOGICAL PROBLEM

The fundamental problem from a modern perspective was given classical expression by Immanuel Kant: "There are certain cases in which man can be convinced that it cannot be God whose voice he thinks he hears; when the voice commands him to do what is opposed to the moral law, though the phenomenon seem to him ever so majestic and surpassing the whole of nature, he must count it a deception." He adds: "The myth of the sacrifice of Abraham can serve as an example: Abraham, at God's command, was going to slaughter his own son—the poor child in his ignorance even carried the wood. Abraham should have said to this supposed divine voice: that I am not to kill my beloved son is quite certain; that you who appear to me are God, I am not certain, nor can I ever be, even if the voice thunders from the sky."[72]

Immanuel Kant's pronouncement is often cited by modern commentators[73] but seldom taken seriously. Brevard S. Childs would simply rule inconvenient questions out of court by dogmatic fiat: "To raise the psychological question as to how Abraham knew it was from God, or the historical question as to whether the sacrifice of children was once a part of Hebrew religion, is to distract the interpreter from the witness of this text."[74] On the contrary, it is to ask for essential clarification of the witness of the text. Claus Westermann counters Kant by arguing that "the command is spoken out of this context of familiar mutual trust. Horrible, inhuman, it is nevertheless the word of his trusted God. . . . This is the reason Kant was unable to understand what is meant here. . . . for him, it is possible to abstract the word as 'that which is said,' from the speaker."[75] But the issue raised by Kant is precisely the difficulty of identifying the speaker as God, a problem that Westermann fails to acknowledge at all. Timo Veijola objects that Kant makes revelation redundant, since the moral law is already known.[76] But this objection does not relieve the difficulty of recognizing revelation: "It is of the essence of religious statements that one cannot evaluate their ultimate claim to truth by objective standards. Rather, one is convinced on the basis of one's own experience—or not. Abraham had the firm unshakeable certainty that this God would prove himself to be the true God even when he demanded from humans that which made no sense."[77] But every fanatic has an unshakable certainly that his or her conviction is right. Such a subjective court of appeal provides no way of distinguishing the saint from the lunatic.

A different kind of objection is raised by Walter Moberly. He notes that in the modern world anyone who claimed to have been told by God to kill a child "would find no credence for such claims from any responsible person, believer or non-believer." He continues: "There is a modern tendency, encouraged (in different ways) by people of the stature of Kant and Kierkegaard to suppose that this modern moral judgment must also apply to the story in its ancient context. Yet such an approach is a classic example of anachronism. . . . Our first point, about the nature of testing, indicates that the story is to be seen as a positive moral example."[78] But a positive moral example for whom? The people of ancient Israel, or modern Jews and Christians? And if it is to be seen as a positive moral example for modern people, must we not correlate it with modern values? The moral issue in the interpretation of Genesis 22 is not whether Abraham acted rightly in his context, but whether his action can still serve as "a positive moral example" in the modern world. Anachronism is a two-edged sword. It defends the ancient story from judgment by modern moral standards, but only at the cost of rendering it irrelevant to modern ethics. The same is true of the argument from cultural relativism. Many people are now skeptical of Kant's idea of a universal moral law.[79] This skepticism, however, hardly extends to the case of child sacrifice, at least not in the Jewish or Christian traditions.

The most cogent objection to the Kantian criticism is based on the literary nature of the text: it is inappropriate to ask how Abraham recognizes the word of God, since the divine command is simply a datum of the story. The historicity of the incident, or indeed of Abraham, is scarcely an issue of debate any more. The stories of Genesis can reasonably be taken as examples of early prose fiction, in the manner advocated by Robert Alter.[80] We may take the story as a history-like narrative and accept God as a character in the story. If our goal is the literary appreciation of an ancient text, this is quite sufficient. The problem arises if we try to move from the realm of the literary to that of theology or ethics, because this usually entails a claim of the truth or nonfictional character of the text. Karl Barth has often been invoked as a model for such a literary-theological reading. In the words of David Kelsey, "It is as though Barth took scripture to be one vast loosely structured non-fictional novel—at least Barth takes it to be non-fictional."[81] But it is precisely the claim that the Bible is non-fictional that is problematic. Similar claims have been made by literary critics, such as Erich Auerbach and Meir Sternberg. Erich Auerbach writes that "without believing in Abraham's sacrifice, it is impossible to put the narrative of it to the use for which it was written. . . . the Bible's claim to truth . . . is tyrannical."[82] Sternberg holds that the Bible requires "literal belief in the past. It claims not just the status of history, but as Erich Auerbach rightly maintains, of *the* history."[83] I suspect, however, that these views are influenced by the long-standing reverence for the Bible as Scripture more than by any literary properties of the biblical text.

In any case, it is no longer possible to defend the historicity of the stories of Abraham.[84] If the "truth" of the story is to be maintained, it cannot be the historical truth. Walter Moberly puts the issue well: "The question about the truth, or otherwise, of the story cannot be answered except by engaging with the beliefs and values that the story portrays. Is it true to the character of God, and is it true to the nature of human life?"[85] Moberly claims that "those who stand in some kind of continuity with the ancient community of faith which cherished and wrote the story, and who themselves cherish it as part of scripture will be inclined to affirm that the story is true."[86]

It is difficult, however, to see how anyone who stands in either the Jewish or the Christian tradition can affirm the beliefs and values of Genesis 22 without serious reservation. One can, to be sure, affirm the reliability of God's promise and the faithfulness of God in a general way, but to do so is only to engage the beliefs and values of the story on a superficial level. For the story affirms that God can demand child sacrifice and that it is praiseworthy for a person to comply with this demand. Many religions worship a "hungry God," and one might well argue that this is a valid revelation of divinity.[87] But this image of the deity was subsequently repudiated even in the biblical tradition.[88] The story commends the faith or obedience of Abraham, without the consummation of the deed. But as the Epistle of James rightly insisted, "faith without works is dead" (Jas 2:26). The faith of Abraham cannot be divorced from the deed he was willing to do, and consequently it cannot be invoked as a positive moral example for the modern world. The story can still be cherished as part of the heritage of Judaism and Christianity, and as a thought-provoking moral tale. To cherish a story, even as Scripture, is not necessarily to accept its values but to engage them in honest critical reflection.

CHAPTER 5

THE DEVELOPMENT
OF THE EXODUS TRADITION

N o event is more central to Israelite and Jewish identity, as expressed in the canonical Hebrew Bible, than the Exodus from Egypt. Accordingly, it has been central to most constructions of biblical theology, and its primacy has usually been taken for granted in reconstructions of Israelite history and the history of Israelite religion. In recent years, however, the historicity of this event has been called into question in two ways. First, the current consensus of archaeologists is that the new settlements in the central highlands in the Iron Age, which are usually taken to be Israelite or proto-Israelite, did not result from invasion or immigration, but that the material culture was essentially Canaanite.[1] Consequently, defenders of the Exodus have to reduce its scope, so that it only involved a small group that had no impact on the material culture, or suggest that the biblical story conflates several mini-exoduses that took place over a few centuries. Second, the traditional "maximalist" account of biblical origins assumed that the Bible incorporates a J source that was written down in the tenth century B.C.E. and preserved traditions that derived from the premonarchic period. Many scholars, however, now question whether a J source can be identified at all, and even those who defend it often date it later than the tenth century (although there are still some exceptions).[2] Consequently, the accounts of the Exodus are now thought to be further removed from the supposed events than previously believed, by several centuries. Moreover, the legendary features of several episodes in the book of Exodus are obvious. There are some grounds, then, for speaking of the Exodus as an invented tradition. Most scholars, however, would still grant that there is some historical memory at the root of the tradition, however much it may have been enhanced over time. The question on which I would like to focus here is not the ultimate origin of the tradition, but whether we can identify some stages in its development. Specifically, I want to examine the earliest evidence for the use of the

Exodus as the story of pan-Israelite origins, and also the relation of the Exodus to the Sinai tradition and the origins of the cult of Yahweh. I will pursue these questions in dialogue with the work of Karel van der Toorn and Rainer Albertz.

VAN DER TOORN

Van der Toorn and Albertz have given us two distinct models for thinking about the place of the Exodus in Israelite tradition. Van der Toorn draws a sharp distinction between the localized, family-based religion of the premonarchic period and the state religion that only arises with the monarchy.[3] His argument that the Exodus served as the charter myth of the northern kingdom seems to me well founded, since it is supported not only by the Deuteronomistic account of 1 Kings 12 but also by the prominence of the Exodus in the prophecies of Amos and Hosea.[4] Van der Toorn is careful to distinguish between the use of the tradition and its origin.[5] He grants that both the Egyptian name of Moses and the data concerning the presence of Western Asiatic people in Egypt in the thirteenth century favor the historicity of an Exodus of some kind. But the tradition about such an Exodus was no more than a local Ephraimite tradition before the rise of Jeroboam. The adoption of the Exodus as a charter myth, we are told, represents an innovation by comparison with the earliest phase of Israelite state religion.[6] Under Saul, the state religion had consisted of little else than the application of the traditional notions of family religion to the nation as a whole. Van der Toorn has no place for a celebration of the Exodus by the assembled tribes of Israel before the monarchy. The Elohistic traditions of the Pentateuch reflect the prominence of the myth in northern Israel. The existence of a Yahwist source is not denied, but it is taken to be later than the Elohist.[7]

ALBERTZ

The position of Rainer Albertz differs from that of van der Toorn in several respects.[8] First, with regard to the literary sources, he accepts the complex analysis of Erhard Blum, which recognizes only Deuteronomistic and Priestly compositions, while acknowledging that these drew on older materials of uncertain provenance. According to this analysis, only a small amount of the pentateuchal material, "the remains of a Moses narrative" in Exodus 1–5, goes back to the early monarchy. The narrative of the plagues and Exodus is said to come from the exilic period. The outline of the Exodus-Sinai tradition as we now have it is no older than the Deuteronomic reform. Prior to that, we are told that "the Exodus-Sinai tradition probably played a leading role only among the tribes of central Palestine and in the northern kingdom."[9] Albertz concludes this rather devastating literary analysis by saying that "we will have to qualify quite considerably the conception of the beginnings of Israel presented by the Pentateuch." But then he adds an amazing comment: "In principle, however, this conception is not to be doubted, since a whole series of special features which Yahweh religion displays can be explained only from the extraordinary social conditions in which it came into being."[10] It seems to me, however, that if the literary analysis of Albertz and Blum is accepted we have every reason to doubt the reliability of the biblical conception of Israelite origins, and that the special features of Yahweh religion can be understood as evolving slowly over several centuries, largely in the period of the monarchy and the exile. Even if we are not as radical as Blum on the literary issues, the centrality of the Exodus in the premonarchic period is open to question.

JEROBOAM

Let us begin with Jeroboam, who seems to offer us one reliable point of reference in the development of the tradition. Not only do we have the testimony of the Deuteronomist that Jeroboam established a cult that focused on the Exodus, but, as Albertz has noted, "the sequence of events in Exod 2:11ff. displays striking parallels to the revolt of Jeroboam and probably comes from the northern kingdom of this period."[11] Jeroboam, we are told, was in charge of the forced labor of the house of Joseph (1 Kgs 11:28) when he rebelled against Solomon. The prophecy of Ahijah that allegedly prompted his rebellion is clearly a Deuteronomistic composition, but it is unlikely that the Deuteronomist invented the link between Jeroboam and the Exodus. The Judean historian generally tries to discredit the northern leader and would not have created any analogies between him and Moses, which might cast him in a favorable light, or sought to portray him as maintaining the Exodus tradition, which is also foundational in Deuteronomic theology. But the analogies with Moses go some way toward explaining Jeroboam's choice of the Exodus as his charter myth. Yahweh had just brought him up from the land of Egypt. He had not been a slave there, but his secession from Jerusalem effectively freed the house of Joseph from Solomon's and Rehoboam's forced labor. The context of Jeroboam's revolt suggests that the motif of liberation was indeed integral to his use of the Exodus as charter myth.[12]

Could Jeroboam have invented the story of the Exodus out of whole cloth? Probably not. Here I am in agreement with both van der Toorn and Albertz. A story that was not known at all would hardly have commanded the allegiance of the northern tribes. Besides, the story is by no means a simple allegory for Jeroboam's revolt. The name of Moses is generally accepted as pointing to an authentic Egyptian connection, although, to my knowledge, it does not occur as an independent name in Egyptian sources.[13] Some scholars go so far as to identify Moses specifically with one Beya, who was chancellor of Egypt in the early twelfth century B.C.E.,[14] but this conjecture goes far beyond the evidence. Asiatic slaves were employed in Ramesses' building projects, and the Leiden Papyrus refers to Apiru in this connection. Papyrus Anastasi V, from the end of the thirteenth century, records the pursuit of slaves who had fled into the Sinai wilderness.[15] Jan Assmann has suggested that the story of the plagues may reflect a faint recollection of an actual epidemic during and after the reign of Akhenaten.[16] The late Egyptian account of Israelite origins in Manetho associates the origin of the inhabitants of Judea with the expulsion of the Hyksos and claims that they were inflicted with leprosy.[17] Several scholars have argued that, in the words of Baruch Halpern, "Israelite lore has tapped a stream of tradition the headwaters of which stem from that time."[18] None of the evidence adduced directly supports the historicity of the Exodus story, but it shows that various motifs in that story fit the local color of Egypt in the mid- to late second millennium. It is not implausible that some slaves who escaped from Egypt should have settled in the mountain country of Ephraim. Some such memory would seem to be required by the biblical tradition, even if there is no reliable extra-biblical evidence to corroborate it.

Do we need to suppose that Jeroboam had available to him anything more than scattered traditions of escape from slavery, including, perhaps, a story about an individual named Moses? Or, more to the point, have we any evidence that he had in fact a more elaborate tradition at his disposal? The books of Joshua, Judges, and Samuel come to us through the hands of Deuteronomistic editors. Nonetheless, there are remarkably few references to the Exodus in Judges and Samuel.[19] Joshua, to be sure, is presented as the continuation of the Exodus story, but little if anything in that book can be taken to reflect premonarchical traditions.[20] It has been argued that Joshua 3–5 preserves traditions from a premonarchic cult at Gilgal.[21] But even if we assume that the Deuteronomist drew on cultic traditions, it is not apparent why these traditions should be traced back to the premonarchic period. Joshua 24 reports a covenant renewal ceremony at Schechem, at which Joshua recalls the Exodus. An older generation of scholars saw here evidence of a cultic assembly of a tribal league.[22] It is now recognized, however, as a Deuteronomistic composition, a late construct of how early Israel should have been.[23] Even the Deuteronomistic historian does not attribute any significant interest in the Exodus to Saul, David, or Solomon. Both van der Toorn and Albertz agree, rightly, that neither biblical nor archaeological evidence supports the existence of a central sanctuary, or a central cult, in the premonarchic period.[24] The oldest cultic festivals, described in the Book of the Covenant, are agricultural festivals. Albertz argues that these festivals were transformed by the experience of liberation from Egypt. The reinterpretation in light of the Exodus is clear enough in Deuteronomy and Leviticus. Albertz points out that already in Exod 23:14 and 34:18 the feast of unleavened bread is associated with the Exodus, but how confident can we be that these texts preserve premonarchic tradition?[25] Is it not more likely that festivals would be associated with the Exodus after that story had been adopted as the charter myth of the state? In short, there seems to me to be no reliable evidence of pan-Israelite celebration of the Exodus prior to the time of Jeroboam.

This is not to say that there was no celebration of the Exodus at all before the monarchy. Our evidence does not permit a confident negative conclusion any more than it permits a confident positive one. In part, the problem concerns the degree of unity that we can attribute to Israel before the rise of Saul. There may well have been a local celebration of the Exodus, at Gilgal or elsewhere. But the Exodus seems to have been given a new centrality in Israelite cult when Jeroboam set up his calves at Bethel and Dan.

THE ORIGIN OF YAHWISTIC RELIGION

Albertz, however, argues that the experience of the Exodus was definitive for Yahwistic religion: "The origin of Yahweh religion is indissolubly connected with the process of the political liberation out of Egypt."[26] Consequently, all worship of Yahweh might be thought to presuppose this experience. This judgment is grounded in the prophets and Deuteronomy and guided by admirable sympathy for liberation and the pursuit of justice. As a historical judgment on the early history of Israel, however, it is open to question.

Both Albertz and van der Toorn recognize that there is good evidence that the worship of Yahweh was originally associated with a mountain to the south of Palestine, somewhere in Midian.[27] Sinai was the mountain of theophany long before it was the mountain of the law. The poetic texts (Judges 5; Deuteronomy 33; Psalm 68; Habakkuk 3) that recount the march of the divine warrior from the south do not mention the Exodus. Conversely, the events of Sinai are usually passed over in the summaries of the early history of Israel, even in the Deuteronomic corpus (Deuteronomy 26; Joshua 24; Judges 11, etc.).[28] This has led some to the conclusion that one group of early Israelites experienced the Exodus, while a different group encountered Yahweh at Mt. Sinai. Albertz objects that "such differentiations create more problems than they can solve" and asks how the assumption of different groups can explain the fact that Exodus and Sinai are connected through Yahweh and Moses.[29] I am inclined to agree with van der Toorn, however, that the Israelites learned of Yahweh from Kenites or Midianites, but that it is unlikely that they did so outside of the borders of Palestine.[30] Kenites and Midianites were traders, and the cult of Yahweh was probably brought north along the caravan routes. In view of the tradition-historical separation of Exodus and Sinai, it is unlikely that the cult of "the one of Sinai" entailed any consciousness of political liberation or was necessarily bound up with a memory of slavery in Egypt. Yahweh was initially a mountain storm-god. He was also a "man of war" to whom the Israelites looked for aid in battle. There is plenty of evidence of devotion to this God in Judges and Samuel. The judges fight the "wars of the Lord." Those who had experienced an escape from Egypt might well attribute their success to this warrior God. According to the biblical account, those who brought the cult of Yahweh to Palestine were themselves fugitives from Egypt who had witnessed a mountain theophany. But the oldest poetic celebrations of the God of Sinai do not mention the Exodus. I infer from this that the cult of Yahweh among the Israelites did not derive historically from the experience of the Exodus but from the accounts of the theophany of a mountain god in the wilderness and his perceived efficacy in battle. If this is so, then we can no longer say that "the origin of Yahweh religion is indissolubly connected with the process of the political liberation out of Egypt."[31] The Exodus may not have been taken as definitive of the God of Israel before it was adopted as the charter myth of the northern kingdom by Jeroboam.

The line of argument that I am following here, which I take to be in essential agreement with Karel van der Toorn, suggests that the Exodus had not assumed its central place in Israelite religion before the monarchy. The Exodus plays no significant part in the Deuteronomistic narratives about David and Solomon. Neither does it figure in the oracles that can reasonably be attributed to Isaiah of Jerusalem. The question then arises, was the Exodus celebrated at all in Jerusalem prior to the Deuteronomic reform?

THE SOURCES OF THE PENTATEUCH

This question brings us back to the disputed issue of the formation of the Pentateuch and the existence of a Yahwist source. The traditional source criticism of von Rad and Noth supposed that the Yahwist narrative combined stories of the patriarchs with that of the Exodus, including the revelation of the law on Mt. Sinai, and that this narrative was composed in Jerusalem in the tenth century B.C.E. If this hypothesis is correct then Jeroboam would only have adapted an account of Israelite origins that was also maintained in Jerusalem.

The composition of the Pentateuch, and specifically the source criticism of Exodus, are complex questions that go beyond the bounds of this discussion. The main effect of pentateuchal criticism of the last twenty years or so seems to me to be to destroy all confidence in any reconstruction of the process. Nonetheless, I will hazard a few observations.

1. It seems to me that the distinction of J and E material in Genesis is beyond reasonable doubt, but this is not the case in Exodus. The classic analysis of Noth attributed only scattered fragments to the E source, although he expressed the opinion that "on the whole E represents rather an earlier stage in the history of tradition than J."[32] The recent attempt of W. H. Propp, in his Anchor Bible commentary on Exodus, to assign more material to the Elohist source only underlines the arbitrariness of the process.[33] Moreover, Rolf Rendtorff's observation on the lack of continuity between Genesis and Exodus seems to me to be one of the more persuasive revisionist comments on the pentateuchal material.[34] The two books simply deal with different kinds of material. The disjunction is not removed by the introduction of the Joseph story as a bridge between them. Consequently, arguments about the date and provenance of J and E that are based on Genesis do not necessarily apply to the material in Exodus. In short, while J and E narratives of Exodus may have existed, it is difficult to reconstruct them and assign them dates with any confidence.

2. The main outline of the Exodus story surely predates both D and P.[35] It is not immediately apparent, however, that the J material in Exodus is necessarily either very old or of southern origin. The lack of interest in the Exodus in Jerusalem traditions before Josiah (primarily the book of Isaiah) must cast some doubt on the existence of a Jerusalem-based J narrative before the eighth century.

3. The most probable occasion for the construction of the Exodus story as a foundation myth was the establishment of the northern kingdom. The

northern myth, however, does not seem to have included the giving of the law on Mt. Sinai as part of the Exodus story. The implied audience of Amos seems to be blissfully unrestrained by awareness of covenantal demands. Even Hosea, who understands the relationship between God and Israel in quasi-covenantal terms does not associate the giving of the law with the Exodus. I am still inclined to think that the combination of the themes of Exodus and Sinai, including the law, is pre-Deuteronomic, but it is not yet presupposed in the eighth-century prophets.

CONCLUSION

In light of these comments, I find myself drawn to the conclusion that the notion of a "liberated Israel," informed by the experience of the Exodus, in the premonarchic period is a modern myth. Not only is it not sustained by modern historical analysis, but it derives little support from the primary biblical account of that period, the book of Judges. The folktales that underlie that book suggest a world of warring tribes, with impulsive charismatic leaders but little socioeconomic idealism. Liberation certainly was a motif in the "charter myth" of the northern kingdom. Like many narratives of national liberation, however, the Israelite one seems to have admitted of a triumphalist, self-satisfied understanding. Or so one might infer from the book of Amos. The myth of liberation from forced labor in Egypt did not immediately become the catalyst for radical social reform. We find a distinct emphasis on liberation in the Exodus narrative traditionally ascribed to the Yahwist (Exod 3:7-8), but it is only with Deuteronomy that the whole understanding of the laws becomes permeated with the recollection of having been slaves in the land of Egypt. This Deuteronomic sensitivity was presumably informed by the preaching of the eighth-century prophets, but it marked a new stage in the creation of the Exodus tradition.

The Priestly tradition marked yet another stage in the tradition when it insisted that "it is to me that the Israelites are servants: they are my slaves whom I freed from the land of Egypt, I the Lord your God" (Lev 25:55). The Holiness Code formulated its own vision of socioeconomic liberation in the jubilee laws. But for the Priestly tradition, the obligation entailed by the Exodus was primarily the pursuit of holiness and only incidentally the pursuit of socioeconomic justice.[36]

The development of the Exodus tradition, then, was not a simple matter, but a process that developed through several stages over many hundreds of years. The historian of religion must forego the theological urge to speak of the essence of Yahwistic religion, or even of the essence of the Exodus tradition. What the Bible has preserved for us is a layered tradition, of which even the oldest layers have only an ambiguous relationship to historical events. Despite the voluminous arguments of Brevard Childs, even the "canonical shape" of this tradition is not clear.[37] As Rainer Albertz has noted, the composition of the Pentateuch seems to have involved a spirit of compromise, so that both the socially oriented laws of Deuteronomy and the ritualistic laws of Leviticus are preserved side by side.[38] One consequence of this is that theological disputes cannot be settled readily by either historical or exegetical arguments. Jon Levenson's critique of liberation theology is based on the Priestly theology of Exodus, which is undeniably present in the biblical text.[39] But the liberation theologians can claim an equally valid basis in Deuteronomy and the eighth-century prophets.[40] Neither viewpoint represents the whole biblical tradition. Moreover, I would argue that neither the Priestly nor the Deuteronomistic theologies can claim to represent the original impulse of Yahwistic religion. That impulse came from traditions of mountain theophanies in the wilderness of Sinai, which had no intrinsic relation to the Exodus, and belong to the prehistory of the biblical text rather than to its history.

CHAPTER 6

THE EXODUS AND
BIBLICAL THEOLOGY

The Book of Exodus occupies a pivotal place in any attempt
to construct a theology of the Hebrew Bible or First Testament. While the Bible
encompasses several strands of tradition,[1] and attempts to relate everything to a
"center" of biblical theology are invariably reductive, the Exodus stands out as the
most influential story of the origin of Israel and as the setting for the authoritative
Mosaic law. In the foundational importance assigned to it within the Bible, it is
rivaled only by the theme of creation and the complex of material associated with
David and Zion.

But how should Exodus be interpreted? The story has a "history-like"
character, but nowhere in the biblical corpus has "the collapse of history" been
more painfully obvious in this generation.[1] While some evangelical scholars (see,
e.g., Kenneth Kitchen) and liberation theologians[2] still speak naïvely of the Exodus
as something that "actually happened," the credibility of such assertions has been
irreparably undermined in academic biblical scholarship. On the one hand, the
archaeological work, to which biblical theologians of the mid-twentieth century
looked for confirmation, has cast severe doubts on the entire biblical account of
the early history of Israel.[3] On the other hand, the amalgam of literary genres
found in the book of Exodus inspires no confidence in their value as historical
sources. The Song of the Sea, widely regarded as the oldest witness to the central
event of the Exodus, is a hymn, which, at least in its present form, encompasses
the Conquest as well as the Exodus.[4] Attempts to reconstruct history from such
material are dubious at best. Even if one is inclined, as I am, to grant that a story of
national origins that begins with a state of slavery is likely to have some historical
nucleus, we are very far from being able to reconstruct what happened with any
confidence.

It is no wonder, then, that biblical theologians have increasingly substituted the category "story" for "history" in speaking of the Exodus.[5] A story may include historical elements. It can also make use of myth and legend. Its truth is not measured by its correspondence with verifiable fact. It is a work of imagination, whose value lies in the degree to which it captures something typical about life in concrete detail. No doubt, many people find a story such as the Exodus more compelling if they believe it is rooted in historical fact. Such an "aura of factuality" is often held to be especially important in religious texts.[6] But in the case of the Exodus, the historical evidence is too scanty and controverted, and so we shall have to make do without the aura of factuality.

To say that the Exodus is a story, however, does not resolve the problems of interpretation; it only helps to frame them. If this is a classic religious text, as it surely is, with the power to shape people's lives,[7] then the shape of the story becomes crucially important. In fact, the major theological debates about Exodus in the past century have been concerned primarily with the shape of the story, or, more precisely, with the relation between the narrative that occupies the first part of the book and the laws that dominate the second half. One such debate centered on Gerhard von Rad's thesis that the traditions about the Exodus from Egypt and those about the giving of the law at Mt. Sinai were originally distinct. A second, more recent, debate has centered on the use of the Exodus in Latin American liberation theology.

THE SEPARATION OF EXODUS AND SINAI

Von Rad argued that it was only at a comparatively late date that the complex of tradition relating to the giving of the law on Mt. Sinai was inserted into the canonical picture of the saving history.[8] His argument was twofold. First, the great block of Sinai traditions that stretches from Exod 19:1 to Num 10:10 is both preceded and followed immediately by traditions about Israel at Kadesh. This point had been vigorously argued by Julius Wellhausen.[9] Second, he noted that the various poetic recitations of Israelite history that he dubbed the "Credos" make no mention of the events at Sinai.

This thesis has been criticized on various grounds. The identification of Kadesh traditions before and after the Sinai complex is open to dispute. E. W. Nicholson argues, for example, that "what we have in Exod 15:22—18:27 is a rather loosely connected series of originally self-contained stories," only one of which (Exod 17:1-7) can be associated with Kadesh. The "Credos," which von Rad believed to be the oldest nucleus of biblical narrative, are now widely regarded as Deuteronomic summaries.[10] The separation of Exodus and Sinai seemed to be definitively refuted by George Mendenhall's (1955) discovery of parallels between the Sinai covenant and Hittite suzerainty treaties, although Mendenhall's theory was far from commanding universal assent.[11] In the treaties, history was used to provide a prologue to the stipulations that were the heart of the document. On this analogy, the historical narrative of the Exodus was only the prelude to the giving of the law, and meaningless without it, a point made most lucidly by J. D. Levenson.[12]

As far as the history of traditions is concerned, von Rad's thesis had considerable merit, even if his own arguments were not decisive. The oldest references to Sinai regard it as the abode from which Yahweh issues forth as divine warrior to lead his people to the promised land.[13] Von Rad thought the giving of the law at Mt. Sinai was already incorporated in the Yahwist narrative in the tenth century. Recent scholarship has cast great doubt on the antiquity of the J source and entertained the notion that the continuous pentateuchal narrative was first strung together no earlier than the exile.[14] Mendenhall's covenant form is not exemplified in the Sinai narrative in Exodus. The best parallels are found in Deuteronomy, and so the suspicion arises that Assyrian treaties may be more immediately relevant to the biblical covenant than the older Hittite ones.[15] Recently, Thomas Dozeman has argued that Sinai came to be identified as the mountain of the revelation of the law only by priestly redactors in the exilic or early postexilic periods.[16] Whether such a late date is justified or not, there is good reason to regard the association of Sinai with the giving of the law as secondary and to think that the oldest recitations of Israel's foundational history did not include the giving of the law.

The theological issues raised by von Rad's thesis, however, went far beyond the history of traditions. The implication of the thesis was that a separation could be made between Exodus and Sinai, as between gospel and law. The Lutheran overtones of this position were unmistakable. Wellhausen, who was notoriously prejudiced against the Jewish law, had held essentially the same thesis. Yet, whatever the prejudices of these scholars, they raised a fundamental question for biblical theology. Where is the locus of authority to be situated? Does it lie in the oldest traditions, or are these superseded by the canonical biblical text? Is a biblical theologian bound by the canonical text in its fullness, or are we at liberty to build our theologies on some traditions and disregard others? These questions inevitably arise in Christian theology that attempts to appropriate the First Testament without undertaking the full "yoke of the Law," especially in its Levitical form. Essentially the same question arises in the case of liberation theology, where there is no reason to suspect any Lutheran bias.

LIBERATION THEOLOGY

Although liberation theologians frequently appeal to the Exodus, they have made very few attempts to exegete the text in detail (although we do have the study by Gottwald and the volume edited by van Iersel and Weiler). Gustavo Gutiérrez devotes only a few pages to the Exodus in his *Theology of Liberation*, but he articulates some basic principles of liberation exegesis. First, he insists that creation, not the Exodus, is the first salvific act in the Bible. The Exodus, then, is to be viewed in the context of creation. Hence its significance transcends the historical people of ancient Israel. Second, it is fundamental that Exodus is viewed as a social and political event: "The Exodus is the long march towards the promised land in which Israel can establish a society free from misery and alienation. Throughout the whole process, the religious event is not set apart."[17] Finally, "The Exodus experience is paradigmatic. It remains vital and contemporary due to similar historical experiences which the People of God undergo."[18] Gutiérrez grounds the paradigmatic understanding of the Exodus by placing it in the context of creation. The historical particularity of the event is not denied, but it must also be transcended if the text is to speak to people in other historical locations. The grounding in creation is not strictly necessary. As Walter Brueggemann has observed, "The most convincing warrant for such a usage is the undeniable fact that it is so used, that its adherents find it to 'work.'"[19]

In a similar vein, J. Severino Croatto interprets the Exodus as a sociopolitical event that remains revelatory for contemporary Latin America, just as it was for ancient Israel. "We are enjoined to prolong the Exodus event because it was not an event solely for the Hebrews but rather the manifestation of a liberative plan of God for all peoples. According to a hermeneutical line of thinking, it is perfectly possible that we might understand ourselves *from* the perspective of the biblical Exodus and, above all, that we might understand the Exodus *from* the vantage point of our situation as peoples in economic, political, social, or cultural 'bondage.'"[20]

The liberationist understanding of the Exodus has recently been subjected to a sharp critique by Jon Levenson.[21] The critique is somewhat distorted by the fact that it is based on the work of George Pixley, who has offered a Marxist critique of Israelite society that goes far beyond the more typical liberationist view of Gutiérrez or Croatto.[22] (Levenson's criticism of Pixley for substituting a dubious and hypothetical history for the biblical text does not seem to me to apply to the work of Gutiérrez or Croatto.) Levenson's basic criticisms do apply, however, to the entire liberationist project; they concern "the categories in which the Exodus should be conceived."[23] In the case of the Exodus, we are told, "*what for* matters more than *what from*."[24] Levenson notes that slavery is not mentioned in the Song of the Sea. Instead, the Song celebrates the kingship of Yahweh. The Exodus constitutes the basis for the covenant: "Then the Lord commanded us to observe all these statutes" (Deut 6:24). One form of servitude is replaced by another: "For it is to me that the Israelites are servants: they are my servants whom I freed from the land of Egypt" (Lev 25:55). There is no intrinsic objection to slavery, as can be seen from the Book of the Covenant, which provides for slavery in its very first law. At most, there is an objection to excessive cruelty and harsh treatment, but "the question may be asked whether God would have freed Pharaoh's slaves at all if they had not happened to be the descendants of Abraham, Isaac, and Jacob, to whom God had promised a land of their own."[25] "The point is not that it is Israel's *suffering* that brings about the exodus, but that it is *Israel* that suffers."[26] Levenson grants that a "preferential option for the poor" can be found in the biblical text, but he insists that it must always be balanced with acknowledgment of the election of Israel.

Now, there is reason to doubt that Levenson has done justice here to the liberation theologians. Even though slavery is not mentioned in the Song of the Sea, the book of Exodus leaves no room for doubt about the occasion of the Exodus: "I have observed the misery of my people who are in Egypt; I have heard their cry on account of their taskmasters. Indeed I know their sufferings, and I have come down to deliver them from the Egyptians and to bring them up out of that land to a good and broad land, a land flowing with milk and honey" (Exod 3:7-8). The liberationists are quite right that Exodus is first of all liberation from slavery and oppression.

Moreover, I see no reason why a liberationist should deny that the goal of the Exodus is the kingdom of God, or even servitude to God. As Brueggemann observes, "No one I know imagines that the Exodus results in autonomous independence."[27] The point is that this involves a new social order. While the social order described in the Book of the Covenant is not as egalitarian as some Marxist liberationists, such as Pixley, would have it, it is light years away from the regime of Pharaoh in Egypt. The liberationists do not deny that the Exodus leads to a covenant, or that it brings obligations with it, but they see those obligations in social and political terms, as "the beginning of the construction of a just and fraternal society."[28] Levenson is grossly misleading when he compares the liberationists with the Anglo-Israelite movement in the nineteenth century, which held that the British were the true Jews.

The real point at issue here is whether a theology of the Exodus must embrace the particularity of the election of Israel rather than see the Exodus as a metaphor for the liberation of all peoples, and whether it must accord equal validity to all the laws, Leviticus as well as Deuteronomy, simply because they are commanded and not only because of their humanitarian character. Levenson is strangely inconsistent when he endorses the use of the Exodus paradigm by Martin Luther King, Jr., while rejecting the similar analogical use by the liberation theologians. The fact that Pixley adopts a questionable and hypothetical reconstruction of Israelite origins does not invalidate the basic liberationist analogy between the slaves in Egypt and the poor in Latin America. While liberation theology does not necessarily require a separation of history and law, such as von Rad's tradition-history implied, it does require the freedom to depart from the particularity of the laws found in the Torah and to be selective about the kind of laws that retain paradigmatic significance.

TRADITION AND CANON

The conflict of interpretations between liberation theology and its critics brings us back to the question of the locus of authority in biblical theology, or—to put it another way—the manner in which the biblical text should be construed for theological purposes. In recent biblical theology there have been two principal ways of addressing this question. On the one hand, there is the tradition-historical approach, which is associated especially with von Rad, but which admits of several variations.[29] On the other, there is the emphasis on "canonical shape" championed by Brevard S. Childs and recently endorsed by Jon Levenson.[30] To be sure, these are not the only possible ways in which the biblical text can be construed. Much biblical theology in the past century has been preoccupied with the search for a "center" around which the rest of the biblical material can be organized.[31] I believe that this quest has proven futile. Many of the prominent issues in biblical theology, however, such as the relation between the testaments or the problem of history, can be viewed in various ways depending on whether the basic vantage point is provided by a synchronic canonical perspective or by a diachronic tradition-historical approach.

The particular form of tradition-history practiced by von Rad is now dated, in the sense that its shortcomings have been exposed.[32] Even if one were to grant the antiquity of the so-called historical credos, as few now would, they cannot bear the weight that von Rad laid on them in *Old Testament Theology*. To his credit, von Rad tried to pay more attention to other aspects of the biblical text, notably the Wisdom literature, in his later work. There are also vestiges of traditional Christian typology in von Rad's work, which are problematic in the context of an ecumenical theology.[33] The tradition-history approach, however, can be adapted in ways that avoid these shortcomings.

One model of post–von Radian tradition-based theology has been provided by James A. Sanders, although he speaks of a "canonical process" rather than of tradition.[34] Sanders views "canon" not from the perspective of divine revelation, but with a view to its function in the human community:

> Canon functions, for the most part, to provide indications of the identity as well as the life-style of the on-going community which reads it. The history of the biblical concept of canon started with the earliest need to repeat a common or community story precisely because it functioned to inform them who they were and what they were to do even in their later situation.[35]

While Sanders puts the primary emphasis on "story," much the same could be said for laws, hymns, oracles, or proverbs. This material was passed on from generation to generation because it spoke to the needs of the people and was adaptable enough to address changing situations. This process was not concluded either with the Second Testament or with the closing of the biblical canon but continues in various ways down to the present: "Each generation reads its authoritative tradition in the light of its own place in life, its own questions, its own necessary hermeneutics. This is inevitable."[36]

In a somewhat similar vein, but from a distinctly Jewish perspective, Michael Fishbane has written on how the traditions of Israel "could also have turned into a closed and lifeless inheritance without the courage of the tradents of biblical teachings to seize the *traditum* and turn it over and over again, making *traditio* the arbiter and midwife of a revitalized *traditum*."[37] He notes that this ongoing process is both constructive and deconstructive, as it both affirms the authority of the received text and simultaneously implies its insufficiency for the needs of the present.[38] Sanders's model has been criticized for lacking theological criteria, and the criticism is justified if one is looking for a contemporary normative theology.[39] As a description of the way in which tradition is actually transmitted, however, his account is cogent. If our question concerns the fidelity of a biblical theology to the biblical text, there is much to be said for Sanders's model as a framework for the discussion.

Brevard Childs is as keenly aware as Sanders is of the multiplicity of traditions encompassed in the biblical text, but he denies that the prehistory of the text has theological significance: "The history of the canonical process does not seem to be an avenue through which one can greatly illuminate the present canonical text."[40] His approach is concisely described as follows by his former student Gerald Sheppard:

> Childs prefers to speak of a "canonical approach," highlighting how the "canonical shape" of a biblical book established possibilities and limits to its interpretation as a part of Jewish and Christian scripture. He starts with "the final text" of scripture, without uncritically accepting the *textus receptus,* and makes observations about how diverse, even contradictory, traditions share a canonical context together. Rather than allowing the reader to pick and choose what elements of traditions seem the most appealing, this canonical context deepened the demand for interpretation in specific ways and in certain significant theological directions.[41]

Levenson's critique of the liberationist interpretation of Exodus is based on essentially the same premises. The liberationists do not read Exodus in its "canonical context," where the liberation from Egypt culminates in the giving of the full Mosaic law, but are selective in their emphasis on social and political liberation.

I do not dispute that Levenson's understanding of the Exodus is in accordance with the biblical text, embracing the full Torah with both its Priestly and its Deuteronomic components. I want to suggest, however, that there may be other ways of reading the text that can also claim to be authentically biblical in their theology. Neither the Bible itself nor Jewish nor Christian tradition requires that the text be always read in the holistic way that Childs prescribes. Childs's notion of canonical shape must be seen in the context of the "New Criticism" that was much in vogue in literary circles in the recent past, even though he himself rejects the association.[42] This is not to deny that attention to "canonical shape" may be helpful, just as attention to historical context can be beneficial, but only to deny that there is any theological imperative in the matter.

THE USE OF THE EXODUS IN THE PROPHETS

By way of renewing the case for tradition criticism as a context for biblical theology, I propose to direct attention to the way the Exodus is used and interpreted within the Hebrew Bible itself. First, it may not be amiss to dwell on the obvious: the Exodus is never treated simply as a matter of ancient history. Already in Deuteronomy, the Israelites are told that the covenant was not just for that generation but for all generations to come: "It is not with you only that I make this covenant and this oath, but also with those who stand with us this day before Yahweh, our God, as well as with those who are not here with us today" (Deut 29:14-15).[43] The repetition of the Exodus story in the Passover to this day enjoins that each person should look on herself or himself as if she/he came forth from Egypt. The Exodus, as Gutiérrez pointed out, is paradigmatic. Within the biblical corpus, the paradigmatic use is inevitably associated with the history of Israel and the chosen people, but it is never stipulated that no one else may think of her/himself as having been a slave in the land of Egypt. The classic quality of the story lies precisely in its adaptability and in its ability to transcend its original historical and ethnic setting.

The oldest witness that we have to the Exodus tradition within the Bible is the eighth-century prophet Amos. There are three references to the Exodus in the book of Amos, at 2:10, 3:1, and 9:7. The first two of these may well be secondary, Deuteronomic, additions, but are no less part of the Exodus tradition for that.[44] The third passage, however, has the unmistakable ring of the iconoclastic prophet: "Are you not like the Cushites to me, sons of Israel? says the Lord. Did I not bring Israel up from the land of Egypt and the Philistines from Caphtor and Aram from Kir? Hence the eyes of the Lord are against the sinful kingdom. I shall destroy it from the face of the earth."[45] It is clear from this passage that the Exodus from Egypt was commemorated in the cult at Bethel, against which Amos directed much of his preaching. Amos does not question the Exodus itself, but he radically relativizes it by suggesting that other peoples have parallel experiences.[46] Amos, then, lends no support to particularist Israelite interpretations of the Exodus. His God is the God of all peoples and is responsible for everything that happens in history. (Cf. Amos 3:6—does disaster befall a city unless the Lord has done it?)

The fact that Amos threatens that the sinful kingdom will be wiped off the face of the earth points to another crucial aspect of his understanding of the Exodus: it entails responsibility. It is much disputed whether the notion of a covenant, wherein there is an intrinsic link between the Exodus and the laws of Sinai, was already part of Israelite religion in the eighth century.[47] The worshipers at Bethel do not appear to have made such a connection between history and law. But Amos certainly made such a connection. In this respect, the two "secondary" references to the Exodus are faithful to the thought of the prophet. Amos 2:10 berates the Israelites for trampling the poor into the dust of the earth, even though "I brought you up from the land of Egypt and led you forty years in the wilderness." Amos 3:1-2 is more concise: "You alone have I known of all the families of the earth. Therefore I will punish you for all your iniquities." It is not apparent that the moral obligations arise from the Exodus. Amos holds other peoples responsible for their iniquities too.[48] But insofar as the Exodus confers any distinction on Israel, it is a distinction in responsibility, not in privilege. The iniquities in question, the matters for which Israel is especially accountable because of the Exodus, are primarily related to social justice. Some of the crimes mentioned can be construed as issues of purity or ritual (e.g., 2:7, "father and son go in to the same girl"), but sacrificial observance is pointedly dismissed ("did you offer me sacrifices and offerings the forty years in the wilderness, O house of Israel?" 5:25). Amos most probably did not know the laws of Leviticus, but his understanding of the moral requirements of the Exodus could scarcely accommodate them.

The moral obligations entailed by the Exodus tradition are also at the heart of the "covenant-lawsuit" of Micah 6.[49] Speaking in God's name, the prophet recites all that God has done for Israel. Then he switches to the persona of the worshiper. With what shall I come before the Lord? Various kinds of sacrificial offering, including the human firstborn, are considered, before the oracle concludes: "He has told you, O mortal, what is good; and what does the Lord require of you but to do justice, and to love kindness, and to walk humbly with your God" (Mic 6:8). The notion that some commandments are greater than others and capture the essence of biblical morality was neither original nor peculiar to Jesus of Nazareth (Matt 22:34-40; Mark 12:28-34; Luke 10:25-28). The reduction of the law to two main principles, of duty to God and to human beings, is especially characteristic of Hellenistic Judaism.[50]

The socially oriented preaching of Amos is not the only lens through which the Exodus may be read, but Amos is a biblical, Israelite author. His reading of the Exodus cannot be dismissed as either Christian confessionalism or Marxist ideology. A theology that treats the Exodus in a manner similar to Amos is surely within the bounds of biblical legitimacy.

Implicit in Amos's critique of the way the Exodus was used in his time is the belief that the God of Israel is also the creator who controls the affairs of all peoples. Creation is prior to Exodus in the narrative of the Bible and provides the backdrop against which the Exodus must be seen.[51] The association of Exodus and creation can be seen most vividly in Second Isaiah.[52] The anonymous prophet of the exile uses the Exodus as the paradigm for understanding the liberation of the Jewish exiles from Babylon in his own day. He reminds his listeners how the Lord "makes a way in the sea, a path in the mighty waters" (43:16), but goes on to bid them "do not remember the former things, or consider the things of old. I am about to do a new thing" (43:18-19). The emphasis is not on the past, but on the reenactment of the Exodus in the present. The paradigmatic, mythic character of the Exodus is more apparent in Isa 51:9-11, where it is juxtaposed not only with the new exodus from Babylon but also with the primordial battle of creation:

> Was it not you who cut Rahab in pieces, who pierced the dragon?
> Was it not you who dried up the sea, the waters of the great deep?
> who made the depths of the sea a way for the redeemed to pass over?

The juxtaposition suggests that the two events are alike, if not identical. The power manifested in the Exodus is the same power manifested in creation. While the paradigm is applied here to the deliverance of the Jewish people from Babylon, it is cosmic in principle and so potentially applicable in other times and places.

The universal implications of the creation story are most fully realized in the Wisdom of Solomon, which is not part of the Hebrew Bible but is nonetheless a pre-Christian Jewish work. The wisdom tradition was slow to address the specific history of Israel. The first attempt at a sapiential hermeneutic of the Torah is found in Ben Sira, in the early second century B.C.E. The Wisdom of Solomon, however, addresses the subject more systematically. It is characteristic of Wisdom's treatment of history that no names are mentioned. Instead, we read of "an unrighteous man" (Cain) or "a righteous man" (Noah). Wisdom is interested not in historical specificity, but in typical examples.[53] The Exodus is described as follows:

A holy people and blameless race wisdom delivered from a nation of oppressors. She entered the soul of a servant of the Lord and withstood dread kings with wonders and signs. She gave to holy people the reward of their labors; she guided them along a marvelous way, and became a shelter to them by day and a starry flame through the night. She brought them over the Red Sea and led them through deep waters; but she drowned their enemies and cast them up from the depth of the sea. (Wis 10:15-18)

In this sapiential hermeneutic, the emphasis is neither on Israel nor on oppression, but on the notion of a holy people. The author assumes that Israel is the holy people par excellence, but nonetheless the people are delivered qua holy people, not because God had a covenant with their ancestors. Wisdom's reading of the Exodus is not without its problems. The implication that deliverance was "the reward of their labors" is hard to justify from the text of Exodus. But the book provides an ancient and venerable precedent for reading Exodus as a paradigm that transcends the historical specificity of Israel. The liberation theologians then have good biblical warrants for arguing that the Exodus paradigm is not the exclusive property of Israel or Judaism.

CONSTANTS AND CONSTRAINTS

It is not our purpose here to rehearse the whole history of the Exodus tradition within the biblical corpus.[54] The examples cited, however, support Sanders's contention that "each generation reads its authoritative tradition in the light of its own place in life, its own questions, its own necessary hermeneutics." There is, then, no single normative way to read the Exodus story, or, to put it another way, the Exodus is not only a *traditum*, but also a *traditio*.[55]

There are, however, some parameters within which the Exodus story is read in the biblical tradition. First, it is assumed that the Israelites are the slaves. No biblical author reads the story from the perspective of Pharaoh. It is highly probable that the cult at Bethel, which drew down the wrath of Amos, celebrated the Exodus in a triumphalistic way. Such a celebration is never sanctioned in the biblical text. Rather, the typical appeal to the tradition is to remind the Israelites that they were slaves in the land of Egypt.

Second, the biblical authors insist that the Exodus carries moral obligations with it. The nature of these obligations is spelled out in various ways, from Micah's terse command to do justice and love kindness to the full complex of pentateuchal law. Several prophets dispense with (or were unaware of) the ritual and purity laws of Leviticus. Nobody, however, can dispense with the demand for justice and kindness. Some commandments occupy a more central place in the tradition than others.

Nonetheless, we should be wary of attempts to identify biblical theology too narrowly with any one normative kerygma. The Latin American emphasis on the theme of liberation is well grounded in the biblical texts, and the analogical application of this theme to other settings is entirely legitimate. But the recognition of the theme of liberation as central does not arise inevitably from the biblical text. Rather, it arises from the conjunction of the text with the political situation of the interpreters and from a set of values that is informed by a wide range of sources, including but not confined to the Bible.[56] The same could be said of any normative biblical theology, Jewish or Christian. There are limits to the range of valid interpretations, but there is also a legitimate diversity of ways in which the Bible can be read. No one has a monopoly on biblical authority.

CHAPTER 7

THE BIBLICAL VISION
OF THE COMMON GOOD

THE RELEVANCE OF SCRIPTURE
TO THE MODERN DEBATE

In their Pastoral Letters on The Challenge of Peace and Catholic Social Teaching and the U.S. Economy, the bishops of the U.S. National Catholic Conference begin with reflections on the teaching of Scripture. Since the relevance of the biblical texts to contemporary problems is not always obvious, it is well to begin here with some reflections on the significance and force of this appeal to Scripture.

Scriptural citations are a conventional part of ecclesiastical rhetoric. Since Vatican II they have generally replaced the traditional appeals to natural law as the basic moral grounding for Catholic social teaching.[1] The citation of Scripture is usually taken to imply a claim to transcendent authority, like the claim previously based on natural law. Indeed, Catholic moral teaching often gives the impression of exploiting the claim to divine revelation, without then being bound by the content of that revelation. From the viewpoint of critical biblical scholarship, however, the Bible cannot support the claim to transcendent authority. The study of the Bible over the last two centuries has amply demonstrated that it is the record of a historic people, through the vicissitudes of its very particular history. The social message of the Bible, like everything else in it, is historically conditioned and relative. The Bible can no more provide us with objective, transcendent moral certainties than can natural law.

Nonetheless, the Bible is relevant to our present discussion for two reasons. The first is broadly humanistic. The biblical ethic has had a profound and long-lasting influence on human civilization especially in the West. It deserves our consideration on its own merits, just as Plato's *Republic* or any other classic text from the past does.[2] The second is specific to the Catholic, or other Christian, community. Christianity is not a deposit of timeless truth but a religious tradition that derives its identity from continuity with the past. The Bible is the foundational document of that tradition and so occupies a fundamental place in the definition of Christian identity. This does not oblige us to accept everything in the Bible, but de facto if we were now to reject the Bible completely we would have cut ourselves off from the root of our tradition and it would be misleading to persist in calling ourselves Christian at all.

The Bible, then, is a controlling factor in deciding what constitutes Christian, or Catholic, social principles. Principles should not be called Christian unless they are in continuity with the Bible in some significant way.

To decide what is in continuity with the Bible, however, is neither simple nor straightforward. The Bible consists of historically specific texts that were composed to address the problems of the day in the ancient Near East. Nowhere is this more apparent than in the pentateuchal laws on social and economic matters, where we encounter such provisions as "when a man sells his daughter as a slave" (Exod 21:7). Any modern appropriation of the Bible must find a way to distinguish between "what it meant" and "what it means,"[3] between the specific ancient laws and the principles that can be adapted to new situations. The problem of historical distance cannot be bypassed by mystifying appeals to the status of the canon or the role of the spirit.[4]

The Bible itself offers some clues as to how it may be adapted to new circumstances. It is not a unified composition but the collected documents of a tradition that spans more than a thousand years. Already in the laws of the Mosaic covenant we can distinguish between the apodictic laws of the Decalogue, which provide sweeping general principles ("thou shalt not kill," "thou shalt not steal"), and the casuistic laws, which tailor these principles to fit varying circumstances.[5] ("Whoever strikes a man so that he dies shall be put to death. But if he did not lie in wait for him . . . then I will appoint for you a place to which he may flee" [Exod 21:12-13].) We can also see how biblical laws evolved in the various pentateuchal codes and how the prophets interpreted traditional law in specific situations. There are, then, biblical warrants for seeking to distinguish between the historically specific biblical laws and their underlying principles. The bishops are well advised when they maintain that our attention should focus not on the specifics of biblical law but on "the Bible's deeper vision of God, of the purpose of creation, and of the dignity of human life in society."[6] Nonetheless, it is only through the specific applications that we can properly grasp the underlying principles. The Bible is not a perfectionist document that is content with proposing moral ideals. It is, rather, the record of a tradition that constantly addressed specific problems and was concerned with practical results.[7] There is no foolproof method for correctly inferring the right application of biblical principles to new situations. Nonetheless, the tradition demands that the attempt be made. The bishops are at least faithful to the biblical process in attempting to address concrete contemporary problems.

THE PLACE OF SOCIAL ETHICS IN THE BIBLE

On questions of social and economic justice, it is primarily the Hebrew Scriptures that demand our attention. The teaching of Jesus in the New Testament is, to be sure, greatly concerned with the problems of wealth and poverty, especially in the Gospel of Luke, as the bishops note. Yet Jesus was not a legislator, and his teachings bear mainly on the conduct of individuals. He presupposes a vision of the social order that he inherited from his Jewish tradition and which is today the common heritage of Jews and Christians.

There is no doubt that a vision of the social order is at the very heart of biblical faith. There is at present little consensus on the historical question of how Israel emerged as a distinct entity in Canaan.[8] There is widespread agreement, however, that earliest Israel was distinguished by its particular social order, most especially by the fact that for a time "there was no king in Israel" (Judg 19:25). The great law codes of the Pentateuch had their origin in this early period. They are not royal proclamations but tribal law. They certainly underwent development at later times but they remained independent of royal authority. The Hebrew Bible has often been characterized as "salvation history" or as "revelation in history." It might equally well be characterized as "revelation in law." One scholar, Norman Gottwald, has gone so far as to argue that Yahweh, God of Israel, should be understood primarily as a symbol for an egalitarian model of society.[9] Gottwald's formulation is extreme, but he is right that the worship of Yahweh was understood from the outset to imply a commitment to certain social values.

THE COVENANT

The laws of the Pentateuch are presented in the context of a covenant between the god Yahweh and the people Israel. Modern scholarship has shown that this covenant was conceived on the model of international treaties in the ancient Near East, specifically of vassal treaties whereby one people became subject to another.[10] These treaties followed a conventional format, three aspects of which concern us here.

First, there was a historical prologue which rehearsed the events that led up to the making of the treaty and clarified the reasons for it.

Second, there were stipulations—the specific behavior required by the treaty. The subject or vassal must pay tribute, support the overlord in time of war, and not become the vassal of any other lord. In return the overlord promised to protect his subjects.

Third, the treaty was confirmed by curses and blessings, of which the gods were guarantors.

There was, then, a simple logic to the covenant form. The essence of the relationship was defined by the stipulations or requirements. The history, on the one hand, and the curses and blessings, on the other, supplied a supporting framework that was conducive to the observance of the laws.

The covenant between Yahweh and Israel was focused on the right of the people of Israel to possess their land. The historical retrospective claimed that they had received the land as a gift from Yahweh. The greatest curse with which they were threatened was loss of the land. Their continued enjoyment of the land was contingent on their observance of the covenant laws.

DIVINE OWNERSHIP OF THE LAND

The most fundamental principle of biblical ethics is the belief in the reality of a God who is lord of the covenant. Vassals in the ancient Near East pledged their loyalty exclusively to one overlord and even promised to "love" that lord in the practical sense of faithful allegiance. Israel, with equal exclusivity, pledged its loyalty to Yahweh. Deuteronomy is especially insistent on this point: "Hear, O Israel, Yahweh is our God, Yahweh alone, and you shall love Yahweh your God with all your heart, with all your soul and with all your might" (Deut 6:4). The land was a gift of God, not something Israel had earned, or to which it had an intrinsic right: "Beware lest you say in your heart, My power and the might of my hand have gotten me this wealth! You shall remember Yahweh your God for it is he who gives you power to get wealth" (Deut 8:17-18). The land is ultimately the property of Yahweh. This point is expressed most directly in Lev 25:23: "The land shall not be sold in perpetuity for the land is mine; for you are strangers and sojourners with me." Consequently, there are constraints on the ways in which the human tenants may use the land.

The religious faith of ancient Israel is not widely shared in contemporary America. Few, even of those who profess to share it, conceive of divine ownership of the land with the realistic seriousness of Leviticus. The belief in divine ownership can no longer serve as a common basis for public dialogue. If we wish to relate this principle to contemporary issues, we must demythologize it, that is, we must understand it in terms of its practical consequences for Israelite society. Most basically, the emphasis on the unity of God symbolized the unity of the people. The command to love God entailed a command to serve the common good, or in biblical idiom, to love one's neighbor as oneself. The affirmation that the land belonged to God meant that in principle it belonged to all, not only to all the people at any given time but also to all generations. The covenant was addressed to the entire people of Israel, and the morality of individuals was viewed only in that context.

THE SABBATICAL LAWS

The practical implications of divine sovereignty for social ethics were spelled out in the pentateuchal law codes. Perhaps the most striking stipulations are the so-called sabbatical laws.[11] The idea of the sabbath rest is familiar from the Decalogue. It is attested by the prophet Amos in the eighth century (Amos 8:5) and so is verifiably ancient. It was not prescribed for the leisure of the wealthy. The commandments repeatedly insist that it also applies to "your manservant, or your maidservant or your cattle, or the sojourner who is within your gates." Exod 20:11 gives a theological reason for the commandment: "For in six days the Lord made heaven and earth, the sea and all that is in them, and rested on the seventh day." Elsewhere, however, we find a more socially oriented explanation: "Six days you shall do your work, but on the seventh day you shall rest; that your ox and your ass may have rest, and the son of your bondmaid and the alien may be refreshed" (Exod 23:12). Deuteronomy is more emphatic: "The seventh day is a sabbath to the Lord your God; in it you shall not do any work, you, or your son, or your daughter, or your manservant, or your maidservant, or your ox, or your ass, or any of your cattle, or the sojourner who is within your gates, that your manservant and your maidservant may rest as well as you. You shall remember that you were a servant in the land of Egypt" (Deut 5:13-14). In this latter case the rationale is evidently to prevent the exploitation of servants or slaves.

In the Book of the Covenant (Exod 20:22—23:33), which is usually regarded as the oldest of the pentateuchal codes,[12] the sabbath rest is extended to the land: "For six years you shall sow your land and gather in its yield; but the seventh year you shall let it rest and lie fallow, that the poor of your people may eat; and what they leave the wild beasts may eat. You shall do likewise with your vineyard, and with your olive orchard" (Exod 23:10-11). It is not certain whether the whole land was originally supposed to observe the law simultaneously, or whether it could be staggered for individual fields.[13] Deuteronomy 15 clearly envisages a fixed sabbatical year for the remission of debt, but does not mention letting the land lie fallow. The practical difficulty of a fixed sabbatical year is obvious. It is acknowledged in Leviticus 25: "And if you say, 'what shall we eat in the seventh year if we may not sow or gather in our crop?' I will command my blessings upon you in the sixth year, so that it will bring forth fruit for three years" (Lev 25:20-21). This answer is idealistic rather than practical, and this is even more true of the Levitical legislation about the jubilee year in the same chapter.[14] We simply do not know how, or how far, the law was observed. After the exile, Nehemiah tried to enforce observance of both the sabbath and the sabbatical year (Neh 10:31), but the only time we read of the actual observance of a sabbatical year is in the time of the Maccabees (1 Macc 6:49, 53).

Regardless of the actual observance, the intention of the law was evidently to protect the land from exploitation. There is also the implication that the natural fruit of the land belongs to all the people, and so the poor could enjoy it at least every seventh year. These intentions are reflected in several laws in Deuteronomy: the forgotten sheaf is to be left for the sojourner, the vineyard and olive trees should not be gleaned a second time (24:19-22), the ox that treads the grain should not be muzzled (15:4).

The practicality of the sabbatical laws, even for antiquity, is open to some question. The objectives, however, were important and remain matters of concern for our own time: how do we preserve the land for future generations and how do we provide for the poor in society? The biblical laws do not provide a viable method for solving these problems in the modern world, but they suggest an attitude that is a prerequisite of any solution. The landowners of ancient Israel were forbidden to think primarily in terms of their individual profits but were directed to think instead of the common good. They were not to grasp at everything they could. The ideal was to have enough and to leave whatever was extra for others.

A second area where the distinctive methods of the Hebrew Bible can be seen concerns the treatment of slaves.[15] Lev 25:39-46 explicitly forbids Israelites to take their fellow Hebrews as slaves, for the obvious reason: "For they are my servants, whom I brought forth out of the land of Egypt" (25:42). Instead, they should be treated as hired servants. Like many of the social laws of Leviticus, this one probably reflects a (fairly late) ideal, rather than actual practice. The older laws in the Covenant Code (Exod 21:2-6) and in Deuteronomy (15:12-18) allow the possession of Hebrew slaves but require that they be released in the seventh year.[16] This law provides a good illustration of the importance of historical context. The logical implication of the Exodus story, which was clearly perceived in Leviticus, was not drawn out in Exodus or Deuteronomy. It is difficult to know for sure whether this was due to a lack of vision or was rather a compromise with the prevailing custom. Deuteronomy clearly provides for an element of compromise. At the outset of Deuteronomy 15 we read that "there will be no poor among you . . . if only you will obey the voice of the Lord" (15:4). Yet the next passage in 15:7 begins "if there is among you a poor man" and follows with the realistic admission that "the poor will never cease out of the land" (15:11). The next passage (15:12) deals with the case where people are forced by poverty into slavery. The Deuteronomic writers did not expect, or even attempt, to eliminate poverty, but only to set limits to it and thereby to alleviate it.

A third law that may serve to illustrate biblical social ethics concerns lending practices.[17] All the pentateuchal law codes prohibit taking interest from fellow Israelites (Exod 22:24; Lev 25:35-37; Deut 23:20), although it is permitted to take it from foreigners (Deut 27:21). It was permitted to take pledges, but again there were restrictions. For example, the creditor was forbidden to enter the debtor's home to seize the pledge, and garments taken in pledge should be returned before nightfall (Deut 24:10-13). We can infer from the prophets that this law was not always observed, but the intention is clear. Moreover, debts were supposed to be remitted in the seventh year. In all, biblical law was not conducive to a profitable banking industry. Here again, we must distinguish between the objective and the means used to attain it. It is evident from Deut 15:9 that the sabbatical release sometimes backfired, making it more difficult to obtain a loan at all.[18] The objective, however, was to do whatever would actually help to relieve the poverty of the debtors.

Some variation and development can be seen in the biblical laws, but the general principles are clear enough. On the one hand, they place restrictions on the aggrandizement of individuals, and on the other, they provide protection for the weaker members of the society.

There is evidently a strong egalitarian impulse in the Israelite tradition, based on the recollection that "we were slaves in the land of Egypt." Yet at no point do the laws envisage a complete elimination of wealth and poverty. It is assumed that there will always be rich and poor. The objective is rather to maintain equilibrium. Accordingly, every provision was made to keep the allotted lands within the family or tribe even if the individual owner had to part with them.[19] The laws were designed to prevent monopolies and situations that could force the poor into slavery.

THE RATIONALE FOR SOCIAL ETHICS

The preceding sample of biblical laws may suffice to show that a communitarian ethic was at the heart of the religion of Israel. The good of the individual was always viewed in the context of the community. The welfare of the community determined the welfare of the individual. We must now consider the kinds of rationale on which this ethic rests.

In the context of the Sinai covenant, three warrants are provided for obedience to the commandments: divine command, appeal to consequences, and appeal to history.

The appeal to divine command is perhaps the most obvious warrant for the covenantal laws. Fundamental though it was in antiquity, this appeal can bear no weight in a modern retrieval of biblical ethics. The point here is not only that people are now less likely to accept the force of such an appeal. More fundamentally, we now recognize that the claim to divine authority was conventional for lawgivers in the ancient Near East.[20] Such claims were a rhetorical device that could be used to legitimate any ideology. Within the Bible, divine authority sanctions the slaughter of the Canaanites as well as the release of slaves. This warrant offers no way of distinguishing which principles have enduring validity. It does not provide a constructive basis for a modern discussion.

The most serviceable warrant for ethical behavior in the Bible is the appeal to consequences. The "bottom line" of the covenant is that obedience is rewarded with a blessing; disobedience is punished with a curse. In this sense the covenant appeals to the enlightened self-interest of the community. We should emphasize that self-interest here is communal self-interest; there is no question of opposing the interest of the individual to that of the community in the biblical laws. We should also emphasize the importance of the adjective "enlightened." The covenant claimed to disclose a moral order in history that was not always evident in the short term. Appreciation of the force of the covenant required the wisdom to take a long-term view. In this regard the Sinai covenant is fundamentally similar to the other great ethical tradition of ancient Israel, the Wisdom literature, which, as is well known, relied on a highly pragmatic theory of reward and punishment.[21]

The other warrant supplied by the covenant, the appeal to history, also includes an element of enlightened self-interest. The typical reminder that "you were slaves in the land of Egypt" implies the possibility that you might find yourselves in that situation again. Accordingly, as you would that men should do to you, so should you do. The recollection of Israel's particular history, then, serves as a reminder of human commonality. No one is exempt from the possibility of being a slave or an alien. There is also an appeal to the intuition of human sympathy here, but this in turn rests on the recognition that we are all vulnerable to the vicissitudes of life.

The various warrants of the Sinai covenant are complementary and not in tension. It is important to recognize that biblical law does not rest only on an apodictic appeal to divine authority. There is also an attempt to persuade, by recollection of the past and by positing a moral order in history, so as to argue that obedience to the divine commandments was, in fact, in the enlightened self-interest of the people.

ILLUSTRATIONS FROM THE PROPHETS

The practical implications of the covenantal social ethic can be seen most clearly in the preaching of the eighth-century prophets. While it may be that the pentateuchal laws reflect to some degree the practice of premonarchic Israel, it is quite clear that different social patterns prevailed in the monarchic period.[22] The upper classes began to expand their holdings and force the smaller owners off the land. We get our first illustration of the problem in the story of Naboth's vineyard in 1 Kings 21. The king of Samaria wanted the vineyard "for a vegetable garden, because it is near my house." However, Naboth was unwilling to sell or exchange his ancestral heritage. The queen, Jezebel, resolved the problem by having Naboth stoned and his land confiscated. Elijah the prophet pronounced a blistering curse on the king, but he was powerless to prevent the seizure of the land. This incident seems to be all too typical of the situation addressed by the eighth-century prophets such as Isaiah and Amos.[23] "Woe to those who join house to house, who add field to field, until there is no more room and you are made to dwell alone in the midst of the land" (Isa 5:8). The expansion of the rich was only the converse of the oppression of the poor. Amos denounces those who "sell the righteous for silver, and the needy for a pair of shoes" and "trample the head of the poor into the dust of the earth." The people "lay themselves down beside every altar upon garments taken in pledge, and in the house of their god they drink the wine of those who have been fined" (Amos 2:6-8). Small landowners were forced to sell themselves into slavery because of their debts. The expanding landowners were more interested in vineyards and wine than in producing the staples of life to feed the peasants.

The charge that Amos and Isaiah bring against the rich of their day is not only that they are doing wrong to the poor but that they are violating the common good. By the common good I mean that which is ultimately in the best interest of all the society, rich and poor. Specifically, they claimed that social injustice would cause the Assyrian invasions, which would lay waste to both Israel and Judah, bring an end to the northern kingdom of Israel, and send its ruling class into exile. Ironically, then, the rich in Israel were fashioning their own destruction by their behavior.

A MORAL ORDER IN HISTORY?

We touch here on another basic presupposition of the Israelite social ethic: the belief that there is a moral order in history. The Mosaic covenant was founded on the belief that the material welfare of the people was directly influenced by their moral behavior. This belief is pervasive in the account of the so-called Deuteronomistic history from Judges to Kings and also in the prophetic books. It gives the social ethic of the Bible a pragmatic, consequentialist orientation.

Here again the biblical presupposition is not widely held today, and indeed the moral order of history was perceived to be problematic as early as the Book of Job. The belief that history, even the history of the people of Israel, follows a covenantal pattern has been undermined by the apparent randomness of weal and woe through the centuries. We should not, however, go to the other extreme and posit utter randomness. Human actions do indeed influence the course of events, even if the correlation is not as simple as the covenant would seem to suggest.

When the prophet Isaiah said that Assyria was the rod of Yahweh's anger (Isa 10:5) to punish Israel and Judah, he was speaking in mythological idiom of divine intervention in history. Modern critical historiography requires that events be explained in terms of human causality, and thus Isaiah's analysis must be demythologized. Since the prophet spoke of God acting through human agents (the Assyrians), this move does no real violence to the biblical text. Isaiah saw the root of Judah's problems in the pride of its rulers, who aspired to superhuman status by the pursuit of wealth and military power. He denounced attempts to form international alliances, which served only to attract the punitive force of Assyria (Isa 31:1-3). In the prophetic view the rulers were led to oppose Assyria, and so court disaster, by their desire for power and status as an independent nation. The same ambition led to social exploitation within the society, so that wealth could be concentrated in the hand of the rulers. There was then an intrinsic connection between internal social abuses and the policies that led to confrontation with Assyria. This analysis of history was probably oversimplified, since it takes too little account of Assyrian greed and aggression, but it was not entirely mistaken. The social abuses in eighth-century Israel and Judah were related to the political actions that led to national disaster.

The biblical view of a moral order in history cannot now be affirmed without qualification, but it should not be completely dismissed either. Precisely because we see the greater complexity of historical causality, we should recognize that economic policies are interwoven with other social and political issues, and the social ethic we espouse may indeed have reverberations throughout other areas of society. The biblical view of history can at least serve as a reminder that social and economic problems cannot be isolated from the political welfare of the society as a whole.

THE SOCIAL IDEAL

The prophetic critique of individualist profiteering in monarchic Israel shows that even in the ancient world there were competing visions of the national interest. In one view, the national interest entailed independence and respectability as a nation and the development of wealth and luxury for the upper classes. Amos sketches this ideal vividly, though only to denounce it, when he describes "those who are at ease in Zion and feel secure on the mountain of Samaria, the notable men of the first of the nations . . . those who lie upon beds of ivory, and stretch themselves upon their couches and eat lambs from the flock and calves from the midst of the stall; who sing idle songs to the sound of the harp, and like David invent for themselves instruments of music; who drink wine in bowls, and anoint themselves with the finest oils" (Amos 6:1-6). These people could probably be described more sympathetically by someone less passionate than Amos. Their luxury was not intrinsically evil: it was simply their view of the good life. Equally, those who "joined house to house and field to field" (Isa 5:8) and had "a thousand vines worth a thousand pieces of silver" (Isa 7:23) could be viewed as the progressive developers of their day. Their wealth presumably brought some employment, and some of it must have trickled down to their servants. They had succeeded in creating wealth, which was unknown to premonarchic Israel. Yet the prophets were outraged by the inequity it involved.

Their outrage arose from a different set of values. The issue was not only whether the peasants of Israel were better housed and fed as slaves under the monarchy or as free landholders in the earlier period (although such considerations were important). There was also the question of human dignity, which was violated by slavery and even by the extreme contrast between rich and poor. The prophetic ideal was that each family live under its own vine and its own fig tree (Mic 4:4). Theirs was an ideal of material sufficiency, but not of luxury, and also of the dignity of independence.

Neither the prophets nor the legislators of the Bible condemn wealth as such, and all regard material prosperity as a good. There is no preferential option for poverty in the Hebrew Bible. Both the legislators and the prophets are opposed to developments that magnify the gap between rich and poor. In a society with limited resources, if some people have more, others must have less. Given the inherent self-ishness of human nature, one cannot assume that the rich will take care of the poor. The biblical legislators realized the need to protect the rights of the poor by laws. The experiences of the prophets show that laws alone were not enough. When there is an extreme division of wealth and power, injustice is virtually inevitable. The prospect of a just society then depends not only on legislating rights for the poor but also on restraining the acquisitive instinct of the rich and promoting an ethic of moderation. This ethic is radicalized considerably in the New Testament Sermon on the Mount, where we are urged to consider the birds of the air and the lilies of the field. Jesus was not legislating for a society as Deuteronomy was, but his message about fundamental attitudes to material goods also goes to the root of the problem of social inequity.

The laws of the Pentateuch often provide protection for the weaker members of society—the widow, the orphan, the alien, etc. The major prophets, too, regularly speak up for the rights of the poor. Accordingly the modern slogan, "a preferential option for the poor," has some biblical warrant—most evidently in the case of a prophet like Amos. The phrase is less appropriate for the pentateuchal laws—Lev 19:15 admonishes: "You shall not be partial to the poor or defer to the great but in righteousness shall you judge your neighbor." The bishops adopt the slogan with a qualification that "option for the poor" "is not an adversarial slogan that pits one class against another. Rather, it states that the deprivation and powerlessness of the poor wounds the whole community."[24] In short, the "option for the poor" is a strategy for restoring the balance to the common good. It is, of course, the poor and vulner-able members of a society, "the widow, the orphan, and the alien," who need special legislation and the voice of a prophet to protect them. The presupposition of biblical ethics, however, is that the treatment of these people will ultimately determine the welfare of the nation as a whole.

CONCLUSION

The laws of the Pentateuch and the preaching of the prophets were born out of the very practical attempts of the people of Israel to regulate their society. They constitute a religious vision, founded on a belief in divine sovereignty and divine ownership of the land. The religious vision, however, is not an apodictic demand for altruism but claims to represent the best interest of the community and of the individuals in it. The special provision for the poor and the restraint and moderation in the pursuit of material goods are recommended because they ultimately enhance the peace and prosperity of all.

Modern attempts to retrieve this biblical vision encounter many obstacles. On the one hand, there is the innate propensity of human nature to short-sighted individualism—a tendency that was also present in ancient Israelite society, as we know from the prophets. On the other hand, the problem is aggravated in modern times by the decline of belief not only in a sovereign God but in any moral order in the universe or in history. Beginning with the New Testament, Christianity relied on belief in an apocalyptic judgment, beyond the bounds of history, to provide the ultimate sanctions for ethics.[25] Apocalyptic imagery remains an important resource for the Christian tradition,[26] but if we want our ethic to serve as the basis for public discussion of economic policy, we need to demonstrate its value for this world too.

While the biblical conceptions of a moral order must now be qualified and revised, the attempt to ground ethics in the ultimate self-interest of the community is of fundamental importance. Enlightened self-interest is undoubtedly the most widespread rationale for all kinds of policies in contemporary American society. It often results in policies that are short-sighted and individualistic, but the fact that self-interest is often misconstrued is not a reason why it should be abandoned as a rationale for ethics. Pragmatic appeals to self-interest are fully in accord with biblical principles. The claim of the biblical tradition, however, is that concern for the poor and restraint in using material goods are ultimately in the best interest of all sectors of the community. The challenge to both the contemporary ethicist and the economist who want to maintain this biblical tradition is to validate this claim in contemporary terms, by identifying the benefits that would accrue to society as a whole from the pursuit of the common good.

PART THREE

WISDOM AND
BIBLICAL THEOLOGY

CHAPTER 8

THE BIBLICAL PRECEDENT
FOR NATURAL THEOLOGY

In 1970, B. S. Childs published what may well be regarded as the obituary of the movement that had dominated biblical theology in the preceding decades. That theology was most succinctly expressed in G. E. Wright's formulation. It laid great stress on the objectivity of God's acts in history and saw the task of theology as simply the recitation of biblical history, with explanatory glosses for the modern age. Wright was candid in admitting that some areas of the Bible were less amenable to this theology than others. Specifically, "in any attempt to outline a discussion of biblical faith, it is the wisdom literature which offers the chief difficulty because it does not fit into the type of faith exhibited in the historical and prophetic literatures. In it there is no explicit reference to, or development of, the doctrine of history, election or covenant." The weakness of biblical theology in this respect was inevitably noted, by James Barr among others, and by 1971 James Crenshaw could claim that "the crisis which has struck at the very foundations of biblical theology was prompted in part by a failure to give more than a passing nod to the wisdom literature, and has helped to create an atmosphere within which a careful look at wisdom is inevitable."[1]

At the same time developments in modern theology have invited a shift in perspective from Wright's idea of biblical theology to something more compatible with the wisdom literature. Walter Brueggemann noted, in 1970, that "the wise teacher affirmed that *authority for life is discerned in experience*" and that "Harvey Cox has recently observed that this is a clue to all the 'New Theologies.' . . . Such a factor suggests the appropriateness of wisdom for our current theological task."[2] While Wright's insistence on the objectivity of God's acts in history was viable in a climate of neo-orthodoxy, one of the leading theologians of the 1960s wrote that "secularization has rendered our inherited biblical faith as irrelevant and meaningless as man's other myths and religions."[3] Since these theologians raised the question of "the reality of God and so of the possibility, meaningfulness and validity of any religious faith and of any theological discourse at all," they obviously could not begin by assuming the objectivity of God's acts as described in the Bible. Rather, "theology literally must begin from the beginning, it must deal with its own most basic foundations. And however much one may be guided by one's great teachers, that means starting as best one can on one's own and at the level of concrete experience."[4]

The disenchantment with "biblical theology" and the reorientation to concrete experience cannot be dismissed as another passing fashion of the turbulent sixties. More recent theologians, such as David Tracy, who profess "disenchantment with disenchantment" do not return to simple proclamation but seek a theology drawn from two sources, "Christian texts," on the one hand, and "common human experience and language," on the other.[5] The "Christian texts" are, of course, indispensable for a theology that wishes to distinguish itself as Christian, but they do not simply take precedence over "common human experience." The various sciences that study human experience must be allowed to reach their own conclusions in accordance with their own canons of evidence and without dogmatic interference. This is what Van Harvey has called "the morality of scientific knowledge," which "requires that one embrace that knowledge which presently best explains certain phenomena unless one has evidence and reasons of the same logical type for rejecting it."[6] Since this morality of knowledge is respected in all other disciplines and in everyday life, it must be respected in theology too. Even the Christian theologian cannot demand that the study of human experience violate its own principles to reach a dogmatic conclusion. A correlation between traditional faith and common human experience is necessary, but the assumption that the tradition simply supplies the answers to the problems of experience cannot be accepted.[7]

However, the respect for the autonomous study of human experience, which Harvey attributes to a "revolution in the morality of knowledge,"[8] has a long and venerable history, although its perceived implications may differ from one period to another. It is implied already in the earliest religious philosophy of the Greeks and the criticism of the Homeric gods.[9] The idea of a "natural" as opposed to "mythical" theology is found in the Roman author Varro in the first century B.C.E., who is cited by Augustine.[10] In the Christian tradition, natural theology has been said to consist "in those theologically important conclusions of reason from generally accessible data which are confirmed by, or at least compatible with, Christian doctrine".[11] These conclusions are correlated to Christian beliefs, but at least in principle are reached by the independent workings of reason. It is, of course, undoubtedly true that Thomas Aquinas and every other practitioner of natural theology was in fact influenced by Christian prejudices and presuppositions, but, as John Cobb has stressed, "he would have us judge his work on purely rational grounds."[12] The natural theologian does not merely seek intellectual justification for faith but attempts to account for human experience in as rational a manner as possible.

Natural theology, whether in the classical form of Thomas Aquinas or according to the "revisionist model" recently proposed by David Tracy, proceeds on the unprovable but necessary presupposition of any Christian theology, that an autonomous analysis of human experience will prove compatible with the "Christian texts," or more positively, "that a proper understanding of the explicitly Christian faith can render intellectually coherent and symbolically powerful that common secular faith which we share."[13] We are not concerned, in this essay, with either confirming or refuting that presupposition but merely with drawing attention to the Jewish wisdom literature as an area within the Judeo-Christian, biblical tradition where an analysis of common human experience and a correlation with a normative religious tradition are explicitly attempted. As a genuine specimen of natural theology within the biblical corpus, the wisdom material deserves closer attention from both "biblical" and "natural" theologians than it has hitherto received.[14]

The significance of the wisdom literature for the theological enterprise may be illustrated by four theses:

1. Wisdom is an integral part of the Judeo-Christian, biblical tradition.
2. Wisdom is concerned to articulate the religious dimension of universal human experience.
3. An attempt to correlate the universal religious experience with the specific traditions of Israel is found, especially in the later wisdom books.
4. Analogies with the wisdom literature suggest that elements of natural theology can also be found within the remainder of the Bible.

1. Wisdom is an integral part of the biblical tradition.

Despite the presence of wisdom books in the biblical canon, this thesis is by no means universally granted. Many scholars regard wisdom as an "alien body" in the OT[15] and question its theological legitimacy and value. The problem is essentially that noted by Wright; the wisdom books prior to Sirach ignore the themes of history, covenant, and election that are usually perceived as central to the historical and prophetic books. The question is how these indisputable differences should be evaluated.

The biblical status and theological value of wisdom has been most recently disputed by H. D. Preuss.[16] Preuss denies that there is any significant difference in viewpoint between Jewish and other Near Eastern wisdom and proceeds to question whether the God of wisdom can be identified with the distinctive God of prophecy. It is important to distinguish between the evidence adduced by Preuss, which is basically accurate, and the theological interpretation that he bases on it.

In fact, Preuss has rendered a considerable service to scholarship by his thorough critique of the allegedly distinctive traits of Hebrew wisdom. Hartmut Gese had argued that in Egyptian wisdom the chain of Act and Consequence (the *Tun-Ergehen-Zusammenhang*) was fixed by a metaphysical order, but that in Proverbs this conception is overthrown by the ability of Yahweh to act freely.[17] Preuss objects that the proverbs in question are a confession of the human inability to understand the order of the world and human affairs rather than an affirmation of God's freedom to depart from that order.[18] Similar expressions of human helplessness before God are found in Egyptian wisdom.[19] Even the "fear of the Lord," a phrase that does not seem to have been derived from pagan wisdom, does not express a phenomenon peculiar to Yahwism, but only the humility that is characteristic of all ancient wisdom.[20]

Preuss's uncompromising insistence on the overwhelming conformity of the earliest Hebrew wisdom to that of the Gentiles is thoroughly documented and convincing. However, he proceeds to draw a theological conclusion that wisdom is alien to the OT and an illegitimate resource for theology and worship. The extreme character of Preuss's position is shown by his rejection of the psalms that mention creation (8, 19a, 29, and 104) as "originally not authentic Israelite texts."[21] Preuss seems unaware of the extent to which the uniqueness of Israel's faith has been qualified by recent study.[22] If such crucial elements in Israelite tradition as the revelation at Sinai and the crossing of the Sea embodied conceptions and images derived from Canaanite myth,[23] we must wonder whether any biblical material is sufficiently distinctive and pure to qualify for Preuss's canon. While Yahwism had its distinctive features, like every individual religion, the view of biblical faith as something "wholly other" than all other forms of religion cannot be maintained.[24] Consequently, continuity with Gentile wisdom cannot in itself disqualify the Jewish wisdom literature as an expression of Yahwistic faith.

Preuss rightly reminds us that the mere use of the name Yahweh does not guarantee that the conception of God in wisdom is compatible with that of the prophets.[25] There is no doubt that the wisdom books speak of God in ways different from those of the prophetic writings. But is it not possible to speak of the same God "in many and various ways," as the Epistle to the Hebrews might suggest? Preuss himself has stressed the variety of conceptions of God within the OT.[26] We might add that the variety often involves clear and irreconcilable contradictions even within the prophetic corpus. Prophetic conflict in the OT is not merely between true and false prophets, but also between canonical prophets such as Haggai and Trito-Isaiah.[27] A Christian theologian who seeks to define the "true" biblical religion by reference to the NT is confronted by the very different theologies of the individual evangelists and Paul. The fact that wisdom is at variance with the prophets is not exceptional in view of the diversity found throughout the Bible. The use of the name Yahweh at least implies a claim that the route of wisdom leads to the same terminal as the admittedly different route of prophecy. If the NT could allow Paul to appreciate the worship of the "unknown God" at Athens, the "prophetic" Christian theologian should not be too hasty to preclude a wisdom literature that names its God Yahweh.

The debate on the "biblical character" of wisdom, or its "theological place in the Old Testament," has suffered from the confusion of two distinct questions. The first concerns the possible influence of the historical traditions of Israel on the wisdom books. The second concerns the legitimacy of wisdom as a way of speaking of the God of the Judeo-Christian tradition. Both critics and defenders of the wisdom tradition have tended to assume that it can only be legitimated in terms of some doctrine found in the Pentateuch or prophets. The most popular legitimation has been that proposed by Walther Zimmerli, who found a warrant for wisdom in the creation story of Genesis 1–3.[28] Zimmerli's suggestion involves an important reminder that the framework of the OT is broader than the history of Israel, but Roland Murphy is surely right when he voices the suspicion that this approach may be too apologetic.[29] Further, the wisdom books do not claim legitimation by reference to Genesis. The earliest wisdom literature derives its authority from human experience and the inherent character of wisdom, but not from any external source under God. In fact there is no reason why it should seek external legitimation, in the doctrine of creation or elsewhere, unless we make the unjustifiable assumption that the historical and prophetic books exhaust the possible ways of speaking of God. It is precisely in the failure of the wisdom literature to legitimate itself by reference to the specific traditions of Israel that we recognize a fundamental trait of natural theology, the attempt to give an autonomous account of the common human experience independently of special revelation.[30]

2. Wisdom articulates the religious dimension of universal human experience.

The essentially religious character of wisdom, even in its earliest stages, has won increasing recognition in recent years.[31] Yet there also persists a more traditional view of wisdom as nonauthoritarian, nonrevelational, and secular. Each of these characterizations of wisdom has been seriously undermined in recent study. We will consider them briefly before we turn to the more positive religious characteristics of wisdom.

The view of wisdom as nonauthoritarian has been championed above all by Zimmerli.[32] In fairness to Zimmerli it should be noted that he has not claimed that wisdom is void of authority: "Certainly we cannot say that counsel has no authority. It has the authority of insight. But that is quite different from the authority of the Lord who decrees."[33] Now several scholars have argued that the prophets were not as apodictic as we sometimes think, but also tried to *persuade* their hearers, and conversely that the sage who instructed his son was far from engaging in an open-minded conversation. Wisdom sayings in Israel as in Egypt are always presented as authoritative pronouncements that only the fool would neglect.[34] Nevertheless, Crenshaw's claim that "between 'Thus saith the Lord' and 'Listen my son to your father's advice' there is no fundamental difference" is surely exaggerated.[35] There is at least the difference in perspective noted by J. C. Rylaarsdam—wisdom is horizontal, prophecy vertical.[36] The difference is not in *amount* of authority but in the *kind* of authority. While the sage undoubtedly supposed that his authority came from God, he did not claim a special revelation. His wisdom is derived from human experience and accessible to all, for "who has ascended to heaven and come down?" (Prov 30:4). By contrast, the prophet is only authoritative if he "has stood in the council of the Lord" (Jer 23:18). Both prophet and sage could appeal to the authority of tradition, but here again the nature of the authority can differ. For the prophet it is a tradition of special revelations and interventions of God in history. For the sage it is the tradition of common human experience. In principle, the advice of the sage could at least be confirmed by common human experience. It is not, however, less authoritative for that reason, nor is it less religious.

The question of authority, then, merges with the question of revelation. Wisdom attaches little importance to visionary experiences or prophetic revelations. Yet personified Wisdom "cries aloud in the street" (Prov 1:20)[37] and seeks out listeners. Von Rad has termed the "call" of Wisdom in Proverbs 8 the "self-revelation of creation."[38] We may content ourselves with the more explicit references of the text to the self-revelation of Wisdom. In either case, the message of Wisdom is a revelation that is beyond human control and is experienced as a gift. However, this revelation is given "on the heights beside the way" and "beside the gates in front of the town" (Prov 8:2-3). It is available to all and presupposes no prophetic ecstasy. It is not an extraordinary phenomenon but is a dimension of human experience that is in continuity with the processes of listening and understanding in everyday life.

"Revelation" in this sense does not necessarily imply the intervention of a personal God nor the disruption of the normal processes of nature. Martin Heidegger has oriented his philosophy to the "Disclosure of Being" and shown that this conception of Being that discloses or reveals itself was fundamental to the earliest Greek philosophy.[39] Heraclitus proclaimed the Logos in prophetic tones, and Parmenides describes his discovery of Being in the language of divine revelation.[40] While it is true that Yahweh is the ultimate source of all revelation in the wisdom literature, yet it is Wisdom, not Yahweh, that calls out in Proverbs 1–9. The direct speech of God at the end of the Book of Job is a striking and deliberate exception to his usual reticence in the wisdom books and is universally admitted to represent a crisis in wisdom, not the normal sapiential mode of revelation. Even then God directs Job back to the works of nature from which a religious understanding of the universe must normally be inferred. Revelation in the wisdom books is a religious experience but not (or only exceptionally) a direct encounter with a personal God. It is found rather in the depth dimension of the common human experience of the world and of life.

The frequency with which the wisdom literature has been categorized as "secular" results from the failure of traditional biblical scholarship to recognize the religious dimension of language, which does not speak of an anthropormorphic God. In Rylaarsdam's words, since the outlook of the sages is "a horizontal one," "their ethical teaching appears less religious than that of the prophets."[41]

No scholar would suggest that the sages of Israel were nonreligious, and there is no doubt that they had some form of belief in Yahweh. Rather, in the words of W. McKane, the question is "whether the fear of God was an effective part of their wisdom."[42] McKane defends the view that the practitioners of wisdom "have to take the world as they find it, and that in their approach to its complex reality they do not permit themselves the luxury of religious or ethical assumptions.[43] In short, he envisages a separation of spheres. The wise men recognized a time and place for religion but distinguished this from the pursuit of their everyday affairs.[44] Gerhard von Rad has warned that "one cannot assume this opposition of real world and religiosity among ancient peoples."[45] However, the issue is clouded by the tendency of both scholars to equate religiosity with the specific influence of Israelite history and institutions rather than recognize it as a dimension of "secular" experience in its own right. McKane's thesis on the secularity of wisdom is based on the contrast between prophets and wise men. Von Rad's approach to the subject is more complex.

In his volume *Wisdom in Israel*, von Rad sometimes implies that the more specifically Israelite views of religion are normative for wisdom. First there was "fear of Yahweh." Then "in its shadow wisdom is assigned its place."[46] Wisdom "was a response made by a Yahwism confronted with specific experiences of the world."[47] We are given the impression that faith in Yahweh preceded wisdom, which was only developed in response to a new view of the world that emerged with the so-called Solomonic enlightenment.[48] In his zeal to defend the authenticity of wisdom within Yahwism, von Rad succumbs to the common temptation to "justify" wisdom in terms of an antecedent faith. If the wisdom books show freedom in their understanding of the world, it is "a freedom to which they were entitled precisely by their faith in Yahweh."[49] As we have noted already, the wisdom books never feel the need to justify themselves in this manner. They make no reference to a knowledge of Yahweh other than what is developed within the principles of wisdom itself. There is nothing to suggest that wisdom is in any sense an offshoot of the religion of Israel. Rather, the knowledge and fear of Yahweh that plays a crucial role in the wisdom books is grounded in the religious experience of the wise throughout the Near East for centuries before Israel was born.

The religious character of wisdom must not be confused with the influence of the history and institutions of Israel. Even when the sages speak of Yahweh, they speak of him in language derived from universal human experience. The knowledge of Yahweh is not equated with special revelation, but with a dimension of common experience. Accordingly the religious character of wisdom must be appreciated in universal experiential categories.

The Religious Dimension of Wisdom. Despite his occasional tendency to "baptize" wisdom as an offshoot of the historical faith of Israel, it is von Rad, more than any other, who has outlined the religious dimension of wisdom. Two concepts are of cardinal importance, the human sense of *limit* and the recognition of *cosmic order.* Both these concepts have played central roles in religion both in antiquity and in modern times.

The sense of human limitation is pervasive in the wisdom literature.[50] Humanity has little control over events, and even the wise have little knowledge: "Do not boast about the next day, for you do not know what a day may produce" (Prov 27:1). Ultimately life itself is limited. At most a wise man can hope for length of days.[51] However, it is precisely in the experience of limit that the sages encounter Yahweh. It is over against God that the finitude of humanity is perceived. "There is no wisdom, no understanding, no counsel against Yahweh" (Prov 21:30). "Many plans are in a man's mind, but Yahweh's decree endures" (Prov 19:31). "The plans of the mind belong to man, but the answer of the tongue comes from Yahweh" (Prov 16:1). This sense of limitation provides the framework for humility and ethical behavior: "Do not think you are wise; fear Yahweh and avoid evil" (Prov 3:7).

This acceptance of human finitude is one of the fundamental and universal attitudes of religion. The entire Bible from the Fall to the Apocalypse rings with reminders that "you are but a man, and no god" (Ezek 28:2).[52] The cardinal sin in the Greek tradition was the *hybris* that precipitates tragedy. The wisdom of Delphi was summed up in the maxims "know thyself" and "nothing too much," sober cautions to heed the limitations of humanity. In modern times some of the most successful attempts to isolate the core of religious experience—Schleiermacher's "feeling of absolute dependence" and Otto's sense of the wholly other and the *mysterium tremendum*—have underlined the finitude of humanity.[53] So David Tracy can justifiably write that "all significant implicitly religious characteristics of our common experience (the 'religious dimension') will bear at least the 'family resemblance' of articulating or implying a limit-experience, a limit-language, or a limit-dimension."[54]

Accordingly, von Rad's conclusion that the wise men "always reckoned with God as a limiting factor and as incalculable" is not surprising.[55] Von Rad goes on to ask, "What more could they [the wise men] have done than keep setting up these somber signs on the frontiers of this area? . . . They are aware that the area which man can grasp with his rational powers [ratio] and fill out with his being is really small. Wherever he turns, before he is aware of it, he is once more confronted with the perfectly incalculable element in the action of Yahweh."[56] It is this incalculable element that Hartmut Gese would attribute to a distinctively Israelite perception of the freedom of God.[57] In fact it expresses a sense of dependence and finitude that is common to all religious experience. The fact that the limiting power may be known by names other than Yahweh in other religious traditions does not detract from the religious value of the concept.

The experience of limit is also central to the various contradictions that put the meaning of life in question and give rise to religious doubt; the contradictions between the hope of immortality and the experience of mortality, hope of justice and experience of injustice, the imperfections of life and the ideals of religion. Modern anthropological studies have made much of the tendency of religions to mediate these contradictions by constructing myths that obscure the contrasts and lessen the starkness of the limit.[58] However, as Dominic Crossan has shown, there are also types of religious writing that are designed to strengthen the awareness of limit (and of contradiction) rather than obscure it.[59] Crossan suggests that parables create rather than mediate contradiction and argues for the same function in the OT stories of Jonah and Ruth. Within the wisdom corpus two major works may be said to underline the contradictions of life and remind us without compromise of human finitude. There are the "negative" wisdom books of Job and Qoheleth.[60] Job's confession that "I uttered what I did not understand" (42:3) and Qoheleth's insistence on the emptiness of life bear striking witness to the inescapable fact of human finitude.

However, all religious language (including Job and Qoheleth) is founded on the assumption that there is some greater reality that transcends human limitations. Accordingly, the other wisdom books are not content to merely set up somber signs of the frontiers but also attempt to speak positively of transcendent reality. As scholars have increasingly agreed in the last two decades, the sapiential perception of transcendent reality is closely bound up with the idea of cosmic order.[61]

The Concept of Order. The concern for order in the wisdom literature has been identified especially in two complexes of ideas. First, there is the so-called Act-Consequence relationship, and second, the personification of wisdom.

There is no doubt that the insight that certain acts (or attitudes)[62] have necessary consequences is fundamental to proverbial thinking from the earliest times. This fact underlies the common assertion that the idea of retribution is central to wisdom thinking.[63] In an influential article in 1955, Klaus Koch questioned the appropriateness of this assertion insofar as it implied a juridical model of reward and punishment and the submission of human actions to an external norm.[64] Instead Koch argued for a *"schicksalwirkende Tatsphäre"* (a sphere of fate-determining action), in which act and consequence were bound by an immanent necessity. The role of Yahweh consists of "midwifery" since he supervises and brings to completion the working out of this order.[65] The merit of Koch's observations lies in noting the impersonal character of this system, whether one refers to it as retribution or not. While Yahweh is undoubtedly personal, his personality does not modify the order of justice. We do not read in Proverbs of a God who "repents" or has mercy.[66] The "retribution" of Yahweh can also be expressed in impersonal terms as the consequence of human acts. The sages perceive no tension between the impersonal character of this order and their belief in a personal God,[67] but their explicit starting point is human experience, not mythological formulations of an anthropomorphic God, or special revelations. The sages identified God in their perception of the order of the universe but they retained to a great extent the impersonal formulation of common human experience.

The association of God with order, and specifically with moral order, was not peculiar to Jewish wisdom literature. The affinities with other Near Eastern conceptions, especially the Egyptian notion of Maat, are well known and have been reviewed in detail elsewhere.[68] The attempt to identify God with a rigid pattern of sin and punishment has often rightly been criticized, both as an unworthy conception of God and as a falsification of human experience. Such rigid dogmatism is undoubtedly found in the wisdom tradition—the friends of Job provide the most obvious example. However, the principles of wisdom did not necessarily lead to such dogmatism. In the book of Proverbs dogmatic assertions that "the righteous will never be removed, but the wicked will not dwell in the land" (10:30) must be tempered to some extent by the reminder that no one knows what a day may produce (27:1). The conviction of a definite order must be held in balance by the knowledge of human limitations, which render that order inaccessible on occasion. The consciousness of limit and the attendant mystery of life may have been suppressed on occasion by a dogmatic conception of order, but both factors are still evident in the wisdom literature that has survived.[69]

Personified Wisdom. While a conception of cosmic order is implicit in the analogies and causal connections of the earliest proverbs, it is not yet formulated explicitly as a metaphysical principle. The representation of order is considerably advanced by the introduction of the personified figure of Wisdom, especially in Proverbs 1–9.[70] The relevance of this figure to the discussion of order is indicated by the influence of the Egyptian Maat on Proverbs 8.[71] However, the much-discussed question of the religio-historical origins of the idea is less important for our purpose than the function of that idea within Israelite wisdom.[72]

Von Rad has rightly objected to the common idea that Wisdom is a hypostasis, or a personification, of an attribute of Yahweh.[73] The figure of Wisdom was not suggested by speculation on the attributes of God, but by the sense of a pervading order in the world. This is evident in Job 28 where the question, "But, where shall wisdom be found?" is prefaced by a recitation of various manifestations of order in the world. It is typical of the book of Job that "man does not know the way to it" (28:13), but only God knows its place. The establishment of wisdom is specifically related to the ordering of creation: "When he gave to the wind its weight and meted out the waters by measure, when he made a decree for the rain and a way for the lightning of the thunder; then he saw it and declared it, he established it, and searched it out" (28:25-27). The hymn in Proverbs 8 also underlines the affinity of Wisdom with creation: "When he established the heavens I was there" (8:27). Whether the word 'amôn in Prov 8:30 should be understood as "master workman" (RSV) or "darling" ('amûn, von Rad), it is clear that the primary locus of Wisdom is "his inhabited world" (8:31). Wisdom is perceived in the paths and city gates, in the street and in the markets, in the contrast of a good wife and an adulteress. It is the principle of order for the individual, which leads to peace, prosperity, and life. Its absence leads to "panic," which "strikes like a storm" (1:26-27). It is true that the statement that "The Lord by wisdom founded the earth" (3:19) suggests that wisdom is also an attribute of Yahweh, but it is known to humanity through creation, not through direct speculation on God. Prov 3:19 is not deduced from the nature of God, but inferred from the order of nature.

Similar (but not, of course, identical) conceptions occur in various religions and philosophies. The parallels with the Egyptian concept of Maat are well known.[74] Other concepts that are not historically related also provide useful analogies: the Being of Parmenides, the Logos of Heraclitus and the Stoics, or in recent times the notion of Being in Heidegger's philosophy. In more immediately theological language, we might compare Tillich's "ground of our being." All these differ, to be sure, but share the sense of a dimension of the universe that "calls" humanity to authentic life.[75] The term "wisdom" is, of course, deliberately ambiguous. In normal usage it is a human attribute, the faculty of understanding.[76] But in Proverbs 1–9 it is also an entity independent of humanity that calls out and encounters us. The person who responds to the call is "wise." Wisdom, then, is that dimension of the universe that corresponds to and forms both the ground and ultimate fulfillment of the human power of understanding. It is not said to be projected on the universe but to be already there, even before the rest of the world was made. However, the very ambiguity of the term "wisdom" should warn us of the difficulty in making any sharp separation between the human thinking process and what we perceive as "reality," between meaning projected and meaning encountered.[77]

Wisdom is not God. This distinction separates Jewish wisdom from some other conceptions of cosmic order, such as the Stoic Logos, but we should remember that the Egyptian Maat was still daughter of Re and could be bestowed by him. The insistence of Proverbs that Wisdom is a creature is probably due to the traditional Israelite insistence on monotheism. Yet the dealings of humanity with God can also be formulated as relations with Wisdom. If God is "a shield to those who walk in integrity" (Prov 3:7), it is because he "gives wisdom," and "wisdom will come into your heart . . . delivering you from the way of evil." The sage not only counsels his son to keep the commandments but also to "get wisdom; get insight. Do not forsake her and she will keep you" (4:5-6). Wisdom gives life and riches (3:16) even as God does. In short, the figure of Wisdom provides a way of speaking of the experience of God without recourse to special revelation, and without portraying God in anthropomorphic terms. By extrapolating from the human experience of wisdom, the sages can speak, in a limited way, of the nature of God and the world. Since they do not equate Wisdom with God they do not claim to have exhausted the mystery of life or eliminated the transcendence of God or the human sense of limit.

The term "order" is not found in the vocabulary of wisdom but is nevertheless appropriate for the experience of the world expressed in the linking of Act and Consequence and in personified Wisdom. This experience is religious, but, once again, it is the religious dimension of common human experience. It does not claim legitimation by reference to any special revelation or to the history of Israel. The fact that the Jewish figure of personified Wisdom was probably modified by traditional Israelite conceptions does not alter the fact that the sages did not invoke the authority of special revelation but attempted to give an independent account of universal human experience.

3. Wisdom attempts a correlation with the specific traditions of Israel.

We noted at the beginning of this essay that the traditional conception of natural theology involves not only the analysis of human experience but also the correlation of that analysis with the specifically Christian tradition. In the later Jewish wisdom books we find an explicit attempt to correlate the wisdom account of human experience with the specifically Israelite tradition.

In the book of Proverbs such a correlation is already implied in the use of the name Yahweh. While the knowledge of God in the wisdom literature is not derived from the history of Exodus and Sinai, the sages affirm that the God they speak of independently is indeed the same. However, this correlation is minimal and provides no guidelines for the integration of specifically Israelite material with the universal observations of wisdom.

It is generally agreed that the first serious attempt at correlation with the wisdom literature is found in the book of Sirach. Sirach provides a review of the history of Israel in the "Praise of the Fathers" in chapters 44–50, and in 24:23 concludes the proclamation of personified wisdom by declaring flatly, "All this is the book of the covenant of the Most High God, the law which Moses commanded us."

Because of the latter statement, especially, Sirach has often been considered a milestone in the "nationalization of wisdom."[78] We might more fittingly speak of a universalization of Israelite tradition. The mere identification of wisdom and the law does not necessarily mean that wisdom is subordinated to the law. In fact the equation permits various conclusions.

There is indeed an attempt to nationalize wisdom in the OT, but it is not found within the books usually classified as wisdom literature. The clearest example is provided by Ezra, who is said equivalently to have the law of his God or the wisdom of his God in his hand (Ezra 7:14, 25). Here "wisdom" is merely a synonym for the law. In Deut 4:6 where the law is also described as wisdom, the revealed law also evidently takes precedence.[79] The later development of this tradition can be seen in the book of Baruch. In Bar 3:9-37 there is a hymnic passage on the place of wisdom, analogous to Job 28. In Bar 4:1, as in Sir 24:23, wisdom is equated with "the book of the commandments of God." However, Baruch continues by urging his readers, "Do not give your glory to another or your advantages to an alien people. Happy are we, O Israel, for we know what is pleasing to God" (4:3-4). The implication here is that the law contains all necessary wisdom and the Jews do not need to look to other manifestations. In effect wisdom is replaced by the law, as in Deuteronomy and Ezra.

There are no such implications in Sirach. While Sirach can say, "If you desire wisdom, keep the commandments" (1:26), his book consists of wisdom sayings and is not simply an invocation of the law.[80] Rather, "all wisdom is the fear of the Lord and in all wisdom there is fulfillment of the law" (19:20). The equation of wisdom and the law does not lead to the rejection of non-Jewish wisdom as superfluous. Rather, it broadens the concept of the law to include all forms of wisdom.[81] The wise man will not hate the law (33:2), but he will not confine himself to the literal law either. The special Jewish revelation is compatible with and must be complemented by the wisdom that derives from common human experience.[82]

The review of history in the "Praise of the Fathers" reflects a similar attitude. Sirach fully endorses the historical tradition of Israel, but he is not interested in the once-for-all quality of historical events, nor indeed in events at all. History has become for him a mine of examples of righteous behavior. Some righteous men have left a name; others have not (44:8-9). What matters to Sirach is the recurring phenomenon of righteous men and the example provided thereby.

The transformation of history into a series of illustrations of a universal principle is carried even further in the Wisdom of Solomon. Beginning in chapter 10 there is a review of the history of Israel, but no proper names are used.[83] Instead, we find repeated references to "a righteous man" or "an unrighteous man." In 10:4 the righteous man is patently Noah; in 10:5, Abraham; in 10:6, Lot; in 10:10, Jacob, and so forth. Wisdom is not interested in the historical differences among these figures but only in the repeated manifestation of a universal type. In this way the history of Israel becomes a series of typical illustrations of the common human experience.[84]

Finally, the most elaborate attempt in ancient Judaism to relate the specific traditions of Israel to universal human experience is found in the writings of Philo. Drawing on a Stoic notion, Philo could formulate his principle explicitly—"that the world is in harmony with the Law, and the Law with the world, and that the man who observes the law is constituted thereby a loyal citizen of the world.[85] In short, the Jewish law is one formulation of the law of nature and can be faithfully translated into the language of other such formulations, e.g., Platonic philosophy. Philo achieves his translation by an allegorical interpretation of the law that is often forced and far-fetched. However, the details of his interpretation cannot detract from the significance of his attempt to relate the scriptural tradition to the common human experience, an attempt that anticipated the major program of Western theology and philosophy through the Middle Ages.[86]

4. Wisdom and the remainder of the biblical corpus

The fourth thesis, that analogies with the wisdom books suggest that elements of natural theology can be found in the rest of the OT, can only be briefly noted here. There has been a proliferation in recent years of studies that claim "wisdom influence" on prophetic or historical books.[87] The basis for these studies lies in the observation of many similarities between these books and the wisdom literature and the use of typical wisdom forms such as proverbs and analogies. It is unfortunate that the dominant interest of biblical scholarship in historical questions of origin and redaction leads to the assumption that such similarities must be due to the influence of wisdom teachers on Amos[88] or whatever biblical writer is in question. The relationship between two books or bodies of literature need not be genealogical. It can also be phenomenological, in the sense that different works can draw independently on similar aspects of the common human experience.[89]

James Crenshaw has rightly objected that if one views wisdom as "practical knowledge of the laws of life and of the world, based on experience," then "it is little surprise to discover wisdom everywhere, for what literature does not grow out of and reflect experience?"[90] However, when we view this question against the background of the neo-orthodox emphases of recent biblical theology it becomes significant. The parallels among wisdom and the prophets and historical books prove no more than the common basis of all this literature in human experience. But that very fact is a salutary reminder that the Word of God is expressed in human language, and even the most revelatory, supernaturalist theology cannot dispense with common human experience. So-called wisdom elements in prophetic and historical books bear witness to the inevitable dependence of any special revelation on analogies with common human experience.[91]

CONCLUSION

The purpose of this essay has been to draw attention to the significance of the wisdom literature as a resource for the ongoing enterprise of natural theology. This is not to suggest that the sages of Israel were modern theologians in disguise. Even apart from the immense differences between their worldview and ours, it is obvious that a systematic or even critical theology in the modern sense cannot be found in the wisdom books. Still less does this essay advocate a "flight to wisdom" as the haven for biblical theology in a secular age.[92] Wisdom cannot in any sense supersede the historical and prophetic materials that constitute the great bulk of the OT. If the "Biblical Theology Movement" erred by neglecting wisdom, no purpose is served by inverting that error.

Nevertheless, there are certain fundamental aspects of the sages' approach to reality that are common to natural theology in all ages. Specifically, the sages attempted to discern the religious dimension of common, universal human experience without appeal to special revelation or the unique experience of one people. This religious dimension was correlated with the distinctively Israelite tradition but it was not subordinated to it. The history and law of Israel did not replace universal wisdom, although the sages claimed that they did complement and illustrate it.

The task of modern exegesis may fairly be described as that of showing the relevance of the ancient biblical material to the universal, contemporary human experience. That task embraces all the biblical material, not just wisdom. However, the wisdom tradition may be of particular interest to the exegete insofar as it provides an explicit precedent for the correlation of revelation and experience within the biblical corpus.

CHAPTER 9

PROVERBIAL WISDOM AND THE YAHWIST VISION

"The books of Wisdom in the Bible are somewhat compromised: they are informed by a rigorous calculation designed to lead to prosperity. If Solomon really wrote any of these books he was as repellent to perceptive Yahwists as Poor Richard to D. H. Lawrence." This evaluation of Hebrew wisdom by literary critic Herbert Schneidau is shared by many biblical scholars. It is usually based on prior theological considerations: wisdom is suspect because of its foreign origin (H. D. Preuss) or its failure to refer to the "mighty acts of God" toward Israel (G. E. Wright).[1] While Schneidau stresses "the essentially foreign" character of wisdom, he is more directly concerned with the nature of the material itself. The "prudent calculation" of wisdom is perceived as incompatible with a "rigorous Yahwist vision." The Yahwist vision is understood by Schneidau in literary terms. The "enduring heritage of the Bible's literary forms" is typified by prophecy and parable.[2] These forms are characterized by a "demythologizing" and "debunking" thrust. While myth "charts paths of meaningfulness" and is probably "the most efficient means man has of stabilizing his societies," the Bible "demands that we acknowledge how precarious is our grasp of any meaning at all" and is characterized by "ambivalence towards culture of any kind, but particularly one's own."[3] By contrast, proverbial wisdom is notoriously dedicated to the idea that order pervades the world of appearances[4] and to "the project of making a continuous whole out of one's existence."[5] It would seem then that Schneidau has substantial reason to regard Solomonic wisdom as repellent to his vision of rigorous Yahwism.

Schneidau's view of the essential spirit of Yahwism is widely shared by biblical scholars. Strikingly similar views have been independently formulated by Malcolm W. Clark (with particular reference to OT prophecy) and J. D. Crossan (with a focus on NT parables).[6] Yet no one would claim that prophecy and parable are the only authentically biblical forms of speech. Biblical religion, like any other, can be understood as an exercise in "world-building,"[7] which involves the development of positive beliefs, traditions, and institutions. Schneidau does not deny that the Bible has its myths but claims that

> whenever mythology developed in Hebrew history, it was inherently more unstable than the mythologies of the surrounding cultures, and those of other cultures generally, because it had, as it were, short half-lives, because the Yahwist vision was always latent within them, ready to erode the comfortable assumption that they shared in Yahweh's sacredness. Each form of mythologizing aroused its generation of critics—i.e., prophets—sooner or later. Even such institutions as the Law, which was manifestly an attempt to stabilize and sacralize the social ideology and thus substitute for myth, eventually became liable to demythologization.[8]

In short, Schneidau's thesis is not that Yahwism dispensed with positive structures, but that its own basic myths and traditions contained within them an impetus to "anti-structure."[9] This impetus is located especially in the use of a "historicizing style"[10] that dominates much of the biblical material. While the biblical narratives are not necessarily "historical" in the sense of reliable factual reports, and are perhaps more accurately classified as "story" than as "history,"[11] they are not presented as timeless truths but are set in the constant flux of historical change. The basic biblical paradigm of the Exodus celebrated a dramatic change in the status of a people and a disruption of the power structure of the ancient world. The Exodus remained a symbol of the possibility of unexpected change, a reminder that God could again do "a new thing," making a path through the sea and rivers in the desert (Isa 43:16-20). In Voegelin's phrase, "history is the Exodus from civilizations,"[12] and no institutions or systems are immune to its eroding power. The Exodus was no doubt often viewed positively in ancient Israel as a guarantee of divine favor and election. However, the Exodus tradition itself contained the seeds of the debunking critique of Israel's complacency, and so could be utilized critically by a prophet such as Amos.

The wisdom tradition in the OT is a self-contained body of literature that is independent of the traditions of Israel's history.[13] Like the historical and legal traditions, it can be viewed as an exercise in world building, the construction of an ordered view of reality. The house on seven pillars (Prov 9:1) eloquently symbolizes the stability of the sages' world. The pursuit of world order in the wisdom tradition culminates in the affirmation of a metaphysical wisdom that "in full might reaches from end to end and orders all things graciously" (Wis 8:1) and "holds all things together" (Wis 1:7).[14] However, the wisdom tradition also produced its literature of dissent.[15] Job and Qoheleth question traditional assumptions in a manner as radical as any prophet or parabler. Even Schneidau, interestingly, claims that the message of Qoheleth, that all human achievements are vanity and chasing after wind, is in fundamental accord with the Yahwist vision and "could come from any book of the Bible."[16] The wisdom that is "repellent to perceptive Yahwists" must be found elsewhere, presumably in the more positive collection of Proverbs. Schneidau does not ask whether the positive proverbial tradition might contain the seeds of a debunking tendency, in the same way that the historical traditions of the Bible are said to have the prophetic vision latent within them. Yet this possibility surely must be explored before wisdom can be compared or contrasted with other biblical traditions.

THE NATURE OF PROVERBS

There is widespread agreement that "the basic unit of gnomic apperception is the saying, either proverb or aphorism."[17] Proverbs, as André Jolles insisted, are not primarily didactic. Rather, they are retrospective and express a conclusion from experience.[18] Such simple statements are plentiful in the book of Proverbs:

> A rich man's wealth is his strong city;
> their poverty is the ruin of the poor. (10:15)

> Where there are no oxen there is no grain
> but abundant crops come by the strength of the ox. (14:4)

> A well-fed person will disdain honey
> but to one who is hungry even the bitter is sweet. (27:7)[19]

These statements are purely declaratory and do not imply either approval or protest. They are not themselves hortatory, although they can clearly become the basis for exhortation.

To say that such sayings are "basic" is not to suggest that they are the oldest stratum of proverbs. While there have been several attempts to identify chronological layers by distinguishing the simpler forms from the more complex,[20] such attempts have not been successful. Comparison with Egyptian wisdom literature has shown that even the longer instructions in Proverbs 1–9 are not necessarily late.[21] The "basic" character of the simple statement is logical rather than chronological. The didactic and hortatory sayings of Proverbs presuppose such declaratory observations. The advice of the sages is not deduced from divine law, but inferred from their observations. In some cases the motivation is explicit:

> Do not neglect your own friend or your father's . . .
> a near neighbor is better than a distant brother. (27:10)

> Be careful to know your own sheep
> and give attention to your flocks,
> for possessions do not last forever
> nor will a crown endure to endless generations. (27:23-24)

Here the exhortations are clearly based on the assertions made in the second half of the sayings. Other observations clearly imply advice. If it is true that "he who sends a fool on an errand cuts off his own feet" (26:6), it is superfluous to add that one should not send a fool on an errand. If a man who meddles in another's quarrel is like one who seizes a passing cur by the ears (26:17), meddling is evidently to be discouraged. In short, the basic declaratory character of the sayings pervades even the hortatory sentences. The ethics of Proverbs are inferred from observations such as are articulated in the sayings.

The prominence of declaratory sayings easily creates the impression that proverbial wisdom is positivistic. By positivism I understand the "assumption that we have an easily accessible standard of 'external reality' against which to measure any of our utterances"[22] and that reality is univocal and unambiguous and yields single, simple, solid, and fixed meanings. This view of proverbs is reflected in Gerhard von Rad's statements that "in their own way and within their own sphere they simply wish to establish something positive, something unquestionably valid," and that "undoubtedly it often required lengthy observation of similar processes until gradually it became possible to recognize certain natural laws. . . . this wisdom poetry never abandoned the strenuous attempt to derive some kind of order from the world and then to give it a fixed form."[23] These statements suggest that proverbial wisdom is positivistic in two respects: that it wishes to establish "something unquestionably valid" and to discern "natural laws" by which other positive facts can be discovered. We will argue that both these suggestions require modification.

PROVERBS AND PARADIGMS

We may begin by noting that proverbs combine concreteness and specificity on the one hand (von Rad's "something positive") with some degree of generalization (which von Rad relates to a search for natural laws). However, it is characteristic of proverbs that the specificity and generality are fused in the single saying. To say that "a well-fed person will disdain honey" is concrete but is not confined to an individual instance. It implies that well-fed people habitually disdain honey, and so the proverb is relevant to recurring situations. However, it also suggests a pattern that can be illustrated without any reference to food or honey. Whoever has plenty of anything is hard to please. Again, the saying that there is no grain where there are no oxen may be apt in a situation remote from agriculture. Results are not achieved where resources are inadequate. The concrete proverb is evidently more striking than the abstract generalization, but its value depends on its range of applicability.

However, the specificity of the proverb has a further implication. It ensures that the proverb falls short of the natural laws to which von Rad refers. The proverb does not necessarily claim that in every case where there are no oxen the barn will be empty. The typical consequence, articulated in the proverb, may still admit of exceptions. This point is all the more apparent in view of the lack of any attempt to establish consistency between the different proverbs. The insights expressed in the different sayings are simply juxtaposed without regard for their mutual implications. In one celebrated case (26:4-5) two sayings that flatly contradict each other are placed side by side. As Robert Scholes remarked à propos of Jolles: "Brought together, 'Look before you leap' and 'He who hesitates is lost' can hardly function as guides to conduct."[24] Proverbs provide insights of general validity, but they do not tell us when they may be appropriately applied. Their generality is limited. So William McKane rightly comments that proverbs have "a special kind of concreteness, in virtue of which their meaning is open to the future and can be divined again and again in relation to a situation which calls forth the proverb as apt comment," and he adds that "a 'proverb' can be generalized and the generalization does some justice to it, but it forecloses the meaning and destroys the hermeneutical openness which derives from its original concreteness." Jolles even goes so far as to say that proverbs resist all generalization and abstraction.[25]

As limited generalizations, then, proverbs might be more appropriately described as paradigms than as laws. The applicability of the proverb, like paradigmatic myths or historical situations, rests on partial similarities but does not require identical correspondence. Bruno Snell has noted that this reliance on partial or limited similarity is fundamentally at variance with all kinds of positivism:

> Neither the primitive magic mentality nor the type of thought which follows scientific lines is able to appreciate the nature of the mythical or, for that matter, the historical paradigm. For whatever the differences between them, neither approach admits any comparisons which are not based on absolute identity. . . . In the sciences, only that which really "is" has any validity. . . . But what we find in myth, in poetry and in history, namely the establishing of precedents for human actions and fortunes, to give them a broader and more universal significance, is rooted in a totally different category of speech.[26]

Since any given proverb may or may not be appropriate in a particular situation, their truth is conditional and relative, not absolute. They cannot be taken as unambiguous statements of "that which really is."

THE USE OF ANALOGY

A further consideration that qualifies the positivism of the proverbial sayings is the frequency with which they resort to metaphor and analogy:[27]

> Like cold water to a weary throat
> is good news from a distant land. (25:25)

> Like a dog returning to his vomit
> is a stupid man who repeats his folly. (26:11)

> Like a bird that strays far from its nest
> is a man who strays from his place. (27:8)

Here again, similarity is not identity. The correspondences in question are no more than partial. The comparisons are not mandatory or necessary. As Max Black has argued: "The metaphor selects, emphasizes, suppresses and organizes features of the principal subject by implying statements about it that normally apply to the sub-sidiary subject."[28] The analogy between the dog and the stupid man is not simply given in experience but is selected and designed to highlight a perspective on the fool that might not be otherwise evident. In Ian Ramsey's terms, such comparisons are not "picture models," "reproducing identically those properties common to model and original which, for the particular purpose in mind, are importantly relevant."[29] Rather, they are "disclosure" or "analogue" models, which do not posit identity but only suggest a structure or "web of relationship." Such analogies "are not made defin-ing or descriptive in any categorical or doctrinal sense, but they are simply suggestive in an explorative effort to find a way in which the reality apprehended can be thought about or made marginally intelligible."[30] Such comparisons have a tentative or explor-atory character. They suggest new ways of looking at an object, which may disclose certain features of it but do not exhaust it or constitute the only way of looking at it. The validity or usefulness of such a model can only be assessed by the degree to which it fits our experience or "chimes in with the phenomena."[31] It does not provide a univocal, positivistic criterion for measuring reality.

The similarity between the fool and the dog is not an obvious one, and can only be perceived if we ignore several features in which the two differ. It is characteristic of proverbs that they bring together and compare things that initially seem very differ-ent. This tendency is especially evident in the so-called numerical sayings:

> Three things there are which are too wonderful for me,
> four which I do not understand:
> the way of a vulture in the sky,
> the way of a serpent on the rock,
> the way of a ship out at sea,
> and the way of a man with a girl. (30:18-19)

The four things in question do not initially seem to have much in common. Von Rad observes: "The aim of this form of proverb is always the same, the collection of things which are similar where the assertion of similarity is the real surprise element."[32] Even when the matters in question are less disparate than Prov 30:18-19, the common ele-ment cannot be perceived without ingenuity. Prov 30:24-28 lists four creatures that are small but exceedingly wise—ants, badgers, locusts, and lizards. Their "wisdom," however, is quite diverse (and, in the case of badgers and lizards, dubious). While the list of four creatures might be conceived as part of a rudimentary attempt to master the world by *Listenwissenschaft*, we should note that the saying does not attempt to list creatures that are related in any obvious way—e.g., things that crawl or that hoard food. The criteria for the "wisdom" of these creatures are too loose to serve any serious purpose of classification. Rather, the saying is a playful exercise in ingenuity that tries to find something in common between lizards and locusts.

Many scholars have suggested that the numerical proverbs (and some others) were originally transmitted as riddles.[33] We can easily imagine the form of such rid-dles: e.g., "what four things are small but exceedingly wise?" If the answer to such a question were obvious, the riddle would lose its interest. It is designed to test the "wisdom" of the respondent, whether that wisdom derives from ingenuity or from learned mastery of a store of proverbs. The less obvious the answer, the better the riddle, and the less obvious the analogy, the more interesting the proverbial saying.

The delight in showing relationships between diverse entities is closely related to the phenomenon of allegory. The numerical saying in Prov 30:18-19 is followed directly by Prov 30:20:

> The way of an adulteress is this:
> she eats, then she wipes her mouth
> and says, "I have done no harm."

The allegorical reference to "eating" might be taken as a mere euphemism. However, it also enhances the saying by suggesting an analogy between her attitudes to sex and to a casual meal. Insofar as that analogy is surprising, it prompts reflection by the reader or hearer. Other allegories, where no euphemism is needed (e.g., the famous allegory of old age in Qoheleth 12), similarly prompt reflection by suggesting unusual analogies for the matter under discussion.

Von Rad has rightly observed that the veiled manner of allegorical speech "arouses reflection precisely through its veiled character."[34] This is also true of the numerical proverb, and even of the simple comparison of the fool to a dog returning to its own vomit. The force of the comparisons involved in any of these cases depends as much on its surprise quality as on the aptness of the comparison itself. In noting the similarity between numerical sayings, allegories, and riddles, von Rad further remarks that riddles are "playing at discovering the truth. One person hides or disguises the truth, the other brings it out of concealment into the light."[35] This remark may be misleading, if it is taken to suggest that "the truth" is definite, distinct, and univocal. In the example cited by von Rad, "What is heavier than lead? and what is its name except Fool?" (Sir 22:14), there is surely no suggestion that Fool is the only possible right answer. Similarly, when the sage announces that three things are too wonderful for him and four he does not understand, we should not conclude that these are the only things that evade his knowledge. While the numerical formula should not be read as an indefinite three or four, and the sage evidently has just four things in mind,[36] the fact remains that the number is in no sense definitive. In short, any of the analogies in the proverbial sayings are arbitrary to a degree and could be replaced by others. Undoubtedly the sages believed that the analogies had a basis in "reality"—that the fool really was like a dog and so forth. However, this does not mean the analogies were fixed and univocal. Any two things could be validly compared by a sage of adequate wit and ingenuity.

The fact that surprising analogies and veiled speech are especially prominent and effective suggests that the "playing" at hiding and discovering truth may be more serious than von Rad realized. The Russian formalists emphasized *defamiliarization* as the essence of good literature.[37] The strange and surprising analogy provides a jolt that can shake off the "lethargy of custom" and permit a new perception and appreciation. The purpose of such surprises is not to suggest that the new analogy is definitive—that we should always think of a fool as a dog or that vultures, serpents, ships, and lovers really form a distinct class. Rather, the goal is a "perceptual shift" that "involves not a replacing of one group of data with another, but rather a basic restructuring of the same material."[38] The purpose is to defamiliarize our routine ways of looking at fools (or lovers) and enable us to see them anew in a fresh perspective. In this sense the surprising quality of the analogy is as important as the aptness of the comparison itself.

Schneidau celebrates such defamiliarization or alienation of meaning as a central aspect of biblical Yahwism. Crossan has stressed its role in the parables of Jesus.[39] Our consideration of the use of metaphor and analogy suggests that defamiliarization also plays a part in the proverbial sayings.

It is, of course, an irony of literature that the more popular and well known a work becomes, the less it can hope to mediate a fresh perspective and the more commonplace its insights appear. Even the greatest poetry becomes banal if it is memorized and incessantly repeated. Proverbs are particularly vulnerable on this count since "the choice phrase, displaying that perfect aptness and originality of the good proverb, so lends itself to continuous repetition that it soon becomes trite."[40] Hence, proverbs are often thought to represent a static, simplified view of reality as familiar and commonplace. However, triteness is not an intrinsic quality of proverbs but only a consequence of excessive repetition. As we have seen, proverbs frequently "defamiliarize" their insights by unusual analogies and veiled speech. Further, the reliance on generalizations and analogies that are only partial gives proverbs an open-ended character and invites a critique of any attempt to use proverbial wisdom as an exhaustive or definitive formulation of reality.

THE LIMITS OF WISDOM

The limited and relative character of all human knowledge is in fact clearly acknowledged in the proverbs themselves. Von Rad, especially, has noted that mention of God frequently occurs in connection with human limitation. Prov 21:30-31 may serve as an example:

> There is no wisdom, no understanding, no counsel against Yahweh.
> The horse is made ready for the day of battle
> but the victory belongs to Yahweh.

Or, in Prov 16:1:

> The plans of the mind belong to man,
> but the answer of the tongue comes from Yahweh.[41]

Von Rad rightly points out that these sayings do not "simply stand as exceptions on the perimeter."[42] They point to limits that can be encountered at any time in life and that are intrinsic to the human condition. The limitations are quite radical. The plans of the mind cannot guarantee the attainment of results, nor even an appropriate "answer of the tongue" that adequately expressed what is intended. No degree of mastery of the rules and maxims of wisdom can confer absolute certainty. Life retains a mysterious and incalculable element, and it is precisely in this incalculable area that Yahweh is encountered.

The sayings that give expression to the limitations of wisdom correspond to a surprising degree to the critique of wisdom in the OT prophets. If Jeremiah can insist that the wise man should not glory in his wisdom (Jer 9:23), the sages know that there is more hope for a fool than for one who thinks himself wise (Prov 26:12).[43] If the god of the prophets "makes the wise men turn back and makes their knowledge foolish" (Isa 44:25), the sages also know that there is no wisdom or counsel against Yahweh (Prov 21:30). The emphasis on the unpredictability of Yahweh accords well with Schneidau's understanding of the Yahwist vision, with which we began. Von Rad's conclusion, that these "limit" proverbs "set the pupil in the midst of the constant oscillation between grasp of meaning and loss of meaning,"[44] claims for proverbial wisdom a function strikingly similar to that claimed by Schneidau for prophetic Yahwism: to show "how precarious is our grasp of any meaning at all."[45]

The limit proverbs we have cited all define humanity over against Yahweh. We might suspect, then, that the affinities between these sayings and prophetic Yahwism is a result of specific Yahwistic influence and does not arise from the intrinsic logic of proverbial wisdom. This viewpoint has been argued especially by Hartmut Gese,[46] who argues that the proverbs that refer to Yahweh are introduced by a redactor and depart radically from the closed chain of act and consequence that dominates Egyptian and older Israelite wisdom. Von Rad does not distinguish the "Yahweh" proverbs as a redactional stage but argues that they show that "the understanding of the world which these teachers had was . . . based quite specifically on faith in Yahweh the God of Israel."[47]

The suggestion that the acknowledgment of human limitation and divine unpredictability is due to the specific influence of Yahwism has been decisively refuted by Preuss. The same ideas occur frequently in Egyptian wisdom.[48] Amen-em-opet 19:16 provides a typical example: "One thing are the words, which men say, another is that which the god does."[49] A Babylonian proverb reflects that "the will of a god is difficult to find out."[50] More fundamentally, the same insight can be expressed in Egyptian, Babylonian, and Israelite traditions in terms of human experience without reference to a god at all: "Man knows not what the morrow is like" (Amen-em-opet 19:13) or "Do not boast about the next day, for you do not know what a day may produce" (Prov 27:1) or "Will the early corn thrive? How can we know? Will the late corn thrive? How can we know?"[51]

THE UNPREDICTABILITY OF EXPERIENCE

These sayings about the uncertainty of the future point to the real roots of the sages' limitation. It is a commonplace that proverbs appeal to experience. They make no claim to supernatural revelation or to any other extrinsic source of authority. They may on occasion appeal to tradition (e.g., Job 8:8), but such a claim still rests on the experience of one's predecessors. Hence, we often find sayings presented as personal observations:

> I passed by the field of a lazy man
> and by the vineyard of a man of little sense.
> See weeds were growing up everywhere. (Prov 24:30-34)

> I was young and have grown old,
> but I have never seen the righteous forsaken. (Ps 37:25)[52]

Von Rad may well be right that we have here a traditional stylistic form rather than biographical information,[53] but the authority of the sayings rests nonetheless on the appeal to experience. Inevitably, then, they can be disputed on the basis of a contradictory experience. So the rebellious Job stands as squarely in the wisdom tradition as his opponents when he challenges them to show him where he erred (6:24) and defends his own conviction that he is righteous despite his sufferings. While the sages attempt to find rules and orders for experience, any rule will admit of exceptions. We have seen already that proverbs stop short of claiming universal validity and thereby differ from natural laws. However, the permanent possibility that an exception may be encountered limits seriously the validity of generalizations and requires a constant openness to new experience. The case of Job does not prove that sufferers are habitually righteous, but it disrupts the general assumption that they must be sinful. Again, Qoh 9:13-16 does not suggest that wise men are always despised, but the sage claims to have found at least one case where wisdom did not prove better than strength. Again,. the human tendency to generalize is thwarted. We find a similar tendency in the parables of Jesus, which always speak of individual instances and never of general rules. We are not asked to believe that no priest or Levite would help a wounded man and that every Samaritan would. It is sufficient that one such case can be envisaged. Then we can no longer presume how either priests or Samaritans will perform. The occurrence of exceptional cases has the effect of defamiliarization, of breaking routine assumptions, and leads to the "perceptual shift" that enables us to grasp individual experiences afresh.

The permanent possibility of new, unpredicted experiences points to the fundamental historicity of human existence. By "historicity" here I mean the fact that we exist in time and that time is a process of change that cannot be frozen by generalizations. Since proverbs are not universally valid laws but admit of exceptions, their applicability depends on the identification of the right time. The realization that all rules and generalizations are relativized by time and that contradictory insights and values all have their time is most forcefully expressed in the famous passage in Qoh 3:1-8 but is not a product of skepticism, since it is also central to the positive wisdom of Sirach that God "made the times and the feasts different" (33:8).[54] The variability of the times and uncertainty of the future imposes an inescapable limit on any wisdom based on experience, irrespective of its contact with Yahwism.

In short, the orientation of proverbial wisdom to historical, time-bound experience has a similar effect to that claimed by Schneidau for the "historicizing style" of the narrative sections of the OT. Both the proverbial sayings and the "historical credos" were undoubtedly designed to construct a positive view of reality, but each contained the seeds of a debunking tendency that repeatedly undermined or modified the generalizations of the tradition.

COMMON CREATUREHOOD

One further aspect of proverbial wisdom that was conducive to a debunking tendency was the conviction of the basic equality of all human beings: "Rich and poor have this in common, Yahweh made them both" (Prov. 22:2; cf. 29:13). This sentiment, with an attendant concern for the poor, is commonplace throughout the Near Eastern wisdom literature.[55] The insight is closely related to the uncertainty of the future—wealth is fleeting and whoever relies on it is riding for a fall (Prov 11:28). Qoheleth perceived that wealth gives no protection against the passing years and that the value of wealth depends on the power to enjoy it (Qoh 6:1-3). The parable of the rich man who hoped for security in the barns he had built makes a similar point (Luke 12:16-20). Not only do rich and poor share a common creaturehood, but they also share a common fate in death. The effect of these observations is a radical relativizing of the value placed on social status. Creaturehood and mortality are the shaky foundations on which all human structures are built.

The relative character of social distinctions is a constant theme in the narrative and prophetic books of the OT. However stratified their society may have become, the Israelites were haunted by the reminder that they had been "slaves in the land of Egypt." This reminder was a vital component in the corrosive Yahwist vision that Schneidau identifies as latent in every Israelite attempt to build institutions and structures.

Although the sages define creaturehood over against Yahweh as creator, their sense of a common humanity cannot be claimed as a peculiar product of Yahwism. Victor Turner's studies of African tribal rituals have shown that a similar conviction, that a common human bond underlies social distinctions, can be found in situations remote from Yahwistic influence. It is significant that Turner discovers his fleeting glimpses of a common human bond in symbols and rituals of "anti-structure" that show the limits of the various structures in which society is organized.[56] Similarly, in the wisdom tradition the common creaturehood of humanity emerges most clearly from the consideration of the limitation and transience of all things human.

CONCLUSION

Our discussion began with the apparent contrast between proverbial wisdom, which is oriented to asserting order and meaningfulness in experience, and the Yahwistic vision typified by prophecy and parables, which tends to question and undermine the established structures. We have argued that although proverbial wisdom is predominantly constructive and cannot be compared directly to either prophecy or parables, it is thoroughly comparable with the historical traditions that were basic to Yahwism. Both the historical credos and the maxims of wisdom could on occasion become rigid and dogmatic. Both, however, contained within themselves the seeds of a debunking tendency. In both cases these seeds can be found in a sense of the historical transience of human existence that exposes the limitations of all human knowledge.

The affinities between proverbial wisdom and the Yahwistic vision are potentially important for biblical theology. First, they show that the familiar dichotomy between wisdom and biblical history cannot be maintained. While the proverbs show no interest in the historical credos of Israel, their understanding of human existence is acutely conscious of the flux of time. Other scholars have, of course, argued for affinities between wisdom and the historical books.[57] Usually, however, the argument has been framed in terms of influence of an alleged wisdom movement on the historical writers. Our argument here does not presume such influence but only shows that similar thought patterns were at work in both historical and sapiential traditions.

Second, and consequent to this, the Yahwist vision was not so sharply discontinuous with its neighboring cultures as often alleged.[58] A comparable view of historicity and its implications can be found in the proverbial wisdom that was the common heritage of the ancient Near East.

CHAPTER 10

NATURAL THEOLOGY AND BIBLICAL TRADITION
The Case of Hellenistic Judaism

Natural theology is traditionally associated with Catholic sensibilities and was given official endorsement by the First Vatican Council, which affirmed that "God, the beginning and end of all things, can be known with certainty by the natural light of human reason from the works of creation."[1] Conversely, the Reformed tradition has typically responded to this subject with a resounding "Nein," articulated most famously by Karl Barth, who identified "real theology" as the revelation in Jesus Christ and the exposition of Scripture and declared that "'natural theology' does not exist as an entity capable of becoming a separate subject within what I consider to be real theology—even for the sake of being rejected."[2] It is remarkable, then, that the only biblical scholar to devote a book to natural theology and biblical faith in recent times should be a Scottish Presbyterian, James Barr, admittedly a Scot whose intellectual lineage should be traced to David Hume rather than to John Knox.[3] Barr's book is in large part a critique of the Barthian rejection of natural theology. His constructive thesis is quite modest: elements of natural theology can be found throughout the Bible, and biblical revelation cannot be cleanly separated from it.[4] He defined natural theology broadly, as the view that "'by nature,' just by being human beings, men and women have a certain degree of knowledge of God and awareness of him, or at least a capacity for such awareness; and this knowledge or awareness exists anterior to the special revelation of God made through Jesus Christ, through the Church, through the Bible."[5] I believe that this definition is defensible and that Barr is essentially right in his thesis,[6] but his argument is open to criticism on the grounds that historically natural theology has meant something more specific and systematic than this. Moreover, while natural theology and biblical revelation have often been combined, in various ways, there remains some tension between them on the level of their basic presuppositions, and serious questions remain about their logical compatibility.

THE ORIGIN OF NATURAL THEOLOGY

The Latin expression *theologia naturalis* entered the vocabulary of Christian theology through Augustine's *City of God*, books 6–8. Augustine borrowed the term from the Roman encyclopedist M. Terentius Varro, who distinguished three *genera theologiae: mythicon, physicon, and civile*.[7] The first kind was that of the poets, the second of the philosophers, and the third of the state. Since Varro used Greek terminology for two of these kinds, it is likely that the distinctions had been introduced by some Hellenistic philosopher, probably Stoic.[8] Augustine appealed to "the custom of speech" for translating *physikon* as *naturale*, and so he presumably was not the first to introduce the term.[9] Varro favored the threefold distinction, because he wished to uphold the civic religion while repudiating mythic theology.[10]

Greek philosophers were also familiar, however, with a simple twofold distinction between the one *physei theos* (god by nature, or in actuality) and the many *thesei theoi* (gods produced by human invention).[11] This was more congenial to Augustine, who acknowledged no significant difference between mythical and political theology. He was far more respectful to natural theology, the domain of the philosophers, which began with Thales and the Ionian naturalists and reached its high points in the philosophies of Plato and the Stoics. Varro's concept of natural theology was essentially Stoic; it was a comprehensive concept of the cosmos animated by a world soul. The Platonists, however, impressed Augustine more, because they acknowledged a transcendent God, "creator not only of this visible world, which is often called heaven and earth, but also of every soul"; Augustine concluded by echoing the words of St. Paul in Rom 1:20: "That which is known of God he manifested to them when his invisible things were seen by them, being understood by those things which have been made; also his eternal power and godhead by whom all visible and temporal things have been created."[12]

The natural theology of the Greeks differed from the elements of natural theology scattered in the Hebrew Bible (for example, in the wisdom literature) by its sustained, systematic character. It was a developed attempt to explain the nature of the cosmos by philosophical reasoning. It did not yield a single unified doctrine, of course. The different philosophical schools were in lively debate with each other, and their doctrines underwent modification as they developed.[13] Natural theology was a process rather than a doctrine. It was the attempt to arrive at the knowledge of God by reflection on the natural order.

Augustine was not the first to appreciate that the Greek philosophers had discovered truths that might be affirmed by worshipers of the God of Israel and by the Christian church. Already in the second century b.c.e. the Jewish philosopher Aristobulus argued that Plato had derived his wisdom from the law of Moses,[14] an ideal still entertained by Augustine. The first extended attempts to integrate the philosophical theology of the Greeks with the religion of Israel, however, were made around the turn of the era in Alexandria and are preserved in the works of Philo and in the deutero-canonical Wisdom of Solomon.

Philo credited Moses with "an account of the creation of the world, implying that the cosmos is in harmony with the Law, and the Law with the cosmos, and that the man who observes the law is constituted thereby a loyal citizen of the cosmos, regulating his doings by the purpose and will of Nature, in accordance with which the entire cosmos itself also is administered."[15] Philo expounds this correspondence in his voluminous writings, which constitute what has been properly recognized as a precursor of Christian theology in its classical forms.[16] The Wisdom of Solomon, in contrast, is a rhetorical rather than a philosophical treatise, and it is much less systematic than the works of Philo. But it is also much more succinct, and for that reason it throws into sharper relief some of the tensions that arise when Greek natural theology is combined with a traditional, confessional belief in the election of Israel. In the following remarks, I will focus primarily on the Wisdom of Solomon, although the problems are essentially the same in the case of Philo.

WISDOM AND GREEK PHILOSOPHY

The author of the Wisdom of Solomon found his common ground with Greek philosophy in the idea of wisdom. In the Book of Proverbs, wisdom had already been spoken of as the first of the works of the Lord and had been given a role in the process of creation. Ben Sira had gone further, identifying it with the law. In the Wisdom of Solomon the idea of wisdom is developed with a philosophical vocabulary that was simply not available to the Hebrew writers. Much of this vocabulary is Stoic, and it serves to associate wisdom with the Logos or *Pneuma*, which the Stoics envisaged as a world soul, "a breath pervading the whole world."[17] Wisdom is similarly identified with the spirit of God that holds all things together (Wis 1:7). The Stoic overtones are especially clear in 7:22—8:1, where wisdom is described as a spirit that penetrates all things because of its pureness, reaches from one end of the earth to the other, and orders all things well.

The Stoic Logos was an immanent deity, identical either with the world itself or with the active force within it. The author of the Wisdom of Solomon, like Augustine later, insisted on a transcendent creator God, who "created the world out of formless matter" (11:17). Wisdom, then, was an intermediary figure, described as "a pure emanation of the glory of the Almighty . . . a reflection of eternal light" (7:25-26), in language that is indebted to Platonic tradition. An older generation of scholars doubted that the Jewish author understood his philosophical sources; they suspected that he had read a little of everything but failed to grasp the coherence of the various philosophical systems.[18] It is now generally recognized, however, that the philosophical background of his thought, as also of Philo's, should not be sought in classical Stoicism or Platonism but in the Middle Platonism that flourished around the turn of the era and was exemplified in Antiochus of Ascalon, who influenced Cicero.[19] The Middle Platonists modernized Platonic teaching by appropriating ideas and formulations from the Peripatetics and Stoics. They affirmed a transcendent deity, and also an intermediate realm between this deity and the visible universe. Conversely, Middle Stoic philosophers in the same period, exemplified by Posidonius, made a place for God in the Stoic system, over against the cosmos.[20] These philosophical trends are often described as eclectic, although the appropriateness of that somewhat pejorative adjective has been questioned by John Dillon.[21]

In any case, the combination of Platonic and Stoic ideas in the Wisdom of Solomon should not be taken as evidence of philosophical superficiality on the part of the author. He was simply reflecting the philosophical trends of his day, and in this respect he was not different from Philo.

THE KNOWLEDGE OF GOD

The philosophical presuppositions of the author of the Wisdom of Solomon evidently allowed for the possibility that human beings could arrive at the knowledge of God without the aid of special revelation. The book gives conflicting signals, however, about the likelihood of success. We read in chapter 9: "The reasonings of mortals are wretched, and our devices precarious; for a perishable body weighs down the soul, and this tent of clay encumbers a mind full of cares. We barely make inferences concerning what is on earth and laboriously discover what is at hand; who then has tracked out what is in the heavens?" (9:14-16). In a famous passage in chapter 13, the author vacillates as to whether human beings are culpable if they fail to arrive at the knowledge of the true God:

> Vain by nature were all who were ignorant of God and were unable to know the Existent One (*ton onta*) from the good things that are seen, or to recognize the Craftsman through attention to his works. . . . If through delight in the beauty of these things they took them to be gods, let them know how much superior is the Master of these things, . . . for from the greatness and beauty of created things is their author correspondingly (*analogōs*) perceived. Yet little blame attaches to these, for they too perhaps err in spite of their search for God and their desire to find him. . . . Yet even they are not to be excused, for if they were so resourceful as to be able to infer the "Universe," how is it they did not sooner discover the master of these things? (Wis 13:1-9)

In the end, the author decides that these people are not free from blame, but he evidently has considerable sympathy for them.

The notion that "the heavens tell forth the glory of God" (Ps 19:1) has honorable precedents in the Hebrew Bible.[22] Since the reality and primacy of the God of Israel are almost universally taken for granted in the Bible, however, the problem of arriving at a knowledge of God is never addressed. When the rival claims of different deities are assessed in Second Isaiah, the appeal is to history as the arena of vindication. It is only when Jewish tradition comes in contact with Greek philosophy that the possibility of a systematic theology based on the study of nature arises. Wisdom of Solomon 13 must be viewed, like Philo's works, in the context of Hellenistic philosophical debates.

The Greek debate about the relation of God, or the gods, to nature and the cosmos had its origin in the rise of naturalistic philosophy in the fifth century.[23] At the extreme of this development, the atomists Leucippus and Democritus found no role for gods in the workings of the universe or in human life. Most philosophers, however, retained a role for a god or gods and held that this role must be inferred from the workings of the universe. Plato, in his *Laws*, took issue with those who found the sources of being in the natural elements and regarded the gods as existing not by nature but by convention and law.[24] He argued that the soul was prior to the body, and that the souls of the planets and other heavenly bodies were gods, "whether as living beings inside bodies arranging the whole universe or in some other way."[25] In *Timaeus* Plato posited a craftsman or demiurge who was responsible for the creation of the universe, and who could be referred to as God. Jewish writers like Philo and later Christian theologians would find Plato's *Timaeus* especially congenial in their attempts to construct a philosophical theology.[26]

The Stoics use much of the same terminology as Plato. But their God is immanent and may even be identified with the cosmos itself, or with its commanding faculty or mind.[27] Nonetheless, the Stoic manner of argumentation is rather similar to what we find in the Wisdom of Solomon. Cleanthes saw the chief cause of belief in God as "the regularity of the motion, the revolution of the heavens, and the individuality, usefulness, beauty, and order of the sun, the moon, and all the stars. The mere sight of these things . . . was proof enough that they are not products of accident," concluding that "it is by some mind that these great motions of nature are controlled."[28] Or again: "We alone of living creatures know the risings and settings; and the courses of the stars, . . . and contemplating the heavenly bodies the mind arrives at a knowledge of the gods."[29] Stoics and Platonists were in agreement that the order of nature required the existence of a divine mind. They disagreed as to whether the divinity was immanent or transcendent.

Consequently, the Jewish belief in a transcendent creator God could be located in the context of Greek philosophical debate. Philo wrote, in his treatise on the Decalogue, that

> a great delusion has taken hold of the larger part of mankind. . . . Some have deified the four elements, earth, water, air and fire, others the sun, moon, planets and fixed stars, others again the heaven by itself, others the whole world. But the highest and the most august, the begetter, the Ruler of the great World-city, . . . the Pilot who ever steers all things in safety, Him they have hidden from sight.[30]

Here, Philo is taking issue with Stoicism, but he could find support for his position in the Platonic tradition, which affirmed the role of the Demiurge and the priority of the soul. We find the same philosophical debate in the work of Augustine several centuries later.

The author of the Wisdom of Solomon regards those philosophers who worship the creation rather than the creator as culpable to some degree. This implies that at least some knowledge of God is attainable in principle by human reason, an implication also found in Rom 1:19-20.[31] In view of the disparagement of human reason in Wis 9:14-17, success would seem to be unlikely without the divine gift of wisdom.

Hence the author's vacillation as to whether those who fail in the quest should be condemned. Philo also argued that the philosophers who seek the true God and fall short deserve respect, while those who engage in mere idolatry deserve nothing but contempt.[32] Yet it is clear that neither Philo nor the author of Wisdom arrived at their knowledge of God simply by philosophical reasoning. Rather, they appealed to natural theology for confirmation of what they affirmed on the basis of tradition or of what they held to be divine revelation. Evidently, their use of philosophy had to be selective, but they could at least claim that their beliefs were compatible with a respected philosophical position.

THE POLEMIC AGAINST IDOLATRY

Thus far, the relationship between Jewish wisdom and Greek philosophy would seem to be quite harmonious and to suggest a quite congenial relationship between the two cultures. But this is not the whole picture. The account of wisdom in philosophical terms is found primarily in the middle section of the Wisdom of Solomon, especially in chapters 7–9. The other sections of the book, however, present a much less harmonious picture of relations between Jews and the Gentile world, so much so that one scholar has recently characterized the attitude evident in the book as a whole as one of "cultural antagonism."[33] Chapters 1–5 dramatize the case of the righteous man who is persecuted unto death by the wicked. It is likely that the account reflects the conflicts between Jews and Greeks in Alexandria in the first century C.E. Most of chapters 10–19 are devoted to reflections on the exodus, with relations between Jews and Gentiles again presented in antagonistic terms. Chapters 13–15 constitute a sustained polemic against idolatry that has recently been described as a "passionate invective against Gentile religion."[34] There is, then, some tension between strands of universalism and of particularism, both of which are undeniably present in the book.

The view in which the Wisdom of Solomon would be characterized as "cultural antagonism," or would be seen as an attack on Gentile religion as such, does not do justice to the rapprochement with Greek philosophy that is at the heart of the book, and such a view specifically misses the philosophical context of the polemic against idolatry. While that polemic was aimed against common pagan practice, the Jewish apologists could hope to find a sympathetic hearing among some Greek philosophers. There had been a growing tendency toward monotheism in Greek philosophy since the fifth century B.C.E.[35] Critiques of idolatry can be found already in the fragments of Heraclitus and Xenophanes. Antisthenes, a pupil of Socrates and teacher of Diogenes, taught that there were many gods by convention but only one by nature. Numerous critiques of idolatry can be found in the writings of Stoics and Cynics around the turn of the era.[36] The critiques of idolatry in the Wisdom of Solomon or in the works of Philo do not represent an unqualified opposition to the Gentile world. Rather, they represent a strategy of making common cause with enlightened Greeks who despised popular superstition, especially the crass forms of idolatry practiced in Egypt.[37]

This strategy had implications that were social and political as well as theological. Jews of the kind represented by the author of the Wisdom of Solomon and by Philo desperately sought acceptance by the cultured Greeks of Alexandria and sought to distance themselves from the Egyptians.[38] In part, this was a matter of social class. Philo's family was especially distinguished and quite probably enjoyed the privilege of Roman citizenship, which was not shared by the mass of Alexandrian Jews.[39] Philo's brother, Gaius Julius Alexander, was an influential financier. His nephew would rise to be prefect of Egypt, thus reaching the pinnacle of power in the Roman administration of the province.[40] There can be little doubt that Philo had had the benefit of an education at a gymnasium,[41] and the author of the Wisdom of Solomon would have had similar training, even if he does not display a comparable grasp of philosophy. Such Jews had natural affinities with upper-class Greeks. Hence, Philo's famous argument that "stranger, in [his] judgment, must be regarded as suppliants of those who receive them, and not only suppliants but settlers and friends who are anxious to obtain equal rights (*isotimia*) with the burgesses and are near to being citizens because they differ little from the original inhabitants."[42] It was in this social class that natural theology had its appeal, since it offered Jew and Greek a common identity as citizens of the cosmos.

Roman policy in Egypt, however, was not supportive of this agenda. The Romans distinguished between citizens and noncitizens more sharply than the Ptolemies had.[43] Noncitizens were excluded from the gymnasium and were subject to the *laographia,* or poll tax. This tax was especially resented by Jews, since it effectively denied their claim to parity with the Greeks and classified them with the despised Egyptians. Conversely, the Greeks jealously guarded their status and resented and opposed the aspirations of the Jews. The first pogrom in history took place in Alexandria in the time of Caligula. The conflict was temporarily resolved under Claudius, who guaranteed the right of the Jews to live according to their own customs but stated emphatically that they lived in a city not their own and warned them not to aspire to more than they already had.[44] A more extensive conflict in 66 c.e. severely damaged the Jewish community. After the great diaspora revolt of 115–17 c.e. the community was virtually wiped out. The elements of cultural antagonism that emerge in the reflections on the exodus in the Wisdom of Solomon must be seen in the context of this developing conflict.

A HOLY PEOPLE?

Ostensibly, the discussion of the exodus in Wisdom of Solomon 10–19 is concerned with the working of wisdom in the cosmos and the universal distinction between the righteous and the wicked. Since the story of the exodus is used as illustration, however, the author seems to identify the Israelites with the righteous and their enemies with the wicked. Consequently, many commentators speak of "undisguised particularism" in this part of the book and find that God is "partial to the Jews and inimical to their enemies."[45] Israel is never mentioned by name. Instead, it is called "a holy people and blameless race" (10:15), but also "your people" (12:19; 16:2, 3, 5, etc.), "your children" (16:10, 21, 26; 18:4), "the holy children" (18:9), "the holy nation" (16:2), "your holy ones" (18:2), and even "the son of God" (18:13). The title last mentioned, which has its biblical basis in Exod 4:22-23, echoes Wis 2:13-20, where the righteous man claims to be son of God, claims that God is his father. But ethnic continuity is also a factor. In Wis 18:6 the Israelites of the exodus are referred to as "our ancestors."

It appears, then, that the story of the exodus has not been reduced to an allegory of the righteous and the wicked but retains its traditional force as ethnic history, reflecting the ethnic antagonisms not only of ancient times but also of Roman Alexandria. David Winston is surely right when he says that "the ancient Egyptians and Canaanites . . . served the author [of Wisdom] as symbols for the hated Alexandrians and Romans of his own day."[46] The Wisdom of Solomon is not exceptional in this regard. Even Philo, the most universalistic of all Jewish writers, entertains a fantasy of nationalistic triumph in his work *De praemiis et poenis*. In both the Wisdom of Solomon and Philo's work, however, the occasional nationalistic notes clash with the philosophy of *philanthrōpia* that both writers explicitly endorse.

The adjective *philanthrōpia* occurs three times in the Wisdom of Solomon. It is used twice to characterize Wisdom (1:6; 7:23). In 12:19, the mercy of God is cited as evidence that the righteous ought to be "philanthropic." God's mercy is grounded in creation: "You love all things that exist and detest none of the things that you have made, for you would not have made anything if you had hated it . . . You spare all things, for they are yours, O Lord, you who love the living, for your imperishable spirit is in all things" (11:24–12:1). By this logic, God should love the Egyptians as well as the Israelites.

The notion of *philanthrōpia* was a Stoic concept, grounded in the affinity between the divine and the human established by the Logos. "The world is as it were the common dwelling place of gods and men, or the city that belongs to both; for they alone have the use of reason and live by justice and by law."[47] Among human beings there should be no division: "The much admired republic of Zeno . . . is aimed at this one main point, that our household arrangements should not be based on cities or parishes, each one marked out by its own legal system, but we should regard all men as our fellow citizens and local residents, and there should be one way of life and order, like that of a herd grazing together and nurtured by a common law."[48] Seneca recognized that "there are two communities—the one, which is great and truly common, embracing gods and men, in which we look neither to this corner nor to that, but measure the boundaries of our state by the sun; the other, the one to which we have been assigned by the accident of our birth."[49] For Philo, "all we men are kinsmen and brothers, being related by the possession of an ancient kinship, since we receive the lot of the rational nature from one mother."[50] Even the Stoics did not think that universalism eliminated all need for discrimination. Zeno, for example, declared "the good alone to be true citizens or friends or kindred or free men."[51] For the Stoics and the Cynics, however, there could be no assumption that these distinctions coincided with ethnic lines (nor, indeed, with membership of a particular organization such as the Christian church).

For Jews in the Hellenistic world, in contrast, such an assumption was part of their cultural heritage, and it was not easily discarded. Jews were often accused of an antisocial and misanthropic way of life, even by people who were not ill disposed to them.[52] Hecataeus comments on their "unsocial and intolerant mode of life" (*apanthrōpon tina kai misoxenon bion*), although his account was generally positive.[53] Diodorus Siculus attributed the intervention of Antiochus Epiphanes in Jerusalem to advice that he should wipe out the Jews, "since they alone of all nations avoided dealings with any other people and looked upon all men as their enemies."[54] These charges were amplified in anti-Jewish polemics of Alexandrian Greeks in the Roman period.[55] In large part, these charges arose from the impression of exclusiveness created by dietary laws, refusal to intermarry, and refusal to worship the same gods as everyone else.

Apologists for Judaism such as Philo labored to explain, both to the Jews themselves and to any Gentile who might listen, that these Jewish practices were really in the best interests of humanity and served the purpose of *philanthrōpia*.[56] Philo devoted a lengthy exposition to the *philanthrōpia* of Moses and his laws in *De Virtutibus* 51–174. Yet even the argument for the *philanthrōpia* of Judaism often entails a claim of Jewish superiority.[57] "The Jewish nation," writes Philo, "is to the whole inhabited world what the priest is to the State,"[58] and in an ideal world, "each nation would abandon its peculiar ways, and throwing overboard [its] ancestral customs, turn to honouring our laws alone."[59] Ethnic affiliation alone did not qualify anyone as righteous, and conversion was certainly possible. "In reality," wrote Philo, "the proselyte is one who circumcises not his uncircumcision but his desires and sensual pleasure and the other passions of the soul. For in Egypt, the Hebrew nation was not circumcised."[60] Philo might have agreed with Paul that "he is not a real Jew who is one outwardly nor is true circumcision something external and physical. He is a Jew who is one inwardly, and real circumcision is a matter of the heart, spiritual and not literal" (Rom 2:28-29). Yet Philo, unlike Paul, was unwilling to dispense with literal circumcision, or with the special importance of "Israel according to the flesh."

The same is most probably true of the author of the Wisdom of Solomon. His intentions were indeed universalist, and his God hated none of the things that he had made. The high priest is able to intercede for humanity, "for on his long robe the whole world was depicted" (Wis 18:24).[61] For a Jew in first-century Alexandria, however, this was a difficult ideal to maintain. Custom and tradition led him to associate righteousness with the observance of the Jewish law, however modified. Conversely, the enemies of the Jews were "an accursed race from the beginning," and their wickedness was inbred (12:10-11). The pagan world offered few if any exemplars of virtue. When the Jewish community came increasingly under attack, the inclination to draw the lines between the holy people and the accursed foreigners was irresistible. In so doing, the Jews were only reciprocating the hostility they encountered from their Gentile neighbors, who, in the words of the Wisdom of Solomon, "practiced a more bitter hatred of strangers" (Wis 19:13). The Greeks of Alexandria were not noted for *philanthrōpia* or for philosophical idealism.

CONFLICTING THEOLOGICAL AUTHORITIES

One conclusion that we might draw from the experience of Hellenistic Judaism is that there is an inevitable, though not necessarily complete, correspondence between theology and social location. Natural theology appealed primarily to the upwardly mobile Jews of Alexandria, who wanted to embrace Greek culture without abandoning their own religion. In fairness, it should be noted that their embrace was highly selective. The philosophical theology of Stoics and Platonists was highly critical of popular Hellenistic culture, and the Jewish theologians were also critical in their appropriation of philosophy. But the Alexandrian Greeks were not predominantly philosophers. Their leaders in the early Roman period were demagogues who had no scruples about enflaming ethnic animosities for their political ends. When the Jewish community found itself under attack, the age-old story of the exodus spoke more eloquently to their situation than did Platonic philosophy, and the promise of deliverance by an unabashedly partial deity offered greater hope and sustenance than the notion of a universal spirit did. Unfortunately, that hope was not fulfilled. Neither the universalist theology of wisdom nor the antagonistic revelation of the exodus could sustain the community when it came into conflict with the power of Rome.

It would be too simple, however, to attribute the tension between universalism and particularism that we find exhibited in the Wisdom of Solomon entirely to social circumstances. Neither Stoicism nor Middle Platonism had any place for a concept of divine election, or for a special and exclusive divine revelation. These ideas were deeply ingrained in Jewish scripture and tradition, and neither the author of Wisdom nor Philo was prepared to dispense with them. Philo could only maintain his contention of the harmony between the law and the cosmos by allegorical exegesis, and however acceptable that kind of exegesis was in antiquity, it seems transparently artificial now. It is certainly possible to draw illustrations of philosophical points from the biblical record and, equally, to use philosophical arguments in support of biblical ideas (as Paul does in Romans), but ultimately either revelation or reason must hold the deciding vote. The two do not mesh as easily as Philo would have us believe. In the end, either the biblical revelation becomes merely a source of illustrations of universal claims, or natural theology is reduced to a supporting role, overruled at crucial points by particularist preference.

Religions usually manage to live with a certain number of tensions and contradictions. The Jews of Egypt in the Hellenistic period were unfortunate, insofar as they were overtaken by social conflicts that rendered moot their universalist aspirations and forced them to concern themselves with ethnic survival. But the tension between universalism and particularism uncovered in the Wisdom of Solomon was no minor theological problem. It was a crack in the foundations of Western theology, and it continues to threaten the stability of the edifice down to modern times.[62] That crack could be papered over with allegory in much of Philo's writing, but its eventual exposure by the pressures of history was probably inevitable. Natural theology may have much in common with biblical revelation, and the two can coalesce on occasion as Barr and others have argued, but ultimately they rest on quite different presuppositions, and they can never be fully reconciled.

PART FOUR

APOCALYPTIC LITERATURE

TEMPORALITY AND POLITICS IN JEWISH APOCALYPTIC LITERATURE

Apocalyptic texts are, broadly speaking, of two kinds. On the one hand, there are the historically oriented apocalypses, such as the book of Daniel, which synthesize the sweep of history and describe a judgment of cosmic proportions. On the other hand, there are the heavenly journeys, such as we find in *2 Enoch* or *3 Baruch*, which pay little if any attention to cosmic eschatology and focus rather on the fate of the soul after death. There are, to be sure, mixed types, including, notably, the book of Revelation, in which the seer is taken up to heaven (4:1-2) and which does not dwell on the periods of history but is nonetheless primarily concerned with the judgment of this world.[1] I shall be concerned with the apocalypses of the historical/cosmic type, primarily with Jewish texts but also with the book of Revelation, which has deep and obvious Jewish roots. The view of history found in these texts has much in common with what is called millenarianism in modern anthropological studies. While this view of history is characteristic of one kind of apocalypse, it is not peculiar to the genre. My concern here is with the view of history rather than with the genre strictly defined.

The notion of a millennium as a milestone of eschatological importance, with the related concepts of millenarianism and the like, entered the Western lexicon from the book of Revelation. Revelation describes the end of history in several stages: first Christ descends from heaven and destroys "the beast and the kings of the earth with their armies" (chapter 19). Then the Devil is imprisoned, and "those who had been beheaded for their testimony to Jesus" come to life and reign with Christ for a thousand years (chapter 20). This is the millennium proper. We should note that the millennium in the book of Revelation follows the Second Coming; the end of history as we know it is at the beginning rather than the end of this period. At the end of the thousand years, there is a second climax of history. Satan is released, and there is a final battle and a second, general, resurrection. After this, the visionary sees "a new heaven and a new earth" and "the new Jerusalem coming down from heaven" (chapter 21). The new Jerusalem will enjoy the immediate presence of God, who is both its temple and its light. People will bring into it the glory and honor of the nations, but nothing impure will enter it. It will be watered by a river flanked on either side by the tree of life.

The book of Revelation may be the only apocalypse in the New Testament, but it was heir to a literary tradition of nearly three hundred years in Judaism, stretching back to the time before the Maccabean revolt. In the memorable phrase of Harold Bloom, it is a belated book (part of a belated testament) that draws together different strands of tradition and attempts to synthesize them.[2] (The adjective should not be taken as derogatory, regardless of Bloom's intention; it merely indicates the place of the book in an unfolding tradition. The same belated character is evident in the roughly contemporary Jewish apocalypses of *4 Ezra* and *2 Baruch*.) Not all of these inherited traditions sit easily together. Specifically, there is some tension between the emphasis on resurrection with its promise of other-worldly existence (for the first heaven and the first earth had passed away) and the vision of a new Jerusalem, come down from heaven but established on earth. This tension can be traced back to the earliest apocalypses, which promise an earthly kingdom, or the renewal of the earth on the one hand, and life with the angels for the elect on the other. These traditions frame one debate about the political relevance of apocalyptic literature: Is it world affirming or world denying? Does it aspire to restoration of a just order on earth, or does it condemn the earth to destruction and look for justice in heaven? This debate about the political implications of apocalyptic literature intersects with another one about its social location.

The great bulk of recent scholarship on apocalyptic or millenarian literature subscribes to some variant of deprivation theory; it holds that apocalyptic visions compensate for the deprivation of poverty or oppression. So, for example, Max Weber held that deprived groups were especially attracted to the "promise from the future which implies the assignment of some function, mission, or vocation to them. What they cannot claim to be, they replace by the worth of that which they will one day become."[3] Karl Mannheim distinguished between ideology and utopia. The proponents of ideology are bound by interest to existing societal structures. The utopian mentality, in contrast, is characteristic of "certain oppressed groups," which are "so strongly interested in the destruction and transformation of a given condition of society that they unwittingly see only those elements in the situation that tend to negate it."[4] More recently, scholars have invoked the more elusive category of "relative deprivation" of those whose value system is endangered.[5] Kenelm Burridge begins his study, *New Heaven, New Earth,* with a quotation that speaks of "communities that feel themselves oppressed."[6] Deprivation theories have figured prominently in studies of biblical apocalyptic (and proto-apocalyptic) literature, notably in the work of Paul Hanson.[7]

These deprivation theories have come under fire from various quarters in recent years. Stephen Cook has mounted an extensive critique of deprivation theories as applied to Jewish apocalypticism and has argued that Zechariah 1–8 "evidences a millennial and messianic worldview among priests in power in the early days of the restoration" and infers that "an apocalyptic worldview need not be a fringe phenomenon."[8] More recently, Albert Baumgarten has argued that we must recognize two types of millennial movements: that of the deprived on the one hand, and on the other, "the triumphant version which emerges as a result of events which produce the conviction that we humans and God are now marching together towards the most glorious of all possible new worlds."[9] As examples of the latter type, Baumgarten also appeals to Haggai and Zechariah, but also, more controversially, to the Maccabees. The second letter prefixed to 2 Maccabees expresses the hope that "God . . . will soon have mercy upon us and will gather us from everywhere under heaven into his place, for he has rescued us from great evils and has purified the place" (2 Macc 2:18). In Baumgarten's view, this is "one of the classic formulations of expectations for the events of the final redemption."[10] Neither of these arguments is entirely persuasive. Haggai and Zechariah are hardly prime exemplars of apocalyptic literature. Moreover, while these prophets occupied central roles in Judean society after the exile, the whole society was peripheral in the context of the Persian empire. The apocalyptic character of the Maccabean movement is even more questionable. Usually the word "millenarian" is taken to have more strongly utopian implications than are in evidence in the books of Maccabees, despite their aspiration to national restoration. The issue raised by Cook and Baumgarten is important, however, as it poses the question as to whether apocalyptic visions are always necessarily a medium of the powerless. There is in fact evidence that millennialism can also serve the purposes of the powerful, although this does not seem to be the case in ancient Judaism or early Christianity. In what follows, I would like to distinguish three different modalities of millennial expectation: the triumphalism of imperial power regarded as the fulfillment of history; the deferred eschatology of those who look for an eventual utopia but are submissive to the current powers for the present; and the revolutionary perspective of radical, imminent expectation. I regard the last of these as the typical originating impulse of millennial expectation in the ancient Jewish and early Christian apocalypses, but it has often been transmuted into the other modalities in the course of history.

THE MILLENARIANISM OF THE POWERFUL

The political uses of apocalyptic literature are grounded in its view of history. The typical apocalyptic view of history may be illustrated by two famous passages in the book of Daniel, which speak of a sequence of four world empires, followed by a definitive, lasting, kingdom of God. In Daniel 2, Daniel narrates and interprets Nebuchadnezzar's dream of a vision of a huge statue. The parts of the statue are represented by metals of declining quality, reminiscent of the declining ages of human history in Hesiod's *Works and Days*.[11] The head is of gold, the chest and arms of silver, the middle and thighs of bronze, and the feet of iron mixed with clay. Daniel interprets the dream so that Nebuchadnezzar is the head of gold, but after him come kingdoms of declining quality. In the end, however, "a stone not cut by hands" demolishes the statue and becomes a great mountain. This, we are told, represents a kingdom set up by God that shall never be destroyed or left to another people. A similar sequence of kingdoms, depicted in very different imagery, appears in Daniel's own vision in chapter 7. Here the kingdoms are represented by hybrid beasts that rise from a turbulent sea, and the fourth is the fiercest of all (in contrast to chapter 2, where the fourth kingdom is weakest). In this case the kingdoms are subjected to divine judgment and the fourth beast is thrown into the fire, while an everlasting kingdom, encompassing the dominion of all the kingdoms under heaven, is given to the people of the holy ones of the Most High (Dan 7:27). In Daniel, the four earthly kingdoms are implicitly identified as Babylon, Media, Persia, and Greece.[12] In later Jewish tradition, beginning with the apocalypse of 4 Ezra at the end of the first century C.E., the sequence is adapted so that the fourth kingdom is Rome.[13] Rome was also taken as the fourth kingdom in traditional Jewish and Christian interpretation.

In the book of Daniel, the four-kingdom schema is revolutionary. All the kingdoms of this world are ultimately overthrown and replaced by the kingdom of God. But this view of history as a succession of kingdoms was not a Jewish invention, nor did it necessarily have revolutionary overtones. The Greek historian Herodotus, in the fifth century B.C.E., spoke of the succession of Assyria, Media, and Persia.[14] This list reflects a Near Eastern rather than a Greek perspective and probably had its origin in propaganda about the superiority of the Persian empire, which was thought to be the culmination of the series. With the coming of Alexander, or more likely with the succession to Seleucid rule in Syria and Asia Minor,[15] the sequence was expanded to include Greece. A further expansion appears several times in sources from the Roman era. A clear formulation is attributed to an otherwise unknown historian named Aemilius Sura:

> The Assyrians were the first of all races to hold power, then the Medes, after them the Persians, and then the Macedonians. Then, when the two kings, Philip and Antiochus, of Macedonian origin, had been completely conquered, soon after the overthrow of Carthage, the supreme command passed to the Roman people.[16]

The references are to the Second Punic War (218–201 B.C.E.) and the defeat of the Seleucid Antiochus III at the battle of Magnesia in 190 B.C.E. and of Philip V of Macedon at Cynoscephalae in 197 B.C.E. The dating, however, is in dispute, and such an early occurrence in Roman literature would be anomalous.[17] The schema is found in several later authors, both Greeks who were friendly to Rome, such as Dionysius of Halicarnassus (10 B.C.E.),[18] and Romans, such as Tacitus.[19] Typically, these authors show how the Roman empire outstripped all that had gone before it and entertain no foreboding of its eventual demise.

The idea that Rome was the fifth empire in the sequence did not necessarily mean that it was an eschatological kingdom or that its reign would last forever.[20] But such pretensions were not alien to Roman sensibility. In the opening book of Virgil's Aeneid, Jupiter reveals to the mother of Aeneas the future course of history, culminating in the establishment of Rome by Romulus: "For these [the Romans] I set neither bounds nor periods. Dominion without end [*imperium sine fine*] I gave to them" (*Aeneid* 1.278–79). This revelation is supposedly given while Aeneas still has many trials before him, but in fact it is written by Virgil, from the perspective of fulfillment in the Augustan age. In the words of Hubert Cancik, "This promise indeed reflects the end of history. . . . The epoch that was to come (*venturum saeculum*), is now arrived. This is how the fulfilled eschatology of a victor sounds. The realized apocalypticism serves, like myth, as a justification of empire."[21]

Nor were the Romans the first people in the ancient world to dream of an everlasting kingdom. The Babylonian prophecies published in the second half of the twentieth century also speak of the rise and fall of kingdoms. One of these, the Uruk Prophecy from the Neo-Babylonian period, says (apparently with reference to Nebuchadnezzar II): "After him, his son will arise as king in Uruk and rule the entire world. He will exercise authority and kingship in Uruk and his dynasty will last forever. The kings of Uruk will exercise authority like the gods."[22] Political eschatology, the hope that a particular human kingdom would last forever, has deep roots in the political propaganda of the ancient world.

Even the Romans, however, realized that the succession of world kingdoms cast some doubt on the permanence of any empire, even that of Rome. One rather poignant instance of such reflection is attributed to the Roman general Scipio, in his account of the destruction of Carthage, in 146 B.C.E. The city burned for seventeen days, then it was ploughed and sown with salt and cursed, so that it would never be rebuilt. Yet we are told that Scipio wept as he looked at the ruined city:

> After being wrapped in tears for long, and realizing that all cities, nations and authorities must, like men, meet their doom, that this happened to Ilium, once a prosperous city, the empires of Assyria, Media and Persia, the greatest of their time, and to Macedonia itself, the brilliance of which was so recent, either deliberately or the verses escaping him, he said:
>
> > A day will come when sacred Troy shall perish
> > And Priam and his people shall be slain (*Il.* 6.448–49).
>
> And when Polybius, speaking with freedom to him, for he was his teacher, asked him what he meant by these words, they say that without any attempt of concealment he named his own country, for which he feared when he reflected on the fate of all things human. Polybius actually heard him and recalled it in his history.[23]

Scipio, however, was exceptional in recognizing that his own victorious Rome was as vulnerable to the passage of time as were its predecessors.

Despite the arguments of Steven Cook and Albert Baumgarten regarding the millennialism of the powerful, there are no good Jewish analogues to Virgil's celebration of *Roma aeterna*. The simple fact is that Jews never came close to enjoying worldwide dominion on the Roman scale. Hence, there are no triumphalist Jewish apocalypses. Neither the Hasmoneans nor the Herodians made use of the genre. The

Jewish apocalyptic writings that have come down to us from antiquity are consistently utopian in character (in Mannheim's sense), typically written under foreign dominion, or in some cases produced in circles that were marginal within Jewish society. The hope for an eschatological judgment and utopian kingdom, however, could admit of some variation in attitude to Gentile rule in the present. We can see this variation in the subtle differences between the second and seventh chapters of the book of Daniel.

ESCHATOLOGY DEFERRED

In Daniel 7, the condemnation of foreign rule is unequivocal. The Gentile kingdoms are beasts risen from the chaotic sea, all are subjected to judgment, and the climactic fourth beast is condemned to the fire. The situation in chapter 2 is quite different. Here Daniel is acting in the service of the Babylonian king, whom he addresses with respect and even flattery:

> You, O king, the king of kings, to whom the God of heaven has given the kingdom, the power, the might, and the glory, into whose hand he has given human beings, wherever they live, the wild animals of the field, and the birds of the air, and whom he has established as ruler over them all—you are the head of gold. (Dan 2:38)

This is hardly revolutionary rhetoric. If subsequent kingdoms are inferior to that of Nebuchadnezzar, that too could be taken as flattering to the king. In fact, the king is troubled not at all by the prospect that all these kingdoms will eventually be destroyed. From his perspective, this is eschatology deferred.[24] While hope deferred makes the heart sick, judgment deferred provides reassurance in the present.

The rub, of course, is that Daniel 2 was not actually written in the Babylonian era, but some centuries later, under the fourth kingdom (whether Ptolemaic or Seleucid), and it does not report the actual dream of a Babylonian king, but a Jewish fabrication. Consequently, Daniel Smith-Christopher argues that this should be regarded as a "dream of the disenfranchised,"[25] which envisions an alternative reality in which God reverses present conditions. This is undoubtedly true, but the manner in which the dream is presented lacks the urgency of apocalyptic visions such as Daniel 7. Daniel continues in the service of the Gentile king for the present. The hope for an eschatological judgment and kingdom is compatible with acceptance of Gentile rule for a time, and even encourages a quietistic attitude, since the temporary rule of the foreign kingdoms is accepted as God's will.

The different political implications that could be drawn from the four-kingdom schema can be seen from the reinterpretation of Daniel in two works from the end of the first century c.e. In the apocalypse of *4 Ezra*, the visionary sees an eagle coming up from the sea and is told that it represents "the fourth kingdom that appeared in a vision to your brother Daniel. But it was not explained to him as I now explain it to you" (*4 Ezra* 12:11-12). The difference is that the fourth kingdom is now identified as Rome, represented by the eagle. In the vision, the eagle is confronted by a lion, representing the Davidic messiah, who

> will denounce them for their ungodliness and for their wickedness, and will display before them their contemptuous dealings. For first he will bring them alive before his judgment seat, and when he has reproved them, then he will destroy them. (*4 Ezra* 12:32-33)

4 Ezra is alluding to Daniel 7 rather than to chapter 2, and like Daniel's vision conveys a sense of urgency and imminent judgment. In contrast, Josephus, the Jewish historian living in Rome, devotes considerable space to paraphrasing Daniel, but skips over chapter 7 entirely. He does, however, comment at some length on Nebuchadnezzar's dream (*Ant.* 10:195–210). He interprets the first kingdom as Babylon, the second as a rule of "two kings" (apparently taking Media and Persia as one kingdom), the third kingdom as "from the west" (clearly the Greek), and so the fourth kingdom must be Rome, as in *4 Ezra* and in later rabbinic sources, although Josephus refrains from making the identification explicit. (He does state later that Daniel predicted the coming of Rome and the destruction of the temple [*Ant.* 10:276].) He describes this as an iron kingdom (ignoring the mixture of clay) and notes that iron is harder than gold, silver, or bronze. He then comments that "Daniel also revealed to the king the meaning of the stone, but I have not thought it proper to relate this, since I am expected to write of what is past and done and not of what is to be" (*Ant.* 10:210). He adds that anyone can learn about it by reading the book of Daniel. Most scholars have attributed Josephus's reticence about the coming kingdom to his concern that he not offend his Roman hosts. The paraphrase of Daniel 2 has no revolutionary implications. It affirms the rise and fall of kingdoms and leaves the mysterious kingdom of God in the indefinite future. Josephus, in Rome, identified with the tales about Daniel the courtier rather than with Daniel the apocalyptic visionary.[26] In the words of Steve Mason, his "firm belief in the rise and fall of empires results, as it did for Daniel, in a pacifistic political outlook."[27] The kingdom will come when God ordains it; in the meantime Jews must be subject to their foreign masters.

Later rabbinic tradition looked on Daniel's loyalty to the Babylonian king with some misgivings. In Daniel 4, when Daniel interprets Nebuchadnezzar's second dream, he tells the king, "May the dream be for your enemy and its interpretation for your foe" (Dan 4:16). One midrash denies that a Jewish hero could have such concern for a Babylonian king and insisted that this remark was addressed to God: "Rather, Daniel looked upward and said, 'My Lord, my Master, may the dream and its interpretation be fulfilled on Nebuchadnezzar, your enemy and your foe.'"[28] The Talmudic tractate *Baba Batra* accepted the plain sense of the text but insisted that Daniel was punished for giving advice to Nebuchadnezzar.[29] In these cases, at least, the rabbis failed to appreciate the logic both of Daniel and of Josephus that loyal service to a foreign power is compatible with the hope for its eventual overthrow.

The interpretation of Nebuchadnezzar's dream in Daniel 2 is somewhat atypical of Jewish apocalyptic literature, because of its setting. It is reported in the context of a court tale and only associated secondarily with the apocalyptic visions of the Maccabean era. These visions are usually experienced by Jewish heroes and interpreted for them by angels. Yet the structure of Nebuchadnezzar's dream has much in common with apocalyptic views of history. In fact, apocalyptic hopes for a judgment and a utopian kingdom have often been deferred. Most Christians who affirm the Second Coming do not expect it any time soon. The function of texts varies with the situation in which they are read, and we should not assume that apocalyptic motifs and themes always have the same political implications. The revolutionary implications of the kingdom of God have often been muted in both Jewish and Christian tradition.

RADICAL ESCHATOLOGY

It remains true, however, that most of the extant Jewish apocalyptic literature is rather fiercely critical of the political powers of the day and adopts a critical and revolutionary stand point. Daniel 7, *4 Ezra* 12, and the book of Revelation are all cases in point. It has sometimes been suggested that the four-kingdom schema served such a revolutionary purpose also for other Near Eastern peoples besides the Jews who had been conquered by Greece or Rome. In the words of Joseph Swain:

> Were the history of this troubled time from 250 to 150 better known, we would undoubtedly learn the names of many little Judases—many of them long before the great Judas—who arose in different parts of the vast Seleucid empire.[30]

The Persian *Bahman Yasht* describes the rulers of the fourth kingdom as "divs [evil spirits] with disheveled hair," and this has reasonably been taken as an allusion to the Macedonians, who are usually represented with disheveled hair in Persian iconography.[31] But the *Bahman Yasht* admittedly contains material from a much later time, and so its witness to the Hellenistic period is problematic.[32] There is no dispute, however, that the four-kingdom schema could lend itself to revolutionary propaganda. The political implications of such a view of history depend on where the authors, or readers, locate themselves on the time scale. For Romans of the early empire, Rome represented the culmination of the ages, the dominion that would not pass away. For most Jews, and probably most of Rome's eastern subjects, it was the oppressive fourth kingdom, whose destruction was eagerly awaited. In Karl Mannheim's terms, the same view of history could be adapted to support either an ideological or a utopian vision.

In the remainder of this essay I would like to probe the revolutionary character of the apocalyptic literature a little further by asking how it imagined the downfall of the kingdoms of the world and the new order that would take their place. This literature is generally characterized as quietistic and other-worldly. Christopher Rowland, however, has called attention to "the importance of future hope for changing the world manifest in some movements for radical change in Christian history" and suggested that these movements are not an aberration but "an authentic outworking of central themes in the biblical tradition" and specifically in the apocalypses.[33] We shall reflect a little on the ways in which Jewish apocalypses, which were a significant factor in the context in which Christianity emerged, aspired to change the world and imagined the transformation.

THE QUIETISM OF THE APOCALYPSES

The great majority of Jewish apocalypses are quietistic in the sense that they expect that the world will be changed by divine intervention rather than by human action. The statue in Nebuchadnezzar's dream is shattered by a stone that is cut "not by human hands." The beasts from the sea are destroyed by divine judgment, not by human insurrection, and in Daniel 10–12 the decisive battle is fought in heaven. In the book of Revelation, the victory is achieved by the blood of the lamb and the testimony of the martyrs. The readers are urged to accept their destiny: "If one is to be taken into captivity, into captivity one goes; if one is to be slain with the sword, one is to be slain with the sword," or if the variant reading be accepted, "if one kills with the sword, with the sword one must be killed."[34] There are exceptions to this quietism in the corpus of Jewish apocalypses. The collection of writings that make up *1 Enoch* include an allegorical pseudo-prophecy of Israelite and Jewish history, known as the *Animal Apocalypse*. The prophecy reaches its climax in the Maccabean era. Judas Maccabee is depicted as a ram with a great horn. He is beset by shepherds and birds of prey but is helped by an angelic "man." This apocalypse is evidently supportive of the Maccabean revolt,[35] but even here the victory is only obtained when "the Lord of the sheep," God, comes and strikes the earth in his anger.

Another Enochic apocalypse from the same era, the *Apocalypse of Weeks*, predicts a judgment, executed by righteous human beings with the sword (*1 Enoch* 91:12). In these cases, the righteous human beings act in synergism with God or the angelic hosts. More typically, however, the role of the righteous is patient waiting and endurance. The wise teachers in Daniel 11 give understanding to the multitude, but some of them fall (are killed) "so that they may be refined, purified, and cleansed, until the time of the end" (Dan 11:35), while the Maccabees, if they are acknowledged at all, are dismissed as only "a little help." The *Testament (Assumption) of Moses* from the same period tells of a man named Taxo who, in a time of persecution, tells his seven sons to fast for three days and on the fourth to go with him to a cave and die rather than transgress the commandments, "for if we do this and die, our blood shall be avenged before the Lord" (*Testament of Moses* 9:7). Taxo, arguably, was trying to "force the end" or hasten the judgment, but his way of doing it is not by fighting but by purifying himself and submitting to death, relying on the biblical promise that God will avenge the blood of his servants.[36] The glorification of the martyrs in the book of Revelation rests on the same logic, even if Revelation does not advocate that one seek martyrdom quite as actively as Taxo did.[37]

THE NEW ORDER

It is of the essence of apocalyptic hope that the new order is ultimately brought about by divine intervention. This does not require that the new order itself necessarily have an other-worldly character. The *Book of the Watchers,* which occupies the introductory place in *1 Enoch,* envisions a restoration of the earth in blessed fecundity, but this is referring to the restoration after the Fallen Angels and the Flood in primeval times, and the real future is at most foreshadowed typologically. Daniel hopes for "kingship and dominion and the greatness of the kingdoms under the whole heaven" (7:27), although he does not elaborate the nature of the new kingdom. The *Apocalypse of Weeks* is more concrete, although extremely terse: the righteous "will acquire houses because of their righteousness" (*1 Enoch* 91:13). *4 Ezra* allows for a messianic age on earth, and the book of Revelation concludes with a vision of the New Jerusalem coming down from heaven. The vision of the New Jerusalem is a more elaborate vision of renewal on earth than anything we find in the Jewish apocalyptic writings except perhaps in the fifth *Sibylline Oracle,* which envisions a Jerusalem whose walls extend as far as Joppa (*Sib. Or.* 5.252). There was, of course, a long-standing tradition of Jewish eschatology that had as its focus the restoration of the land of Israel, and specifically of Jerusalem. Motifs from this tradition are often incorporated in the apocalypses, especially in belated apocalypses such as *4 Ezra* and Revelation. I would argue, however, that a restored earthly order is never the primary focus of these apocalypses, and that other concerns always take precedence.[38]

The images of earthly renewal that we have briefly acknowledged must be seen in the fuller context of the works in which they appear. The restoration of the earth appears relatively early in the *Book of the Watchers* (chapter 10). The greater part of the book is devoted to Enoch's ascent to heaven and then to his guided tour of remote places, where he sees such things as the chambers of the dead and the places that have been prepared for the final judgment. Daniel concludes with a prediction of resurrection and a promise that the wise will shine like the stars. The hope for a kingdom on earth is complemented by hope for exaltation of individuals to heaven. In the *Apocalypse of Weeks,* the righteous wield the sword and acquire houses in the eighth week, but in the ninth the world is written down for destruction and in the tenth the first heaven will pass away and a new heaven will appear. In *4 Ezra,* the messiah reigns for four hundred years, but then he dies and then there are seven days of primeval silence followed by a resurrection. In Revelation, the New Jerusalem appears after the thousand-year reign and after the new heaven and new earth have appeared. It is still imagined in this-worldly terms: "the nations will walk by its light and the kings of the earth will bring their glory into it" (Rev 21:24). But it is part of a new creation, after the present course of history has come to an end.

All of these writings are passionately concerned with the earthly political order, but their concern does not find its primary expression in the construction of a new world order. More typical is a disjunction between the corruption and oppression of this world and the purity and incorruption of the heavenly world on the one hand or the future age on the other. In the words of *4 Ezra,* "the Most High made not one world, but two" (*4 Ezra* 7:50). The *Epistle of Enoch* (the last major component of *1 Enoch*) rages against earthly injustice by proclaiming woes against those who build their houses with sin and acquire gold and silver (*1 Enoch* 94:7). Their wealth, we are assured, will be taken away, but the epistle does not say, as we might have expected, that it will be given to those they have persecuted. Rather, the hope of the righteous is that they will shine like the stars of heaven and that the gate of heaven will be opened to them (*1 Enoch* 104). This hope is shared, in various formulations, by all the apocalypses from Daniel to *4 Ezra* and Revelation. It is this hope that gives the apocalyptic literature an other-worldly character. It should not be thought to imply any lack of concern with the affairs of this world, but only to bear on the kind of alternative to present reality that is imagined.

THE SENSE OF AN ENDING

The main political impact of the apocalyptic literature lies not in any program it may imply for the future but in its rejection and condemnation of the present order. Many of the most memorable images in apocalyptic literature are depictions of the evil empire—such as Daniel's fourth beast of the whore of Babylon in Revelation. The essential message is that an end will come upon this empire. Nowhere is the downfall of the mighty imagined with such glee as in the Christian apocalypse, the book of Revelation, where an angel standing on the sun calls the birds of heaven to "the great supper of God, to eat the flesh of kings, the flesh of captains, the flesh of the mighty—the flesh of all . . . both small and great" (Rev 19:18). The condemnation extends to all the kingdoms of this world, but in the original apocalyptic compositions it is quite specific: it relates to the Seleucid kingdom in Daniel and to the Roman empire in Revelation.

The negative, sometimes vengeful, tone of passages like Revelation 19 conveys a rather unpleasant impression of apocalyptic literature, as something that is only destructive, not constructive. The novelist D. H. Lawrence wrote scathingly of the Apocalypse:

> By the time of Jesus, all the lowest classes and mediocre people had realized that never would they get a chance to be kings, never would they go in chariots, never would they drink wine from gold vessels. Very well then—they would have their revenge by destroying it all. "Babylon the great is fallen, is fallen, and is become the habitation of devils." And then all the gold and silver and pearls and precious stones and fine linen and purple, and silk and scarlet—and cinnamon and frankincense, wheat, beasts, sheep, horses, chariots, slaves, souls of men—all these that are destroyed in Babylon the great—how one hears the envy, the endless envy screeching through this song of triumph![39]

But while Lawrence was hardly a member of the ruling class, he had internalized the attitude of empire and had neither empathy nor sympathy with the subjects of Rome (or of the British empire of his day). For John of Patmos, Rome was not so much the splendor to be envied as an oppressive weight that had to be removed before a free and just world could even be imagined. He could do little more than proclaim an end to empire, say no to its demand for submission.

The "no" of the apocalyptist is not a Barthian *Nein* to nature and this world as such. Rather, it is a political "no," a rejection of a particular world order. While it hardly offers a political program, its efficacy should not be underestimated. In the words of the long-time American activist Daniel Berrigan, "it is the same no that has shaken thrones and the enthroned where they sit. It is Bonhoeffer's no, and Parks' . . . Mandela's and Vaclav Havel's."[40] It was not for nothing that the Emperor Augustus had oracles collected and burnt.[41] The apocalyptic vision was the denial and contradiction of *Roma aeterna,* the official eschatology of empire.

We return here to the point from which we started. Imperial propagandists and apocalyptic dissenters had similar views of the structure of history—a sequence of transitory kingdoms followed by a definitive rule that would last forever. The crucial difference was one of vantage point and location on the time scale. For the triumphalist, the final kingdom has already arrived; for the visionary, the kingdom of the present is passing away. Whether the advent of a final kingdom is imminent or deferred to some time in the future does not make an essential difference so long as the conviction is real that an end to the present order is assured. Writing in Nazi Germany in 1939, Walter Benjamin argued, "That things 'just keep going on' is the catastrophe."[42] Like the authors of Daniel and Revelation, he realized that the most urgent desideratum was the end of the present course of affairs, whatever might follow. If Benjamin had been an apocalyptist, however, he would have added that it would not *weitergehen* indefinitely. However powerfully entrenched the Nazi regime might have seemed to be, its end was inevitable.

It is, of course, a notorious fact that the kingdom predicted in apocalyptic visions never comes, and so apocalypses are often criticized for nourishing illusions. The illusion, however, only relates to the new order. The conviction that "Babylon will fall" has always been proved right, eventually, even if the fulfillment is sometimes deferred for hundreds of years. One might argue that the power of the apocalyptic genre as it was developed in Judaism and early Christianity depends on the permanent delay of the *parousia.* When the final kingdom is thought to have come, utopia becomes ideology and the revolutionary spirit of the apocalypses is betrayed.[43] (This is true of the Augustinian view that the thousand-year reign is realized in the church, just as much as in political ideologies that claim millennial fulfillment.) The insight from which the apocalyptic vision draws its enduring vitality is not the illusory certainty of a new kingdom, but the temporality of all human existence. The Roman Scipio grasped the insight that all earthly power must pass more profoundly than did Daniel, but the Jewish visionary shared it to a significant degree. But while the temporality of power made Scipio sad, it gave hope to Daniel and John of Patmos and has continued to give hope to the oppressed down through the centuries, even if the dream of a utopian kingdom remains elusive.

Speaking in this cradle of empire and colonialism,[44] I cannot resist concluding with a loose adaptation of the four-kingdom schema, found in an anonymous

Irish poem from the eighteenth century, translated by Frank O'Connor with the title "Hope." It seems to me to grasp as well as any formulation the sense of temporality that is at the root of all apocalyptic hope, even if lacks the apocalyptic conviction of Daniel or Revelation:

> Life has conquered; the wind has blown away
> Alexander, Caesar, and all their power and sway;
> Tara and Troy have made no longer stay;
> Maybe the English too will have their day.[45]

A Chechnyan poet today might substitute the Russians for the English. Some Palestinians no doubt would substitute the Israelis, and various peoples in the third world would substitute the Americans. For the insight of Scipio remains as true now as it was when he gazed on the ruins of Carthage. However unreliable apocalyptic predictions may be, whether they set a date for the "end" of history or promise a glorious kingdom, we can be quite certain that all human empire, including that which we enjoy, is doomed to pass.

CHAPTER 12

THE BOOK OF TRUTH
Daniel as Reliable Witness to Past and Future in the United States of America

WITH ADELA YARBRO COLLINS

THE RECEPTION OF DANIEL
IN MILLENARIAN THEOLOGY[1]
ADELA YARBRO COLLINS

The leaders of the American colonies were in large part conscious heirs of the Reformation. They spoke of having an "errand" or mission to fulfill in the new land: to create a society that would conform to the commandments of God and thus lead to the fulfillment of the divine plan, the millennium. As Ruth Alden Doan puts it, "The millennial hope reflected back to give pattern and meaning to the present. . . . [W]hat had been a tradition of millennial dissent in Europe became a foundation of cultural orthodoxy in America."[2]

Like their counterparts in England, the heirs of the Reformers in the colonies attempted to unlock the mysteries of the prophetic texts of the Bible by coordinating the history of the Church with secular history. The book of Daniel played a major role in this Protestant effort to construct a usable past. Thomas Parker, for example, a pastor in Massachusetts, published a book in 1646 entitled *Visions and Prophecies of Daniel Expounded.* In this book he argued that the fourth kingdom of Daniel 2, represented by the iron legs of the image in Nebuchadnezzar's dream, was the Roman kingdom, which, in his view, continued in the Roman Catholic Church. He interpreted the stone as the kingdom of the Saints that is to be set up at the time of the fall of the Antichrist, with whom he identified the Pope or the papacy.[3] As the stone is cut out by no human hand, so the saints "are cut out . . . without hands, that is, by the only power and finger of God. . . . Thus they began to be cut out, *anno* 1160, in the Waldenses, and continue so unto this day."[4] Later he says that the Waldenses professed the same doctrine "that we do now."[5]

He also interpreted the fourth beast of Daniel 7 as the Roman empire.[6] He discovered in v. 8, the description of the little horn before which three horns were plucked up by the roots, a prophecy of the first Crusade, proclaimed by Pope Urban II in 1095. He called this the first War of the Antichrist.[7] Parker interpreted the statement in v. 25 that the fourth beast shall wear out the saints of the Most High as an allusion to the second War of the Antichrist, the one against the Waldensian Protestants that began in 1160 and which, as he saw it, was still continuing.[8]

He interpreted the ram of Daniel 8 as the Persian empire and the goat as the Greek.[9] He concluded that the little horn mentioned in v. 9 is the Antichrist, that is, the Pope. The casting down of the stars is interpreted as the War against the Waldensians and the cessation of the daily sacrifice as the taking away of the true doctrine and worship.[10]

Parker explained the two thousand three hundred evenings and mornings of Dan 8:14 in two ways. First, he argued that they are half as many complete days, namely, one thousand one hundred and fifty. And, he declares, days are years.[11] He equates this period of time with the 1,260 years of the Apocalypse of John and the time, times, and a half a time of Dan 12:7. All these periods refer to the activity of the Antichrist, the time of the removal of true doctrine and worship. Parker proposed that the beginning of the 1,150 days, based on Dan 8:14, be placed in the year 360. This date is apparently a round number representing the reign of Pope Damasus, who, Parker states, was "the first Pope that ent[e]red in after the manner of an Antichrist." This remark probably refers to his violent struggle for the papacy against Ursinius and his supporters. The end of the period then falls in 1510, "when by Luther the Sanctuary began to be purged." The second calculation is based on his view that four mornings and evenings complete one day according to the Jewish reckoning. Thus, the 2,300 mornings and evenings of Dan 8:14 stand for 575 complete days. These then signify 575 years. In this case, Parker suggested beginning with the year 1075, because around that time Hildebrand, Pope Gregory VII, rose above the emperor, Henry IV. According to this calculation, the end of the reign of the Antichrist would be in 1650, which Parker called "the first yeer [sic] of the great Purgation of the Sanctuary."[12] This date was only a few years into the future from the time at which he was writing.

With regard to the prophecy of the seventy weeks in Daniel 9, Parker noted that it was revealed to Daniel at the time of the evening sacrifice. It may be, he says, that the unsealing of it is reserved to the evening of the world.[13] He argued against the view, commonly held by Christians of his time, that the prophecy relates to the times between the Babylonian Captivity and the passion of Christ or the destruction of Jerusalem. His own interpretation is that the seventy weeks of years concern the restoration of the spiritual Jerusalem, the Church of Christ, from Babylon and servitude of the Antichrist.[14] The beginning of the seventy weeks, "from the going forth of the word to restore and build Jerusalem," is the word preached by the Waldenses, beginning in 1160.[15] "The coming of an anointed one, a prince," after seven weeks or forty-nine years is identified with the rising up of certain princes in war against the Pope in defense of the Waldenses in 1209. Parker also considers the possibility that the seventy weeks of years begin with the activity of Wycliffe, the English reformer, for which he gives the date 1370.[16] If one begins with the Waldensians, the sixty-two weeks would end in 1642. But if one starts with Wycliffe, they would end in 1804.

Finally, in dealing with the variety of numbers of years given in Daniel and related works, Parker concludes that the end of the time of the Antichrist will be either in 1649 or in 1859; that is, either in a few years from the time at which he was writing or in two hundred years or so from that time.[17]

According to Parker, the millennium began when the Saints rose up in their own defense, attacking the Antichristians and pronouncing them excommunicate. God approved their word by sending upon the Antichristians the first six plagues, related to the first six bowls of the book of Revelation. The period of time associated with these plagues is equivalent to the millennium, and Parker considered this process to be going on in his own time. After a short interval for the gathering of all nations, the Antichristians would be utterly cut off by the seventh bowl. The first four bowls and thus the millennium began either with the Mohammedan plagues upon Christendom in general in 620 or with the judgments upon the German Roman Empire, beginning in 820. The fifth bowl is associated with Wycliffe and the sixth with Luther. The thousand years will end either in 1649 or in 1860. Following the millennium will be the New Jerusalem, which will involve a new heaven and a new earth. Parker interpreted this image as the heavenly state that will follow upon the general resurrection and the last judgment. He interpreted Paul's prophecy of the conversion of the Jews in Romans 11 spiritually and applied it to "the faithful in general."[18] For Parker, therefore, the millennium was nearly entirely past, and the end of this world was near.

According to Reiner Smolinski, no fixed apocalyptic hermeneutic existed in the seventeenth century in Europe or in the American colonies. There was no consensus on the spatial location of the golden age, whether it would be a literal time of fulfillment on earth or a spiritual one in heaven. Some believed that the millennium belonged to the past, others to the present, and still others to the future. For most of the seventeenth century, both those inclined to a spiritual or allegorical reading of the prophecies and those inclined to a literal reading spoke of "an inchoate, progressively unfolding millennium of mortals who would not attain eternal life until judgment day, in the second resurrection."[19]

Jonathan Edwards, the main theologian of the First Great Awakening in New England, which took place between 1734 and 1743, followed the Augustinian interpretation of his predecessors in allegorizing the first resurrection as a spiritual conversion of individuals. He was similar to his predecessors also in viewing the millennium as incipient: "a mixture of the saints in heaven ruling through their spiritual successors over their mortal and sinful counterparts on earth." The corporeal resurrection would not occur until judgment day.[20]

Later in the eighteenth century, millennial rhetoric and fervor were dedicated to the Revolution, in a process that once again linked divine providence to the destiny of the nation.[21] David Austin, for example, a Yale graduate and Presbyterian minister in Elizabethtown, New Jersey, argued in 1794 that the United States of America is the "stone cut out of the mountain" soon to cover the whole earth (Dan 2:31-45). Young America is that prophetic "kingdom of the stone," born on July 4, 1776.[22] He argued further, based on visions he had received, that Christ would return to the earth on the fourth Sunday of May 1796, a prophecy he thought confirmed by the American and French Revolutions.[23]

The American Revolution was followed by displacement and hardship and by geographic and demographic expansion. The evangelical churches created a broad coalition that dominated society religiously and culturally. This alliance manifested its energy in the Second Great Awakening, a series of revivals in the first third of the nineteenth century that entailed social reform and benevolent organizations.[24] It was in this context that the Millerite or Adventist movement emerged.

William Miller was the son of a devout Baptist woman and a farmer who had fought in the Revolutionary War. His maternal grandfather was a Baptist minister. Miller grew up in New York state and married a woman from a nearby town across the border in Vermont. In his wife's more sophisticated circle, Miller became a Deist. After fighting in the War of 1812 and mourning the death of his father, Miller and his wife moved to New York, and he returned to the Baptist faith of his youth. He was a farmer by profession yet very studious. He was a Calvinist of the Old School, believing that Christ atoned only for the elect and opposing the idea of free will after the sin of Adam. Unlike the Presbyterians, however, and like his fellow Baptists, he did not value an educated clergy and, although he was an avid student of the Bible, he knew no Hebrew or Greek. The King James version was his sacred text.[25]

Although Miller became a professing Christian, he continued to be influenced by the Enlightenment ideal of rationalism. He sought empirical support for his faith and found it in a particular hermeneutical theory, partly inherited and partly of his own devising. Like his contemporary, Alexander Campbell, founder of the Disciples of Christ, Miller concluded that the key to the validity of the Scriptures could be found in the Bible itself. His notion of scientific study of the Bible would demonstrate its consistency and thus its divine origin.[26]

He worked out fourteen rules of interpretation, the last and most important of which was faith that the Bible is the word of God.[27]

He devised his method by 1816 and had decoded the entire Bible by 1818. Like Parker, he discovered that three kingdoms had already fallen, and the last, the Roman, with which he also associated the Roman Catholic Church, had yet to fall.[28] He concluded that the fourth kingdom had already passed into its last state.[29] Miller rejected the idea of some of his contemporaries that the Jews must return to Israel and be converted before the return of Christ.[30] Like Parker, he "found that the promises respecting Israel's restoration are applied by the apostle to all who are Christ's."[31] He also rejected the idea that the millennium was past or present.[32] Rather, he expected the literal, personal return of Christ and the actual destruction of this world by fire upon Christ's return.[33] This earth, "melted by fervent heat at Christ's coming," would then "according to the promise . . . become the new earth, wherein the righteous will forever dwell. . . . [A]t his coming the bodies of all the righteous dead [would] be raised, and all the righteous living be changed from a corruptible to an incorruptible, from a mortal to an immortal state. . . . [T]hey [would] all be caught up together to meet the Lord in the air, and [would] reign with him forever in the regenerated earth. . . . [T]he bodies of the wicked will then all be destroyed, and their spirits reserved in prison until their resurrection and damnation."[34] He concluded that the only millennium "taught in the word of God" is the thousand years between the first resurrection and that of the rest of the dead and that it must follow, not precede, the personal coming of Christ and the regeneration of the earth.[35] Thus most of the events of the last days would occur simultaneously. The only event that would follow the millennium was the actual damnation of the wicked dead, which would eliminate all evil and establish righteousness for eternity.[36]

Miller was also deeply interested in the chronology of the Scriptures. Unlike Parker, Miller agreed with the opinion that the seventy weeks of Daniel 9 had already been fulfilled. He dated the end of these 490 years to the death of Jesus in 33 C.E. Like Parker, however, he believed that the 2,300 days of Dan 8:14 were not yet fulfilled. In fact, this was the key passage for his calculation of the date of the awesome event of the coming of Christ. He took the expression "two thousand three hundred mornings and evenings" to mean 2,300 days, and took these as figurative days meaning years.[37]

The key to calculating the End lay in determining the beginning point of the 2,300 years. Since, he argued, God would not bestow upon us a useless revelation, this point must be revealed in Scripture. In the introduction to the prophecy of the seventy weeks, Gabriel exhorts Daniel to understand the vision. Miller inferred that the vision in question was that of the ram and the he-goat in Daniel 8.[38] He concluded, therefore, that the 2,300 years had the same beginning as the seventy weeks of Daniel 9. According to Dan 9:25, the seventy weeks began with "the going forth of the word to restore and build Jerusalem." Miller connected this event with the statement in Ezra 7:7 that Ezra and other exiles returned to Jerusalem in the seventh year of Artaxerxes the king. He identified this king with Artaxerxes I, called Longimanus, and concluded that the date was 457 B.C.E. Most scholars today would identify the seventh year of this king as 458 B.C.E.[39]

Since Dan 12:12 implies that the End will come after 1,335 days, Miller sought to reconcile this period of time with the 2,300 days. Ignoring the 1,290 days of Dan 12:11, Miller concluded that the 1,335 days of v. 12 began with the taking away of the continual burnt offering and the setting up of the abomination that makes desolate, mentioned in v. 11. He interpreted the abomination as papal supremacy and determined that it began in 508 C.E. The ten toes of the statue of Daniel 2 were usually interpreted as ten kingdoms that had invaded the Roman empire. Miller claimed that the last of these was baptized in 508. This date, in Miller's view, marked the end of pagan Rome.[40] Both of these periods of time, therefore, the 2,300 years and the 1,335 years, would terminate in 1843. In his own words, "I was thus brought, in 1818, at the close of my two years' study of the Scriptures, to the solemn conclusion, that in about twenty-five years from that time all the affairs of our present state would be wound up; that all its pride and power, pomp and vanity, wickedness and oppression, would come to an end; and that, in the place of the kingdoms of this world, the peaceful and long-desired kingdom of the Messiah would be established under the whole heaven."[41]

Miller did not begin immediately to proclaim the time of the End publicly. From 1818 until 1823 he tested his theory and considered objections to it. One of these was, of course, the passage in Mark 13:32 and parallels stating that no one knows the day or the hour of the coming of Christ, only the Father. How then could the Bible reveal the time of the advent? When he examined the context of this saying he saw at once that we are informed how we may know when it is near, "even at the doors; consequently, that text could not teach that we could know nothing of the time of that event."[42] He then "began to speak more clearly [his] opinions to his neighbors, to ministers, and others."[43]

Miller began to proclaim and explain his views to the public in the autumn of 1831.[44] In the 1830s Miller spoke to congregations by invitation in New York and New England. His ideas gave rise to a popular crusade that followed upon the revivals of the Second Great Awakening. His combination of empirical verification and pietist Biblicism converted and recruited many among his audiences.[45] The idea that anyone could sit down with his or her Bible and correlate the word of God with history for himself or herself was appealing to democratic Americans. They needed no clerical or professional mediator. His approach also seemed to be compatible with the ideals of accessible scriptures, common sense, and Francis Bacon's inductive method.[46]

In 1839, Miller met Joshua V. Himes, who undertook to support Miller's proclamation financially.[47] From this point on, the message began to be promulgated in major cities and Miller's ideas began to be printed and distributed widely. According to Paul Boyer, "The Millerites also pioneered organizational and publicity techniques that would provide a model for later popularizers of apocalyptic belief. They used the latest techniques of mass communication—the new high speed printing presses of the day—to produce their tracts, posters, charts, periodicals, and hymnals."[48] Apocalyptic preachers of our own time use the media of television and the Internet. Millerites used visual aids to convince and instruct their audiences. Often the statue of Daniel 2 would be portrayed with dates in the margins, all leading to the last date, 1843.[49]

As Stephen O'Leary has noted, the proclamation of a near end produces expectation in the audience of specific details.[50] Whereas some Millerites did not believe in calculating the date of the End at all and others doubted that 1843 was the correct date, the original expression "about the year 1843" was regarded as too general by many of Miller's followers. Toward the end of 1842, Miller issued a statement that, in accordance with the Jewish computation of time, Christ would come between March 21, 1843, and March 21, 1844.[51] When Christ had not returned by the dawn of March 22, 1844, the movement experienced its first significant disappointment and apparent disconfirmation. Some attempted to recalculate the chronology. Others inferred that the Lord was testing the believers' faith. Missionary efforts continued, but at a slower pace. Outsiders ridiculed the movement mercilessly. Finally, at a camp meeting in New Hampshire in August 1844, Samuel S. Snow argued that Christ would return on the Day of Atonement, the tenth day of the seventh month in the Jewish reckoning, for the final atonement of all sin. He calculated that in 1844 that day would fall on October 22. This new date was soon widely accepted within the movement.[52] Miller himself did not want to approve the October 22 date, but Himes and others pressured him to do so. According to Rowe, "illness and disappointment had weakened Miller physically and emotionally, and perhaps his longfelt lack of confidence moved him to hope desperately that others were correct." For whatever reason, he endorsed the new date just two weeks beforehand.[53]

With the dawn of October 23, 1844, came the Great Disappointment. Most of those involved in the movement returned to the evangelical denominations. Others joined another sect, for example, the Shakers, who spiritualized the coming of Christ. A few, undeterred, engaged in calculating a new date. Others declared that something significant did in fact occur on October 22, but it was a spiritual event, not the end of the world.[54] Among ex-Millerites whose faith in the advent did not decline arose a movement that eventually became the Seventh-Day Adventist Church, which continues to thrive today.[55]

The opponents of Millerism tied the movement so closely to the date of 1843 that a simplistic picture of it survives to this day.[56] But recent scholarship, drawing upon the work of Emile Durkheim, has shown that groups defined as dissenters or outsiders, by their very deviance, perform a service to society by providing an incentive to the orthodox or insiders to formulate their own ideas and values more clearly and to redefine the boundaries of consensus. This Durkheimian view of nineteenth-century American culture supports the conclusion that the Millerite movement made an important contribution by precipitating a "boundary crisis." On the one hand, the Millerites were attempting to retrieve a portion of the Puritan vision. On the other, as Ruth Alden Doan expressed it, "Immanence had begun to seem more compelling than transcendence, subjective experience more believable than objective force."[57] The Millerites advocated a radical supernaturalism, a position that lost prestige with the failure of the End to arrive on the predicted date. From the 1850s to the 1870s, the focus was on issues associated with the Civil War. In the aftermath of that war, radical supernaturalism experienced a revival. What would become the Fundamentalist movement began to take shape in Bible conferences in the 1870s and later. This movement drew force and focus from controversies over evolution and biblical criticism.[58]

FUNDAMENTALISM AND LIBERALISM

John J. Collins

The Fundamentalist Movement

The book of Daniel has had its most dramatic impact in American life in groups like the Millerites and in the popular work of Hal Lindsey,[59] where it is read as a guide to imminent, catastrophic events. There is another strand of the reception of Daniel in North America, however, that concerns the book's witness to the past rather than to the future. The book has played its part in disputes about the inerrancy of the Bible and more generally in the disputes between Fundamentalists and Modernists in the early twentieth century and in the aftershocks of those disputes, which can still be felt on the American scene.

The doctrine of biblical inerrancy is associated especially with the theology developed at Princeton Theological Seminary in the nineteenth and early twentieth centuries. Princeton Seminary was founded in 1811. At its centenary celebration, its president, F. L. Patton, asserted that "Princeton Seminary . . . simply taught the old Calvinistic Theology without modification. . . . there never was a distinctively Princeton theology. Princeton's boast . . . is her unswerving fidelity to the theology of the Reformation."[60] Nonetheless, the Old Princeton Theology is remembered as a distinctive phenomenon in American Protestantism. The first professor of the seminary, Archibald Alexander, was influenced by the philosophical school known as Scottish "Common-Sense Realism," which was widely popular in America in the late eighteenth and early nineteenth centuries. This philosophy was democratic and anti-elitist and was based on the assumption that the human mind can grasp the real world directly. It was formulated in the eighteenth century in response to the epistemological theories of John Locke, which made the process of knowing seem more complicated by interposing "ideas" between the mind and reality, and to the skepticism of David Hume. Thomas Reid, the principal formulator of this philosophy, insisted that the common sense of humankind was the surest guide to the truth.[61] Reid admired the seventeenth-century philosopher Francis Bacon, who advocated a strictly empirical method that consisted of the careful observation and classification of the facts known to common sense. This philosophy had no room for sophisticated theories about the construction of reality but held a rather simplistic view of truth and falsehood, which was very attractive in democratic America.

The theology developed by Alexander and his successors at Princeton was "scientific" in the Baconian sense. Charles Hodge claimed that "if natural science be concerned with the facts and laws of nature, theology is concerned with the facts and principles of the Bible."[62] Hodge apparently thought of the theologian working with the data of Scripture as a scientist working with nature. Implicit in this approach was the assumption that the Bible provides reliable facts to begin with, and this in turn was implied by the doctrine of inspiration.

The classic doctrine of biblical inerrancy in the Princeton theology was formulated by A. A. Hodge[63] and B. B. Warfield in 1881, in response to the rise and spread of critical biblical scholarship. These theologians held "that the Scriptures not only contain but are the Word of God, and hence that all their elements and all their affirmations are absolutely errorless, and binding the faith and obedience of men." Vague or general truths would not suffice. "Infallible thought must be definite thought, and definite thought implies words." Hence they insisted on "the truth to fact of every statement in the Scripture."[64] The proponents thought that this position was grounded in reason. Warfield held that reason was as necessary to faith as light is to photography.[65] Reason, however, operated from the starting point of a very specific idea of revelation.

While the Princeton theologians were not millenarian, their biblical literalism was conducive to a millenarian interpretation of books like Daniel and Revelation. The Princeton theology and popular millenarianism were major factors in the rise of Fundamentalism in the early twentieth century. Biblical literalism increasingly became the norm in the Presbyterian church. Prominent liberals, such as C. A. Briggs, of the Brown-Driver-Briggs dictionary, were driven out of the church. In the years 1910 to 1915 a series of volumes called *The Fundamentals* appeared, taking issue with the views of "Modernists," especially "those infidel professors in Chicago University," such as Shailer Mathews.[66] In the years after World War I there was strident controversy between the conservative "Fundamentalist" and liberal "Modernist" factions, and even between Fundamentalists and less militant conservatives.[67] Within Princeton Seminary there was a feud between the fundamentalist J. Gresham Machen and the conservative but conciliatory Charles Erdman. Matters came to a head at the Presbyterian General Assembly in 1925, when Erdman was elected moderator. He proceeded to establish a commission, which issued reports in the following years stressing that the Presbyterian system admitted diversity of viewpoints in the expression of Christian faith. Princeton Seminary was reorganized so that it was no longer dominated by the theology of inerrancy. A number of Princeton faculty, led by Machen, resigned and founded Westminster Seminary as a conservative alternative. The conflict within the Presbyterian church, then, was a "boundary crisis" just as surely as the Millerite Disappointment. Henceforth a clear line was drawn between Fundamentalists and mainline Christians. While the Fundamentalists may have lost this conflict, however, they by no means disappeared as a result and continue to constitute a thriving subculture in American life down to the present.

The Historical Accuracy of Daniel

The old Princeton theology of Warfield and Machen had implications for biblical interpretation. Even when conservative scholars have not held to strict verbal inspiration, they have been concerned repeatedly to show that the book of Daniel is without error. This is no easy task. The stories of the fiery furnace and the lions' den were fantastic, but the fundamentalist could argue that nothing is impossible with God. It was more difficult to argue, against the available evidence, that Belshazzar was the last king of Babylon or that an otherwise unknown Darius the Mede "received the kingdom" after his demise.

Difficulty, however, can be viewed as a challenge. One of the professors who resigned from Princeton and joined the Westminster faculty was Robert Dick Wilson, who wrote a whole series of Studies in the Book of Daniel, published in two volumes.[68] In the preface to the second volume of the series, which appeared posthumously, Oswald T. Allis, who had also moved from Princeton to Westminster, wrote:

> He [Wilson] believed thoroughly in "scientific Biblical criticism." His method and aim were truly scientific. He was not only willing, but eager to ascertain the facts and all the facts. For he believed and showed again and again that the facts support the high claims of the Bible to entire trustworthiness as the Word of God.[69]

Wilson was one of the first scholars to try to use the Akkadian material that had come to light in the nineteenth century to mount a defense of the authenticity of

Daniel. This new evidence gave some comfort to conservative Christians insofar as it provided evidence that a person named Belshazzar (*Bēl šarra uṣur*) had indeed existed and ruled Babylon for a time. The vindication of the biblical record was not complete. Belshazzar was only the viceroy for his father Nabonidus while the latter was away at Teima. But according to the Verse Account of Nabonidus, the father "entrusted the kingship" to Belshazzar, and for an apologist like Wilson, this was enough. In fairness to Wilson, one can hardly deny that there is some historical memory preserved in the biblical text. But the preservation of a historical name is no guarantee of the historicity of the story in which it occurs, and an apologist like Wilson moved too quickly from mere possibility to definite claim.

The Akkadian texts provide no attestation of Darius the Mede. Wilson was one of the first to suggest that the reference was to Gobryas or Ugbaru, the governor of Gutium, who led the actual capture of Babylon in advance of Cyrus. Like all other identifications of Darius the Mede, this one fails for the simple reason that Gobryas was never called Darius the Mede, although here again there may be some vague underlying memory of the historical conqueror. This identification has had appeal beyond Fundamentalist circles, however. It was endorsed by the archetypical American biblical scholar, William Foxwell Albright,[70] and by no less an authority on Daniel than Klaus Koch![71] Wilson made a positive contribution to scholarship insofar as he compiled pertinent ancient evidence and forced liberal scholars to be rigorous in their arguments. The strained, apologetic character of Wilson's work, however, is evident when he tries to defend the possibility that Belshazzar was in some sense the son of Nebuchadnezzar,[72] or in his refusal to accept that the account of Hellenistic history in Daniel 11 was *ex eventu,* and in his insistence that it was "absolutely within the sphere of ordinary predictive prophecy."[73] However much he might appeal to evidence from the ancient Near East, there was always a presumption in favor of the historical reliability of the biblical text.

Mention of Albright reminds us that the most influential biblical scholar of his era also had strong inclination toward establishing the historicity of the biblical text. For this reason his work was attractive to Fundamentalists, although he was certainly not one himself.[74] The question of the historical reliability of the biblical text dominated American biblical scholarship for much of the twentieth century. In the case of the tales of Daniel 1–6, however, this issue was settled to the satisfaction of most people by the magisterial commentary of J. A. Montgomery, of the University of Pennsylvania, in 1927.[75] It was coincidental, but timely, that Montgomery's commentary appeared just after the great Fundamentalist-Liberal controversy had played itself out with the apparent defeat of the Fundamentalists. Montgomery acknowledged that Wilson's collection of references had merit, but concluded aptly:

> It is a vast pity that apologists have gone so far as they have in attempting to maintain every iota of statement in the book—this in their zeal to support not so much its historical accuracy as its divine infallibility. In consequence they demand an extreme of respect for Daniel, which is not required by conservative critics for the historical

books of the Old Testament or even for the Gospels, in which the play of human limitation and inexactness is generally allowed.[76]

Needless to say, the Fundamentalists were not convinced. There has continued to be a stream of works from both British and American conservatives, tilting away at the windmill of the historical Daniel. The American scholar E. J. Young[77] and the British scholars Donald Wiseman and Kenneth Kitchen come to mind.[78] In recent years the effort has found an organ in Andrews University Seminary Studies, where such scholars as Gerhard Hasel and William Shea have published learned apologetic essays after the manner of Wilson.[79] It is noteworthy that Andrews is an Adventist seminary, in Berrien Springs, Michigan, standing in a tradition that had its origin with the Millerites in the nineteenth century. Despite the efforts of these scholars, however, the theologically conservative Brevard Childs could say that Wilson was "the last great defender of Daniel's traditional authorship" in America.[80]

The attempt to verify Darius the Mede by trying to fit him into the historical record seems to me to be a genre mistake. It tries to construe literature that is imaginative and sometimes fantastic as if it were sober factual reporting. It is no coincidence that Wilson also labored to distance Daniel from the pseudepigraphical apocalypses, such as we find in *1 Enoch*.[81] The objective is to refute the charge that Daniel resembles the literature of the second century B.C.E. more than the classical prophets. Here again Wilson could find some basis for his arguments: the visions of Daniel are closer to those of the biblical prophets than are those of *Enoch*, a fact that may explain why Daniel was included in the canon. The importance of the apocalypses as the appropriate literary context for Daniel was established not so much by Montgomery as by the Irish-born Oxford professor R. H. Charles, in his edition of the Apocrypha and Pseudepigrapha and in his commentary on Daniel.[82] The relevance of the second-century context was reinforced massively by the discovery of the Dead Sea Scrolls. The revival of interest in the Pseudepigrapha, and especially in the apocalyptic literature in the last quarter of the century, has moved the discussion of Daniel away from traditional polemics and located it firmly in the context of Jewish literature of the Hellenistic period.[83] It is significant that the critical consensus on the date and genre of Daniel is accepted without question in the avowedly evangelical Word Biblical Commentary, by the English scholar John Goldingay who is now a professor at Fuller Seminary in California.[84]

The Liberal Interpretation of Daniel

While the liberal, critical interpretation of Daniel has prevailed in academic scholarship, however, it has never gripped the popular imagination in the way that fundamentalist, millenarian readings have. Liberation theologians, and specifically African American theologians, have generally found their inspiration in the book of Exodus. Daniel, and apocalyptic literature in general, has most often been associated with religiously and socially conservative Protestantism. There are some exceptions, especially in recent years. The commentary by Daniel Smith-Christopher, a Mennonite scholar from a strongly pacifistic tradition, in the *New Interpreter's Bible,* moves beyond the standard historical-critical interpretation to read Daniel as "dreams of the oppressed," still relevant to our time.[85] For an illustration of the liberal reception of Daniel beyond the world of professional biblical scholarship, however, I turn to a series of essays by Daniel Berrigan, a Jesuit priest who has been a noted social activist since the time of the Vietnam war.[86]

Berrigan finds Daniel to be "a book about power . . . and about the powerlessness of the believing community, revealed ironically as a new form of power." The selection of Daniel and his companions for special training at the Babylonian court is an attempt to co-opt them for "the adventure of empire." Their decision to refuse the food of the king is not a matter of *kashrut* but a symbolic gesture of resistance. It is a "no" to the corruption of empire. Berrigan comments:

> We hear it. And we know it is repeated, echoed down the centuries, including our own. We know, or know of, those who die for daring it, that puny monosyllable that no sooner uttered seems lost on the air, a mote. And yet such a word, like "a cloud no larger than a hand," covers the sun. It is the same no that has shaken thrones and the enthroned where they sit. It is Bonhoeffer's no, and Rosa Park's and Franz Jaegerstaetter's, Sojourner Truth's, Mandela's, Vaclav Havel's.

Berrigan does not pause at all over the historicity of Belshazzar or Darius the Mede. Neither is there any attempt to correlate the visions with events of our time or to predict the future. Rather, Berrigan interprets the apocalyptic symbolism in terms of universal truths. So,

> according to the Word of God, conveyed in heavenly imagery here and in the Book of Revelation, there is no such thing as a purely earthbound war. No matter its nature or provocation or slogans or ideology or religious or moral justification, war on earth is above all a spiritual reality. Whether in ancient Persia or in today's Persian Gulf, war is always and everywhere a demonic assault on God. War, therefore, is always and everywhere witnessed—and judged—by God. (Would that the church understood!)[87]

Berrigan notes the correspondence between the *maskilim,* or wise, of Daniel and the Servant of the Lord in Isaiah 53: "The so-called fourth servant song of Isaiah identifies and praises, in the name of Yahweh, this same quality: the wisdom that brings merciful justice to others, often by unmasking, as Martin Luther King, Jr., did, the cleverly concealed injustices that lie under the incantation of 'law and order.'" There is, to be sure, an interpretive leap involved here. Daniel was arguably unmasking foreign rulers as beasts from the sea or manifestations of primeval chaos, but the book scarcely implies a suspicion of law and order as such. For Berrigan, however, the significance of Daniel is not in the details, but in an attitude to political power, which is applied typologically to what he perceives as analogous issues in the modern world.

Berrigan concludes his reflections on Daniel with a consideration of the question that reverberates throughout Daniel, "How long must these things last?": "The only 'answer' given," he says, "is the famous 'time, times and half a time.'"[88] (He ignored the specific numbers of days given in Daniel 12.) Rather than try to calculate the "end" on the basis of this answer, Berrigan emphasizes its mystery:

> A boundary is set against our pretension to seize upon "the end time" and claim it in a show of power, here and now. Let the human know its limits, God's word seems to say—and thus its salvation. Neither we nor any human striving, no matter how virtuous, nor any system or political amelioration—no human effort can usher in the era of justice and peace known as the realm of God. . . . Neither believer nor unbeliever is able to bring the end to pass.[89]

Whether the book of Daniel was originally meant to be so evasive might be questioned, in light of the highly specific predictions it offers. More than two thousand years later, however, Berrigan's emphasis on the evasiveness of Daniel's prediction is a salutary corrective to the kind of futurology that has dominated the Fundamentalist readings of the book.

Conclusion

The book of Daniel has not been especially prominent in American public life, but it has had its moments of glory. These have come primarily in the Dispensationalist movement and in Millerite prophecy and have concerned primarily the eschatological timetable of the book. It has not, however, fueled any radical social movements in America, as it had at various times in European history. Evangelical and Fundamentalist theologians who affirm the eschatology of Daniel and Revelation have been nonetheless socially and politically conservative. Only occasionally, in recent liberationist writing, is the revolutionary potential of the book exploited.

The conservative dominance in the interpretation of Daniel in the United States is bound up with the tradition of literalist interpretation, which has its roots in the positivistic, scientific orientation of American culture, in contrast to the idealism that has often flourished in Europe. Only gradually, in the twentieth century, has the rich symbolism of Daniel, with its deep roots in Near Eastern myth, been appreciated, and even then the appreciation rarely extends beyond the world of academia. It is true that where Daniel is understood symbolically it loses some of the urgency that it had for the Millerites or for Fundamentalists who took its predictions in literal seriousness. In this case, however, we would suggest that the loss is gain. The book of Daniel may no longer be at the center of the popular imagination, but it is more appropriately and satisfactorily appreciated as a document of its time, which is neither an inerrant guide to the past nor a reliable prediction of the future.

CHAPTER 13

THE LEGACY
OF APOCALYPTICISM

In 1970, the German Old Testament scholar Klaus Koch published a slim monograph with the title *Ratlos vor der Apokalyptik*. The book appeared in English a couple years later, but with a significantly different title: *The Rediscovery of Apocalyptic*.[1] The translator, or more likely the publisher, believed in positive thinking. The rediscovery of something sounds like good news. But Koch's original title had a polemical edge. Modern scholarship, he suggested, and more generally the so-called mainline churches, were "clueless" as to what to do with a prominent part of the biblical heritage. He spoke of "Apocalyptic" as a disquieting motif and documented at some length "the agonized attempt to save Jesus from Apocalyptic." Much ink has been spilled on the subject of apocalypticism in the intervening decades, and I would like to think that we have arrived at a much clearer under-standing of the phenomenon. But the embarrassment indicated by Koch's title per-sists, and one need only conjure up the names of Robert Funk or Dominic Crossan to see that "the agonized attempt to save Jesus from apocalyptic" continues apace. Is that embarrassment justified? Or is apocalypticism a valuable component of the biblical heritage?

THE CAUSES OF EMBARRASSMENT

First, it may be well to consider the charges against the defendant. To a great degree liberal suspicion of the phenomenon is related to the popularity of apocalyptic texts in fundamentalist and very conservative circles. This is an issue that lies outside the competence of the biblical scholar as such, and I will touch on it only incidentally. Suffice it to say that the use that some people make of a body of literature does not necessarily exhaust its potential or value. But the charges are also rooted in perceptions of the literature itself. Four kinds of criticism of apocalyptic literature come to mind.

1.	The books of Daniel and Revelation are somewhat exceptional in the biblical canon. Their closest analogues are to be found in the pseudepigraphic literature of ancient Judaism and early Christianity, literature that is unfamiliar not only to the average layperson but also to many biblical scholars. The introductory essay in one recent collection of essays on "Apocalyptic and the New Testament" dismisses this extracanonical literature as "abstruse and fantastic."[2] Even the canonical apocalypses are sometimes characterized as the products of what the late John A. T. Robinson called "a perfervid imagination."

2.	Despite this recognition of the exuberance of apocalyptic symbolism, many people still think that it is supposed to be understood in a highly literalistic way—as interpreted, for example, by Hal Lindsey in *The Late Great Planet Earth*. The late Norman Perrin, in his presidential address to the Society of Biblical Literature in 1973, claimed that apocalyptic symbols were *stenosymbols* that stood in a one-to-one relationship with their referents.[3] He buttressed this claim by referring to the interpretations given within some apocalyptic visions such as Daniel 7, where we are told that the four beasts from the sea represent four kings. Such interpretations were taken to reflect a deficient literary imagination.

3.	Very often, apocalypticism is equated with an obsession about predicting the future, especially the end of the world. The books of Daniel and Revelation have indeed been used for this purpose throughout the history of Christianity (and in the case of Daniel, also of Judaism). The Millerite movement in nineteenth-century America is perhaps the most prominent example of this kind of thinking.[4] Such predictions have been made repeatedly since antiquity and have always proved unfounded. Consequently, apocalypticism is viewed as a source of illusion and false hope, and there is reason to believe that some people in antiquity, such as the majority of the rabbinic sages, already saw it in this light.

4.	Finally, perhaps the most weighty criticism of apocalyptic literature is that it exhibits and fosters a strong moral dualism. The world is divided between sons of light and sons of darkness. The opponents of the good are sons of Belial or Satan. This kind of thinking shows little appreciation for the shades of human behavior and is rightly seen as simplistic. It encourages self-righteousness on the part of those who belong to the sons of light. Since apocalypses typically include judgment scenes, where the wicked are destroyed, often in a violent manner, there is also the fear that these texts may encourage violence by their readers, even if they do not explicitly condone it.

These criticisms of apocalyptic literature are not without foundation. This is indeed difficult and problematic literature. If we read the ancient texts in context, however, it is possible to arrive at a much more sympathetic assessment. This assessment will not amount to a blanket endorsement of apocalyptic values, but it will suggest that there is also much that is positive in the legacy of apocalypticism.

APOCALYPTIC SYMBOLISM

First, the nature of the symbolism. Daniel's great vision of the beasts from the sea is introduced as a dream, visions in his head as he lay on his bed. We do not know whether any of the apocalyptic revelations that have come down to us actually originated in dreams. They are literary compositions, and the dreams are at least retold and consciously shaped. Even if the dream is a literary construct, however, it governs the nature of the symbolism. Dreams are not coherent logical treatises. They are made up of scenes that may be quite disjointed and in which meanings are displaced, and one thing may stand for another. We do not need to be psychiatrists to decipher these dreams, but we do need to know something about Ancient Near Eastern mythology. Anyone who knows the role of the Sea in the Ugaritic myths of the second millennium, or indeed has paid attention to biblical allusions to "mighty waters" or "the dragon that is in the sea" (Isa 27:1) in the Hebrew Bible, will recognize an allusion here.[5] Equally, the "one like a son of man" riding on the clouds of heaven and the white-headed deity before whom he appears recall the figures of Baal and El in the Ugaritic myths.[6] Daniel's vision, in short, is not just a nightmare about strange animals. It is an evocation of an ancient myth that suggests that the forces of life and vitality ultimately triumph over those of chaos and disorder. Equally, the great dragon that is cast down to earth in the book of Revelation does not spring without precedent from the brain of John of Patmos, perfervid or otherwise. Rather, it adapts imagery that had circulated for millennia in the combat myths in which Ancient Near Eastern religions had expressed some of their fundamental convictions about the world.[7] In short, to understand this literature at all one must know something of the traditions to which it alludes. Many of these traditions can be found in the Bible itself, but some are drawn from the surrounding cultures of the Ancient Near East and Hellenistic world. Even when we are armed with this knowledge, however, we should not expect the apocalypses to take the form of rational discourses. These are works of imagination, highly symbolic and imagistic. They function, in the words of Clifford Geertz's famous definition of religion, to establish and shape the mood and motivations of the reader. One of the problems in the modern fundamentalist use of apocalyptic literature is that it lacks this contextual knowledge, and this results in a flat, literalistic interpretation, which is an impoverished view of the literature.

In view of the richly allusive character of apocalyptic visions, the argument that they are intended to be read as "steno-symbols," in Perrin's phrase, is clearly inadequate.[8] It is true that the angel tells Daniel that the four great beasts are four kings that arise on the earth, but that interpretation does not begin to do justice to the vision. Even someone who fails to recognize the mythic allusions in the scene of beasts rising from the sea cannot fail to appreciate that the scene conveys a sense of turbulence and threat that is completely lacking in the interpretation. Moreover, the angel refrained from identifying the beasts specifically. Modern scholars identify them as Babylon, Media, Persia, and Greece, but in antiquity the fourth beast was usually identified as Rome. Later Christians would take it as Muslim Turks. In fact, it is the genius of apocalyptic symbols, like those of much prophetic literature, that they can be reinterpreted endlessly in the light of new circumstances. The fourth beast can be Hitler or Soviet Russia (Reagan's "evil empire") or Saddam Hussein, or whoever is perceived as the villain of the hour. So, far from being steno-symbols, restricted to a single referent, these symbols are essentially multivalent. The elusiveness of these symbols was recognized in antiquity. In a famous passage in *4 Ezra*, written at the end of the first century C.E., Ezra sees an eagle coming up from the sea and is told: "The eagle that you saw coming up from the sea is the fourth kingdom that appeared in a vision to your brother Daniel. But it was not explained to him as I now explain it to you" (*4 Ezra* 12:11-12). Even symbols whose meaning seems to be quite clear, like the whore of Babylon in Revelation, admit of reinterpretation. Because the referents are never identified explicitly in the texts, there is always what Paul Ricoeur has called "a surplus of meaning."[9] The symbol is never exhausted by any one referent.

There is little substance then to the charge that ancient apocalypses show a defective literary imagination. Of course, the literary quality of the apocalypses is uneven, but the best exemplars of the genre, such as Daniel, Revelation, or *4 Ezra*, are works of considerable power. A significant part of their legacy is that they have furnished Jewish and Christian imaginations with symbols and images of exceptional evocative power that have been rediscovered and reemployed through the centuries.

APOCALYPTIC PREDICTIONS

There is somewhat more substance to the charge that apocalypses inspire false hopes and lead to disillusionment. Attempts to predict specific events, or set a date for a definitive end, however, are remarkably rare. Daniel is the most notable exception in this regard. In Daniel 9, Jeremiah's prophecy that Jerusalem would be desolate for seventy years is reinterpreted to mean that the desolation would last seventy weeks of years, or 490 years. This passage was repeatedly taken as a key to the course of history, down into the Middle Ages. In its original context it pointed to a clearly specified time of fulfillment, three and a half years (half a week) after the disruption of the Jerusalem cult. But the numbers lent themselves easily to reinterpretation. After all, if seventy years could mean seventy weeks of years, why should the latter number too not have a symbolic meaning?

The most specific prediction of a date in all of ancient Jewish or Christian apocalyptic literature is found at the end of the book of Daniel. There we are told: "From the time that the regular burnt offering is taken away and the abomination that desolates is set up, there shall be one thousand two hundred and ninety days. Happy are those who persevere and attain the thousand three hundred thirty five days." Two things about these statements are remarkable. First, we are given two different numbers of days, and second, we are not told what should happen at the end of them. Each of the numbers is a little more than three and a half years, the duration predicted at other points in the Book of Daniel. A slightly shorter figure was given in chapter 8: two thousand three hundred evenings and mornings, or 1,150 days. I think the conclusion is inescapable that attempts to specify the number of days were made when the three and a half years were thought to have expired. When the first number of days passed, the calculation was revised. This kind of recalculation is well known in the history of millennial movements. It was documented famously by Leon Festinger in his book *When Prophecy Fails*.[10] What is remarkable in the case of Daniel is that the outdated predictions were allowed to stand in the text. If three different numbers of days are given, too much weight cannot be placed on the literal accuracy of any one of them.

The first number of days in Daniel 8 is clearly related to the defilement of the Jerusalem temple: "For two thousand three hundred evenings and mornings; then the sanctuary shall be restored to its rightful state." According to 1 Maccabees, the temple was restored exactly three years after it was desecrated (1 Macc 1:54; 4:54). At least the later predictions in Daniel must have been made after this had happened. At some point, the author or authors of Daniel no longer regarded the restoration of the temple as the "end" for which they looked, or at least they did not regard the Maccabean restoration as such a fulfillment. A clue to their understanding may be found in the last verse of the book in which Daniel is told to "go your way and rest; you shall rise for your reward at the end of days." The end was now conceived as the time of the resurrection, or what we might call the end of the world as we know it. But if this was the end in view, even the latest prediction in Daniel went unfulfilled, or at least has gone unfulfilled until now.

Daniel, then, would seem to be a paradigm case of the unreliability of apocalyptic predictions. Nonetheless, the book was accepted as canonical Scripture within a generation. Two hundred and fifty years later Josephus would say that Daniel was the greatest of the prophets, because he not only predicted what would happen but said when it would happen. Josephus apparently failed to notice that Daniel's predictions had failed. We can only conclude that Daniel benefited from the same kind of hermeneutic that he had applied to Jeremiah's prophecy of seventy years of desolation. The specific, unambiguous numbers were treated as mysterious ciphers, just as surely as the beasts from the sea.

I do not deny that the author of Daniel tried to predict that something would happen on a specific date. There may be one or two other cases of such predictions in Jewish antiquity, but not many. (The Qumran sect seems to have expected an "end" forty years after the death of the Teacher.) But the failure of the calculation was not thought to invalidate the prediction as a whole. There was something else at issue in Daniel's prediction of the "end."

The book of Daniel is the clearest case we have of an apocalypse written in the throes of persecution. Hence the urgency of the question, how long will these things be? People wanted to know how long their sufferings would last. But all the apocalypses that have come down to us envision a crisis of some sort. In the earliest Jewish apocalypse in the book of Enoch, the crisis is a cultural one. The world was changed by the new mores of the Hellenistic age. The apocalypses of *4 Ezra* and *2 Baruch* look back on the crisis of the destruction of Jerusalem and its temple. There is no good evidence that the book of Revelation was written in a time of persecution, but it nonetheless paints a picture of crisis. There was a perceived crisis, because the author regarded the pretensions of Rome to universal dominion as intolerable. All of these apocalypses portray their crises in cosmic terms. Beasts have arisen from the sea and threaten the order of creation. The dragon has been cast down from heaven and is loosing its fury on earth. But what is crucial to all of them is the sense of an ending, the assurance that closure is at hand. That sense of resolution is far more important than any specific date. Consequently, Josephus and indeed all of Jewish and Christian tradition could overlook the failure of Daniel's prediction in its original context. What mattered was the belief that sooner or later justice would be done. That belief does not admit of verification, short of eschatological verification at the end of history or in the hereafter, but it is fundamental to both Christianity and Judaism. Those who hold to that general faith should not be too quick to dismiss its concrete expression in the apocalyptic literature.

MORAL DUALISM

The idea of a final judgment, however, brings to the fore the problem of moral dualism, which touches, in my view, on the most problematic aspect of apocalyptic literature. Apocalyptic literature typically divides the world into good and evil—sons of light and sons of darkness in the terminology of the Dead Sea Scrolls. The dualism admits of some modification. The scrolls allow that people may have mixed natures, some parts light and some parts darkness. But in the end there is a clean separation. In Daniel some people rise to eternal life and some to shame and everlasting contempt. The book of Revelation envisions the slaughter of all who follow the Beast. There is little appreciation for shades of gray. John of Patmos writes to the angel of the church in Laodicea: "I wish that you were either cold or hot. So because you are lukewarm and neither cold nor hot, I am about to spit you out of my mouth" (Rev 3:15-16).

The problem with this kind of mentality is shown by the one exceptional apocalyptic text that proves the rule. In the Testament of Abraham, the patriarch asks to see the whole inhabited world before he dies, and so he is taken on a chariot ride by the Archangel Michael (chapter 10). But the righteous Abraham is filled with indignation whenever he sees people sinning. So, for example, when he sees "a man and a woman engaging in sexual immorality with each other" he prays that the earth open and swallow them. And because of the efficacy of his prayer, the earth splits in two and swallows them up. After a few such incidents, however, a voice speaks from heaven to the Archangel: "Command the chariot to stop and turn Abraham away, lest he should see the entire inhabited world. For if he were to see all those who pass their lives in sin, he would destroy everything that exists. For behold, Abraham has not sinned and he has no mercy on sinners. But I made the world, and I do not want to destroy any one of them."

The Testament of Abraham has the form of an apocalypse, at least in part, but it is really a parody of the genre. The heroes of Daniel and Revelation may not be quite as sinless as Abraham, but they are unequivocally righteous, and their enemies are unequivocally wicked. Such a view of the world is surely too simplistic.

There are mitigating circumstances that may be adduced in defense of the moral dualism of the apocalypses. Most of them were written in times of crisis that called for extreme rhetoric. Daniel depicts Antiochus Epiphanes, persecutor of the Jews, as a beast that should be thrown into the fire. Few people would object if the image were used with reference to Hitler. But while Hitler was not a unique phenomenon, he was certainly an extreme case. Crises are often in the eye of the beholder, and one person's beast may not seem so bad to someone else. Apocalyptic rhetoric should be used sparingly. The danger is that it may encourage polarization and discourage the kinds of compromises that make it possible for people to live together. It does not provide an ethic for all seasons, although it may be appropriate to some situations.

POSITIVE ASPECTS OF APOCALYPTICISM

Thus far we have been considering the negative perceptions of apocalypticism that are often seen as a cause of embarrassment. Is there, however, a more positive case to be made? Are there ways in which apocalypticism has enriched the Jewish and Christian traditions?

The first and most obvious legacy of apocalypticism in this regard is the store of images that it has supplied to religious language. Think of the whore of Babylon or the four horsemen of the Apocalypse. As we have just noted, this imagery is a double-edged sword. It often lends itself to extreme and intolerant rhetoric. But its power and vividness cannot be denied. It is language that can shape one's view of the world for better or worse. Perhaps its greatest contribution in this regard is that it provides ways of naming evil that go beyond philosophical and theological abstractions and do justice to its concrete reality.

THE APOCALYPTIC WORLDVIEW

Apocalyptic literature is a way of depicting reality. Unlike the prophetic or sapiential literature, it seldom resorts to direct exhortation. It is a visual medium that constructs a view of the world. This view has implications for human behavior, but these are not always spelled out. The goal of this literature is to transform the reader's understanding on a level prior to ethical decision making.

In speaking of an apocalyptic worldview, I am obviously engaging in generalization and abstracting from the specific nuances of individual apocalypses. The essential elements of this worldview are a lively belief in the role of supernatural forces in shaping human behavior and an equally lively belief in the certainty of a final definitive judgment that will not only set matters right on earth (if the earth is thought to endure) but also provide everlasting reward or punishment for individual behavior. Attempts to calculate the time of the "end" such as we have seen in Daniel are incidental to this worldview and not essential.

Does this worldview embody insights that we should accept as true or valid, that capture aspects of the human condition that are less adequately represented elsewhere? Three aspects of the literature seem to me to merit consideration in this regard: first, the sense that human life is subject to forces beyond human control; second, the sense of transience, that all human power is fading and that the world as we know it is passing away; and third, the affirmation of transcendence, the faith that justice will prevail and that certain values demand our ultimate allegiance.

Apocalyptic Determinism

First, the issue of supernatural forces. Apocalyptic literature is often viewed as deterministic, and to some degree it is. History is typically measured out in set periods and can supposedly be predicted centuries in advance. Many critics have drawn the inference that this determinism undermines human responsibility. Martin Buber wrote scathingly of the device of pseudepigraphy, which to his mind typified the difference between prophecy and "apocalyptic":

> The time the prophetic voice calls us to take part in is the time of the actual decision. . . . In the world of the apocalyptic, this present historical-biographical hour hardly ever exists, precisely because a decision by men constituting a factor in the historical-suprahistorical decision is not in question here. The prophet addresses persons . . . to recognize their situation's demand for decision and to act accordingly. The apocalyptic writer has no audience turned towards him; he speaks into his notebook.[11]

Again, with reference to *4 Ezra*, Buber wrote, "Everything here is predetermined, all human decisions are only sham struggles."[12]

Buber, however, seems to have missed the point of most apocalyptic texts. In the book of Daniel, chapter 11, there is a long pseudo-prophecy of Hellenistic history, which serves to show that the persecution of the Jews by Antiochus Epiphanes falls in the penultimate stage of history, shortly before the final denouement. The point is not to relieve human beings of responsibility for decision making but to sharpen the context of the decision. In the time of persecution, the "wise" are those who stand their ground, even though some of them lose their lives in the process. Their choice does not determine the course of events, but it directly determines their own destiny. (In some other apocalyptic texts, such as the Testament of Moses, human decisions seem to have a greater bearing on the course of events.) The message of Daniel is that one should act like these "wise" martyrs; the wisdom of their decision is confirmed by the resurrection in the following chapter. Moreover, apocalyptic visions usually presuppose a synergism between human and superhuman agents. In Daniel, the beasts that rise from the sea represent human kings or kingdoms, but they also suggest that they are embodiments of primordial chaos, the primeval sea that was subdued in the ancient myths. In Revelation 13, the dragon, or Satan, gives his power to the beast that rises from the sea and represents the Roman Empire. In each case, the human ruler is still a responsible agent, but he is thought to tap into other greater forces as well. The same might be said of Hitler. In a modern secular analysis we might identify these forces as cultural, historical, or economic, or even in some cases as the collective psychosis of a people. The idiom is different. But the apocalyptic writers recognized that individuals who make decisions are often shaped by forces that they do not understand, and that those decisions often have effects that go far beyond anything that they intended. The same insight is expressed in a different way in Greek tragedy.

The Sense of Transience

A second insight of the apocalyptic literature that seems to me to have enduring significance is the sense that the form of this world is passing away. One popular motif that recurs in several apocalypses is the sequence of four kingdoms. Nebuchadnezzar may be the head of gold in Daniel's interpretation of the statue in the dream, but eventually he will crumble when the stone strikes the base of the statue. This motif was widespread in the ancient world. The Roman general Scipio is said to have wept at the destruction of Carthage, "realizing that all cities, nations and authorities must, like men, meet their doom, that this happened to Ilium, once a prosperous city, the empire of Assyria, Media and Persia, the greatest of their time, and to Macedonia itself, the brilliance of which was so recent, either deliberately or the verses escaping him, he said: A day will come when sacred Troy shall perish / And Priam and his people shall be slain." When Polybius asked him what he meant, he replied that when he reflected on the fate of all things human he also feared for Rome.[13] Scipio, admittedly, was exceptional in following the idea through to its logical conclusion. More typically, the sequence is thought to culminate in an empire that is immune to decline. In the apocalyptic literature the sequence ends in a kingdom of God, which, at least in some cases, entails a Jewish kingdom on earth. There is nonetheless a powerful sense of the transience of all things human prior to the advent of that final kingdom.

A Lasting Kingdom

The hope for a lasting kingdom that will not pass away, whether in this world or in the next, is, however, an essential part of the apocalyptic worldview. This brings us to the question of transcendence, the belief in something over and above this transient world. In part this belief is born of the demand for justice, which so often is not seen to be done in this world. The belief in an ultimate judgment where things are set right provides the underpinning for decisions in the present. The Jewish martyrs in the Maccabean period could afford to risk or even lose their lives because they were convinced that they would shine like stars at the resurrection. In the Christian book of Revelation those who had been beheaded for their testimony to Jesus are raised first to enjoy the thousand-year reign before the general resurrection. "Over these the second death has no power" (Rev 20:6). It is the second death, and the prospect of the lake of fire, that is to be feared. The first death has lost its sting. Conversely, in the words of St. Paul, "if for this life only we have hoped . . . we are of all people most to be pitied" (1 Cor 15:19).

THE NEED FOR DEMYTHOLOGIZING

The steadfastness of the martyrs, Jewish or Christian, in the face of death remains admirable two millennia later. But the faith on which that steadfastness was based presents more problems in the modern world. These problems have troubled Christians more than Jews, since in Judaism obedience to the law is central, rather than faith. Not surprisingly, the problems have surfaced especially in the study of the New Testament. Rudolf Bultmann saw the problem clearly:

> The whole conception of the world which is presupposed in the preaching of Jesus as in the New Testament generally is mythological; i.e. the conception of the world as being structured in three stories, heaven, earth and hell; the conception of the intervention of supernatural powers in the course of events; the conception of miracles, especially the conception of the intervention of supernatural powers in the inner life of the soul, the conception that men can be tempted and corrupted by the devil and possessed by evil spirits. This conception of the world we call mythological because it is different from the conception of the world which has been formed and developed by science since its inception in ancient Greece and which has been accepted by all modern men.[14]

What Bultmann called the mythological worldview is essentially the worldview of apocalypticism. Bultmann fully accepted the arguments of Schweitzer and Weiss that Jesus was an apocalyptic prophet. He cannot then be accused of "the agonized attempt to save Jesus from apocalypticism." But he argued that the message of Jesus—and this would be true of all the apocalyptic writings—can only be appropriated in the modern world if it is demythologized. Bultmann did this by reinterpreting the text in terms of the existentialist philosophy of Heidegger. He did not simply discard the apocalyptic imagery but understood it as the objectification of subjective feelings and convictions. The existentialist philosophy on which he relied now seems passé. In any case, it was too individualistic to do justice to apocalyptic literature, with its central concerns for political and cosmic justice. But the process of demythologization, it seems to me, does not necessarily entail existentialist philosophy. Like the most religious literature from antiquity, the apocalypses embody a view of the world based on assumptions about cosmology and history that are no longer tenable. Some kind of hermeneutic, or translation in light of modern assumptions, is necessary if these texts are to be meaningful at all.

One common way of dealing with this problem is to focus on the ethical aspects of the message and ignore the mythological wrappings in which it is presented. This strategy has been especially popular in connection with the figure of Jesus. Two hundred years ago, Thomas Jefferson offered a selection of those sayings of Jesus that he judged to be of enduring value. Much of the work associated with the Jesus Seminar seems to tend in the same direction, by attempting to distinguish between the enlightened and enduring teaching of Jesus and the apocalyptic trappings introduced, supposedly, by his followers. In some respects, such a distinction is easy enough to make. The Gospel of Matthew uses an apocalyptic judgment scene, where the Son of Man sits on his throne of glory, surrounded by his angels, to single out some essential features of Christian ethics. The judgment is based on what people have done to "the least of the brethren," on the grounds that it was done also to Christ. This ethical message is logically independent of the judgment scene. Similar teachings are presented elsewhere in the Gospels in other contexts. Much of them can already be found in the legal and sapiential traditions of Israel and the Ancient Near East. But many ethicists would dispute whether an ethical message can be separated so easily from the narrative and symbolic context in which it is embedded. Does not the judgment scene alter the message, if only by adding a sense of urgency that is not found in sapiential or legal texts? The meaning of the judgment scene in Matthew cannot be entirely reduced to the maxim that we should do unto others as we would have others do unto us. It also entails a claim that such an ethic will ultimately be vindicated by whatever means. It is, I think, impossible to argue that any apocalyptic judgment scene is a reliable prediction of the future in its details, if only because of the enormous variety we find in such scenes. But it is, I think, possible to demythologize such scenes so that they are still held to affirm some conviction about ultimate reality, even if it is only seen through a glass darkly and expressed in myths and symbols that attempt to articulate hopes and beliefs that lie beyond the clear grasp of knowledge.

CONCLUSION

The legacy of apocalypticism is a complex one. More than most of the biblical corpus, the apocalyptic texts present problems of intelligibility, because they are woven of allusions to ancient myths, some of which are only partly known to us. Sometimes they offer specific predictions that clearly failed. Even their more general hope for a comprehensive judgment and the coming of a just kingdom of God is by its nature unrealizable within the bounds of history as we know it. In every century since antiquity, such hopes have led some people astray. Worse, apocalypticism fosters a moral dualism that tends to demonize one's opponents and breed intolerance.

Nonetheless, this literature has also displayed extraordinary vitality through the ages. It has been largely immune to disconfirmation. Predicted "ends" have come and gone, but apocalyptic hope persists. Persistence is no guarantee of truth, but it should give us pause if we are minded to relegate apocalypticism to a lunatic fringe of Western society. Why is it that this literature continues to speak powerfully to some people? The reason, surely, is that it articulates in a powerful way a sense of dissatisfaction with this world and keeps alive the hope, however unrealistic it may seem, of a world free from sin and death. Inevitably, this literature appeals especially to those who are alienated in some way from the world around them, whether by poverty and oppression or by more subtle factors such as the sense that their values are not respected, even if they enjoy material comfort. The Heaven's Gate cult was no doubt an extreme example, but it was typically apocalyptic in some ways. One of the members explained the willingness of the group to end their lives in this world in the hope of being raised up to "the level higher than human" by the sad and simple statement: "There is nothing left for us here." Apocalypticism has always appealed most powerfully to such people, and much less so to "those who are at ease in Zion." But then the canon of Scripture is not a single coherent theological document, but a collection of resources that may be helpful to different people on different occasions. As Qoheleth might have said, there is a time for rational wisdom and a time for apocalyptic fantasy. The canon would be poorer if it were limited to whatever is universally valid.

The example of Heaven's Gate, however, leads to a final reflection on the paradoxical nature of apocalyptic hope. As I have noted already, such hopes often seem immune to disconfirmation. Early Christians did not disband when the Second Coming was delayed indefinitely. Daniel was accepted as Scripture even though the end did not come within the three and a half years predicted. The Millerites survived their initial disappointment to give rise to a flourishing Adventist movement. In all these cases, apocalyptic hope continued to nourish people in the face of disappointment. These hopes lead to disaster when people think that the time of fulfillment has come. The community at Qumran, which had long entertained dreams of a final battle of the Sons of Light against the Sons of Darkness but preached pacifism until the "Day of Wrath" should come, seems to have perished at the hand of the Roman army. Rabbi Akiba prematurely hailed Bar Kochba as messiah and was one of many who died at Roman hands in the following years. Numerous other examples can be cited, down to the Native Americans at Wounded Knee and the more recent suicides of the Heaven's Gate cult. Apocalyptic hopes can sustain life when they are anchored in the uncertain future. When they are thought to reflect present realities, they can be disastrous. Ultimately, such hopes must always be tempered by the realization that it is not given to mortals to know the day or the hour.

PART FIVE

CHRISTIAN ADAPTATIONS
OF JEWISH TRADITIONS

CHAPTER 14

JESUS AND
THE MESSIAHS OF ISRAEL

In an article published in 1992, in the Festschrift for David Flusser, Martin Hengel discussed the messianic consciousness of Jesus in the context of Jewish messianic ideas at the turn of the era.[1] In the course of his argument, Hengel gave a rapid overview of Jewish messianic expectations that were current at the time.[2] This article, however, was written before the full corpus of the Dead Sea Scrolls became generally available at the end of 1991. The newly released Scrolls contain several items of importance for the subject of messianism.[3] The new evidence lends remarkable support to one feature of Hengel's presentation, but requires qualifications on some other points. It does not resolve any of the long-standing debates about Jesus of Nazareth, but it should at least help sharpen some of the questions.

A FIXED CONCEPT OF MESSIAH?

Hengel begins his discussion of the *religionsgeschichtliche* problem by repudiating the overly synthesized concept of the Jewish messiah that was taken for granted a century ago and can still be found occasionally in recent handbooks.[4] This unitary concept involved an ahistorical synthesis of ideas found in the late apocalypses of *4 Ezra* and *2 Baruch* and in rabbinic writings, which was then retrojected into the period before 70 C.E. Hengel joined a chorus of modern scholars in rejecting this synthetic approach.[5] Messianic references in the Pseudepigrapha are sparse.[6] There is no evidence of messianism at the time of the Maccabean revolt, and indeed messianic expectations seem to have been dormant throughout much of the Second Temple period.[7] When we find a resurgence of messianism in the Dead Sea Scrolls, we find not just one messiah but, in the classic phrase of 1QS 9:11, the expectation of "a prophet, and the messiahs of Aaron and Israel."

The variety of messianic figures in the Scrolls has been interpreted in various ways. Morton Smith saw "an unreconciled diversity, within single groups, or opinions which are nevertheless considered important, at least by many members of the groups concerned." He concluded that eschatology was "a comparatively arbitrary and individual matter . . . about which the opinions of different members might, and did, differ quite widely."[8] Recently Lawrence Schiffman summed up the situation by finding that "a variety of motifs and beliefs are distributed throughout many different texts in what may appear to be random fashion."[9] He allows two possible explanations: multiple approaches within the group, or gradual evolution over time. In fact, as Schiffman recognizes, while it is possible and even likely that the ideas of the group evolved over time, no attempt to reconstruct the development has been persuasive. Smith was certainly right that the community was not organized on the basis of shared messianic beliefs, but it seems to me that the diversity and randomness of the messianic ideas has been exaggerated. The major Rule books—the Community Rule, the Messianic Rule (1QSa), and the Damascus Document (CD)—are all plausibly understood to refer to two messiahs, and this structure is also supported by the Florilegium (4Q174) and the Testimonia (4Q175).[10] There seems to be some consistency (though surely not a requirement of orthodoxy) in the core sectarian documents. The expectation of a priestly messiah at Qumran was rooted in the priestly ideology of the sect. It does not appear to have been widely shared by other Jews of the time.[11] It is, in any case, only of marginal relevance to the messianic claims of Jesus of Nazareth. Jesus was not a priest, and no one could have identified him as the Messiah of Aaron, as understood in the Scrolls. The fact that a priestly messiah was expected in some circles, however, does not mean that the concept of the royal, Davidic, messiah was fluid or variable.

Here again the Qumran evidence exhibits more coherence than scholars like Smith and Schiffman have been disposed to recognize. References to the Davidic or royal messiah depend on a small number of biblical texts, of which the most influential are Isaiah 11 and Numbers 24.[12] Both of these texts cast the future king in a violent role. According to Isaiah, "He will strike the earth with the rod of his mouth and with the breath of his lips he shall kill the wicked" (Isa 11:4). The star and scepter of Numbers 24 are expected to crush the skulls of the Moabites and Shethites.[13] While some of the messianic passages in the Scrolls only say that the messiah will come and do not elaborate his role, several depict him as a militant figure. The most explicit passage is found in the blessing of "the Prince of the Congregation" in 1QSb, where the Prince is called upon "to dispense justice with [equity to the oppressed] of the land" (Isa 11:4a): "[May you smite the peoples] with the might of your hand and ravage the earth with your scepter; may you bring death to the ungodly with the breath of your lips! [Isa 11:4b] . . . and everlasting might, the spirit of knowledge and of the fear of God [Isa 11:2]; may righteousness be the girdle [of your loins] and may your reins be girded [with faithfulness]" (Isa 11:5). The passage goes on to compare the Prince to a young bull with horns of iron and hooves of bronze, and (probably) to a lion (cf. Gen 49:9). Isaiah 11 is also cited in a militant context in 4Q285 (probably part of the War Rule) and 4QpIs[a]. Balaam's oracle from Numbers 24 is cited in

CD 7:19: "The scepter is the Prince of the whole congregation, and when he comes he shall smite all the children of Sheth." The same oracle is cited in the War Rule (1QM 11:6-7) and in the Testimonia. It should be noted that both Isaiah 11 and Numbers 24 are applied to the "Prince of the congregation," which is a messianic title in the Scrolls. Both these texts are also cited in circles unrelated to Qumran. Psalms of Solomon 17:21-25 asks God to "raise up for them their king, the son of David, . . . to purge Jerusalem from gentiles . . . in wisdom and righteousness to drive out the sinners from the inheritance; to smash the arrogance of sinners like a potter's jar; to shatter all their substance with an iron rod, to destroy the unlawful nations with the word of his mouth." The "word of his mouth" reflects the LXX translation of Isa 11:4. The iron rod and potter's jar are derived from another classic messianic text, Psalm 2 (cf. Ps 2:9). The messianic interpretation of Num 24:17 is found also in Greek-speaking Judaism. The LXX translated "scepter" as "man," and Philo interprets this "man" as a warrior who, leading his host to war, will destroy great and populous nations.[14] Most famously, it was applied to the militant revolutionary Bar Kokhba by Rabbi Akiba (*y. Ta'anit* 68d). Unlike the expectation of a priestly messiah, the notion of a warrior messiah was not peculiar to sectarian circles. This is not to suggest that there was any messianic dogma in Judaism at the turn of the era, to which *everyone* necessarily subscribed. But the concept of a royal messiah was more widespread than any other, and this figure was consistently expected to drive out the Gentiles by force, even if that force had a miraculous quality (e.g., the breath of his lips). The *degree* of messianic expectation probably fluctuated considerably in the first century. There does not, however, appear to have been much variation in the *character* of royal messiah that was expected.[15]

Two other controverted issues relating to the alleged fluidity of messianic concepts require comment: the question of a suffering messiah and the relation between the Davidic messiah and the Danielic "Son of Man."

A SUFFERING MESSIAH?

In his 1992 essay, Hengel regarded the view that there was no suffering messiah in pre-Christian Judaism as "questionable."[16] In this he relied on the report published by J. Starcky in 1963, that an Aramaic text in his lot "seems to us to evoke a suffering messiah, in the perspective opened up by the Servant poems."[17] This text, 4Q541 or 4QAaronA, was finally published by Emile Puech in 1992.[18] Even though the editor concurred with Starcky that this text evokes the Servant of Deutero-Isaiah,[19] it lends no support in fact to the idea of a suffering messiah. The figure described in the text is not actually called a messiah, but he does appear to be an ideal figure, and he can plausibly be correlated with the messiah of Aaron.[20] He is said to atone for all the children of his generation and is therefore presumably a priest, who effects atonement by offering sacrifice. Two aspects of this text have been taken to suggest the suffering servant. First, "his light will be kindled in all the corners of the earth, and it will shine on the darkness." Deutero-Isaiah describes the servant of the Lord as "a light to the nations" in Isa 42:6 and 49:6. This is not said in Isaiah 53. While modern scholarship has pulled out four passages in Deutero-Isaiah and labeled them "servant songs" (42:1-4; 49:1-7; 50:4-9, and 52:13—53:12), these passages were not separated out from their context or associated with each other in antiquity.[21] In view of the atomistic exegesis of Scripture practiced at Qumran, it is not legitimate to assume that an allusion to Isaiah 42 or 49 entails an allusion to Isaiah 53. Being a light to the nations does not necessarily entail suffering at all. There is no question of vicarious suffering or death in 4Q541. The figure described in this text is said to be subjected to lies and slander, but this is suffering of a very different order from that envisaged in Isaiah 53, where the servant is "led like a lamb to the slaughter" (v. 7) and "cut off from the land of the living" (v. 8). Another, very obscure, fragment of 4Q541 contains a phrase that Puech interprets as "[let] not the nail approach him," implying a reference to crucifixion.[22] Even if this is correct, which is by no means certain, the text does not in any case imply that a messianic figure will be crucified, and it entails no allusion to Isaiah 53.[23] The figure in question is more likely to be modeled on the Teacher of Righteousness, who also encountered opposition in his teaching, than on the suffering servant.[24]

When the Scrolls became generally available in fall 1991 there was also a short-lived controversy about a fragment of 4Q285, which was taken to say that certain people "will kill the Prince of the Congregation, the Bran[ch of David]."[25] Analysis of the text soon revealed that the passage could be translated more plausibly as "the Prince of the Congregation, the Bran[ch of David] will kill him."[26] The fragment alludes to Isaiah 11, and the reference to the messiah must be understood in this context. This passage then, lends support to the usual picture of the militant messiah rather than to a Christlike suffering figure. The Scrolls provide no evidence for a suffering or dying messiah before the time of Jesus of Nazareth.

MESSIAH, SON OF MAN AND SON OF GOD

A more complex issue is raised by the relation between the Davidic messiah and the Danielic "Son of Man." Here there is indeed a confluence of traditions that were originally distinct.[27] The Similitudes of Enoch (*1 Enoch* 48:10; 52:4) uses the word "messiah," anointed one, with reference to the figure elsewhere called "that Son of Man" or "the Righteous One."[28] The reference in 48:10, which has the king and the mighty fall prostrate before the Lord of Spirits and his anointed, may be an allusion to Psalm 2. The Son of Man acts as judge, which is also a royal function. But the assimilation of the Son of Man to the Davidic messiah in the Similitudes is quite limited. The Son of Man does not appear on earth, and he is not portrayed as the fulfillment of other messianic prophecies. The fusion of traditions is more advanced in *4 Ezra* 13. Here Ezra sees a figure rising out of the sea and flying with the clouds, a clear allusion to Daniel 7.[29] But then he takes his stand on a mountain and slays those who come against him by emitting "from his mouth as it were a stream of fire, and from his lips a flaming breath" (cf. Isa 11:4). Further, in the interpretation of the vision we read that "he will stand on the top of Mount Zion . . . and he, my son, will reprove the assembled nations for their ungodliness" (13:35, 35; cf. Psalm 2). The "man from the sea" in *4 Ezra* 13 functions as the Davidic messiah typically functions in Jewish literature of this era. He slays the Gentiles with the breath of his lips and restores Israel on Mt. Zion. The Davidic lineage of this figure is probably implied in the appellation "my son" (cf. 2 Samuel 7; Psalm 2).[30] The preceding chapter (*4 Ezra* 12) explicitly identifies the messiah as the one "whom the Most High has kept until the end of days, who will arise from the posterity of David" (v. 32). *4 Ezra* modifies the traditional notion of the messiah primarily by emphasizing his mysterious origins: despite his Davidic descent, he is "revealed" at the end of days. The Danielic imagery suggests a transcendent, supernatural origin, which also had some basis in the royal Psalms of the Hebrew Bible (Psalms 2, 45, 110).

The Dead Sea Scrolls are conspicuously lacking in references to Daniel 7 and to the figure of the "Son of Man."[31] There is, however, one text which may possibly offer an interpretation of this figure: the controversial 4Q246 or Son of God text.[32] This text refers to a figure who is called "Son of God" and "Son of Most High." Scholarly opinion is divided as to whether he is a positive, most probably messianic, figure,[33] or a negative figure, such as a Seleucid king.[34] The editor, Emile Puech, insists that both interpretations are possible.[35] The argument that the figure is negative rests on a construal of the logical progression of the text. The reference to the "Son of God" is followed by a situation where "people will trample on people and city on city, until the people of God arises [or: until he raises up the people of God]." There is a lacuna before the word "until" that strengthens the impression that this is a point of transition in the text. Those who read the text on the assumption that events are reported in chronological sequence infer that the "Son of God" belongs to the time of distress, and so must be a negative, evil figure. This inference is unsafe for two reasons. First, it is quite typical of apocalyptic literature that the same events are repeated several times in different terms. Apocalypses such as Daniel, the Similitudes of Enoch, *4 Ezra*, *2 Baruch*, and Revelation all juxtapose multiple visions that go over the same ground with different imagery. Within the single chapter of Daniel 7, the same events are presented first in the form of a vision, then in two successive interpretations, so that the kingdom is given, in turn, to the "one like a son of man," to the holy ones of the Most High, and finally to the people of the Holy Ones. I have argued elsewhere that 4Q246 should be read in this way, so that the coming of the "Son of God" parallels the rise of the people of God rather than precedes it.[36] It is true that the repetitions in Daniel 7 are occasioned by the process of interpretation, and this is not overtly the case in 4Q246.[37] The Qumran text does, however, refer to a vision in col. 1, and part of the difficulty of reading it is that we cannot be sure of its precise literary genre. We shall consider shortly the reasons for relating this text to Daniel 7. If these are accepted, the repetitions in Daniel 7 are highly relevant to our understanding of 4Q246. Even if the parallel with Daniel 7 is not accepted, however, a second consideration should warn against the simple sequential understanding of the text. The appearance of a savior figure does not inevitably mean that the time of strife is over. In Daniel 12:1 the rise of Michael is followed by "a time of anguish, such as has never occurred since nations first came into existence." In *4 Ezra* 13, the apparition of the man from the sea is followed by the gathering of an innumerable multitude to make war on him. We should note that the statement about the people of God is ambiguous. It can be read either as "the people of God will arise (*y'qûm*)" or as "he will raise up the people of God (*y'qîm*)." If the latter reading is correct, the nearest antecedent is the one who will be called "Son of God," although it is certainly also possible that God is the subject. It is possible then that the text envisages an interval of warfare between the apparition of the deliverer and the actual deliverance. So, while the order of the text may suggest prima facie that the figure who is called "Son of God" belongs to the era of wickedness, this is not necessarily the case.

Two other factors strongly suggest that the one who is called "Son of God" is accepted as a positive figure in this text. First, the title is never disputed, and no judgment is passed on this figure after the people of God arise. This would be truly extraordinary if the figure in question were an imposter. In contrast the hybristic pretensions of Antiochus Epiphanes in Daniel 8 and 11 lead directly and very explicitly to his downfall.[38] Second, by far the closest parallel to the titles in question is explicitly messianic. In Luke 1:32 the angel Gabriel tells Mary that her child "will be great, and will be called the son of the Most High, and the Lord God will give to him the throne of his ancestor David. He will reign over the house of Jacob forever, and of his kingdom there will be no end." In 1:35 he adds: "He will be called the Son of God." The Greek titles "son of the most High" and "Son of God" correspond exactly to the Aramaic fragment from Qumran. (Note also the reference in both texts to an everlasting kingdom.) The fact that these parallels are found in the New Testament does not lessen their relevance to the cultural context of the Qumran text.[39] Despite the claim of Puech that these honorific titles could apply "to any other king whatever," neither he nor anyone else has been able to adduce a parallel of comparable precision from any other source.[40] The use of these titles for a messianic king had a clear warrant in biblical texts such as 2 Samuel 7 and Psalm 2 and is also supported by the Florilegium (4Q 174:11–12), which interprets 2 Sam 7:12-14 ("I will be a father to him and he will be a son to me") as referring to the branch of David at the end of days.[41]

I have elsewhere suggested tentatively that the "Son of God" figure may be a reinterpretation of the "one like a son of man" in Daniel 7.[42] While this suggestion cannot be proven and must remain tentative, it is not gratuitous or without any foundation.[43] There are clear allusions to Daniel in col. 2, line 5 ("its/his kingdom is an everlasting sovereignty"; cf. Dan 4:31; 7:14). Another possible reference to Daniel 7 is the use of the word *dwš*, trample, at col. 2, line 3. The same verb is used with reference to the fourth beast in Daniel 7. Moreover, the setting of the document, where someone falls before a throne and interprets a vision, is reminiscent of Daniel. There is, then, reason to consider the possibility that the Son of God text is a reinterpretation of Daniel 7, and that the "Son of God" figure is related to the people of God as the "one like a son of man" is related to the people of the holy ones in Daniel 7. The suggestion remains inconclusive, however, since the Qumran text is clearly not a systematic interpretation of Daniel 7.

If the "Son of God" text is read as messianic, it fits nicely with everything we have seen about the Davidic/royal messiah in the Scrolls. He functions as a warrior to subdue the Gentiles: God will make war on his behalf and cast peoples down before him. If the hypothesis is entertained that this figure also corresponds to the Danielic Son of Man, then the fusion of traditions would seem to be similar to what we have found in *4 Ezra*. The divine origin of the figure is emphasized, but he functions on earth as a militant messiah, in a way that owes more to the traditional understanding of the royal messiah than to the imagery of Daniel.

Despite its admitted variety, the evidence of the Scrolls provides a persistent profile of the Davidic/royal messiah. The most striking aspect of this profile is the militancy it involved. It was a primary requirement of the messiah that he overcome the Gentile enemies of Israel. Precisely here lies the anomaly of the messianic claims of Jesus of Nazareth, as Albert Schweitzer already saw.[44] There is little evidence of a militant Jesus in the Gospels.[45] Yet it is undeniable that he was crucified as King of the Jews and that the title Christ, Messiah, was already established as a virtual personal name by the time of St. Paul.

A PROPHETIC MESSIAH?

In his 1992 article, Hengel wrote that no Old Testament text could be more aptly applied to Jesus than Isa 61:1f., the text that Luke chooses for Jesus' inaugural sermon at Nazareth (Luke 4:17-19).[46] Precisely this passage from Isaiah is featured in the text from Qumran that may throw the most light on the messianism of Jesus of Nazareth. This is the so-called Messianic Apocalypse, 4Q521, of which the longest fragment begins "heaven and earth will obey his messiah."[47] This passage is heavily dependent on Psalm 146, but departs from the psalm at one significant point. The psalm refers to the Lord "who made heaven and earth, the sea and all that is in them," but it has no mention of a messiah. The purpose of this innovation is not immediately clear, as the Qumran text goes on to say that God will release captives, give sight to the blind, etc., just as God does in the psalm. Again, at 4Q521:12, it is God who will heal the wounded, give life to the dead, and preach good news to the poor. God is normally the one who raises the dead in Jewish tradition (e.g., in the Eighteen Benedictions), but it is surprising to find God as the subject of preaching good news. This is normally the work of a herald or messenger.

This passage in 4Q521 is based on Isa 61:1: "The spirit of the Lord God is upon me, because the Lord has anointed me; he has sent me to preach good news to the poor, to bind up the brokenhearted, to proclaim liberty to the captives and release to the prisoners; to proclaim the year of the Lord's favor and the day of vengeance of our God." In Isaiah, the speaker is a prophet; there is nothing to indicate that this passage is any different from the rest of the book of Isaiah in this respect.[48] He also claims to be anointed, a *mēšíaḥ.* While the anointing of prophets is unusual in the Hebrew Bible,[49] prophets are called "anointed ones" in the Dead Sea Scrolls.[50] In 11QMelchizedek, the herald who preaches good news is identified as "the anointed of the spirit."[51] It seems likely that God also acts through an agent in 4Q521, and this would explain the introduction of the "messiah" in the first line of the fragment.[52] In fact, some of the works attributed to God in 4Q521 are called "the works of the messiah" in Matt 11:2.

Puech assumes that the messiah whom heaven and earth obey is the kingly messiah, but this is mere assumption, unsupported by any indication in the text.[53] If our suggestion that the "messiah" is God's agent later in the passage is correct, then the messiah is more likely to be an eschatological prophet in the manner of Elijah. The royal messiah is never said to raise the dead. Elijah was credited with raising the dead during his historical career (1 Kings 17) and is sometimes cast as the one who will raise the dead in rabbinic literature.[54] Moreover, the statement that "heaven and earth will obey his messiah" makes excellent sense if the anointed one is Elijah redivivus. Ben Sira says of Elijah: "By the word of the Lord he shut up the heavens and also three times brought down fire" (Sir 48:3). The two olive trees in Revelation 11, which have authority to shut up the sky so that no rain may fall and to turn the waters into blood, are usually identified as Elijah and Moses.[55]

On this reading, 4Q521 provides a rare account of the role of the messianic prophet.[56] It is of immediate relevance to the messianic claims of Jesus of Nazareth. In a passage that derives from the Sayings Source, Q, Jesus responds to the question of the Baptist: "Go and tell John what you hear and see: the blind receive their sight, the lame walk, the lepers are cleansed, the deaf hear, the dead are raised, and the poor have good news brought to them" (Matt 11:2-5; Luke 7:22). Three items on this list are shared by 4Q521: giving sight to the blind, raising the dead, and preaching to the poor.[57] The parallel is all the more striking as both the Qumran and NT texts include the raising of the dead, which was not mentioned in Isaiah 61. It is precisely this element that suggests the role of Elijah redivivus. The Gospels are careful to undo this impression and assign the role of Elijah to the Baptist (Matt 11:10; Luke 7:27). There are, nonetheless, indications in the Gospel record that some people entertained the possibility that Jesus might be Elijah. So in Mark 6:14-15 various people identify Jesus to Herod as John raised from the dead, Elijah, or "a prophet," and again in Mark 8:27 Jesus' question, "who do people say that I am?" receives the answer, "John the Baptist, and others, Elijah, and still others, one of the prophets" (cf. also Mark 6:4; John 6:14).

It is far easier to see how Jesus might have been regarded as an anointed (that is, divinely commissioned) prophet than as a messianic king.[58] The problem is why someone who appeared and acted as a prophet should be crucified as King of the Jews and venerated as the Davidic messiah after his death.[59] Kingship and prophecy were not incompatible, and David himself was sometimes regarded as a prophet, but it does not follow that someone would be regarded as Davidic messiah because he was a prophet.[60] Indeed, Donald Juel has argued with some cogency that "when such alleged nonroyal messianic tradition is used to interpret Mark, however, the passion narrative makes no sense."[61]

There is indeed a gap between the nonmilitant, nonroyal career of Jesus as reported in the Gospels and his death and subsequent veneration as king-messiah, and it may not be possible to bridge it. Nonetheless, a few suggestions may be offered as to how a prophet came to be thought of as a king. Preaching that the kingdom of God was at hand was surely a factor in this transition. The Romans, at least, were not concerned with fine distinctions between prophets who preached about a kingdom and pretenders who aspired to rule; some Jews may also have had difficulty in maintaining the distinction. Both prophets and pretenders were threats to the Roman order and were dispatched summarily. Josephus tells of a number of both royal pretenders and prophetic figures who led abortive movements in the first century C.E.[62] He admits that the prophets were different from militant revolutionaries such as the *sicarii* but argued that they had the same detrimental effect on the peace of the city: "Deceivers and imposters, under the pretence of divine inspiration fostering revolutionary changes, they persuaded the multitude to act like madmen, and led them out into the desert under the belief that God would there give them tokens of deliverance."[63] He repeatedly associates the prophets with the violent revolutionaries in such a way as to blur the distinction between them.[64] In the case of the Egyptian prophet, the categories are blurred further. This figure allegedly rallied a crowd of about thirty thousand people and led them to the Mount of Olives. In his *Jewish War,* Josephus claims that the intention was to force an entry into Jerusalem, so that the Egyptian could become ruler of the citizens. In the *Jewish Antiquities,* however, he says that the Egyptian expected the walls of Jerusalem to fall down at his command.[65] In short, he was a prophet, who expected a sign of deliverance, rather than a practical revolutionary.[66] Josephus may have intentionally exaggerated the militancy of the Egyptian in *Jewish War*. But the disparity of the accounts may also reflect genuine uncertainty about the objectives and motives of a charismatic figure with a multitude of followers. If Jesus actually performed the triumphal entry into Jerusalem as reported in the Gospels, similar confusion might have arisen as to whether he was signifying the imminent coming of the messiah or claiming to be the messiah himself.[67]

Such confusion was not necessarily limited to unsympathetic outsiders. Enthusiastic followers of a prophet might also expect him to personally bring about what he foretold. In the Gospel accounts, Jesus appears reticent about his own claims but unwilling to contradict claims made in his behalf. An intriguing modern parallel is provided by Menahem Schneerson, the Lubavitcher rebbe of Crown Heights, New York, who died in 1994.[68] Schneerson taught as prophecy that the *moshiach* was on his way,[69] but many of his followers believed that he himself was the messiah. Schneerson made no such claim, but he did little to discourage the belief. There is, of course, no necessary analogy between Jesus and either Schneerson or Josephus's Egyptian, but they offer some possibilities for imagining how a figure who was primarily a prophet came to be regarded as the messianic king. If the contemporaries of Schneerson are unable to know the mind of the rebbe, or be sure as to whether he thought himself to be the messiah, we should hardly be surprised that we are unable to establish the self-identity of Jesus.

We should not be surprised that most Jews of the time did not recognize Jesus as the Davidic messiah. He simply did not fit the expectations that were most widely associated with that role. But his followers were convinced that he was God's anointed. When he patently did not drive out the Gentiles or restore the kingdom of Israel, they found other ways of affirming his messianic status. One such way was to identify him with the Danielic Son of Man who would come as judge on the clouds of heaven. Whether Jesus had spoken of such a Son of Man, or whether he had identified himself with him, is too complex an issue to be broached here.[70] It must suffice to say that the notion that Jesus would come on the clouds of heaven could hardly have made much sense to his followers before his death, when he was present with them on earth. After his death, however, the Son of Man paradigm provided a way of imagining how Jesus could come again and fulfill messianic prophecies that were conspicuously unfulfilled in his lifetime. The book of the New Testament where Jesus most fully fulfills the traditional role of the royal messiah is the book of Revelation. There he comes from heaven on a white horse, wearing a robe dipped in blood. "From his mouth comes a sharp sword with which to strike down the nations, and he will rule them with a rod of iron" (Rev 19:15). The traditional picture of the Davidic messiah is qualified here, as it is in the roughly contemporary *4 Ezra* 13.[71] Jesus comes from heaven, as the figure in *4 Ezra* comes from the sea. But both are warrior messiahs. Jesus of Nazareth shed no blood in Jerusalem as the Davidic messiah was expected to do. In Revelation, however, the traditional paradigms prevail over anything that could be construed as historical memory in shaping the portrayal of Jesus as messiah of Israel.

CHAPTER 15

JEWISH MONOTHEISM
AND CHRISTIAN THEOLOGY

"In the beginning was the Word" reads the opening verse of the Gospel of John, "and the Word was with God, and the Word was God." In the context of the Gospel, it is clear that the Word is identified with Jesus of Nazareth, the charismatic preacher who had been crucified by the Romans some sixty years before the Gospel was written. John's Gospel is exceptional in the New Testament for the explicitness of its claim that Jesus was divine. Nonetheless, it is both the culmination of a trend within Judaism and a good indicator of the course Christian theology would take in the following centuries. This development would accentuate the gap between emerging Christianity and Judaism.

By nearly all accounts, by the end of the first century C.E. strict monotheism had long been one of the pillars of Judaism.[1] John takes pains to show how unacceptable Jesus' claim of divinity was to Jews. "For this reason the Jews were seeking all the more to kill him, because he was not only breaking the Sabbath, but was also calling God his own Father, thereby making himself equal to God" (John 5:18). This Gospel is traditionally attributed to one of the Jewish disciples of Jesus. Even though that attribution is problematic, the Christian movement had unquestionably originated in the heart of Judaism little more than half a century earlier. Yet, in the opinion of one modern scholar, John's version of a divine Jesus is so elevated that observant Jews at the beginning of the first century C.E.—including the first apostles—could not have believed in such a figure.[2] The question is, How was it possible for first-century C.E. Jews to accept this man Jesus as the preexistent Son of God and still believe, as they surely did, that they were not violating traditional Jewish monotheism? How did this development come about?

WAS JUDAISM MONOTHEISTIC?

Jewish monotheism, which gave birth to the Christian movement, was not as clear cut and simple as is generally believed. Several kinds of quasi-divine figures appear in Jewish texts from the Hellenistic period that seem to call for some qualification of the idea of monotheism. We will consider three categories of such figures—angels or demigods, exalted human beings, and the more abstract figures of Wisdom and the Word (Logos).[3]

Angelic Figures

The latest book of the Hebrew Bible contains a passage that had great significance for early Christians. In the book of Daniel, the visionary sees that "thrones were set in place and an Ancient One took his throne, his clothing was white as snow, and the hair of his head like pure wool; his throne was fiery flames, and its wheels were burning fire" (Dan 7:9). The Ancient One is the God of Israel, even though some of his features, like his white hair, are reminiscent of the ancient Canaanite god El. The ancient rabbis were troubled by the plural term "thrones," which indicates that at least one other figure will be enthroned. Indeed, a second figure makes his entrance a few verses later:

> I saw one like a son of man
>   coming with the clouds of heaven.
> And he came to the Ancient one
>   and was presented before him.
> To him was given dominion
>   and glory and kingship,
> that all peoples, nations and languages
>   should serve him.
> His dominion is an everlasting dominion
>   that shall not pass away,
> and his kingship is one
>   that shall never be destroyed. (Dan 7:13-14)

Monotheistic theologians commonly interpret the "one like a son of man" as a symbol for Israel.[4] The figure does indeed represent Israel in some sense, but the manner in which he is presented cannot be brushed aside so lightly.[5] Elsewhere in the Hebrew Bible, a figure riding on the clouds is always the Lord, the God of Israel.[6] Daniel's imagery has its background in ancient Canaanite mythology, in which the god Ba'al rides the clouds and is distinct from the venerable, white-bearded El. In Daniel's vision, the second heavenly figure, the rider on the clouds, is most plausibly identified as the archangel Michael, who is introduced as "the prince of Israel" later in the book (Dan 10:13). Canaanite mythology is thus transformed; it is not entirely dead.[7] In later Jewish tradition, this text from Daniel proved controversial because it provided a basis for the idea that there are "two powers in heaven."[8] The rabbis rejected this idea as heretical, but nonetheless it was evidently held by some Jews—as well as by Christians.

The "one like a son of man" in Daniel is what we might call a super-angel. This kind of figure appears quite regularly in Jewish texts around the turn of the era.[9] Consider the following passage from Psalm 82 in the fragmentary Melchizedek scroll from Qumran Cave 11: "*Elohim* [God] has taken his place in the divine council; in the midst of the gods he holds judgment." The Scroll then provides a gloss on the quoted passage: "Its interpretation concerns Belial and the spirits of his lot [who] rebelled by turning away from the precepts of God . . . and Melchizedek will avenge the vengeance of the judgments of God."[10] The *elohim* who rises for judgment in the divine council is here identified as Melchizedek (the identification is probably even more explicit in a later, fragmentary, passage). Another text, the Testament of Amram, tells us that Melchizedek was one of the names for an angel who was also known as Michael and the Prince of Light; this good angel was paired with the evil angel Melchiresha, also known as Belial or the Prince of Darkness.[11] Both Michael and the Prince of Light appear in other Qumran scrolls, most notably the War Scroll. What is striking about Melchizedek in the Cave 11 text is that he is identified as an *elohim*, a god. But, in fact, this usage is not exceptional. The great Jewish scholar Yigael Yadin pointed out many years ago that the beings we call angels are called *elim*, gods, in the War Scroll,[12] and the same usage can be found in the Songs of Sabbath Sacrifice, an early mystical text also found at Qumran.[13]

Given the appearance of such semidivine figures in Jewish texts, the term "monotheism" is not entirely felicitous as a description of Jewish beliefs in this pre-Christian period. Yet it is not entirely inappropriate either. These texts always distinguish clearly between the supreme God and his angelic lieutenant. In the Qumran War Scroll, for example, a passage about the Prince of Light is quickly followed by a question addressed to God: "Which angel or prince can compare with thy succor?" (col. 12). It is also true that these principal angels are not usually worshiped, but the issue of worship is not as straightforward as is sometimes supposed. The "one like a son of man" in Daniel is given dominion and glory and kingship, and all peoples serve him. Whether this constitutes worship would seem to be a matter of definition.

The "one like a son of man" underwent some development in Jewish tradition, quite apart from the adaptation of this imagery in Christianity.[14] In the Similitudes of Enoch,[15] a work of uncertain, but clearly Jewish, origin and probably dating to the first century C.E., the visionary sees "one who had a head of days, and his head was white like wool, and with him there was another whose face had the appearance of a man and his face was full of grace, like one of the holy angels" (*1 Enoch* 46:1). The latter figure is subsequently referred to as "that Son of Man." It is said of this figure that "his name was named" before the sun and the stars. He is hidden with God, only to be revealed at the judgment. Later, in the judgment scene, this figure is, like God, set on a throne of glory, and the kings of the earth are commanded to acknowledge him (*1 Enoch* 60–62). Finally, at the end of the Similitudes, Enoch is lifted aloft into the presence of that Son of Man; he is then greeted by an angel, who tells him, "You are the Son of Man who is born to righteousness" (*1 Enoch* 71:14). Whether this means that Enoch himself is identified with the same Son of Man he had seen in his visions is disputed. The passage can also be translated as "you are a son of man [that is, a human being] who has righteousness." It is also possible that this passage is a later addition to the text, intended to counter the Christian claim that Jesus was the Son of Man by identifying this figure with the Jewish prophet Enoch. In any case, this non-Christian Jewish text provides an intriguing example of the exaltation of a human being to the heavenly realm.

This tradition of the super-angel reached a climax several centuries later, in another Jewish text known as *3 Enoch* or *Sepher Hekalot*.[16] A figure known as Metatron, Prince of the Divine Presence, is "called by the name of the Creator with seventy names . . . [and is] greater than all the princes, more exalted than all the angels, more beloved than all the ministers, more honored than all the hosts and elevated over all potentates in sovereignty, greatness and glory" (*3 Enoch* 4:1). Metatron is given a throne like the throne of glory (*3 Enoch* 10:1) and is even called "the lesser YHWH" (*3 Enoch* 12:5). When Aḥēr, one of the four sages reputed to have ascended to Paradise in the early second century C.E., sees Metatron seated as a king with ministering angels beside him as servants, Aḥēr declares, "There are indeed two powers in heaven!" (*3 Enoch* 16:3). Because of this, we are told, Metatron is dethroned and given sixty lashes of fire.

Metatron's punishment suggests that there was some controversy about his exalted status at the time *3 Enoch* was written. But the tradition that he had a throne in heaven could not be suppressed entirely. Metatron is still identified with Enoch, son of Jared, who was taken up to heaven before the flood (see Gen 5:24). Evidently, Metatron is a later development of the Son of Man figure in the Similitudes of Enoch and has attained an even more exalted rank in the intervening centuries.

Exalted Human Beings

The case of Enoch brings us to a second kind of divine being under the Most High God: the exalted human being. In Daniel 12, the righteous martyrs of the Maccabean era are promised that they will shine like the brightness of the firmament and be like the stars forever and ever. In *1 Enoch* 104, this imagery is clarified: "You will shine like the lights of heaven . . . and the gate of heaven will be opened to you . . . for you will have great joy like the angels of heaven . . . for you will be companions to the host of heaven."

In the idiom of apocalyptic literature, the stars are the angelic host. When the righteous dead become like the stars, they become like the angels; in the Hellenistic world, to become a star was to become a god. We find a reflection of this way of thinking in a Jewish wisdom text attributed to the Greek gnomic poet Phocylides. The author expresses the hope "that the remains of the departed will soon come to the light again out of the earth, and afterwards become gods."[17] This does not mean, of course, that the righteous dead are on a par with the Most High God (or with the Olympian gods) or that worship should be directed toward them (although the dead have been worshiped in many cultures). But it does indicate that the line separating the divine from the human in ancient Judaism was not as absolute as is sometimes supposed.

Some exalted human beings were more important than others. In the second century B.C.E., an Alexandrian Jew named Ezekiel wrote a Greek tragedy about the exodus. In the play, Moses has a dream:

> I dreamt there was on the summit of Mt. Sinai
> a certain great throne extending up to heaven's cleft,
> on which there sat a certain noble man
> wearing a crown and holding a great scepter
> in his left hand. With his right hand
> He beckoned to me, and I stood before the throne.
> He gave me the scepter and told me to sit
> on the great throne. He gave me the royal crown,
> and he himself left the throne.
> I beheld the entire circled earth
> both beneath the earth and above the heaven,
> and a host of stars fell on its knees before me;
> I numbered them all,
> They passed before me like a squadron of soldiers.
> Then seized with fear, I rose from my sleep.[18]

The figure on Mt. Sinai who vacates his throne for Moses can only be God. If Moses sits on God's throne, then he is in some sense conceived of as divine. While the dream is part of a literary work, there can be little doubt that it reflects wider traditions about Moses. These traditions are also apparent in the *Life of Moses* by the first-century C.E. philosopher Philo, also an Alexandrian Jew. In Exod 7:1, God tells Moses: "I have made you a god to Pharaoh." Philo correspondingly writes that "Moses was named god and king of the whole nation."[19] It has been suggested that "god" in this passage is an allegorical equivalent for "king,"[20] but the choice of the term "god" can hardly be incidental. While Philo insisted that "He that is truly God is one," he also recognized other divine entities, such as the Logos, that existed under God.

Another case of qualified divinization concerns the Davidic messiah. The notion that the Davidic king was the son of God is well established in the Hebrew Bible in 2 Sam 7:14 and in Ps 2:7. It was only natural then that the coming messianic king should also be regarded as the Son of God. The Florilegium from Qumran (4Q174) explicitly interprets 2 Sam 7:14 in a future, messianic, sense: "I will be a father to him and he will be a son to me. He is the Branch of David, who will arise . . . at the end of days." A fragmentary Aramaic text (4Q246), popularly known as "The Son of God Text," predicts the coming of a figure who will be called "Son of God" and "Son of the Most High"; this figure is probably the Davidic messiah, though some scholars dispute this interpretation.[21] To say that the king was the son of God, however, does not necessarily imply divinization. Israel, collectively, is called God's son in the book of Exodus and again in Hosea, and the "righteous man" is identified as God's son in the Wisdom of Solomon, a first-century C.E. Jewish text from Alexandria. There are other traditions, however, that suggest a more exalted status for the messianic king.

Rabbi Akiba is said to have explained the plural "thrones" in Dan 7:9 as "one for God, one for David."[22] In the Psalms, traditionally attributed to David, there seems to be a clear scriptural warrant for the enthronement of the messiah: "The Lord said to my Lord, sit at my right hand" (Ps 110:1). In fact, however, the first messianic interpretation of this text is found in the New Testament (Mark 12:35-37; Acts 2:34-36). In the Similitudes of Enoch, the Son of Man figure is also called "messiah," although he does not appear to have an earthly career. Another Jewish apocalypse, *4 Ezra*, written at the end of the first century C.E., interprets Daniel's "son of man" vision in terms of a figure who rises from the sea on a cloud, takes his stand on a mountain, and defeats the Gentiles in the manner of the Davidic messiah. This figure is also called "my son" by God. The Similitudes and *4 Ezra* are witnesses of a tendency to conceive of a quasi-divine messiah in Jewish texts of the first century C.E.

A final example of exalted humanity involves a very fragmentary text from Qumran (4Q491), in which the speaker claims to have "a mighty throne in the congregation of the gods" and to have been "reckoned with the gods (*elim*)."[23] We cannot be sure who the speaker is supposed to be; suggestions have ranged from the Teacher of Righteousness[24] to some later sectarian teacher to the messianic High Priest. It does seem clear, however, that the speaker is not an angel or other heavenly creature but an exalted human being. It is not unusual in hymns from Qumran for the hymnist to claim that he enjoys the fellowship of the heavenly host, but this text seems to claim a higher degree of exaltation. Once again, we find that a human being could be reckoned among the *elim* or gods. Even in a conservative Jewish community like Qumran, such an idea was not taboo.

Wisdom and Logos

Our third category of quasi-divine being or entity is the personification of Wisdom, which was identified with the Greek philosophical concept of Logos (Word or Reason) in the Hellenistic period. According to Prov 8:22, "God created [the female figure Wisdom] at the beginning of his work, the first of his acts of long ago," and she then accompanied him in the creation of the world. In the book of Ben Sira, written in the early second century B.C.E., Wisdom increasingly resembles the Creator: "I came forth from the mouth of the Most High, and covered the earth like a mist. I dwelt in the highest heavens, and my throne was in a pillar of cloud. Alone I compassed the vault of heaven and traversed the depths of the abyss" (Ben Sira 24:3-5). According to the Wisdom of Solomon, written around the turn of the era in Alexandria, Wisdom brought Israel out of Egypt and holds all things together. Ben Sira's statement that Wisdom came forth from the mouth of the Most High already hints at the identification of Wisdom with Word, which is made explicit in the Wisdom of Solomon.

The Word, or Logos, had another set of connotations in Greek philosophy. The Stoics conceived of the Logos as an immanent god—the principle of rationality in the world—and as a kind of world soul. (It can also be called Spirit or Pneuma, although it is understood as a fine material substance.) The Jewish philosopher Philo adapted this concept of the Logos for a Jewish theology that acknowledged a transcendent creator God.[25] For Philo, the Logos is "the divine reason, the ruler and steersman of all" and it stands on the border that separates the Creator from the creature.[26] But this Logos is also said to be a god. In his *Questions on Genesis,* Philo asks: "Why does [Scripture] say, as if of another God, 'In the image of God he made man' and not 'in His own image'? Most excellently and veraciously this oracle was given by God. For nothing mortal can be made in the likeness of the Most High One and father of the universe, but only in that of the second God, who is His Logos." Here Philo unabashedly calls the Logos a "second God," and this is not the only passage in which he gives the title "God" to the Logos,[27] though he also refers to it as an angel or as God's first-born son.

Does Philo then believe in two Gods? He addresses this question explicitly in his treatise *On Dreams* 1.227-229, where he comments on a passage in the Greek Bible that reads, "I am the God who appeared to thee in the place of God" (Gen 31:13). Philo writes:

> And do not fail to mark the language used, but carefully inquire whether there are two Gods; for we read "I am the God that appeared to thee," not "in my place" but "in the place of God," as though it were another's. What then are we to say? He that is truly God is one, but those that are so called by analogy are more than one. Accordingly the holy word in the present instance has indicated Him who truly is God by means of the articles, saying "I am the God," while it omits the article when mentioning him who is so called by analogy, saying "who appeared to thee in the place" not "of the God" but simply "of God."[28]

Philo does not seem to regard the use of "God" as a designation for the Logos as improper,[29] although he clearly distinguishes between the supreme God and the intermediary deity.

So was Judaism monotheistic in the Hellenistic period? The evidence we have reviewed comes from the two areas of Judaism, apocalyptic circles in Palestine, including but not limited to the Dead Sea sect, and the Hellenized Alexandrian Judaism of Philo. Not all Jews shared these ideas and beliefs, but they are, nonetheless, indisputably Jewish.

In this literature, the supremacy of the Most High God is never questioned, but there is considerable room for lesser beings who may be called "gods," *theoi* or *elim.* Moreover, both the authors of the apocalyptic literature and Philo single out one preeminent divine or angelic being under God—a super-angel—called by various names in the apocalyptic texts and identified as the Logos by Philo.

It is often said that the practice of monotheism is shown in Jewish worship, which was reserved for the Most High God and did not extend to lesser divinities or angels. It is certainly true that the official sacrificial cult in Jerusalem was monotheistic, and no evidence indicates that any being other than the God of Israel was worshiped in synagogue services. There is some evidence, however, for the veneration of angels.[30] Christian authors such as Clement of Alexandria and Origen claimed that Jews worshiped angels, and both apocalyptic and rabbinic text prohibit the worship of angels. Presumably, the prohibitions would not have been necessary if the practice had been unknown. There is also some evidence for the practice of calling on angels in prayer, especially in the context of magic. None of this, however, implies that there was an organized, public cult of angels or that the religious authorities sanctioned such activities.

More significant for our purposes is the kind of honor bestowed on the "one like a son of man," in Daniel 7, who is given "dominion and glory and kingship, that all peoples, nations, and languages should serve him" (Dan 7:14). Similarly, in the Similitudes of Enoch we are told that "all those who dwell on the dry ground will fall down and worship" before that Son of Man (*1 Enoch* 48:5). The passage continues, however, by stating that they will bless, praise, and celebrate with psalms the name of the Lord of Spirits—so there is some doubt as to whether the worship is directed at the Son of Man or the Lord God. According to the "Son of God Text" from Qumran, when war ceases on earth, all cities will pay homage either to the "Son of God" or to "the people of God." Although the homage in this passage involves political submission, worship in the ancient world was often considered analogous to submission to a great king.

Both the "Son of Man" passages and the "Son of God Text" are eschatological—they describe the future. They do not imply that there was any actual cult of either the "Son of Man" or the "Son of God." But they do suggest that some form of veneration or homage could be directed to these figures in the eschatological future.[31] Each of these figures, to be sure, can be understood as God's agent or representative, so that homage given to them is ultimately given to God. But these passages also show that the idea of venerating God's agent, at least in the eschatological future, was not unthinkable in a Jewish context.

WAS CHRISTIANITY MONOTHEISTIC?

The veneration of Jesus by his first-century c.e. Jewish followers should be somewhat less surprising in light of the foregoing evidence. Those who believed that Jesus was righteous and unjustly executed would naturally believe that he was exalted to heaven after his death. But more was at issue in the case of Jesus. He was crucified as King of the Jews, which means that he was viewed by the Romans as a messianic pretender and, presumably, by some of his followers as a messianic king. In Luke 24:19, the disciples talk "about Jesus of Nazareth, who was a prophet mighty in deed and word before God and all the people, and how our chief priests and leaders handed him over to be condemned to death and crucified him. But we had hoped that he was the one to redeem Israel." Their bewilderment over Jesus' death is then relieved by the belief that he has risen from the dead.

Whatever the nature of the resurrection experience, it is undeniable that the belief in it arose very shortly after Jesus' death. The resurrection was taken as confirmation that Jesus was indeed the messiah, even though he had not restored the kingdom to Israel, as some had hoped. According to Paul, Jesus was "declared [or appointed?] to be Son of God with power according to the spirit of holiness by resurrection from the dead" (Rom 1:4). Although Jesus had unfinished business as messiah, this anomaly was explained by appeal to Daniel 7: Jesus was the "one like a son of man" who would come again on the clouds of heaven. Like the Similitudes of Enoch, the Gospel of Matthew envisions the Son of Man, Jesus, seated on a throne of glory and presiding over the Last Judgment (see Matthew 25:31). In the Gospels, Jesus is said to have spoken of himself as the Son of Man who would come on the clouds of heaven, but it is more likely that he was so identified by the disciples after his death, when he was no longer present on earth.

According to the Gospel of John, the claim that Jesus was Son of God was blasphemous to his Jewish contemporaries: "We have a law, and according to that law he ought to die because he has claimed to be the Son of God" (John 19:7). Despite this statement, the claim to be the son of God was not inherently blasphemous in a Jewish context. In the Wisdom of Solomon, it is the righteous man who claims to be the child of God and boasts that God is his father (Wisdom of Solomon 2:13, 16). To claim to be the son of God, in a Jewish context, was not to claim to be equal to God. Nor was it blasphemous to claim that someone was the messiah, the promised heir to the Davidic line. According to Jewish tradition, the great Rabbi Akiba hailed the revolutionary Simeon Bar Kokhba as the messiah, about a century after Jesus. Rabbi Akiba proved to be mistaken, but he was not deemed a heretic. Some Jews apparently believed that the Son of Man, and later the exalted Metatron, was the human patriarch Enoch exalted to heaven. Even the extreme claim of the Gospel of John that the Word was God could be defended in a Jewish context by appeal to Philo's distinction between the analogical use of "God" without the article, which could refer to the Logos, and "the God," with the article, which was reserved for the Most High (although it is by no means clear that the author of John's Gospel intended such a distinction).

Nonetheless, the claim in the Gospel of John that "the Father and I are one" is without parallel in Judaism.[32] By the end of the first century c.e., the exaltation of Jesus had reached a point where it was increasingly difficult to reconcile with Jewish understandings of monotheism.

The apocalyptic understanding of Jesus reaches its New Testament climax in the book of Revelation. There John sees "one like a Son of Man, clothed with a long robe and with a golden sash across his chest. His head and his hair were white as white wool, white as snow; his eyes were like a flame of fire" (Rev 1:13-14). The figure in question, Jesus, combines attributes of both the "one like a son of man" and the "Ancient one" of Daniel 7.[33] He has become difficult to distinguish from the God of Israel.[34]

In some part, the tendency to identify Jesus with the God of Israel began with early Christians attempting to claim for Jesus everything that Jews would claim for an intermediary figure.[35] But then it went further; Jesus was the Son of God in a unique sense, and this claim was expressed in Hellenistic idiom in stories of his birth from a virgin. Revelation 12 relates a fragment of a Jewish myth in which the archangel Michael does battle with a dragon in heaven, a variant of a combat myth that was widespread in the ancient Near East. In Revelation, however, we are told that it is by the blood of the Lamb (the crucifixion of Jesus) that the dragon is defeated (Rev 12:11).[36] Michael fights the battle, but Jesus gains the victory. Similarly, the Epistle to the Hebrews is at pains to insist that Jesus is superior to the angels: "For to which of the angels did God ever say, 'You are my son; today I have begotten you'?" (Heb 1:5). Hebrews even applies to Jesus the statement of Ps 110:4, "You are a priest forever after the order of Melchizedek" (Heb 5:6), even though Jesus of Nazareth was not a priest at all. Again, if Hellenistic Judaism venerated the Logos, or Word, as "a second God," the Gospel of John goes one better by claiming that Jesus is the Word and the Word is God.[37]

This proliferation of honorific titles and claims made on Jesus' behalf by the early Christians goes hand in hand with the veneration, or worship, of Jesus in the early church. Paul declared that "at the name of Jesus every knee should bend in heaven and on earth and under the earth, and every tongue should confess that Jesus Christ is Lord, to the glory of God the Father" (Phil 2:10-11). In Revelation, we find the same blessing addressed to the Lamb (Christ) as to "the one seated on the throne" (God): "Blessing and honor and glory and might forever and forever" (Rev 5:13). Now, Revelation pointedly rejects the worship of angels; and John is rebuked twice for prostrating himself before an angel (Rev 19:10; 22:9).[38] Yet Christ has many angelic features in Revelation (especially if the "Son of Man" in Rev 14:14 is identi-fied as Christ).[39] Moreover, the homage paid to Christ in Revelation is reminiscent of the homage paid to the super-angelic Son of Man in Daniel 7: dominion and glory and kingship, so that all peoples, nations and languages should serve him.

The notion that there was a second divine being *under* God was not intrinsically incompatible with Judaism, although the belief that Jesus of Nazareth was such a being undoubtedly seemed preposterous to many Jews. What was incompatible with Judaism was the idea that this second divine being was equal to God. Hence the argument attributed to the Jews in the Gospel of John: According to Jewish law, Jesus ought to die, for he made himself equal to God. Indeed, in the Gospel of John, Jesus is said to claim unabashedly that "the Father and I are one" (John 10:30). Yet this very formulation shows something of the peculiarity of the Christian confession. Jesus is not "a second God" like Philo's Logos; he is one with the Father, so that those who worship both Father and Son can still claim that they worship only one God.

Eventually, Christian theology would be further complicated by the doctrine of the Holy Spirit, which also has its roots in the New Testament and even in pre-Christian Judaism. Over the next few centuries, Christian theologians would labor to find acceptable formulas that would enable them to affirm the divinity of Jesus and the Spirit, but still maintain the unity of God. Along the way, several formulas were rejected as heretical. In the second century C.E., Justin Martyr, following in the footsteps of Philo, spoke of the Logos as "another God" beside the Father; he added that the Logos was other "in number, not in will," and proposed the analogy of one torch lit from another—suggesting different manifestations of the same divine entity.[40] This position led to the Monarchian controversy about the unity of God. The Monarchians adopted the position that the Father and Son are one and the same, two aspects of the same being.[41] A century and a half later, an Alexandrian presbyter named Arius ignited one of the great controversies of Christian antiquity by teaching, in the tradition of Philo, that the Logos was part of the created order and thus was not God in the same sense as the Father. The Council of Nicea, convened by the emperor Constantine in 325 c.e., condemned Arianism as a heresy and adopted the creed that the Son is "one in being [*homoousios*] with the Father" and that the Spirit "proceeds from the Father and the Son."[42] Even people who signed the decree at the time understood these formulas in different ways, and the controversy continued for several centuries.

In traditional Christian theology, the doctrine of the Trinity is a mystery, which entails an admission that it is not entirely amenable to rational logic and understanding. Non-Christians, and many Christians who lack the appetite for metaphysical reasoning, may be forgiven for thinking that this allows for some equivocation, enabling Christianity to maintain contradictory positions without admitting it. Be that as it may, Christianity has never wavered in its claim to be a monotheistic religion. However the different persons of the Trinity are defined, they are to be understood as falling within the overarching unity of God. The notion that God is three as well as one, however, obviously entails a considerable qualification of monotheism.

Both Judaism and Christianity are committed to monotheism, the belief that ultimately there is only one God. Moreover, the break between Christianity and Judaism, particularly in their understanding of monotheistic doctrines, was not as sharp or complete as is sometimes assumed. The Synoptic Gospels can be reconciled quite easily with Jewish understandings of monotheism. The theology of Justin Martyr and Origen, in second-century c.e. Christianity, is not greatly removed from that of Philo, except that the Logos is now believed to be incarnate in the person of Jesus. This was, to be sure, a considerable difference, but the difference lay in the evaluation of a specific historical person rather than in the theological framework of monotheism or di-theism. Philo, for example, could speak of the patriarchs as *empsychoi nomoi,* or "the laws of God incarnate."[43] Only gradually did the Christian understanding of Christ and the Spirit evolve to the point where it was incompatible with any Jewish understanding of monotheism, and this process was only finalized in the fourth century c.e. Even the Nicene Creed (325 c.e.) begins with the confession, "I believe in one God." Despite the logical anomalies of the Trinity, this confession is still repeated in Christian churches to this day.

NOTES

INTRODUCTION

1. See, e.g., J. L. Crenshaw, "The Concept of God in Old Testament Wisdom," in *In Search of Wisdom: Essays in Memory of John G. Gammie* (ed. L. Perdue et al.; Louisville: Westminster John Knox, 1993), 1–18; M. Fox, "World Order and Ma'at: A Crooked Parallel," *JANES* 23 (1995): 37–48; *Proverbs 1–9* (AB 18A; New York: Doubleday, 2000); L. Perdue, *Wisdom and Creation* (Nashville: Abingdon, 1994).

2. James Barr, *History and Ideology in the Old Testament* (Oxford: Oxford University Press, 2000), 32–58.

3. See the discussion of the principles of historical criticism in ch. 1, "Is a Critical Biblical Theology Possible?"

4. See, e.g., Wolfhart Pannenberg, "Problems in a Theology of (Only) the Old Testament," in *Problems in Biblical Theology: Essays in Honor of Rolf Knierim* (ed. H. T. C. Sun and K. L. Eades, with J. M. Robinson and G. I. Möller; Grand Rapids: Eerdmans, 1997), 275–80.

5. K. Stendahl, "Biblical Theology, Contemporary," *IDB* 1 (1962): 418–32.

6. R. Bultmann, *Theology of the New Testament* (2 vols.; New York: Scribner's, 1951, 1955), 2:251.

7. J. D. Levenson, "Historical Criticism and the Fate of the Enlightenment Project," in *The Hebrew Bible, the Old Testament, and Historical Criticism* (Louisville: Westminster John Knox, 1993), 106–26. See my review of Levenson's book in "Historical Criticism and the State of Biblical Theology," *ChrCent* (July 28–August 4, 1993): 743–47. See also the critique by James Barr, *Biblical Theology* (Minneapolis: Fortress Press, 1999), 291–302. My debate with Levenson is continued in the essay, "The Exodus and Biblical Theology," reprinted here as chapter 5. That essay is also reprinted in *Jews, Christians, and the Theology of the Hebrew Scriptures* (ed. Alice Ogden Bellis and Joel S. Kaminsky; SBLSymS 8; Atlanta: Society of Biblical Literature, 2000), 247–61, with a rejoinder by Levenson, pp. 263–75.

8. Levenson, *The Hebrew Bible*, 119.

9. Ibid., 120.

10. Ibid., xiii.

11. Ibid., 80.

12. Ibid., 105.

13. See the classic critique of the Biblical Theology Movement, by B. S. Childs, *Biblical Theology in Crisis* (Philadelphia: Westminster, 1970).

14. See Levenson, "Why Jews Are Not Interested in Biblical Theology," in *The Hebrew Bible*, 33–61.

15. R. Rorty, *Philosophy and the Mirror of Nature* (Princeton: Princeton University Press, 1979); idem, *Consequences of Pragmatism* (Minneapolis: University of Minnesota Press, 1982); idem, *Contingency, Irony, and Solidarity* (Cambridge: Cambridge University Press, 1989). See further W. M. Sullivan, "After Foundationalism: The Return to Practical Philosophy," in *Anti-Foundationalism and Practical Reasoning* (ed. E. Simpson; Edmonton, Alberta: Academic Printing and Publishing, 1987), 21–44.

16. See J. E. Thiel, *Nonfoundationalism* (Guides to Theological Inquiry; Minneapolis: Fortress Press, 1994); P. Ochs, ed., *The Return to Scripture in Judaism and Christianity: Essays in Postcritical Scriptural Interpretation* (Mahwah, N.Y.: Paulist, 1993); S. Hauerwas, N. Murphy, and M. Nation, ed., *Theology without Foundations: Religious Practice and the Future of Theological Truth* (Nashville: Abingdon, 1994).

17. L. Perdue, *The Collapse of History: Reconstructing Old Testament Theology* (Overtures to Biblical Theology; Minneapolis: Fortress Press, 1994). See the discussion of the Exodus in ch. 5 of this volume.

18. G. von Rad, *Old Testament Theology* (trans. D. M. G. Stalker; New York: Harper, 1962–65), 1:106–8.

19. B. S. Childs, *Biblical Theology of the Old and New Testaments: Theological Reflections* (Minneapolis: Fortress Press, 1992), 196–207.

20. W. Brueggemann, *Theology of the Old Testament: Testimony, Dispute, Advocacy* (Minneapolis: Fortress Press, 1997). See also his earlier book, *Texts under Negotiation: The Bible and Postmodern Imagination* (Minneapolis: Fortress Press, 1993); and his article, "Biblical Theology Appropriately Postmodern," *BTB* 27 (1997): 4–9.

21. Brueggemann, *Theology of the Old Testament*, 11.

22. Ibid., 62.

23. Ibid., 65.

24. Ibid., 400–401.

25. I discuss Brueggemann's theology at greater length in my book, *The Bible after Babel: Historical Criticism in a Postmodern Age* (Grand Rapids: Eerdmans, 2005).

26. Brueggemann, *Theology of the Old Testament*, 715.

27. Ibid., 714.

28. Ibid.

29. Ibid.

30. Ibid., n21.

31. See chs. 8 and 10.

32. J. Barr, *Biblical Faith and Natural Theology* (Gifford Lectures for 1991; Oxford: Clarendon, 1993).

33. See the essays in A. Amanat and J. J. Collins, ed., *Apocalypse and Violence* (New Haven: Yale Center for International and Area Studies and the Council on Middle East Studies, 2002).

34. See ch. 4.

35. See my essay, "The Zeal of Phinehas: The Bible and the Legitimation of Violence," *JBL* 122 (2003): 3–21, delivered as the presidential address to the Society of Biblical Literature in Toronto, November 23, 2002, and reprinted as *Does the Bible Justify Violence?* (Facets; Minneapolis: Fortress Press, 2004).

1. IS A CRITICAL BIBLICAL THEOLOGY POSSIBLE?

1. J. Sandys-Wunsch and L. Eldredge, "J. P. Gabler and the Distinction between Biblical and Dogmatic Theology: Translation, Commentary and Discussion of His Originality," *SJT* 33 (1980): 133–58.

2. J. H. Hayes and F. Prussner, *Old Testament Theology: Its History and Development* (Atlanta: John Knox, 1985), 3.

3. E. Troeltsch, "Über historische und dogmatische Methode in der Theologie," in *Gesammelte Schriften* (4 vols.; Tübingen: Mohr, 1913), 2:729–53.

4. V. A. Harvey, *The Historian and the Believer* (New York: Macmillan, 1966), 39–42.

5. W. Wrede, "The Task and Methods of New Testament Theology," in *The Nature of New Testament Theology* (ed. R. Morgan; London: SCM, 1973), 69–70.

6. Ibid., 70.

7. Ibid., 69.

8. Ibid., 70.

9. Harvey, *The Historian and the Believer*, 103.

10. W. Eichrodt, *Theology of the Old Testament* (2 vols.; Philadelphia: Westminster, 1961), 1:32.

11. Ibid.

12. Ibid., 1:33.

13. Ibid., 1:31.

14. J. D. Levenson, "The Hebrew Bible, the Old Testament, and Historical Criticism," in *The Future of Biblical Studies* (ed. R. E. Friedman and H. G. M. Williamson; Atlanta: Scholars Press, 1987), 19–59.

15. B. S. Childs, *Biblical Theology in Crisis* (Philadelphia: Westminster, 1970).

16. G. E. Wright, *God Who Acts: Biblical Theology as Recital* (London: SCM, 1952), 128.

17. Ibid., 117.

18. Ibid., 126.

19. L. Gilkey, "Cosmology, Ontology, and the Travail of Biblical Language," *JR* 41 (1961): 194–205.

20. G. von Rad, *Old Testament Theology* (2 vols.; New York: Harper & Row, 1962–1965), 2:321.

21. J. Barr, *The Scope and Authority of the Bible* (Philadelphia: Westminster, 1980), 11.

22. Harvey, *The Historian and the Believer*, 139–46; S. M. Ogden, *Christ without Myth* (New York: Harper, 1961).

23. Childs, *Biblical Theology in Crisis*; idem, *Introduction to the Old Testament as Scripture* (Philadelphia: Fortress Press, 1979); idem, *The New Testament as Canon* (Philadelphia: Fortress Press, 1984); idem, *Old Testament Theology in a Canonical Context* (Philadelphia: Fortress Press, 1985).

24. Childs, *Introduction to the Old Testament as Scripture*, 56–60, 74–75.

25. Childs, *Biblical Theology in Crisis*, 100–101.

26. Childs, *Introduction to the Old Testament as Scripture*, 77.

27. J. Barr, *Holy Scripture: Canon, Authority, Criticism* (Philadelphia: Westminster, 1983), 49–104; J. Barton, *Reading the Old Testament: Method in Biblical Study* (Philadelphia: Westminster, 1984), 77–103.

28. Childs, *Biblical Theology in Crisis*, 9.

29. H. G. Gadamer, *Truth and Method* (New York: Crossroad, 1982); P. Ricoeur, *Essays on Biblical Interpretation* (ed. L. Mudge; Philadelphia: Fortress Press, 1980).

30. G. Lindbeck, *The Nature of Doctrine: Religion and Theology in a Postliberal Age* (Philadelphia: Westminster, 1984), 34.

31. P. Stuhlmacher, *Historical Criticism and Theological Interpretation of Scripture* (Philadelphia: Fortress Press, 1977), 84.

32. K. Stendahl, *Meanings: The Bible as Document and as Guide* (Philadelphia: Fortress Press, 1984), 22.

33. N. K. Gottwald, *The Tribes of Yahweh: A Sociology of the Religion of Liberated Israel, 1250–1050 B.C.E.* (Maryknoll, N.Y.: Orbis, 1979); E. Schüssler Fiorenza, *In Memory of Her* (New York: Crossroad, 1983).

34. Harvey, *The Historian and the Believer,* 16; A. C. Thiselton, *The Two Horizons: New Testament Hermeneutics and Philosophical Description* (Grand Rapids: Eerdmans, 1980), 78–79.

35. Harvey, *The Historian and the Believer*, 123, citing John Locke.

36. D. Tracy, *The Analogical Imagination: Christian Theology and the Culture of Pluralism* (New York: Crossroad, 1981), 237–46.

37. Ibid., 99.

38. J. Barr, *Fundamentalism* (Philadelphia: Westminster, 1978).

39. J. A. Miles, "Understanding Albright: A Revolutionary Etude," *HTR* 69 (1976): 151–75.

40. Barton, *Reading the Old Testament*, 153–54.

41. Troeltsch, "Über historische und dogmatische Methode in der Theologie," 730.

42. S. M. Ogden, "The Authority of Scripture for Theology," *Int* 30 (1976): 243–45.

43. Wrede, "The Task and Methods of New Testament Theology," 70.

44. J. J. Collins, "Apocalyptic Eschatology as the Transcendence of Death," *CBQ* 36 (1974): 21–43; repr. in *Visionaries and Their Apocalypses* (ed. P. D. Hanson; Philadelphia: Fortress Press, 1983), 61–84.

45. Barton, *Reading the Old Testament*, 8–29; K. Koch, *The Growth of the Biblical Tradition* (New York: Scribners, 1969), 3–16.

46. H. Gunkel, *The Legends of Genesis* (New York: Schocken, 1964), 10.

47. B. G. Caird, *The Language and Imagery of the Bible* (Philadelphia: Westminster, 1980), 7–36.

48. Stendahl, *Meanings,* 4-5; H. Frei, *The Eclipse of Biblical Narrative* (New Haven: Yale University Press, 1974).

49. Barr, *The Scope and Authority of the Bible*, 5.

50. J. Barr, *The Bible in the Modern World* (New York: Harper, 1973), 55.

51. Robert Alter, *The Art of Biblical Narrative* (New York: Basic, 1980), 23–46.

52. Meir Sternberg, *The Poetics of Biblical Narrative* (Bloomington: Indiana University Press, 1985), 25.

53. Ibid., 30.

54. Ibid., 25.

55. E. Auerbach, *Mimesis: The Representation of Reality in Western Literature* (Princeton: Princeton University Press, 1953), 14.

56. J. Neusner, *The Way of the Torah: An Introduction to Judaism* (Belmont, Calif.: Dickenson, 1970), 13–18.

57. Ricoeur, *Essays on Biblical Interpretation*, 75.

58. Ibid., 103.

59. Ibid., 117.

60. D. J. Lull, "What Is Process Hermeneutics?" *Process Studies* 13 (1983): 193.

61. D. H. Kelsey, *The Uses of Scripture in Recent Theology* (Philadelphia: Fortress Press, 1975), 48.

62. Sternberg, *The Poetics of Biblical Narrative*, 32.

63. P. L. Wismer, "The Myth of Original Sin: A Hermeneutic Theology Based on Genesis 2–3" (PhD diss., University of Chicago, 1983), 187–253.

64. Ricoeur, *Essays on Biblical Interpretation*, 93–95.

65. Gottwald, *The Tribes of Yahweh*, 667–709.

66. P. L. Berger, *The Sacred Canopy* (Garden City, N.Y.: Doubleday, 1969).

67. J. D. Levenson, *Sinai and Zion: An Entry into the Jewish Bible* (Minneapolis: Winston, 1985), 42.

2. BIBLICAL THEOLOGY AND THE HISTORY OF ISRAELITE RELIGION

1. Dermot Ryan was Professor of Semitic Languages at University College Dublin from 1957 to 1971, when he was appointed Archbishop of Dublin.

2. G. von Rad, *Old Testament Theology* (trans. D. M. G. Stalker; 2 vols.; New York: Harper & Row, 1962–1965).

3. I am not aware that Dr. Ryan's views on this subject were ever published.

4. J. Sandys-Wunsch and L. Eldredge, "J. P. Gabler and the Distinction between Biblical and Dogmatic Theology: Translation, Commentary and Discussion of His Originality," *SJT* 33 (1980): 133–58.

5. B. C. Ollenburger, "Biblical Theology: Situating the Discipline," in *Understanding the Word: Essays in Honor of Bernhard W. Anderson* (ed. J. T. Butler, E. W. Conrad, and B. C. Ollenburger; JSOTSup 37; Sheffield: Sheffield Academic Press, 1985), 43.

6. Wilhelm Wrede, *Über Aufgabe und Methode der sogenannten neutestamentlichen Theologie* (Göttingen, 1897); repr. as "The Task and Methods of New Testament Theology," in *The Nature of New Testament Theology* (ed. and trans. R. Morgan; London: SCM, 1973), 68–116.

7. W. Eichrodt, *Theology of the Old Testament* (2 vols.; Philadelphia: Westminster, 1961), 1:31–33.

8. G. E. Wright, *God Who Acts: Biblical Theology as Recital* (London: SCM, 1952), 117.

9. B. S. Childs, *Old Testament Theology in a Canonical Context* (Philadelphia: Fortress Press, 1986), 8.

10. L. Gilkey, "Cosmology, Ontology and the Travail of Biblical Language," *JR* 41 (1961): 194–205; J. Barr, *Old and New in Interpretation* (London: SCM, 1966).

11. B. S. Childs, *Biblical Theology in Crisis* (Philadelphia: Westminster, 1970).

12. Modern hermeneutics has repeatedly insisted that there is no interpretation without presuppositions. See especially H. G. Gadamer, *Truth and Method* (New York: Crossroad, 1982); P. Ricoeur, *Essays on Biblical Interpretation* (ed. L. Mudge; Philadelphia: Fortress Press, 1980); and the comments of P. Stuhlmacher, *Historical Criticism and Theological Interpretation of Scripture* (Philadelphia: Fortress Press, 1977).

13. On the principles of historical criticism, see V. A. Harvey, *The Historian and the Believer* (New York: Macmillan, 1966), 13–19, adapting the work of E. Troeltsch, "Über historische und dogmatische Methode in der Theologie," in *Gesammelte Schriften* (4 vols.; Tübingen: Mohr, 1913), 2:729–53. Of crucial importance is Troeltsch's principle of criticism, according to which historical assertions can claim only a greater or lesser degree of probability and must be always open to revision.

14. See J. J. Collins, "The 'Historical' Character of the Old Testament in Recent Biblical Theology," *CBQ* 41 (1979): 185–204.

15. R. A. Oden, *The Bible without Theology* (San Francisco: Harper, 1987), viii.

16. N. K. Gottwald, *The Tribes of Yahweh: A Sociology of the Religion of Liberated Israel, 1250–1050 B.C.E.* (Maryknoll, N.Y.: Orbis, 1979), 667–709.

17. Especially J. Barr, *Holy Scripture, Canon, Authority, Criticism* (Philadelphia: Westminster, 1983), passim.

18. See J. Barton, *Reading the Old Testament: Method in Biblical Study* (Philadelphia: Westminster, 1984), 77–103.

19. Childs, *Old Testament Theology in a Canonical Context*, 15.

20. Many biblical theologians appear to work with dogmatic presuppositions that are not adequately articulated. Rolf Knierim's view of "The Task of Biblical Theology" (*HBT* 6 [1984]: 25–57) is to establish "the criteria of accountability of what is to be confessed." These criteria are not derived from frequency of attestation in the Old Testament or because they occur in particular settings but "because of the decisive theological arguments themselves" (48). Knierim does not explain, however, what makes these arguments decisive.

21. Such a position is advocated by S. Ogden, "The Authority of Scripture for Theology," *Int* 30 (1976): 242–61, among others.

22. I have proposed this view in an essay, "Is a Critical Biblical Theology Possible?" at a meeting at the University of California, San Diego, in May 1986. See chapter 1 above.

23. The work of P. D. Hanson, *Dynamic Transcendence* (Philadelphia: Fortress Press, 1978) and *The Diversity of Scripture* (Philadelphia: Fortress Press, 1982), makes full use of critical scholarship but still construes theology as a confessional activity, in a manner reminiscent of G. E. Wright's "projection of faith into facts." In an academic context, this is open to the charge of mystification, although it may be quite appropriate in an ecclesiastical setting.

24. Some of the more literary approaches to Old Testament Theology are open to criticism on this point, e.g., D. Patrick, *The Rendering of God in the Old Testament* (Philadelphia: Fortress Press, 1981); and T. E. Fretheim, *The Suffering of God: An Old Testament Perspective* (Overtures to Biblical Theology; Philadelphia: Fortress Press, 1984). This is also true of some attempts to apply Process Theology to the Old Testament. See W. A. Beardslee and D. J. Lull, ed., "Old Testament Interpretation from a Process Perspective," *Semeia* 24 (1982).

25. Childs, *Old Testament Theology in a Canonical Context*, 15.

26. J. A. Sanders, "Adaptable for Life: The Nature and Function of Canon," in *Magnalia Dei: The Mighty Acts of God; Essays on the Bible and Archeology in Memory of G. Ernest Wright* (ed. F. M. Cross et al.; Garden City, N.Y.: Doubleday, 1976), 537. See also J. A. Sanders, *Canon and Community* (Philadelphia: Fortress Press, 1983) and *From Sacred Story to Sacred Text: Canon as Paradigm* (Philadelphia: Fortress Press, 1987). Sanders's approach is sometimes confused with that of Childs because of the confusing label "canon criticism," but in fact it is quite different. Sanders's approach is sociological, insofar as he treats the text in terms of the needs of the community. Childs also professes to base his approach on the actual function of the text in the religious community, but there is no evidence that "the canonical form" of the text was a matter of concern for anyone in ancient Judaism or early Christianity.

27. See J. J. Collins, *The Apocalyptic Imagination* (New York: Crossroad, 1984).

28. E. B. Pusey, *Daniel the Prophet* (Oxford, 1865), 75.

29. B. S. Childs, *Introduction to the Old Testament as Scripture* (Philadelphia: Fortress Press, 1979), 616.

30. Ibid.

31. Ibid., 618.

32. On the imagery of Daniel 7, see J. J. Collins, *The Apocalyptic Vision of the Book of Daniel* (Missoula, Mont.: Scholars Press, 1977), 95–106; and J. Day, *God's Conflict with the Dragon and the Sea* (New York: Cambridge University Press, 1985), 151–67.

33. See B. M. Metzger, "Literary Forgeries and Canonical Pseudepigrapha," *JBL* 91 (1972): 3–24.

34. So D. S. Russell, *The Method and Message of Jewish Apocalyptic* (Philadelphia: Westminster, 1964), 133–34.

35. So C. Rowland, *The Open Heaven* (New York: Crossroad, 1982), 245.

36. Plato, *Republic* 382C, 414B, 459D.

37. On the concept of myth in Greek apocalypses, see H. D. Betz, "The Problem of Apocalyptic Genre in Greek and Hellenistic Literature," in *Apocalypticism in the Mediterranean World and the Near East* (ed. D. Hellholm; Tübingen: Mohr, 1983), 577–97.

38. Compare the general proposal of Paul Ricoeur "to place the originary expressions of biblical faith under the sign of the poetic function of language" (*Essays on Biblical Interpretation*, 103).

39. Childs, *Introduction to the Old Testament as Scripture*, 621.

40. See M. Delcor, "Le Dieu des Apocalypticiens," *La Notion Biblique de Dieu* (BETL 41; ed. J. Coppens; Leuven: Leuven University Press/Peeters, 1974), 211–28.

41. On the "repentance" of God, see especially Fretheim, *The Suffering of God*, 45–59.

42. Childs, *Introduction to the Old Testament as Scripture*, 622.

43. So Delcor, "Le Dieu des Apocalypticiens," 215.

44. E.g., R. K. Bultmann, "New Testament and Mythology," in *Kerygma and Myth* (ed. H. W. Bartsch; New York: Harper & Row, 1961), 1–44.

45. Cf. Bultmann, in ibid., 44.

46. E.g., where Daniel is specifically obedient to the Jewish food laws (Daniel 1) Childs does not specify what obedience requires.

47. On the contextual approach to Biblical Theology, see J. Goldingay, *Theological Diversity and the Authority of the Old Testament* (Grand Rapids: Eerdmans, 1987), 29–58.

48. Childs, *Old Testament Theology in a Canonical Context*, 245.

49. See also H. Gese, "Death in the Old Testament," in *Essays on Biblical Theology* (trans. Keith Crim; Minneapolis: Augsburg, 1981), 34–59.

50. See B. Vawter, "Intimations of Immortality and the Old Testament," in idem, *The Path of Wisdom: Biblical Investigations* (Wilmington, Del.: Glazier, 1986), 140–60.

51. G. W. E. Nickelsburg, *Resurrection, Immortality, and Eternal Life in Intertestamental Judaism* (Cambridge: Harvard University Press, 1972), 17–20.

52. J. J. Collins, "The Place of Apocalypticism in the Religion of Israel," in *Ancient Israelite Religion* (ed. P. D. Miller, P. D. Hanson, and S. D. McBride; Philadelphia: Fortress Press, 1987), 549. Reflection on the disappearance of the biblical Enoch may also have played a part in the development.

53. J. J. Collins, "Apocalyptic Eschatology as the Transcendence of Death," *CBQ* 36 (1974): 21–43; repr. in *Visionaries and Their Apocalypses* (ed. P. D. Hanson; Philadelphia: Fortress Press, 1983), 61–84. Compare Childs, *Introduction to the Old Testament as Scripture*, 622.

3. THE POLITICS OF BIBLICAL INTERPRETATION

1. K. W. Whitelam, *The Invention of Ancient Israel: The Silencing of Palestinian History* (London: Routledge, 1996).

2. See, e.g., T. L. Thompson, *Early History of the Israelite People* (SHANE 4; Leiden: E. J. Brill, 1992), 199; P. R. Davies, *In Search of "Ancient Israel"* (JSOTSup 148; 2nd ed.; Sheffield: Sheffield Academic Press, 1997).

3. For accounts of postmodernism in its biblical incarnation, see A. K. M. Adam, *What Is Postmodern Biblical Criticism?* (Guides to Biblical Scholarship; Minneapolis: Fortress Press, 1995), 199; G. Aichele et al. (Bible and Culture Collective), *The Postmodern Bible* (New Haven: Yale University Press, 1995); and R. P. Carroll, "Poststructuralist Approaches: New Historicism and Postmodernism," in *The Cambridge Companion to Biblical Interpretation* (ed. J. Barton; Cambridge: Cambridge University Press, 1998), 50–66. How the use of the label "postmodern" in biblical studies relates to its use in other fields is a question that lies beyond the scope of this essay.

4. J. Barr, *History and Ideology in the Old Testament* (Oxford: Oxford University Press, 2000), 32–58.

5. E. Troeltsch, "Über historische und dogmatische Methode in der Theologie," in *Gesammelte Schriften* (4 vols.; Tübingen: Mohr, 1913), 2:729–53; E. Troeltsch, "Historiography," in *Encyclopedia of Religion and Ethics* (13 vols.; ed. J. Hasting; New York: Charles Scribner's Sons, 1914), 6:716–23; and V. A. Harvey, *The Historian and the Believer* (New York: Macmillan, 1966). See also E. Krentz, *The Historical-Critical Method* (Guides to Biblical Scholarship; Philadelphia: Fortress Press, 1975).

6. I. Kant, "What Is Enlightenment?" in *Critique of Practical Reason and Other Writings in Moral Philosophy* (ed. L. W. Beck; Chicago: University of Chicago Press, 1949), 286–92; Harvey, *The Historian and the Believer*, 39–42.

7. R. G. Collingwood, *The Idea of History* (Oxford: Oxford University Press, 1946), 236.

8. See, e.g., J. D. Levenson, *The Hebrew Bible, The Old Testament and Historical Criticism* (Louisville: Westminster John Knox, 1993), 106–26.

9. This point was made most famously by H. G. Gadamer, *Truth and Method* (New York: Crossroad, 1975). See also A. McIntyre, *After Virtue* (Notre Dame: Notre Dame University Press, 1981); and S. Fish, *Is There a Text in This Class? The Authority of Interpretive Communities* (Cambridge: Harvard University Press, 1980).

10. Harvey, *The Historian and the Believer*, 14–15; and Krentz, *The Historical-Critical Method*, 55–72.

11. Harvey, *The Historian and the Believer*, 14–15.

12. For example, D. M. Gunn and D. N. Fewell, in *Narrative in the Hebrew Bible* (Oxford: Oxford University Press, 1993), 7, say that historical criticism claims "some kind of absolute truth." See the comments of Barr, *History and Ideology in the Old Testament*, 33–34.

13. This is readily admitted. See, e.g., A. K. M. Adam, "Post-Modern Biblical Interpretation," in *Dictionary of Biblical Interpretation* (ed. J. H. Hayes; Nashville: Abingdon Press, 1999), 305.

14. S. Fish, *The Trouble with Principle* (Cambridge: Harvard University Press, 1999). For a recent example in biblical studies, see G. Aichele et al., *Sign, Text, Scripture: Semiotics and the Bible* (Interventions 1; Sheffield: Sheffield Academic Press, 1997), 40.

15. Adam, "Post-Modern Biblical Interpretation," 306.

16. See the nicely ironic comments of Carroll, "Poststructuralist Approaches: New Historicism and Postmodernism," 58–59, on the authoritarian and totalizing ideology of *The Postmodern Bible*.

17. Adam, "Post-Modern Biblical Interpretation," 306.

18. Ibid., 305.

19. Ibid.

20. So my colleague Dale Martin, in oral discussion.

21. Whitelam, *The Invention of Ancient Israel*, 11.

22. See especially W. F. Albright, *From the Stone Age to Christianity: Monotheism and the Historical Process* (New York: Doubleday, 1957); J. Bright, *A History of Israel* (4th ed.; Louisville: Westminster John Knox, 2000).

23. Whitelam, *The Invention of Ancient Israel*, 82.

24. A. Alt, "The Settlement of the Israelites in Palestine," in *Essays on Old Testament History and Religion* (trans. R. A. Wilson; New York: Doubleday, 1968), 175–221.

25. Whitelam, *The Invention of Ancient Israel*, 76.

26. Ibid., 82–83.

27. Albright, *From the Stone Age to Christianity: Monotheism and the Historical Process*, 280–81.

28. Whitelam, *The Invention of Ancient Israel*, 85.

29. N. A. Silberman, "Vision of the Future: Albright in Jerusalem, 1919–1929," *BA* 56 (1993): 13.

30. W. F. Albright, "Why the Near East Needs the Jews," *New Palestine* 32 (1942): 12–13. In view of Albright's explicit Zionism, the implication of anti-Jewish bias in another post-modernist study, B. O. Long, *Planting and Reaping Albright: Politics, Ideology, and Interpreting the Bible* (University Park: Pennsylvania State University Press, 1997), 71–109), is seriously distorted.

31. I. Finkelstein and N. A. Silberman, *The Bible Unearthed* (New York: Free Press, 2001). A convenient summary of the basic data can be found in W. G. Dever, "Israel, History of (Archaeology and the 'Conquest')," in *ABD* 3 (1992): 545–58.

32. G. E. Mendenhall, "The Hebrew Conquest of Palestine," *BA* 25 (1962): 66–87.

33. N. K. Gottwald, *The Tribes of Yahweh: A Sociology of the Religion of Liberated Israel, 1250–1050 B.C.E.* (Maryknoll, N.Y.: Orbis, 1979).

34. Ibid., xxv.

35. Ibid., 214.

36. For a convenient summary, see E. F. Campbell, "The Amarna Letters and the Amarna Period," *BA* 23 (1960): 2–22.

37. Dever, "Israel, History of (Archaeology and the 'Conquest')," 553.

38. Gottwald, *The Tribes of Yahweh*, 215.

39. Whitelam, *The Invention of Ancient Israel*, 113.

40. I. Finkelstein, *The Archaeology of the Israelite Settlement* (Jerusalem: Israel Exploration Society, 1989); and I. Finkelstein, "The Emergence of Israel in Canaan: Consensus, Mainstream and Dispute," *SJOT* 2 (1991): 47–59.

41. See Dever, "How to Tell a Canaanite from an Israelite," in H. Shanks, ed., *The Rise of Ancient Israel* (Washington, D. C.: Biblical Archaeological Society, 1992), 27–60, with responses by Israel Finkelstein, Norman Gottwald, and Adam Zertal.

42. Whitelam, *The Invention of Ancient Israel*, 13.

43. C. Eden, "Review of *The Emergence of Early Israel in Historical Perspective* by R. B. Coote and K. W. Whitelam and *The Archaeology of the Israelite Settlement* by I. Finkelstein," *AJA* 93 (1989): 292.

44. This is true despite the far-fetched suggestion of D. Jacobson, "When Palestine Meant Israel," *BAR* 27, no. 3 (2001): 42–47, who argues that the name comes from the Greek *palaistēs* ("wrestler") and relates to the naming of Israel in Gen 32. Since the name "Palestine" is found already in Herodotus, Jacobson's theory would require Genesis to have been translated into Greek by the fifth century B.C.E.!

45. The point is noted by N. S. Ateek, *Justice, and Only Justice: A Palestinian Theology of Liberation* (Maryknoll, N.Y.: Orbis Books, 1989), but also by some Jewish scholars (e.g., M. H. Ellis, *Toward a Jewish Theology of Liberation* [Maryknoll, N.Y.: Orbis Books, 1991]). See D. J. Pleins, *The Social Visions of the Hebrew Bible: A Theological Introduction* (Louisville: Westminster John Knox, 2001), 168–70.

46. W. G. Dever, "The Death of a Discipline," *BAR* 21, no. 5 (1995): 50–55, 70.

47. A. Schweitzer, *The Quest of the Historical Jesus* (New York: Macmillan, 1964).

48. T. Kuhn, *The Structure of Scientific Revolutions* (2nd ed.; Chicago: University of Chicago Press, 1970). R. F. Shedinger, "Kuhnian Paradigms and Biblical Scholarship: Is Biblical Studies a Science?" *JBL* 119 (2000): 453–71, argues that Kuhn's description of paradigm change has little resemblance to the way biblical studies are done because there is always diversity of opinion in biblical studies. In his view no interparadigm debate is possible in the sciences. Whether this claim is justified with reference to the sciences is not our concern here. There are, of course, differences between scientific and biblical research, but there are analogies too. Kuhn's model is helpful in describing the process by which dominant theories change, whether these theories were ever undisputed or not.

49. For a good discussion of "historians and their facts," see R. J. Evans, *In Defence of History* (London: Granta Books, 1997), 75–102.

4. FAITH WITHOUT WORKS

1. G. von Rad, *Genesis* (trans. J. H. Marks; Philadelphia: Westminster, 1961), 238. See also G. von Rad, *Das Opfer des Abraham* (Kaiser Traktate 6; Munich: Kaiser, 1971).

2. H. Seebass, *Genesis II: Vätergeschichte I (11.27—22.23)* (Neukirchen-Vluyn: Neukirchener Verlag, 1997), 197.

3. H. Gunkel, *Genesis* (trans. M. E. Biddle; Macon, Ga.: Mercer University Press, 1997), 233; H. Graf Reventlow, *Opfere deinen Sohn* (BibS[N] 53; Neukirchen-Vluyn: Neukirchener Verlag, 1968), 66–77.

4. The unity of vv. 1-19 is defended by G. W. Coats, "Abraham's Sacrifice of Faith," *Int* 27 (1973): 389–400; G. W. Coats, *Genesis with an Introduction to Narrative Literature* (FOTL 1; Grand Rapids: Eerdmans, 1983), 152–55; J. Van Seters, *Abraham in History and Tradition* (New Haven: Yale University Press, 1975), 227–40. Van Seters makes an interesting argument that vv. 15-18 give the purpose of the test, but this is only true on the redactional level. The original purpose was to establish whether Abraham feared God.

5. Gunkel, *Genesis*, 238.

6. Reventlow, *Opfere deinen Sohn*, 63.

7. T. Veijola, "Das Opfer des Abraham—Paradigma des Glaubens aus dem nachexilischen Zeitalter," *ZTK* 85 (1988): 149–57.

8. R. Rendtorff, *The Problem of the Process of Transmission in the Pentateuch* (trans. J. J. Scullion; JSOTSup 89; Sheffield: Sheffield Academic Press, 1990); E. Blum, *Die Komposition der Vätergeschichte* (WMANT 57; Neukirchen-Vluyn; Neukirchener Verlag, 1984). Blum discusses the problem of sources in Genesis 22 on p. 323 and suggests that the variation in divine names is intentional.

9. W. Zimmerli, *I. Mose 12–25. Abraham* (ZBAT 1, 3; Zürich: Theologischer Verlag, 1976), 109–10; Seebass, *Genesis II*, 200.

10. B. S. Childs, *Biblical Theology of the Old and New Testaments* (Minneapolis: Fortress Press, 1993), 326–27. Cf. also the discussion of Gen 22:15-18 by R. W. L. Moberly, "The Earliest Commentary on the Akedah," *VT* 38 (1988): 302–23.

11. Gunkel, *Genesis*, 239–40; von Rad, *Genesis*, 238; R. Kilian, *Isaaks Opferung* (SBS 44; Stuttgart: Katholisches Bibelwerk, 1970).

12. C. Westermann, *Genesis 12–36* (Continental Commentaries; trans. J. J. Scullion; Minneapolis: Augsburg, 1985), 355. Von Rad, *Genesis,* 238, grants that "the supposedly oldest version of the narrative was a cult saga" but insists that "this idea is quite foreign to the present narrative."

13. Westermann, *Genesis 12–36, 355.*

14. Ibid.

15. Von Rad, *Genesis,* 234.

16. Ibid., 239.

17. N. Sarna, *The JPS Torah Commentary: Genesis* (Philadelphia: The Jewish Publication Society, 1989), 393.

18. J. D. Levenson, *The Death and Resurrection of the Beloved Son* (New Haven: Yale University Press, 1993), 126.

19. Cf. G. Rouiller, "The Sacrifice of Isaac," in *Exegesis* (ed. F. Bovon and G. Rouiller; Pittsburgh: Pickwick, 1978), 16: "To reduce the sense of the verb to a 'pretense' seems to me considerably to weaken the importance of the testing and the meaning of the text."

20. Coats, "Abraham's Sacrifice of Faith," 399.

21. Westermann, *Genesis 12–36,* 364–65.

22. Sir 44:20; Heb 11:17-19.

23. Seebass, *Genesis II,* 201.

24. Cf. the reconstruction of the basic story by Reventlow, *Opfere deinen Sohn,* 52.

25. For the history of the Christian interpretation of Genesis 22, see D. Lerch, *Isaaks Opferung christlich gedeutet* (BHT 12; Tübingen: Mohr, 1950).

26. Luther's *Commentary on Genesis* (trans. J. T. Mueller; Grand Rapids: Zondervan, 1959), 2:9.

27. S. Kierkegaard, *Fear and Trembling* (trans. W. Lowrie; Princeton: Princeton University Press, 1941), 47–48.

28. The ambiguity of Abraham's answer to Isaac is highlighted in Midrash *Gen. Rab.* 56:4: "At all events God will provide himself the lamb, O my son; and if not, thou art for a burnt-offering my son. So they went both of them together—one to slaughter and the other to be slaughtered." See the comments on this midrashic passage by D. Shulman, *The Hungry God* (Chicago: University of Chicago Press, 1993), 133–39.

29. Coats, "Abraham's Sacrifice of Faith," 394.

30. Von Rad, *Genesis,* 239.

31. Childs, *Biblical Theology,* 394.

32. Blum, *Die Komposition,* 321, recognizes four themes in the original story: testing, the trust of Abraham, the holy place, and child sacrifice. The theme of the holy place is not taken up here as it does not bear on the subject of this essay.

33. Cf. the comment of H. P. Müller, "Genesis 22 und das mlk-Opfer," *BZ* New Series 41 (1997): 237–38.

34. W. Burkert, *Homo Necans: The Anthropology of Ancient Greek Sacrificial Ritual and Myth* (trans. P. Bing; Berkeley: University of California Press, 1983), 21; L. E. Stager and S. R. Wolff, "Child Sacrifice at Carthage—Religious Rite or Population Control?" *BAR* 10 (1984): 31–51.

35. As argued by Sarna, *The JPS Torah Commentary,* 392.

36. At Carthage, urns containing the remains of children and of animals have been found in the same area, and Stager and Wolff suggest "that the burned animals were intended as substitute sacrifices for children" ("Child Sacrifice at Carthage," 39).

37. Levenson, *The Death and Resurrection,* 13.

38. Sarna, *The JPS Torah Commentary,* 393.

39. Ibid.

40. Isa 30:30-33, translation by Levenson, in *The Death and Resurrection,* 9–10.

41. O. Eissfeldt, *Molk als Opferbegriff im Punischen und Hebräischen und das Ende des Gottes Moloch* (Halle: Niemeyer, 1935).

42. M. Weinfeld, "The Worship of Molech and of the Queen of Heaven and Its Background," *UF* 4 (1972): 133–54; J. Day, *Molech: A God of Human Sacrifice in the Old Testament*

(Cambridge: Cambridge University Press, 1989). See also G. C. Heider, *The Cult of Molech* (JSOTSup 43; Sheffield: Sheffield Academic Press, 1985).

43. On the connotations of the phrase, see M. Smith, "A Note on Burning Babies," *JAOS* 95 (1975): 477–79.

44. G. C. Heider, "Molech," in *ABD* (ed. D. N. Freedman; New York: Doubleday, 1992), 4:897. Heider suggests that Isa 30:30-33 implies that the cult is offered to YHWH.

45. Levenson, *The Death and Resurrection*, 11.

46. So also Exod 13:13.

47. Westermann, *Genesis 12–36*, 357.

48. R. de Vaux, *Studies in Old Testament Sacrifice* (Cardiff: University of Wales Press, 1964), 71.

49. Levenson, *The Death and Resurrection*, 9, with reference to the Code of Hammurabi and to the law of the jubilee year in Leviticus.

50. R. M. Hals, *Ezekiel* (FOTL 19; Grand Rapids: Eerdmans, 1989), 136.

51. W. Zimmerli, *Ezekiel 1* (Hermeneia; trans. R. E. Clements; Philadelphia: Fortress Press, 1979), 411.

52. M. Greenberg, *Ezekiel 1-20* (AB 22; New York: Doubleday, 1983), 369.

53. See, further, Levenson, *The Death and Resurrection*, 8.

54. *Sib. Or.* 3:765–66. Cf. Wis 12:5, which polemicizes against the "merciless slaughter of children" by the Canaanites.

55. G. F. Moore, *A Critical and Exegetical Commentary on Judges* (ICC; New York: Scribners, 1901), 299.

56. P. Trible, *Texts of Terror* (Overtures to Biblical Theology; Philadelphia: Fortress Press, 1984), 97, alleges that the making of the vow is an act of unfaithfulness, but the text provides no warrant for this judgment.

57. Ibid., 97, blames Jephtah for failing to trust the spirit of the Lord but attributes his victory in battle to its influence. Should not the making of the vow equally be due to its influence?

58. S. Spiegel, *The Last Trial* (New York: Pantheon, 1967), 28–50. Gen 22:19 mentions that Abraham returned to the young men but does not mention Isaac.

59. See the satirical remarks of L. Kolakowski, "Abraham oder eine höhere Trauer," cited in von Rad, *Das Opfer des Abraham*, 82–83.

60. Sarna, *The JPS Torah Commentary*, 393.

61. Ibid. Emphasis added.

62. J. L. Kugel, *The Bible as It Was* (Cambridge: Harvard University Press, 1997), 171–72. In Pseudo-Philo, *Bib. Ant.* 32:1–2, all the heavenly host was jealous of Abraham.

63. J. C. VanderKam, "The Aqedah, Jubilees, and PseudoJubilee," in *The Quest for Context and Meaning: Studies in Biblical Intertextuality in Honor of James A. Sanders* (ed. C. A. Evans and S. Talmon; Leiden: Brill, 1997), 241–61; G. Vermes, "New Light on the Sacrifice of Isaac from 4Q225," *JJS* 47 (1996): 140–46.

64. Kugel, *The Bible as It Was*, 172.

65. G. Vermes, *Scripture and Tradition in Judaism* (SPB 4; Leiden: Brill, 1961): 193–227; R. J. Daly, "The Soteriological Significance of the Sacrifice of Isaac," *CBQ* 39 (1977): 45–75; J. Swetnam, *Jesus and Isaac* (AnBib 94; Rome: Biblical Institute Press, 1981): 4–80; C. T. R. Hayward, "The Present State of Research into the Targumic Account of the Sacrifice of Isaac," *JJS* 32 (1981): 127–50.

66. P. R. Davies and B. D. Chilton, "The Akedah: A Revised Tradition History," *CBQ* 40 (1978): 514–46; B. D. Chilton, "Recent Discussion of the Aqedah," in *Targumic Approaches to the Gospels* (Lanham, Md.: University Press of America, 1986), 39–49.

67. Daly, "The Soteriological Significance," 51. A parallel account is found in the Fragmentary Targum. Cf. also *Gen. Rab.* 56:8.

68. Vermes, "New Light on the Sacrifice of Isaac."

69. J. VanderKam and J. T. Milik, "Jubilees: 225. 4QpseudoJubilee," in H. Attridge et al., *Qumran Cave 4. VIII. Parabiblical Texts, Part 1* (DJD 13; Oxford: Clarendon, 1994), 149–52.

70. See Swetnam, *Jesus and Isaac.*

71. Jeremiah 23:28: "Let the prophet who has a dream tell the dream, but let the one who has my word speak my word faithfully." There are numerous examples of skepticism toward revelation in Greek and Roman antiquity.

72. I. Kant, "The Dispute between the Philosophical and Theological Faculties," cited by Westermann, *Genesis 12–36,* 354.

73. In addition to Westermann, see Seebass, *Genesis II,* 202.

74. Childs, *Biblical Theology,* 334.

75. Westermann, *Genesis 12–36,* 356–57.

76. Veijola, "Das Opfer des Abraham," 129–30.

77. Ibid., 162, author's translation.

78. R. W. L. Moberly, *Genesis 12–50* (Sheffield: Sheffield Academic Press, 1992), 43.

79. E.g., A. MacIntyre, *Whose Justice? Which Rationality?* (Notre Dame, Ind.: University of Notre Dame Press, 1988).

80. R. Alter, *The Art of Biblical Narrative* (New York: Basic Books, 1981).

81. D. H. Kelsey, *The Uses of Scripture in Recent Theology* (Philadelphia: Fortress Press, 1975), 48. Cf. H. Frei, *The Eclipse of Biblical Narrative* (New Haven: Yale University Press, 1974), vii–viii.

82. E. Auerbach, *Mimesis* (Princeton: Princeton University Press, 1968), 14–15.

83. M. Sternberg, *The Poetics of Biblical Narrative* (Bloomington: Indiana University Press, 1985), 32.

84. Reventlow, *Opfere deinen Sohn,* 7–20. Reventlow is far less skeptical about the Patriarchal Age than most recent critics, but even he grants that the historicity of the individual stories cannot be defended.

85. Moberly, *Genesis 12–50,* 56.

86. Ibid.

87. Cf. Shulman, *The Hungry God.*

88. Blum, *Die Komposition,* 328, thinks that Abraham trusts "that he experiences a God other than the one of the command" (author's translation), but the story shows no qualms about the initial command of God.

5. THE DEVELOPMENT OF THE EXODUS TRADITION

1. See especially I. Finkelstein, *The Archeology of the Israelite Settlement* (Jerusalem: Israel Exploration Society, 1989). Even Finkelstein's critics grant the basic cultural continuity. See W. G. Dever, "Cultural Continuity: Ethnicity in the Archaeological Record and the Question of Israelite Origins," *ErIsr* 24 (1993): 22–33; and the debate among Dever, Finkelstein, and others, in *The Rise of Ancient Israel* (ed. H. Shanks et al.; Washington, D.C.: Biblical Archeology Society, 1992).

2. See especially E. Blum, *Die Komposition der Vätergeschichte* (WMANT 57; Neukirchen-Vluyn: Neukirchener Verlag, 1984); and E. Blum, *Studien zur Komposition des Pentateuch* (BZAW 189; Berlin: de Gruyter, 1990). The late date for the Yahwist has been proposed

by H. H. Schmid, *Der sogenannte Jahwist: Beobachtungen und Fragen zur Pentateuchforschung* (Zürich: Theologischer Verlag, 1976); J. Van Seters, *Prologue to History: The Yahwist as Historian in Genesis* (Louisville: Westminster/John Knox, 1992); and idem, *The Life of Moses: The Yahwist as Historian in Exodus-Numbers* (Louisville: Westminster John Knox, 1994). The traditional view of the Yahwist and Elohist is defended by R. E. Friedman, "Torah," *ABD* 6: 605–22; and idem, *The Hidden Book in the Bible: The Discovery of the First Prose Masterpiece* (San Francisco: Harper: 1998).

3. K. van der Toorn, *Family Religion in Babylonia, Syria and Israel: Continuity and Change in the Forms of Religious Life* (Leiden: Brill, 1996), 236–315.

4. Ibid., 291–300.

5. Ibid., 301.

6. Ibid., 289.

7. Ibid., 258.

8. R. Albertz, *A History of Israelite Religion in the Old Testament Period* (2 vols.; Louisville: Westminster John Knox, 1994), 1:40–94.

9. Ibid.

10. Ibid., 44.

11. Ibid., 43.

12. It is noteworthy, however, that neither Amos nor Hosea mentions slavery in Egypt. The omission is especially striking in Amos, since his message is primarily concerned with social justice. Yet he never tells the Israelites, in Deuteronomic fashion, to remember that they were slaves in the land of Egypt. Both Amos and Hosea, however, seem to know the tradition of wandering in the wilderness. While the authenticity of the relevant passages in Amos might be questioned, the motif is firmly embedded in the poetic oracles of Hosea.

13. Moses is a short form of a theophorous name such as Thut-mose or Amun-mose. See J. Gwyn Griffiths, "The Egyptian Name of Moses," *JNES* 12 (1953): 225–31. Jan Assmann states that the divine name was frequently dropped in Egyptian names and that such a short form would be particularly appropriate for someone who had rejected Egyptian polytheism (*Moses the Egyptian: The Memory of Egypt in Western Monotheism* [Cambridge: Harvard University Press, 1997], 253).

14. E. A. Knauf, *Midian: Untersuchungen zur Geschichte Palästinas und Nordarabiens am Ende des 2. Jahrtausends v. Chr.* (Wiesbaden: Harrassowitz, 1988), 135–41; J. C. De Moor, *The Rise of Yahwism: The Roots of Israelite Monotheism* (BETL 91; Leuven: Leuven University Press/Peeters, 1997), 214–27.

15. A. Malamat, "The Exodus: Egyptian Analogies," in *Exodus: The Egyptian Evidence* (ed. E. S. Frerichs and L. H. Lesko; Winona Lake, Ind.: Eisenbrauns, 1997), 15–26.

16. J. Assmann, *Moses the Egyptian,* 27. Cf. H. Goedicke, "The 'Canaanite Illness,'" *SAK* 11 (1984): 91–105; R. Hendel, "The Exodus in Biblical Memory," *JBL* 120(2001): 601–22.

17. Josephus, *Against Apion,* 1.228–50. E. Gruen, *Heritage and Hellenism: The Reinvention of Jewish Tradition* (Berkeley: University of California Press, 1998), 41–72, argues implausibly that Manetho's version of the Exodus was adapted from a Jewish source.

18. B. Halpern, "The Exodus and the Israelite Historians," *ErIsr* 24 (1993): 89–96. See also his essay, "The Exodus from Egypt: Myth or Reality?" in *The Rise of Ancient Israel*, ed. Shanks et al., 87–113. Similar arguments are made by Assmann, *Moses the Egyptian*; and Hendel, "The Exodus."

19. Judg 6:13, 11:13; 1 Sam 4:8; 2 Sam 7:6, 23.

20. See the tabulation of the pertinent archaeological evidence by W. Dever, "Israel, History of (Archaeology and the 'Conquest')," *ABD* 3 (1992): 548.

21. H. J. Kraus, "Gilgal: Ein Beitrag zur Kultusgeschichte Israels," *VT* 1 (1951): 181–99; J. A. Soggin, "Gilgal, Passah und Landnahme," VTSup 15 (1966): 263–77; F. M. Cross, *Canaanite Myth and Hebrew Epic* (Cambridge: Harvard University Press, 1973), 104.

22. G. von Rad, *Old Testament Theology* (2 vols.; New York: Harper & Row, 1962–65), 16–17, suggested that the story preserved the memory of the founding of "the Old Israelite Amphictyony."

23. Cf. the summary judgment of E. Zenger et al., eds., *Einleitung in das Alte Testament* (Stuttgart: Kohlhammer, 1995), 135: "that no source material can be identified in 23-24" (author's translation).

24. Van der Toorn, *Family Religion,* 246; Albertz, *A History of Israelite Religion,* 82–83.

25. Albertz, *A History of Israelite Religion,* 46.

26. Ibid., 46.

27. Ibid., 49–52; Van der Toorn, *Family Religion,* 283. Cf. also F. M. Cross, "Reuben, First-Born of Jacob," *ZAW* 100 (1988): 50–63; repr. in *From Epic to Canon: History and Literature in Ancient Israel* (Baltimore: Johns Hopkins University Press, 1998), 53–70; M. Weinfeld, "The Tribal League at Sinai," in *Ancient Israelite Religion: Essays in Honor of Frank Moore Cross* (ed. P. D. Miller et al.; Philadelphia: Fortress Press, 1987), 303–14; Knauf, *Midian,* 50–56, 135–41; and De Moor, *The Rise of Yahwism,* 206. De Moor is exceptional in positing a migration of Proto-Israelites from the south (Teman) to Bashan in the middle of the second millennium.

28. G. von Rad, "The Form-Critical Problem of the Hexateuch," in *The Problem of the Hexateuch and Other Essays* (New York, 1966; repr., London: SCM Press, 1984), 1–78.

29. Albertz, *A History of Israelite Religion,* 53.

30. Van der Toorn, *Family Religion,* 284.

31. Albertz, *A History of Israelite Religion,* 46.

32. M. Noth, *A History of Pentateuchal Traditions* (Englewood Cliffs, N.J.: Prentice-Hall, 1972; repr., Chico, Calif.: Scholars Press, 1981), 38n143.

33. W. H. C. Propp, *Exodus 1–18* (New York: Doubleday, 1999), 49–51.

34. R. Rendtorff, "The Yahwist as Theologian? The Dilemma of Pentateuchal Criticism," *JSOT* 3 (1977): 2–9; idem, *The Problem of the Process of the Transmission of the Pentateuch* (JSOTSup 89; Sheffield: JSOT Press, 1990).

35. Cf. E. Nicholson, *The Pentateuch in the Twentieth Century: The Legacy of Julius Wellhausen* (Oxford: Clarendon Press, 1998), 247–48.

36. On the incorporation of social concerns into the Priestly tradition in the Holiness Code, see I. Knohl, *The Sanctuary of Silence: The Priestly Torah and the Holiness School* (Minneapolis: Fortress Press, 1995).

37. B. S. Childs, *Introduction to the Old Testament as Scripture* (Philadelphia: Fortress Press, 1979); idem, *Biblical Theology of the Old and New Testament: Theological Reflection on the Christian Bible* (Minneapolis: Fortress Press, 1993).

38. Albertz, *A History of Israelite Religion,* 468–69.

39. J. D. Levenson, "Exodus and Liberation," in *The Hebrew Bible: The Old Testament and Historical Criticism* (Louisville: Westminster John Knox, 1993), 127–59.

40. See my critique of Levenson in "The Exodus and Biblical Theology," chapter 6 below (originally published in *BTB* 25 (1995): 152–60).

6. THE EXODUS AND BIBLICAL THEOLOGY

1. L. G. Perdue, *The Collapse of History: Reconstructing Old Testament Theology* (Overtures to Biblical Theology; Minneapolis: Fortress Press, 1994), 17–68.

2. A. Fierro, "Exodus Event and Interpretation," in *The Bible and Liberation* (ed. N. K. Gottwald; New York: Orbis Books, 1983), 474.

3. N. P. Lemche, "Israel: History of (Premonarchic Period)," *ABD* 3 (1992): 526–45; W. G. Dever, "Archaeology and the Israelite 'Conquest,'" *ABD* 3 (1992): 545–58.

4. F. M. Cross, *Canaanite Myth and Hebrew Epic* (Cambridge: Harvard University Press, 1973), 112–44; J. Day, *God's Conflict with the Dragon and the Sea* (Cambridge: Cambridge University Press, 1985), 97–101; B. F. Batto, *Slaying the Dragon: Mythmaking in the Biblical Tradition* (Louisville: Westminster John Knox, 1992), 102–27.

5. See Perdue, *The Collapse of History*, 231–47. Also J. Barr, "Story and History in Biblical Theology," *JR* 56 (1976): 1–17; repr. in *The Scope and Authority of the Bible* (Philadelphia: Westminster Press, 1980), 1–17.

6. C. Geertz, *The Interpretation of Cultures* (New York: Basic Books, 1973), 90.

7. D. Tracy, *The Analogical Imagination* (New York: Crossroad, 1981), 99–229.

8. G. von Rad, "The Form-Critical Problem of the Hexateuch," in *The Problem of the Hexateuch and Other Essays* (ed. G. von Rad; New York: McGraw-Hill, 1966), 1–78; idem, *Old Testament Theology* (2 vols.; New York: Harper & Row, 1962–65), 1:187–88.

9. J. Wellhausen, *Prolegomena to the History of Israel* (1878; repr., Atlanta: Scholars Press, 1994), 342–44.

10. D. A. Knight, "The Pentateuch," in *The Hebrew Bible and Its Modern Interpreters* (ed. D. A. Knight and G. M. Tucker; Philadelphia: Fortress Press, 1985), 268.

11. D. J. McCarthy, *Old Testament Covenant: A Survey of Current Opinions* (Richmond, Va.: John Knox, 1973).

12. J. D. Levenson, *Sinai and Zion: An Entry into the Jewish Bible* (Minneapolis: Winston, 1985), 42–45.

13. Wellhausen, *Prolegomena to the History of Israel*, 343–44; Cross, *Canaanite Myth and Hebrew Epic*, 99–105; M. Weinfeld, "The Tribal League at Sinai," in *Ancient Israelite Religion* (ed. P. D. Miller et al.; Philadelphia: Fortress Press, 1987), 303–14.

14. See E. Blum, *Die Komposition der Vätergeschichte* (WMANT 57; Neukirchen-Vluyn: Neukirchener Verlag, 1984); *Studien zur Komposition des Pentateuch* (BZAW 189; Berlin: de Gruyter, 1990).

15. So especially D. J. McCarthy, *Treaty and Covenant* (AnBib 21; Rome: Pontifical Biblical Institute, 1963).

16. T. Dozeman, *God on the Mountain* (SBLMS 37; Atlanta: Scholars Press, 1989), 120–26.

17. G. Gutiérrez, *A Theology of Liberation* (Maryknoll, N.Y.: Orbis Books, 1973), 157.

18. Ibid., 159. Cf. N. Lohfink, *Option for the Poor: The Basic Principle of Liberation Theology in the Light of the Bible* (Berkeley: Bibal, 1987), 27–52.

19. W. Brueggemann, "Pharaoh as Vassal: A Study of a Political Metaphor," *CBQ* 57 (1995): 27.

20. J. S. Croatto, *Exodus: A Hermeneutics of Freedom* (Maryknoll, N.Y.: Orbis Books, 1978), 15.

21. J. D. Levenson, *The Hebrew Bible: The Old Testament and Historical Criticism* (Louisville: Westminster/John Knox, 1994), 127–59.

22. G. V. Pixley, *On Exodus: A Liberation Perspective* (Maryknoll, N.Y.: Orbis, 1987).

23. Levenson, *The Hebrew Bible: The Old Testament and Historical Criticism*, 140.

24. Ibid., 145–46, citing John Howard Yoder.

25. Ibid., 151.

26. Ibid., 152.

27. Brueggemann, "Pharaoh as Vassal: A Study of a Political Metaphor," 28.

28. Gutiérrez, *A Theology of Liberation*, 155. There is a long tradition, independent of liberation theology, that sees the Exodus as a paradigm for political action; see M. Waltzer, *Exodus and Revolution* (New York: Basic Books, 1985).

29. D. A. Knight, *Tradition and Theology in the Old Testament* (Philadelphia: Fortress Press, 1977); P. D. Hanson, *Dynamic Transcendence* (Philadelphia: Fortress Press, 1978); W. Brueggemann, *Old Testament Theology: Essays on Structure, Theme, and Text* (Minneapolis: Fortress Press, 1992); R. Gnuse, "New Directions in Biblical Theology," *JAAR* 62 (1994): 893–918.

30. B. S. Childs, *Biblical Theology of the Old and New Testaments* (Minneapolis: Fortress Press, 1993); idem, *Old Testament Theology in a Canonical Context* (Philadelphia: Fortress Press, 1985); idem, *Introduction to the Old Testament as Scripture* (Philadelphia: Fortress Press, 1979). Cf. Levenson, *The Hebrew Bible: The Old Testament and Historical Criticism*.

31. G. F. Hasel, *Old Testament Theology: Basic Issues in the Current Debate* (4th ed.; Grand Rapids: Eerdmans, 1991), 117–47.

32. Perdue, *The Collapse of History.*

33. See the chapter "Why Jews Are Not Interested in Biblical Theology," in Levenson, *The Hebrew Bible: The Old Testament and Historical Criticism*, 56–61.

34. See especially J. A. Sanders, "Adaptable for Life: The Nature and Function of Canon," in *Magnalia Dei: The Mighty Acts of God* (ed. F. M. Cross et al.; Garden City, N.Y.: Doubleday, 1976); but see also J. A. Sanders, *Canon and Community* (Philadelphia: Fortress Press, 1984).

35. Sanders, "Adaptable for Life," 537.

36. Ibid., 551.

37. M. Fishbane, *Biblical Interpretation in Ancient Israel* (Oxford: Clarendon Press, 1985), 18.

38. M. Fishbane, "Revelation and Tradition: Aspects of Inner-Biblical Exegesis," *JBL* 99 (1980): 361.

39. See J. Barr, "Review of Sanders, *From Sacred Story to Sacred Text: Canon as Paradigm*" (*CRBR*; Atlanta: Scholars Press, 1988), 137–41.

40. Childs, *Introduction to the Old Testament as Scripture*, 67.

41. G. T. Sheppard, "Canonical Criticism," *ABD* 1 (1992): 863.

42. J. Barton, *Reading the Old Testament* (Philadelphia: Westminster Press, 1984), 153–54.

43. Cf. Deut 5:2-3; and von Rad, *Old Testament Theology*, 99–112.

44. See H. W. Wolff, *Joel and Amos* (Hermeneia; Philadelphia: Fortress Press, 1977), 169–70 (on Amos 2:10) and 175 (on Amos 3:1). See, however, the objections of S. Paul, who allows that there is an editorial expansion at Amos 3:1, in *Amos* (Hermeneia; Minneapolis: Fortress Press, 1991), 90, 100.

45. R. Coote is exceptional if not unique in arguing that this is an exilic addition, in *Amos among the Prophets* (Philadelphia: Fortress Press, 1981), 117–20.

46. Cf. Paul, *Amos*, 284, who maintains that the Exodus as such is not a unique event and grants its participants no special priority or immunity.

47. See especially L. Perlitt, *Bundestheologie im Alten Testament* (Neukirchen-Vluyn: Neukirchener Verlag, 1969).

48. J. Barton, *Amos' Oracles against the Nations: A Study of Amos 1.3—2.5* (Cambridge: Cambridge University Press, 1980).

49. See M. DeRoche, "Yahweh's *Rîb* against Israel: A Reassessment of the So-Called 'Prophetic Lawsuit' in the Preexilic Prophets," *JBL* 102 (1983): 563–74. On the authenticity of Micah 6, see J. Blenkinsopp, *A History of Prophecy in Israel* (Philadelphia: Westminster, 1983), 120.

50. See Philo, *On the Special Laws* 2:282; K. Berger, *Die Gesetzauslegung Jesu* (Neukirchen-Vluyn: Neukirchener Verlag, 1972), 137–76.

51. This point is emphasized by Gutiérrez, in *A Theology of Liberation*, 154–57.

52. B. W. Anderson, "Exodus Typology in Second Isaiah," in *Israel's Prophetic Heritage* (ed. B. W. Anderson and W. Harrelson; New York: Harper, 1962), 177–95; C. Stuhlmueller, *Creative Redemption in Deutero-Isaiah* (AnBib 43; Rome: Pontifical Biblical Institute, 1970), 59–68.

53. B. L. Mack, "*Imitatio Mosis*: Patterns of Cosmology and Soteriology in the Hellenistic Synagogue," *SPhilo* 1 (1972): 27–55.

54. Aspects of such a review can be found in S. E. Loewenstamm, *The Evolution of the Exodus Tradition* (Jerusalem: Magnes, 1992).

55. Fishbane, *Biblical Interpretation in Ancient Israel*, 6.

56. For a sober and balanced discussion of this issue, see James Gustafson, "The Place of Scripture in Christian Ethics: A Methodological Study," *Int* 24 (1970): 430–55.

7. THE BIBLICAL VISION OF THE COMMON GOOD

1. See the reviews of Catholic social teaching by Frs. Bartell and Curran in O. F. Williams and J. W. Houck, eds., *The Common Good and U.S. Capitalism* (Lanham, Md.: University Press of America, 1987), 50–69. I am especially indebted to my colleague, Professor Leslie Griffin, for orientation to the issues in contemporary moral theology.

2. Compare David Tracy's definition of a classic as "any text, event or person which unites particularity of origin and expression with a disclosure of meaning and truth available, in principle, to all human beings" ("Theological Classics in Contemporary Theology," *TD* 25 [1977]: 349) and his discussion of the New Testament as a classic, in *The Analogical Imagination* (New York: Crossroad, 1981), 248–304.

3. The phrase of Krister Stendahl, in *Meanings: The Bible as Document and as Guide* (Philadelphia: Fortress Press, 1984), 14.

4. Against the "canonical approach" advocated by B. S. Childs in several books, most notably his *Introduction to the Old Testament as Scripture* (Philadelphia: Fortress Press, 1979).

5. The distinction was formulated by A. Alt, "The Origins of Israelite Law," in *Essays on Old Testament History and Religion* (Garden City, N.Y.: Doubleday, 1968), 101–71. For recent surveys of biblical law, see D. Patrick, *Old Testament Law* (Atlanta: John Knox, 1985); and L. Epstein, *La Justice Sociale dans le Proche-Orient Ancien et le Peuple de la Bible* (Paris: Cerf, 1983).

6. *Pastoral Letter on Catholic Social Teaching and the U.S. Economy* (Washington, D.C.: National Conference of Catholic Bishops, 1985), para. 35.

7. On the "traditio-historical" approach to the Bible, which views the biblical material as a tradition in process, see J. A. Sanders, "Adaptable for Life: The Nature and Function of Canon," in *Magnalia Dei: The Mighty Acts of God* (ed. F. M. Cross et al.; Garden City, N.Y.: Doubleday, 1976), 531–60; and D. A. Knight, ed., *Tradition and Theology in the Old Testament* (Philadelphia: Fortress Press, 1977). Compare the "historical contextual" approach advocated by T. W. Ogletree, in *The Use of the Bible in Christian Ethics* (Philadelphia: Fortress Press, 1983).

8. The main approaches are summarized by N. K. Gottwald, *The Hebrew Bible: A Socio-Literary Introduction* (Philadelphia: Fortress Press, 1985), 261–76.

9. N. K. Gottwald, *The Tribes of Yahweh: A Sociology of Liberated Israel, 1250–1050 B.C.E.* (Maryknoll, N.Y.: Orbis, 1979), 700–709.

10. The initial demonstration was made by G. E. Mendenhall, in *Law and Covenant in Israel and the Ancient Near East* (Pittsburgh: The Presbyterian Board of Colportage, 1955). For

a recent discussion, see J. D. Levenson, *Sinai and Zion: An Entry into the Jewish Bible* (Minneapolis: Winston/Seabury, 1984), 15–86.

11. R. de Vaux, *Ancient Israel,* vol. 1, *Social Institutions* (New York: McGraw-Hill, 1961), 174–77; R. Gnuse, "Jubilee Legislation in Leviticus: Israel's Vision of Social Reform," *BTB* 15 (1985): 43–48.

12. S. M. Paul, *Studies in the Book of the Covenant in the Light of Cuneiform and Biblical Law* (Leiden: Brill, 1970).

13. De Vaux, *Ancient Israel,* 173.

14. Ibid., 175: "There is no evidence that the law was ever in fact applied."

15. Ibid., 80–90.

16. The sabbatical release did not apply to foreign slaves, but Deuteronomy defies ancient Near Eastern custom by forbidding the extradition of runaway slaves (Deut 23:16-17).

17. De Vaux, *Ancient Israel,* 170–73.

18. In the Roman era, Hillel allegedly had to devise a legal ruse to bypass the sabbatical law and make it possible for borrowers to obtain loans. He decreed that a loan would not be canceled in the seventh year if it was secured by a *prosbul* that explicitly declared that it could be collected at any time. See R. A. Horsley and J. S. Hanson, *Bandits, Prophets and Messiahs: Popular Movements in the Time of Jesus* (Minneapolis: Winston/Seabury, 1985), 59–60.

19. De Vaux, *Ancient Israel,* 166–67. See Num 27:9-11 for the law of succession. Daughters could inherit (Num 27:7-8) but had to marry within their tribe. See also Lev 25:25, which requires the next of kin to "redeem" property sold because of poverty, by buying it and keeping it within the tribe. See Jer 32:6-9, where Jeremiah buys the field of his cousin, and the Book of Ruth, where Boaz buys the land of Elimelek.

20. The major ancient Near Eastern law codes can be found in J. B. Pritchard, *Ancient Near Eastern Texts* (Princeton: Princeton University Press, 1955), 159–98.

21. See J. Blenkinsopp, *Wisdom and Law in the Old Testament* (Oxford: Oxford University Press, 1983).

22. An ideal of justice was of course maintained in the monarchic period. See K. W. Whitelam, *The Just King: Monarchical Judicial Authority in Ancient Israel* (Sheffield: JSOT, 1979), 29–37.

23. See R. Coote, *Amos among the Prophets* (Philadelphia: Fortress Press, 1981), 24–32; and B. Lang, "The Social Organization of Peasant Poverty in Biblical Israel," in *Monotheism and the Prophetic Minority* (Sheffield: Almond, 1983), 114–27.

24. *Pastoral Letter,* para. 90.

25. So the famous passage, "I was hungry and you gave me food," is framed in an apocalyptic judgment scene in Matthew 25. See J. R. Donahue, S.J., "The Parable of the Sheep and the Goats: A Challenge to Christian Ethics," *TS* 47 (1986): 3–31.

26. On the relevance of apocalyptic imagery, see J. J. Collins, *The Apocalyptic Imagination* (New York: Crossroad, 1984), 214–15; and A. Yarbro Collins, *Crisis and Catharsis: The Power of the Apocalypse* (Philadelphia: Westminster, 1984), 165–75.

8. THE BIBLICAL PRECEDENT FOR NATURAL THEOLOGY

1. B. S. Childs, *Biblical Theology in Crisis* (Philadelphia: Westminster Press, 1970); G. E. Wright, *God Who Acts: Biblical Theology as Recital* (London: SCM, 1952), 103; J. Barr, *Old and New in Interpretation* (London: SCM Press, 1966), 72–74; J. L. Crenshaw, *Prophetic Conflict* (BZAW 124; Berlin: Walter de Gruyter, 1971), 116.

2. W. Brueggemann, "Scripture and an Ecumenical Life-Style," *Int* 25 (January 1970): 11.

3. L. Gilkey, *Naming the Whirlwind: The Renewal of God-Language* (New York: Bobbs-Merrill, 1969), 26.

4. Ibid., 11.

5. D. Tracy, *Blessed Rage for Order* (New York: Seabury Press, 1975), 43. Tracy labels his position "revisionist" and claims that "some process theologians are the most obvious example of this position; still many other positions—for example such Roman Catholic thinkers as Leslie Dewart, Gregory Baum or Michael Novak or such Protestant thinkers as Langdon Gilkey, Van Harvey, or Gordon Kaufman—seem to fit the same general model" (32).

6. V. Harvey, *The Historian and the Believers* (New York: Macmillan, 1966), 117.

7. Cf. Tracy, *Blessed Rage for Order*, 45-46, in criticism of the well-known principle of Paul Tillich.

8. Cf. Harvey, *The Historian and the Believers*, 103. Harvey's thesis that a revolution has taken place (is taking place?) is not disputed.

9. Cf. W. Jaeger, *The Theology of the Early Greek Philosophers* (Oxford: Clarendon Press, 1947), 1–17; and J. Pépin, *Mythe et Allégorie* (Aubier: Montaigne, 1958), 93–104. Antisthenes, a pupil of Socrates who influenced the Stoics, distinguished one *physei theos* and many *thesei theoi*.

10. Cf. Jaeger, *The Theology of the Early Greek Philosophers*, 2–3. Varro's distinction was derived from a Greek source.

11. J. B. Cobb, *Living Options in Protestant Theology* (Philadelphia: Westminster Press, 1962), 18.

12. Ibid., 19. Aquinas did acknowledge that some convictions could only be known by revelation while they were compatible with reason.

13. Tracy, *Blessed Rage for Order*, 9.

14. By "wisdom material," I intend to refer to the books of Proverbs, Job, Qoheleth, Sirach, and Wisdom of Solomon. Wisdom material in the Psalms and other Old Testament books is not considered here, since such material can only be identified by analogy with the accepted wisdom books. Within the wisdom literature, the books of Job and Qoheleth give rise to a host of special problems, and their relevance to our discussion will only be indicated in passing. The other books may be regarded as different stages of an ongoing tradition, although the Wisdom of Solomon is distinguished by extensive Hellenistic influence.

15. Cf. H. Gese, *Lehre und Wirklichkeit in der alten Weisheit* (Tübingen: J. C. B. Mohr, 1958), 2: "It is acknowledged that the teaching of wisdom represents a foreign body in the Old Testament" (author's translation). Gese argues that wisdom underwent a transformation when it was adopted by Israel.

16. Cf. H. D. Preuss, "Erwägungen zum theologischen Ort alttestamentlicher Weisheitsliteratur," *EvT* 30 (August 1970): 393–417; H. D. Preuss, "Das Gottesbild der älteren Weisheit Israels" (*Studies in the Religion of Ancient Israel,* VTSup 23; Leiden: E. J. Brill, 1972), 117–45; G. E. Mendenhall, "The Shady Side of Wisdom," in *A Light unto My Path: Old Testament Studies in Honor of Jacob M. Myers* (ed. H. N. Bream et al.; Philadelphia: Temple University Press, 1974), 324; see the criticism of this position by R. E. Murphy, "Wisdom and Yahwism," in *No Famine in the Land: Studies in Honor of John L. McKenzie* (ed. J. W. Flanagan and A. W. Robinson; Missoula, Mont.: Scholars Press, 1975), 117–26.

17. Cf. Gese, *Lehre und Wirklichkeit in der alten Weisheit*, 50: "Es ist der Jahwismus gewesen, der die in der altorientalischen Weisheit gegebene Lehre von der schicksalwirkenden Tat durchbrochen und das menschliche Geschick als vor der frei waltenden Gnade Gottes

abhängig gedacht hat." Gese refers to Prov 10:22; 16:1, 9; 20:24; and 21:31. Gese's position is accepted by H. J. Hermisson, *Studien zur Israelitischen Spruchweisheit* (WMANT 28; Neukirchen-Vluyn: Neukirchener Verlag, 1968), 69.

18. Preuss, "Das Gottesbild der älteren Weisheit Israels," 125–28; cf. U. Skladny, *Die ältesten Spruchsammlungen in Israel* (Göttingen: Vandenhoeck & Ruprecht, 1962), 71–76.

19. H. Brunner, "Der Freie Wille Gottes in der Ägyptischen Weisheit," in *Les Sagesses du Proche-Orient Ancien* (Colloque de Strasbourg; Paris: Presses Universitaires de France, 1962), 102–20.

20. Cf. Preuss, "Das Gottesbild der älteren Weisheit Israels," 136–42. "Fear of the Lord" has been considered as a distinctively Yahwistic element by G. von Rad, *Wisdom in Israel* (New York and Nashville: Abingdon Press, 1972), 53–74; C. Bauer-Kayatz, *Einführung in die alttestamentliche Weisheit* (Neukirchen-Vluyn: Neukirchener Verlag, 1969), 31; and Hermisson, *Studien zur Israelitischen Spruchweisheit*, 71.

21. Preuss, "Erwägungen zum theologischen Ort alttestamentlicher Weisheitsliteratur," 413, author's translation.

22. Childs, *Biblical Theology in Crisis*, 47–50.

23. F. M. Cross, *Canaanite Myth and Hebrew Epic* (Cambridge: Harvard University Press, 1973), 93–194; cf. Childs, *Biblical Theology in Crisis*, 70–77.

24. See further the remarks of Murphy, "Wisdom and Yahwism," 123–24, who reminds us that the God of the Fathers was only later identified with the God of the Exodus.

25. Preuss, "Das Gottesbild der älteren Weisheit Israels," 143–44.

26. Ibid.

27. P. D. Hanson, *The Dawn of Apocalyptic* (Philadelphia: Fortress Press, 1975).

28. W. Zimmerli, "The Place and Limit of Wisdom in the Framework of the Old Testament Theology," *SJT* 17(1964), 146–58.

29. Murphy, "Wisdom and Yahwism," 117.

30. Even the identification of Wisdom and the law in Sirach does not suggest that Wisdom is derived from or legitimated by the law, but only that it derives from and leads to the same God.

31. Cf. von Rad, *Wisdom in Israel*; Gese, *Lehre und Wirklichkeit in der alten Weisheit*; H. H. Schmid, *Wesen und Geschichte der Weisheit* (BZAW 101; Berlin: Alfred Töpelmann, 1966).

32. Zimmerli, "The Place and Limit."

33. Ibid., 153.

34. B. Gemser, "The Spiritual Structure of Biblical Aphoristic Wisdom," in *Adhuc Loquitur* (Pretoria Oriental Series 7; ed. A. van Selms and A. S. van der Woude; Leiden: E. J. Brill, 1968), 138–49.

35. Cf. Crenshaw, *Prophetic Conflict*, 123. Crenshaw gives a valuable summary of the entire debate.

36. Cf. J. C. Rylaarsdam, *Revelation in Jewish Wisdom Literature* (Chicago: University of Chicago Press, 1946), 55. This is accepted by both Gemser and Crenshaw.

37. On the similarity of Wisdom to a prophet, see R. B. Y. Scott, *Proverbs; Ecclesiastes* (AB 18; Garden City, N.Y.: Doubleday, 1965), 39.

38. Von Rad, *Wisdom in Israel*, 144–76.

39. Cf. M. Heidegger, *An Introduction to Metaphysics* (trans. R. Manheim; New Haven: Yale University Press, 1959); and the comparison of poetic and religious revelation by O. Paz, *The Bow and the Lyre* (New York: McGraw-Hill, 1975), 101–66.

40. Jaeger, *The Theology of the Early Greek Philosophers*, 112, 94–95.

41. Rylaarsdam, *Revelation in Jewish Wisdom Literature*, 55. We might compare the frequent tendency of scholars to contrast "humanism" and "religion" as if these were mutually exclusive terms. For a defense of the religious dimension of humanism with reference to the wisdom literature, see J. Priest, "Humanism, Skepticism and Pessimism in Israel," *JAAR* 34 (December 1968): 311–26.

42. W. McKane, *Prophets and Wise Men* (SBT 44; London: SCM Press, 1965), 48.

43. Ibid. McKane regards early wisdom as "a wisdom of statecraft."

44. We might compare the thesis of Bruno Malinowski (*Magic, Science and Religion* [Garden City, N.Y.: Doubleday, 1954], 25–36) that the "savage" "has his profane world of practical activities and rational outlook besides the sacred region of cult and belief." More recent anthropological studies have emphasized that there is also a rational element in myths and religious beliefs.

45. Von Rad, *Wisdom in Israel*, 68.

46. Ibid., 67.

47. Ibid., 307.

48. In his major review of von Rad's book ("*Wisdom in Israel* by Gerhard von Rad," *RelSRev* 2, no. 2 (April 1976): 6–12], J. L. Crenshaw asserts that "no such enlightenment existed." There would seem to be evidence for a transformation of Israelite culture at the time of the origin of the monarchy, but at least some types of wisdom (the "clan-wisdom" stressed by Crenshaw) were surely known in Israel before that period.

49. Von Rad, *Wisdom in Israel*, 63.

50. Ibid., 97–110.

51. Cf. B. Vawter, "Intimations of Immortality and the Old Testament," *JBL* 91 (June 1972): 158–71. Vawter rightly rejects the view that a belief in immortality can be found in Proverbs, Sirach, or Psalms.

52. Cf. D. E. Gowan, *When Man Becomes God* (PTMS 6; Pittsburgh: Pickwick Press, 1975), on this theme in the OT.

53. Note also the importance of "limit" or "boundary situations" in the philosophy of Karl Jaspers and Heidegger's insistence that "limit and end are that wherewith the essent begins to be" (*An Introduction to Metaphysics*, 60).

54. Tracy, *Blessed Rage for Order*, 93.

55. G. von Rad, *Old Testament Theology* (vol. 1.; trans. D. M. G. Stalker; Edinburgh: Oliver & Boyd, 1962), 439.

56. Ibid., 440.

57. Gese, *Lehre und Wirklichkeit in der alten Weisheit*, 45–60.

58. Cf. E. Leach, "Lévi-Strauss in the Garden of Eden: An Examination of Some Recent Developments in the Analysis of Myth," in *Claude Lévi-Strauss: The Anthropologist as Hero* (ed. E. N. Hayes and T. Hayes; Cambridge: MIT Press, 1970), 47–60.

59. J. D. Crossan, *The Dark Interval* (Niles, Ill.: Argus Communications, 1975), 47–62. Crossan offers a spectrum of possible stories, ranging from myth, on one extreme, to parable, on the other.

60. These works need not be classified as parables, but they are evidently closer to parable than to myth in Crossan's spectrum.

61. Cf. Gese, *Lehre und Wirklichkeit in der alten Weisheit*, 33–34; Schmid, *Wesen und Geschichte der Weisheit*, 144–68; von Rad, *Wisdom in Israel*, 124–37, 144–76.

62. Skladny, *Die ältesten Spruchsammlungen in Israel* (71–75), correctly points out that attitudes rather than individual actions are often involved and prefers the phrase "Haltung-Schicksal Zusammenhang" (the connection of attitude and consequence).

63. Cf. O. S. Rankin, *Israel's Wisdom Literature* (Edinburgh: T&T Clark, 1936).

64. K. Koch, "Gibt es ein Vergeltungsdogma im Alten Testament?" (repr. in *Um das Prinzip der Vergeltung in Religion und Recht des Alten Testaments,* ed. K. Koch; Darmstadt: Wissenschaftliche Buchgesellschaft, 1972), 130–80.

65. Ibid., 135. Koch explains the verbs *glm* and *hšyb* in this sense.

66. Prov 28:13 says that one who confesses his sins will obtain mercy, but this is only another example of an act that has a necessary consequence. Yahweh does not simply and spontaneously forgive.

67. Gese, *Lehre und Wirklichkeit in der alten Weisheit,* 37.

68. Ibid., 5–50; Preuss, "Das Gottesbild der älteren Weisheit Israels," 120–34.

69. R. B. Y. Scott ("Wise and Foolish, Righteous and Wicked," in *Studies in the Religion of Ancient Israel* [VTSup 23; Leiden: E. J. Brill, 1972], 146–65) reminds us that there exist "differences in viewpoint and objectives among the various contributors to the corpus of wisdom sayings." However, it is doubtful whether the different contributors can be successfully disentangled.

70. These chapters are generally thought to be late (post-exilic), although there is no decisive evidence. James L. Crenshaw, in his review of von Rad ("*Wisdom in Israel* by Gerhard von Rad," 9), suggests that the warning against wicked men set on increasing their spoil and the frequent theme of the foreign adulteress point to a postexilic date, but neither of these points is incompatible with an earlier dating. However, there are no cogent arguments for a preexilic date either.

71. Cf. Kayatz, *Einführung in die alttestamentliche Weisheit.*

72. The most extensive discussion of the religio-historical origins of personified Wisdom is still Helmer Ringgren (*Word and Wisdom* [Lund: Håkan Ohlsson, 1947]).

73. Von Rad, *Wisdom in Israel,* 144–57. The view that Wisdom is a personified attribute has been defended in recent years by R. N. Whybray, in *Wisdom in Proverbs* (SBT 45; London: SCM Press, 1965). On hypostases in general, see G. Pfeifer, *Ursprung und Wesen der Hypostasenvorstellungen im Judentum* (Stuttgart: Calwer Verlag, 1967).

74. Cf. Kayatz, *Einführung in die alttestamentliche Weisheit.*

75. Cf. Heidegger, *An Introduction to Metaphysics,* 93–206.

76. Cf. G. Fohrer, "*Sophia,* III, The Wisdom (Sagacity and Knowledge) of Man," *TDNT* 7 (Grand Rapids: Eerdmans, 1971), 483–89.

77. Cf. P. L. Berger, *The Sacred Canopy* (Garden City, N.Y.: Doubleday/Anchor Books, 1967), for an important discussion of the dual features of projection and objectivity in the human quest for order.

78. Rylaarsdam, *Revelation in Jewish Wisdom Literature,* 18–46; J. Fichtner, "Die altorientalische Weisheit in ihrer israelitisch-jüdischen Ausprägung" (BZAW 62; Giessen: Alfred Töpelmann, 1933), 123–28.

79. This remains true even if the content of the law was influenced by wisdom traditions. Cf. M. Weinfeld, "The Origin of Humanism in Deuteronomy," *JBL* 80 (September 1961): 241–47.

80. Von Rad, *Wisdom in Israel,* 244.

81. In fact Sirach draws extensively on Hellenistic materials. Cf. Th. Middendorp, *Die Stellung Jesu Ben Siras zwischen Judentum und Hellenismus* (Leiden: E. J. Brill, 1973), 7–34; and M. Hengel, *Judaism and Hellenism* (vol. 1; Philadelphia: Fortress Press, 1974), 138–53.

82. Cf. J. Marböck, *Weisheit im Wandel* (BBB 37; Bonn: Peter Hanstein, 1971), 93–96.

83. D. Georgi, "Der vorpaulinische Hymnus Phil 2, 6-11," in *Zeit und Geschichte, Dankesgabe an Rudolf Bultmann* (ed. E. Dinkler; Tübingen: J. C. B. Mohr, 1964), 272.

84. B. L. Mack, "Imitatio Mosis: Patterns of Cosmology and Soteriology in the Hellenistic Synagogue," *SPhilo* 1 (1972): 30–31.

85. Philo, *De opificio mundi* 1.3(1).

86. Cf. H. A. Wolfson, *Philo* (Cambridge, Mass.: Harvard University Press, 1948): 155–64. Philo's debt to the wisdom tradition is stressed by Jean Laporte, in "Philo in the Tradition of Wisdom," in *Aspects of Wisdom in Judaism and Early Christianity* (ed. R. Wilken; Notre Dame, Ind.: University of Notre Dame Press, 1975), 103–42. The influence of wisdom on early Christian theology is stressed by R. L. Wilken, "Wisdom and Philosophy in Early Christianity," in ibid., 143–68.

87. A detailed bibliography can be found in W. Brueggemann, *In Man We Trust* (Richmond, Va.: John Knox, 1972), 134–37.

88. Cf. H.W. Wolff, *Amos the Prophet: The Man and His Background* (tr. F. R. McCurley; Philadelphia: Fortress Press, 1973); and the critique by J. L. Crenshaw, "The Influence of the Wise upon Amos," *ZAW* 79 (1967): 42–52.

89. J. L. McKenzie ("Reflections on Wisdom," *JBL* 86 [March 1967]: 1–9) makes a useful distinction between "wisdom literature" and "wisdom as an approach to reality." However, McKenzie seems to forget his own distinction when he proceeds to designate the historical books as wisdom literature.

90. J. L. Crenshaw, "Method in Determining Wisdom Influence upon 'Historical Literature,'" *JBL* 88 (June 1969): 131.

91. J. B. Cobb (*A Christian Natural Theology* [Philadelphia: Westminster Press, 1965], 11) states: "Even those theologies which explicitly repudiate natural theology have had assumptions or developed implications that should, in fact, be recognized as belonging to the sphere of natural theology."

92. Crenshaw (*Prophetic Conflict*, 121) suggests that "the current flight to wisdom as more palatable to contemporary man may be as futile as Jonah's attempt to escape the Inevitable."

9. PROVERBIAL WISDOM AND THE YAHWIST VISION

1. H. N. Schneidau, *Sacred Discontent* (Berkeley: University of California, 1976), 206–7; H. D. Preuss, "Das Gottesbild der älteren Weisheit Israels," in *Studies in the Religion of Ancient Israel* (VTSup 23; Leiden: E. J. Brill, 1972), 117–45; G. E. Wright, *God Who Acts: Biblical Theology as Recital* (SBT 1, no. 8; London: SCM, 1952).

2. Schneidau, *Sacred Discontent,* 254.

3. Ibid., 12, 10.

4. G. von Rad, *Wisdom in Israel* (New York: Abingdon, 1972); H. Gese, *Lehre und Wirklichkeit in der alten Weisheit* (Tübingen: Mohr, 1958).

5. W. A. Beardslee, "Uses of the Proverb in the Synoptic Gospel," *Int* 24 (1970): 67.

6. M. W. Clark, "Debunking and the Open Society," in *Commitment without Ideology* (ed. C. D. Batson, J. C. Beker, and M. W. Clark; Philadelphia: United Church, 1973), 124–51; J. D. Crossan, *The Dark Interval: Towards a Theology of Story* (Niles, Ill.: Argus, 1975).

7. P. L. Berger, *The Sacred Canopy* (Garden City, N.Y.: Doubleday/Anchor Books, 1967), 3.

8. Schneidau, *Sacred Discontent,* 13–14.

9. To borrow a term of Victor Turner (*Dramas, Fields, and Metaphors* [Ithaca, N.Y.: Cornell University Press, 1974], 45).

10. Ibid., 215.

11. J. Barr, "Story and History in Biblical Theology," *JR* 56 (1976): 1–17.

12. Cited by Schneidau, *Sacred Discontent*, 185.

13. Preuss, "Das Gottesbild der älteren Weisheit Israels"; J. J. Collins, "The Biblical Precedent for Natural Theology," chapter 8 above (originally published in JAARSup 45 [1977]: 35–67).

14. See John J. Collins, "Cosmos and Salvation: Jewish Wisdom and Apocalyptic in the Hellenistic Age," *HR* 17 (1977): 123–34.

15. J. L. Crenshaw, "The Human Dilemma and the Literature of Dissent," in *Tradition and Theology in the Old Testament* (ed. D. A. Knight; Philadelphia: Fortress Press, 1977), 235–58.

16. Schneidau, *Sacred Discontent*, 5.

17. J. L. Crenshaw, "Wisdom," in *Old Testament Form-Criticism* (ed. J. H. Hayes; San Antonio: Trinity University Press, 1974), 231.

18. A. Jolles, *Einfache Formen* (Darmstadt: Wissenschaftliche Buchgesellschaft, 1968; orig. publ. Tübingen: Niemeyer, 1930), 158; Crenshaw, "Wisdom," 231.

19. For further examples, see H.-J. Hermisson, *Studien zur Israelitischen Spruchweisheit* (WMANT 28; Neukirchen-Vluyn: Neukirchener Verlag, 1968), 52–64.

20. O. Eissfeldt, *Der Maschal im Alten Testament* (BZAW 24; Giessen: Töpelmann, 1913); J. Schmidt, *Studien zur Stilistik der alttestamentlichen Spruchliteratur* (Münster: Aschendorff, 1936).

21. R. N. Whybray, *Wisdom in Proverbs* (SBT 1, no. 45; London: SCM, 1965); C. Kayatz, *Studien zu Proverbien 1-9* (WMANT 22; Neukirchen-Vluyn: Neukirchener Verlag, 1966).

22. Schneidau, *Sacred Discontent*, 248.

23. Von Rad, *Wisdom in Israel*, 31.

24. R. Scholes, *Structuralism in Literature* (New Haven: Yale University Press, 1974), 45; cf. J. M. Thompson, *The Form and Function of Proverbs in Ancient Israel* (The Hague: Mouton, 1974), 69–70.

25. W. McKane, *Proverbs* (Philadelphia: Westminster, 1970), 23; Jolles, *Einfache Formen*, 167.

26. B. Snell, *The Discovery of the Mind* (New York: Harper & Row, 1960), 207.

27. Von Rad, *Wisdom in Israel*, 115–24.

28. M. Black, *Models and Metaphors* (Ithaca: Cornell University Press, 1962), 44–45.

29. I. T. Ramsey, *Models and Mystery* (London: Oxford, 1964), 3.

30. B. E. Meland, *Fallible Forms and Symbols* (Philadelphia: Fortress Press, 1976), 130.

31. Ramsey, *Models and Mystery*, 15.

32. Von Rad, *Wisdom in Israel*, 35–36.

33. Thompson, *The Form and Function of Proverbs in Ancient Israel*, 75.

34. Von Rad, *Wisdom in Israel*, 44.

35. Ibid., 37.

36. Wolfgang M. W. Roth, "The Numerical Sequence X/X + 1 in the Old Testament," *VT* 12 (1962): 300–311.

37. Schneidau, *Sacred Discontent*, 267.

38. M. W. Clark, "Debunking and the Open Society," in *Commitment without Ideology* (ed. C. D. Batson, J. C. Beker, and M. W. Clark; Philadelphia: United Church, 1973), 100.

39. J. D. Crossan, *Raid on the Articulate* (New York: Harper & Row, 1976), 40–51.

40. Thompson, *The Form and Function of Proverbs in Ancient Israel*, 14.

41. Cf. also Prov 16:2, 9; 19:14, 21; 20:24.

42. Von Rad, *Wisdom in Israel*, 99.

43. Cf. Prov 28:26; 3:7.

44. Von Rad, *Wisdom in Israel*, 106.

45. Schneidau, *Sacred Discontent*, 255.

46. Gese, *Lehre und Wirklichkeit in der alten Weisheit*, 45–50.

47. Von Rad, *Wisdom in Israel*, 104.

48. H. Brunner, "Der freie Wille Gottes in der Ägyptischen Weisheit," in *Les Sagesses du Proche-Orient Ancien* (Colloque de Strasbourg; Paris: Presses Universitaires de France, 1962), 103–20; Preuss, "Das Gottesbild der älteren Weisheit Israels."

49. James B. Pritchard, ed., *ANET* (2nd ed.; Princeton: Princeton University Press, 1955), 423. Cf. Prov 19:21; 16:9.

50. Thompson, *The Form and Function of Proverbs in Ancient Israel*, 121; W. G. Lambert, *Babylonian Wisdom Literature* (Oxford: Clarendon, 1960), 266.

51. Thompson, *The Form and Function of Proverbs in Ancient Israel*, 121; W. G. Lambert, *Babylonian Wisdom Literature*, 250.

52. See further von Rad, *Wisdom in Israel*, 37.

53. Ibid., 38.

54. See J. L. Crenshaw, "The Problem of Theodicy in Sirach: On Human Bondage," *JBL* 94 (1975): 53.

55. F. C. Fensham, "Widow, Orphan and the Poor in Ancient Near Eastern Legal and Wisdom Literature," *JNES* 21 (1962): 129–39.

56. Turner, *Dramas, Fields, and Metaphors*, 272–99.

57. J. L. McKenzie, "Reflections on Wisdom," *JBL* 86 (1967): 1–9; Clark, "Debunking and the Open Society"; H.-J. Hermisson, "Weisheit und Geschichte," in *Probleme biblischer Theologie* (ed. H. W. Wolff; Munich: Kaiser, 1971), 136–54.

58. Wright, *God Who Acts: Biblical Theology as Recital*; Schneidau, *Sacred Discontent*.

10. NATURAL THEOLOGY AND BIBLICAL TRADITION

1. Concilium Vaticanum I, *Constitutio dogmatica "Dei Filius,"* ch. 2, "De revelatione," available in *Enchiridion Symbolorum* (33rd ed.; ed. H. Denzinger, rev. A. Schönmetzer; Freiburg: Herder, 1965), 588, no. 3004 (1785); cf. p. 593 no. 3026 (1806). The Council, nonetheless, also insisted on supernatural revelation and the necessity of faith.

2. K. Barth, in *Natural Theology: Comprising "Nature and Grace" by Professor Dr. Emil Brunner and the Reply "No!" by Dr. Karl Barth, with an Introduction by J. Baillie* (London: Bles/Centenary, 1946), 67–128, esp. p. 75.

3. J. Barr, *Biblical Faith and Natural Theology* (Gifford Lectures 1991; Oxford: Clarendon, 1993).

4. Ibid., 137.

5. Ibid., 1.

6. Cf. already J. J. Collins, "The Biblical Precedent for Natural Theology," chapter 8 above (originally published in JAARSup 45 [1977]: 35–67).

7. Augustine *City of God* 6.5; cf. 6, 12, where he speaks of three *theologiae: mythice, physice,* and *politice*. For the discussion of this schema, and the relevant texts, see G. Liberg, "Die 'theologia tripertita' in Forschung und Bezeugung," in *ANRW 1: Von den Anfängen Roms bis zum Ausgang der Republik* (ed. H. Temporini; Berlin/New York: de Gruyter, 1972–73), 4:53–115; J. Pepin, *Mythe et Allegorie* (Paris: Etudes Augustiniennes, 1976), 13–32.

8. W. Jaeger, *The Theology of the Early Greek Thinkers* (Gifford Lectures 1936; Oxford: Clarendon, 1947), 3.

9. Augustine *City of God* 6.5.

10. P. Boyancé, "Sur la théologie de Varron," *REA* 57 (1955): 57–84.

11. So, for example, Antisthenes, a pupil of Socrates; see Jaeger, *Theology,* 3.

12. Augustine *City of God* 8.6.

13. For an example of philosophical debate on theological issues, see Cicero's *De natura deorum*.

14. Eusebius *Praeparatio evangelica* 13.12.1. See J. J. Collins, *Between Athens and Jerusalem: Jewish Identity in the Hellenistic Diaspora* (New York: Crossroad, 1983), 175–78.

15. Philo *Opif.* 1§3, trans. F. H. Colson (and G. H. Whitaker), in *Philo* (10 vols.; LCL; London: Heinemann; New York: Putnam's; Cambridge: Harvard University Press, 1929–62), 1.7; for Colson and Whitaker's "world" I have substituted "cosmos."

16. H. Chadwick, "Philo and the Beginnings of Christian Thought," in *The Cambridge History of Later Greek and Medieval Philosophy* (ed. A. H. Armstrong; Cambridge: Cambridge University Press, 1967), 137–57; J. Pelikan, *Christianity and Classical Culture: The Metamorphosis of Natural Theology in the Christian Encounter with Hellenism* (Gifford Lectures 1992–93; New Haven: Yale University Press, 1993), 96.

17. A. A. Long and D. N. Sedley, *The Hellenistic Philosophers* (2 vols.; Cambridge: Cambridge University Press, 1987), 1:275.

18. So C. Larcher, *Etudes sur le Livre de la Sagesse* (EBib; Paris: Gabalda, 1969), 235–36. Cf. P. Heinisch, *Die griechische Philosophie im Buche der Weisheit* (Alttestamentliche Abhandlungen1.4; Münster: Aschendorff, 1908), 155.

19. D. Winston, *The Wisdom of Solomon* (AB 43; New York: Doubleday, 1979), 33. On Middle Platonism, see J. Dillon, *The Middle Platonists: A Study of Platonism, 80 B.C. to A.D. 220* (London: Duckworth, 1977); and T. H. Tobin, *The Creation of Man: Philo and the History of Interpretation* (CBQMS 14; Washington, D.C.: Catholic Biblical Association of America, 1983), 10–19.

20. J. M. Rist, *Stoic Philosophy* (Cambridge: Cambridge University Press, 1969), 202–18.

21. Dillon, *Middle Platonists,* xiv.

22. Barr, *Biblical Faith and Natural Theology,* 81–101. Barr discusses elements of natural theology in Psalms 19, 104, and 119, the wisdom literature, the prophets, and the law.

23. For a concise summary, see M. R. Wright, *Cosmology in Antiquity* (Sciences of Antiquity; London: Routledge, 1995), 166–75.

24. Plato *Laws* 10 (890).

25. Ibid. (899B).

26. Pelikan, *Christianity and Classical Culture,* 96.

27. Diogenes Laertius *Lives and Opinions of Eminent Philosophers* 7.1 §148; Cicero *De natura deorum* 1.15 §39; *SVF* (4 vols.; ed. H. F. A. von Arnim; Leipzig: Teubner, 1903–24), 2.1077.

28. Cicero *De natura deorum* 2.5 §15, trans. H. Rackham, in *Cicero: De natura deorum: Academica* (LCL; London: Heinemann; New York: Putnam's, 1933), 271.

29. Ibid., 2.61 §153.

30. Philo *Decal.* 12 §§52–54, trans. Colson, in *Philo,* 7. 33; cf. Philo *Spec.* 1.3 §§13–20. See Winston, *Wisdom of Solomon,* 248.

31. J. A. Fitzmyer, *Romans* (AB 33; New York: Doubleday, 1993), 273–77. Fitzmyer distinguishes what Paul is saying from the position taken in the First Vatican Council. Paul was speaking of a situation de facto: God is intellectually perceived and known from created things. The Fathers of the Council drew an inference in arguing for the possibility of such knowledge. See also B. J. Brooten, *Love between Women: Early Christian Responses to Female Homoeroticism* (Chicago Series on Sexuality, History, and Society; Chicago: University of Chicago Press, 1996), 222–28, with extensive bibliography.

32. Philo *Decal.* 66.

33. J. M. G. Barclay, *Jews in the Mediterranean Diaspora, from Alexander to Trajan (323 BCE–117 CE)* (Edinburgh: T&T Clark, 1996), 190.

34. Ibid., 191.

35. M. P. Nilsson, *Geschichte der griechischen Religion 2: Die hellenistische und römische Zeit* (Handbuch der Altertumswissenschaft 5, no. 2; Munich: Beck, 1974), 569–78; B. von Borries, *Qvid veteres philosophi de idolatria senserint* (Göttingen: Dieterich, 1918).

36. H. W. Attridge, *First-Century Cynicism in the Epistles of Heraclitus* (HTS 29; Missoula, Mont.: Scholars, 1976), 13–23.

37. M. Görg, "Die Religionskritik in Weish 13,1f.: Beobachtungen zur Entstehung der Sapientia-Salomonis im späthellenistischen Alexandria," in *Lehrerin der Gerechtigkeit: Studien zum Buch der Weisheit* (Erfurter theologische Schriften 19; ed. G. Hentschel and E. Zenger; Leipzig: Benno, 1991), 13–25.

38. See V. Tcherikover, A. Fuks, and M. Stern, *Corpus Papyrorum Judaicarum* (3 vols.; Cambridge: Harvard University Press, 1957–64), 1.1–93; J. M. Modrzejewski, *The Jews of Egypt, from Rameses II to Emperor Hadrian* (Philadelphia: Jewish Publication Society, 1995).

39. Modrzejewski, *Jews of Egypt,* 185. The name Julius borne by Philo's brother and nephew suggests that citizenship had been bestowed on the family either by Julius Caesar or by Augustus.

40. Ibid., 185–90.

41. L. H. Feldman (*Jew and Gentile in the Ancient World: Attitudes and Interactions from Alexander to Justinian* [Princeton: Princeton University Press, 1993], 57–59) shows that Philo had firsthand knowledge of the gymnasium and that he never condemns the institution. A. Mendelson (*Secular Education in Philo of Alexandria* [Monographs of Hebrew Union College 7; Cincinnati: Hebrew Union College Press, 1982], 29) argues that Philo's references to the gymnasium reflect his own education.

42. Philo *Mos.* 1.7 §35, trans. Colson, in *Philo* 6.295.

43. Modrzejewski, *Jews of Egypt,* 161–63.

44. Tcherikover, Fuks, and Stern, *Corpus Papyrorum Judaicarum,* 2.36–55.

45. J. Reider, *The Book of Wisdom* (New York: Harper, 1957), 41.

46. Winston, *Wisdom of Solomon,* 45.

47. Cicero *De natura deorum* 2.47 §154, trans. Rackham, in *Cicero: De natura deorum,* 273.

48. Plutarch *Moralia: On the Fortune or the Virtue of Alexander* 1.6 (329A-B); cf. *SVF* 1. 262.

49. Seneca *De otio* 4.1.

50. Philo *Qu. In Gen.* 2.60, trans. R. Marcus, in *Philo, Supplement* (2 vols.; LCL; Cambridge: Harvard University Press; London: Heinemann, 1953), 1.147 (from the Armenian version of the lost Greek text).

51. Diogenes Laertius *Lives and Opinions of Eminent Philosophers* 7.1 §33, trans. R. D. Hicks, in *Diogenes Laertius: Lives of Eminent Philosophers* (2 vols.; LCL; London: Heinemann; New York: Putnam's, 1925), 2.145.

52. See Feldman, *Jew and Gentile,* 125–31. On the motif of misanthropy directed against the Jews, see now P. Schäfer, *Attitudes towards the Jews in the Ancient World* (Cambridge: Harvard University Press, 1997), 175–77.

53. Diodorus Siculus 40.3.4, trans. F. R. Walton, in *Diodorus of Sicily 12* (LCL; Cambridge: Harvard University Press; London: Heinemann, 1967). Schäfer (*Attitudes towards the Jews,* 17), however, notes that it was Hecataeus who combined for the first time the motif of *misoxenia* and the tradition about the exodus.

54. Diodorus Siculus 34/35.1.1, 53.

55. See J. N. Sevenster, *The Roots of Pagan Anti-Semitism in the Ancient World* (NovTSup 41; Leiden: Brill, 1975). J. G. Gager, *The Origins of Anti-Semitism: Attitudes toward Judaism in*

Pagan and Christian Antiquity (New York: Oxford University Press, 1983), 39–54. The charges are recorded and answered in Josephus's tract *Against Apion*.

56. See A. Mendelson, *Philo's Jewish Identity* (BJS 161; Atlanta: Scholars, 1988), 103–13.

57. Ibid., 128–29.

58. Philo *Spec.* 2.29 §163, trans. Colson, *Philo*, 7.407.

59. Philo *Mos.* 2.7 §44, trans. Colson, *Philo*, 6.471.

60. Philo *Qu. In Exod.* 2.2., trans. Marcus, *Philo, Supplement*, 2.36; for his "sojourner" (from the Armenian version), I have presumed an original *prosēlytos*.

61. Compare Philo *Spec.* 1.12–17 §§66–97, where the truest temple of God is the whole universe.

62. See, for example, the contrast between the experiential-expressive and cultural-linguistic models in G. A. Lindbeck, *The Nature of Doctrine: Religion and Theology in a Postliberal Age* (Philadelphia: Westminster, 1984), 30–45; and the insistence of J. D. Levenson. *The Hebrew Bible, the Old Testament and Historical Criticism: Jews and Christians in Biblical Studies* (Louisville: Westminster John Knox, 1993), 80, that "there is no non-particularistic access" to confessional contexts.

11. TEMPORALITY AND POLITICS IN JEWISH APOCALPYTIC LITERATURE

1. See the analysis of the genre in J. J. Collins, ed., *Apocalypse: The Morphology of a Genre* (*Semeia* 14; Missoula, Mont.: SBL, 1979).

2. For Harold Bloom's theory of influence, see *The Anxiety of Influence: A Theory of Poetry* (Oxford: Oxford University Press, 1983).

3. M. Weber, *The Sociology of Religion* (trans. E. Fischoff; 1922; repr., Boston: Beacon Press, 1963), 106.

4. K. Mannheim, *Ideology and Utopia: An Introduction to the Sociology of Knowledge* (trans. L. Wirth and E. Shils; 1929; repr., New York: Harcourt, Brace & Company, 1936), 40.

5. D. F. Aberle, "A Note on Relative Deprivation Theory as Applied to Millenarian and Other Cult Movements," in *Millennial Dreams in Action: Essays in Comparative Studies* (ed. S. Thrupp; The Hague: Mouton, 1962), 209–14.

6. K. Burridge, *New Heaven, New Earth: A Study of Millenarian Activities* (New York: Schocken Books, 1969), 3.

7. P. D. Hanson, *The Dawn of Apocalyptic: The Historical and Sociological Roots of Jewish Apocalyptic Eschatology* (Philadelphia: Fortress Press, 1975).

8. S. L. Cook, *Prophecy and Apocalypticism: The Postexilic Social Setting* (Minneapolis: Fortress Press, 1995), 153.

9. A. I. Baumgarten, *The Flourishing of Jewish Sects in the Maccabean Era: An Interpretation* (JSJSup 55; Leiden: E. J. Brill, 1997), 165.

10. Baumgarten, *The Flourishing of Jewish Sects*, 171.

11. See J. J. Collins, *Daniel* (Hermeneia; Minneapolis: Fortress Press, 1993), 162–70.

12. The Median kingdom is represented by the unhistorical Darius the Mede (Dan 6:1; 9:1), who is followed by Cyrus the Persian (6:28; 10:1). The "prince of Greece" follows the "prince of Persia" in Dan 10:20.

13. An independent "four-kingdom" schema, with Assyria instead of Babylon in the first place, is found in the fourth *Sibylline Oracle*, a Jewish work that dates from the end of the first century C.E. in its present form. See D. Flusser, "The Four Empires in the Fourth Sibyl and in the Book of Daniel," *Israel Oriental Studies* 2 (1972): 148–75.

14. Herodotus 1.30, 1.95.

15. J. Wiesehöfer, "Vom 'oberen Asien' zur 'gesamten bewohnten Welt': Die hellenistisch-römische Weltreiche-Theorie," in *Europa, Tausendjähriges Reich und neue Welt: Zwei Jahrtausende Geschichte und Utopie in der Rezeption des Danielbuches* (ed. M. Delgado, K. Koch, and E. Marsch; Fribourg, Switzerland: Universitätsverlag; Stuttgart: W. Kohlhammer, 2003) 66–83.

16. Velleius Paterculus 1.6.6. J. W. Swain, "The Theory of the Four Monarchies: Opposition History under the Roman Empire," *CP* 35 (1940): 1–21.

17. It is rejected by Wiesehöfer, "Die hellenistisch-römische Vier-Monarchien-Theorie," who argues that Sura wrote no earlier than the Augustan age. The rise of Roman power was, however, sometimes dated to the second century B.C.E., e.g., by Polybius, who regarded the victory over Perseus of Macedonia at Pydna in 168 B.C.E. as the decisive point.

18. Dionysius of Halicarnassus 1.2.1–4.

19. Tacitus *Historiae* 5.8–9.

20. One Latin author who used the schema, Pompeius Trogus, was critical of Rome and generally anti-imperial. He wrote in the Augustan era. See Swain, "The Theory of the Four Monarchies," 16–17.

21. H. Cancik, "The End of the World, of History, and of the Individual in Greek and Roman Antiquity," in *The Origins of Apocalypticism in Judaism and Christianity* (vol. 1 of *The Encyclopedia of Apocalypticism*; ed. J. J. Collins; New York: Continuum, 1998), 84–125 (119).

22. S. A. Kaufman, "Prediction, Prophecy, and Apocalypse in the Light of New Akkadian Texts," in *Proceedings of the Sixth World Congress of Jewish Studies, 1973* (ed. A. Shinan; Jerusalem: World Union of Jewish Studies, 1977), 221–28 (224). See also P. Höffken, "Heilszeit-herrschererwartung im babylonischen Raum," *WO* 9 (1977): 57–71.

23. Polybius 29.21, from Appian *Punica* 132.

24. See J. J. Collins, "Nebuchadnezzar and the Kingdom of God: Deferred Eschatology in the Jewish Diaspora," in *Seers, Sibyls, and Sages in Hellenistic-Roman Judaism* (JSJSup 54; Leiden: E. J. Brill, 1997), 131–37.

25. D. L. Smith-Christopher, "The Book of Daniel," *NIB* 7, 57.

26. C. T. Begg, "Daniel and Josephus: Tracing the Connections," in *The Book of Daniel in the Light of New Findings* (ed. A. S. van der Woude; BETL 106; Leuven: Leuven University Press, 1993), 539–45.

27. S. Mason, "Josephus, Daniel and the Flavian House," in *Josephus and the History of the Greco-Roman Period* (ed. F. Parente and J. Sievers; SPB 41; Leiden: E. J. Brill, 1994), 161–91 (175).

28. *Tanḥuma* Mishpatim (4), cited by D. Satran, "Early Jewish and Christian Interpretation of the Fourth Chapter of the Book of Daniel" (diss., Hebrew University, Jerusalem, 1985), 123.

29. *b. B. Bat.* 3b–4a; Satran, "Early Jewish and Christian Interpretation," 127.

30. Swain, "The Theory of the Four Monarchies," 8.

31. S. K. Eddy, *The King Is Dead: Studies in Near Eastern Resistance to Hellenism, 334–31 B.C.* (Lincoln: University of Nebraska Press, 1961), 19.

32. On the *Bahman Yasht,* see A. Hultgård, "The *Bahman Yasht:* A Persian Apocalypse," in *Mysteries and Revelations: Apocalyptic Studies since the Uppsala Colloquium* (ed. J. J. Collins and J. H. Charlesworth; JSPSup 9; Sheffield: JSOT Press, 1991), 114–34; A. Hultgård, "Mythe et histoire dans l'Iran: Étude de quelques thèmes dans le Bahman Yašt," in G. Widengren, A. Hultgård, and M. Philonenko, *Apocalyptique iranienne et dualisme quomrânien* (Paris: Maisonneuve, 1995), 63–162.

33. C. Rowland, "'Upon Whom the Ends of the Ages Have Come': Apocalyptic and the New Testament," in *Apocalypse Theory and the Ends of the World* (ed. M. Bull; Oxford: Basil Blackwell, 1995), 38–57 (54).

34. See the discussion of this passage in D. E. Aune, *Revelation 6–16* (WBC 52B; Dallas: Word Books, 1998), 750. See also A. Yarbro Collins, "The Political Perspective of the Revelation to John," in *Cosmology and Eschatology in Jewish and Christian Apocalypticism* (JSJSup 50; Leiden: E. J. Brill, 1996), 198–217.

35. See the commentary by P. A. Tiller, *A Commentary on the Animal Apocalypse of 1 Enoch* (Atlanta: Scholars Press, 1993), 355–66.

36. Deut 32:34-43. See J. Licht, "Taxo, or the Apocalyptic Doctrine of Divine Vengeance," *JJS* 12 (1961): 95–103.

37. A. Yarbro Collins, "The Political Perspective," 207–17.

38. See J. J. Collins, "Apocalyptic Eschatology as the Transcendence of Death," in *Seers, Sibyls, and Sages,* 75–98; and J. J. Collins, *The Apocalyptic Imagination* (2nd ed.; Grand Rapids: Eerdmans, 1998), passim.

39. D. H. Lawrence, *Apocalypse* (1931; repr., New York: Penguin Books, 1976), 118–19.

40. D. Berrigan, "Till the End of Empire," *The Other Side* (July–August, 1990): 10.

41. Suetonius *Augustus* 31.1. On the role of such oracles in oriental resistance to Rome, see in general H. Fuchs, *Der geistige Widerstand gegen Rom in der antiken Welt* (Berlin: W. de Gruyter, 1938); and R. MacMullen, *Enemies of the Roman Order* (Cambridge: Harvard University Press, 1966).

42. W. Benjamin, "N," in *Benjamin: Philosophy, Aesthetics and History* (ed. G. Smith; Chicago: University of Chicago Press, 1989), 64; cited by M. Bull, *Seeing Things Hidden: Apocalypse, Vision and Totality* (London: Verso, 1999), 149.

43. Cf. E. Schüssler Fiorenza, *Justice and Judgement in the Book of Revelation* (Philadelphia: Fortress Press, 1985), 75: "This antagonistic concept of Christian existence does not allow for a realized understanding of redemption and salvation, but demands an eschatological one."

44. This paper was originally delivered at the Oxford Millennium Conference in April 2000.

45. F. O'Connor, *Kings, Lords and Commons: An Anthology from the Irish* (Van Nuys, Calif.: Ford & Bailie, 1989), 108.

12. THE BOOK OF TRUTH

1. I would like to thank my colleague at the University of Chicago, Catherine Brekus, for her bibliographical suggestions regarding the Millerites.

2. R. A. Doan, *The Miller Heresy, Millennialism, and American Culture* (Philadelphia: Temple University Press, 1987), 10.

3. T. Parker, *The Visions and Prophecies of Daniel Expounded* (London: Edmund Paxton, 1646; available through UMI, Ann Arbor, Mich.), 4. See the discussion of Parker by R. Smolinski, "Apocalypticism in Colonial North America," in *Apocalypticism in the Modern Period and the Contemporary Age* (ed. Stephen J. Stein; vol. 3 of *The Encyclopedia of Apocalypticism*; ed. B. McGinn, J. J. Collins, and S. J. Stein; New York: Continuum, 1998), 44–45.

4. Parker, *The Visions and Prophecies of Daniel Expounded,* 7; cf. 15.

5. Ibid., 23.

6. Ibid., 19.

7. Ibid., 22–30.

8. Ibid., 30.

9. Ibid., 39.

10. Ibid., 44–45.

11. Ibid., 49. Later, he cites Gen 6:3; Ezek 4:6; Rev 11:3, 8; and Lev 25:8 in support of the principle that a day is a figure for a year in certain passages; ibid., 54.

12. Ibid., 48–49.

13. Ibid., 50.

14. Ibid., 52–53.

15. Ibid., 57.

16. Ibid., 58–59.

17. Ibid., 134–43.

18. Ibid., 155.

19. Smolinski, *Apocalypticism in Colonial North America,* 39.

20. Ibid., 59.

21. Doan, *The Miller Heresy, Millennialism, and American Culture,* 11.

22. Smolinski, *Apocalypticism in Colonial North America,* 64.

23. S. J. Stein, "Apocalypticism outside the Mainstream in the United States," in Stein, ed., *Apocalypticism in the Modern Period and the Contemporary Age,* 110. For a later example of a similar attitude, see J. H. Moorhead, "Apocalypticism in Mainstream Protestantism," in Stein, ed., *Apocalypticism in the Modern Period and the Contemporary Age,* 77.

24. Stein, "Apocalypticism outside the Mainstream in the United States," 110.

25. D. L. Rowe, *Thunder and Trumpets: Millerites and Dissenting Religion in Upstate New York, 1800–1850* (American Academy of Religion Studies in Religion 38; Chico, Calif.: Scholars Press, 1985), 17–18, 26. On Miller's lack of Hebrew and Greek and his disinterest in a learned clergy, see S. Bliss, *Memoirs of William Miller* (Boston: Joshua V. Himes, 1853), 155–56. For Miller's statement of faith, see ibid., 77–80.

26. Rowe, *Thunder and Trumpets,* 10.

27. Bliss, *Memoirs of William Miller,* 70–72; see also S. D. O'Leary, *Arguing the Apocalypse: A Theory of Millennial Rhetoric* (New York: Oxford University Press, 1994), 116–17.

28. Rowe, *Thunder and Trumpets,* 10–11.

29. Bliss, *Memoirs of William Miller,* 74.

30. Ibid., 72.

31. Ibid., 74, 82.

32. Ibid., 81–82.

33. Ibid., 72.

34. Ibid., 72–73.

35. Ibid., 73.

36. Doan, *The Miller Heresy, Millennialism, and American Culture,* 31; Rowe, *Thunder and Trumpets,* 13.

37. Bliss, *Memoirs of William Miller,* 74. Unlike Parker, Miller did not conclude that these 2,300 years would end at the same point in time as the 1,260 years of the Apocalypse. Like the seventy weeks of Daniel 9, he believed that the 1,260 years had already ended. Miller interpreted the latter as the period of papal supremacy (ibid.). He claimed that the supremacy of the papacy should be reckoned from 538 C.E., by virtue of a decree of Justinian (ibid., 197; Doan, *The Miller Heresy, Millennialism, and American Culture,* 105). Miller dated the end of the supremacy of the papacy to 1798, when Napoleon captured Rome (Rowe, *Thunder and Trumpets,* 68).

38. Bliss, *Memoirs of William Miller,* 96, 193–97.

39. Ibid., 76, 192–93; see the discussion in J. J. Collins, *Daniel* (Hermeneia; Minneapolis: Fortress Press, 1993), 354–55.

40. Bliss, *Memoirs of William Miller,* 76. Here he does not explain this dating but simply says that he followed the "best historians that [he] could consult" (ibid.). In another context,

a letter from Charles Fitch is quoted that includes an inquiry "in what history [Miller] find[s] the fact that the last of the ten kings was baptized in A.D. 508," but Miller's response is not recorded (ibid., 129). The year 508 was understood by the Millerites as the end of pagan Rome (Doan, *The Miller Heresy, Millennialism, and American Culture,* 99).

41. Bliss, *Memoirs of William Miller,* 76.

42. Ibid., 81.

43. Ibid., 83.

44. Ibid., 97.

45. Rowe, *Thunder and Trumpets,* 44.

46. Doan, *The Miller Heresy, Millennialism, and American Culture,* 98–100.

47. Bliss, *Memoirs of William Miller,* 139–40. In Himes's words, "It was at this time that I laid myself, family, society, reputation, all, upon the altar of God, to help him, to the extent of my power, to the end" (ibid., 140).

48. P. Boyer, "The Growth of Fundamentalist Apocalyptic in the United States," in Stein, ed., *Apocalypticism in the Modern Period and the Contemporary Age,* 146–47.

49. Rowe, *Thunder and Trumpets,* 45.

50. O'Leary, *Arguing the Apocalypse,* 109.

51. Bliss, *Memoirs of William Miller,* 170–72. Miller regarded the Jewish year as extending from one vernal equinox to the next (O'Leary, *Arguing the Apocalypse,*105).

52. O'Leary, *Arguing the Apocalypse,* 106; Rowe, *Thunder and Trumpets,* 135.

53. Rowe, *Thunder and Trumpets,* 136.

54. Ibid., 145–46.

55. Stein, "Apocalypticism outside the Mainstream in the United States," 118–19.

56. Doan, *The Miller Heresy, Millennialism, and American Culture,* 39.

57. Ibid., 26, 81–82.

58. Ibid., 212–14.

59. H. Lindsey, *The Late Great Planet Earth* (New York: Bantam, 1973). On Lindsey and other dispensationalist writers of the late twentieth century, see Boyer, "The Growth of Fundamentalist Apocalyptic in the United States," 140–78.

60. "The Centennial Celebration of the Theological Seminary" (Princeton, 1912), 349–50 (cited by E. R. Sandeen, *The Roots of Fundamentalism: British and American Millenarianism, 1800–1830* [Chicago: University of Chicago Press, 1970], 115).

61. See the summary by G. M. Marsden, *Fundamentalism and American Culture: The Shaping of Twentieth-Century Evangelicalism, 1870–1925* (New York: Oxford, 1980), 14–16. Also S. E. Ahlstrom, "The Scottish Philosophy and American Theology," *CH* 24 (1955): 257–72.

62. C. Hodge, *Systematic Theology* (New York, 1874), 1.18 (cited by Sandeen, *The Roots of Fundamentalism,* 117).

63. The younger Hodge was named Archibald Alexander, after the first Princeton professor.

64. A. A. Hodge and B. B. Warfield, "Inspiration," *Presbyterian Review* 2 (April 1881): 237, 234, 243 (cited by Marsden, *Fundamentalism in American Culture,* 113).

65. Marsden, *Fundamentalism in American Culture,* 115.

66. Sandeen, *The Roots of Fundamentalism,* 188.

67. M. E. Marty, *The Noise of Conflict* (vol. 2 of *Modern American Religion*; Chicago: University of Chicago Press, 1986), 155–214.

68. R. D. Wilson, *Studies in the Book of Daniel* (New York: Revell, 1917; Second Series, New York: Revell, 1938). See also his study "The Aramaic of Daniel," in *Biblical and Theological Studies by the Faculty of Princeton Theological Seminary Published in Commemoration of the One Hundredth Anniversary of the Founding of the Seminary* (New York: Scribners, 1912), 261–306.

69. Wilson, *Studies in the Book of Daniel* (Second Series), 3.

70. W. F. Albright, "The Date and Personality of the Chronicler," *JBL* 40 (1921): 112n.

71. K. Koch, "Dareios der Meder," in *The Word of the Lord Shall Go Forth: Essays in Honor of David Noel Freedman* (ed. C. L. Meyers and M. P. O'Connor; Winona Lake, Ind.: Eisenbrauns, 1983), 287–99.

72. Wilson, *Studies in the Book of Daniel* (1917), 117–22.

73. Ibid., 274.

74. See the comments of J. Barr, in *Fundamentalism* (2nd ed.; London: SCM, 1981), 150–52.

75. J. A. Montgomery, *A Critical and Exegetical Commentary on the Book of Daniel* (ICC; Edinburgh: Clark, 1927).

76. Ibid., 72n17.

77. E. J. Young, *The Prophecy of Daniel* (Grand Rapids: Eerdmans, 1949).

78. D. J. Wiseman, T. C. Mitchell, R. Joyce, W. J. Martin, and K. A. Kitchen, *Notes on Some Problems in the Book of Daniel* (London: Tyndale, 1965); D. J. Wiseman, *Nebuchadnezzar and Babylon* (The Schweich Lectures, 1983; Oxford: Oxford University Press, 1985).

79. See the critique of this scholarship by L. L. Grabbe, "Fundamentalism and Scholarship: The Case of Daniel," in *Scripture, Meaning and Method: Essays Presented to Anthony Tyrrell Hanson* (ed. B. P. Thompson; Hull: Hull University Press, 1987), 133–52.

80. B. S. Childs, *Introduction to the Old Testament as Scripture* (Philadelphia: Fortress Press, 1979), 612.

81. Wilson, *Studies in the Book of Daniel* (Second Series), 101–16.

82. R. H. Charles, ed., *The Apocrypha and Pseudepigrapha of the Old Testament* (Oxford: Clarendon, 1913); idem, *A Critical and Exegetical Commentary on the Book of Daniel* (Oxford: Clarendon, 1929).

83. See further J. J. Collins, *Daniel*.

84. J. E. Goldingay, *Daniel* (WBC 30; Dallas: Word, 1988).

85. D. L. Smith-Christopher, "The Book of Daniel," *NIB* (Nashville: Abingdon, 1996), 7:57.

86. D. Berrigan, "Till the End of Empire," *The Other Side* (July–August 1990): 8–14; idem, "Unflinching Faith," *The Other Side* (September–October 1990): 8–17; idem, "A Frightful Vision," *The Other Side* (November–December 1990): 36–43.

87. Berrigan, "A Frightful Vision," 38.

88. Ibid., 40.

89. Ibid., 42.

13. THE LEGACY OF APOCALYPTICISM

1. K. Koch, *The Rediscovery of Apocalyptic: A Polemical Work on a Neglected Area of Biblical Studies and Its Damaging Effects on Theology and Philosophy* (Naperville, Ill.: Allenson, 1972).

2. R. Sturm, "Defining the Word 'Apocalyptic': A Problem in Biblical Criticism," in *Apocalyptic and the New Testament* (ed. J. Marcus and M. Soards; Sheffield: JSOT, 1989), 37.

3. H. Lindsey, *The Late Great Planet Earth* (New York: Bantam, 1973); N. Perrin, "Eschatology and Hermeneutics: Reflections on Method in the Interpretation of the New Testament," *JBL* 93 (1974): 3–14.

4. P. Boyer, *When Time Shall Be No More: Prophecy Belief in Modern American Culture* (Cambridge: Harvard University Press, 1992).

5. J. Day, *God's Battle with the Dragon and the Sea* (Cambridge: Cambridge University Press, 1985).

6. J. Collins, *Daniel* (Hermeneia; Minneapolis: Fortress Press, 1993), 286–94.

7. A. Yarbro Collins, *The Combat Myth in the Book of Revelation* (Missoula, Mont.: Scholars Press, 1976).

8. Perrin, "Eschatology and Hermeneutics: Reflections on Method in the Interpretation of the New Testament."

9. P. Ricoeur, *The Symbolism of Evil* (Boston: Beacon, 1969).

10. L. Festinger, W. Riecken, and S. Schachter, *When Prophecy Fails* (Minneapolis: University of Minnesota Press, 1956).

11. M. Buber, "Prophecy, Apocalyptic and the Historical Hour," in *Pointing the Way* (trans. and ed. M. Friedman; New York: Harper, 1957), 200.

12. Ibid., 201.

13. Polybius 29:21; H. Cancik, "The End of the World, of History and of the Individual in Greek and Roman Antiquity," *Encyclopedia of Apocalypticism* (ed. J. Collins; New York: Continuum, 1998), 108–9.

14. R. Bultmann, *Jesus Christ and Mythology* (New York: Scribners, 1958), 15.

14. JESUS AND THE MESSIAHS OF ISRAEL

1. M. Hengel, "Jesus, der Messias Israels," in *Messiah and Christos* (ed. I. Gruenwald et al.; TSAJ 32; Tübingen: Mohr, 1992), 155–76.

2. Ibid., 164–65.

3. For a comprehensive treatment of the evidence of the Dead Sea Scrolls on the subject of messianism, see J. J. Collins, *The Scepter and the Star: The Messiahs of the Dead Sea Scrolls and Other Ancient Literature* (New York: Doubleday, 1995).

4. E.g., E. Schürer, *The History of the Jewish People in the Age of Jesus Christ, 175 B.C.–A.D. 135* (rev. and ed. G. Vermes, F. Millar, and M. Black; Edinburgh: Clark, 1979), 2:488–547.

5. See especially J. Neusner, W. S. Green, and E. S. Frerichs, eds., *Judaisms and Their Messiahs* (Cambridge: Cambridge University Press, 1987); J. H. Charlesworth, ed., *The Messiah* (Minneapolis: Fortress Press, 1992).

6. J. H. Charlesworth, "The Messiah in the Pseudepigrapha," in *Aufstieg und Niedergang der Römischen Welt* (ed. H. Temporini and W. Haase; Berlin: de Gruyter, 1979), 2/19.1:188–218.

7. J. J. Collins, *The Scepter and the Star*, 31–41.

8. M. Smith, "What Is Implied by the Variety of Messianic Figures?" *JBL* 78 (1959): 72.

9. L. H. Schiffman, *Reclaiming the Dead Sea Scrolls* (Philadelphia and Jerusalem: Jewish Publication Society, 1994), 326. Compare also K. E. Pomykala, *The Davidic Dynasty Tradition in Early Judaism: Its History and Significance for Messianism* (Atlanta: Scholars Press, 1995), 235–46.

10. Of course the interpretation of these texts, and especially of CD, is disputed. See J. J. Collins, *The Scepter and the Star*, 74–101; J. VanderKam, "Messianism in the Scrolls," in *The Community of the Renewed Covenant* (ed. E. Ulrich and J. VanderKam; Notre Dame, Ind.: University of Notre Dame Press, 1994), 211–34; and E. Puech, "Messianism, Resurrection, and Eschatology at Qumran and in the New Testament," in ibid., 235–56.

11. It is supported by some Pseudepigrapha that are ideologically close to the Qumran community: *Jubilees* 31:12-20; *Testament of Levi* 18; and *Testament of Judah* 21.

12. Other important messianic texts include Psalm 2, Genesis 49, 2 Samuel 7, Amos 9, and Jeremiah 23 and 33. See J. J. Collins, *The Scepter and the Star*, 49–73, for fuller discussion.

13. The original meaning of the Hebrew is disputed.

14. Philo, *De praemiis et poenis*. See P. Borgen, "'There Shall Come Forth a Man': Reflections on Messianic Ideas in Philo," in Charlesworth, ed., *The Messiah*, 341–61.

15. Pomykala, *The Davidic Dynasty Tradition*, 232–26, argues for a diversity of royal messiahs in the Scrolls by assuming that a messiah is not Davidic unless he is explicitly said to be so. The messiah of Israel, as paired with the messiah of Aaron, then, is not Davidic. The Prince of the Congregation is Davidic in 4Q285, but not in CD. Even in 1QSb, "a specific connection to the davidic figure is . . . lacking" (p. 242), despite the admitted allusions to Isaiah 11. I find this methodology problematic and its results implausible. On the methodological issue, see further J. J. Collins, "Method in the Study of Messianism," in *Methods of Investigation of the Dead Sea Scrolls and the Khirbet Qumran Site: Present Realities and Future Prospects* (ed. M. O. Wise et al.; New York: New York Academy of Sciences, 1994), 213–29.

16. Hengel, "Jesus, der Messias Israels," 164.

17. J. Starcky, "Les quatres étapes du messianisme à Qumrân," *RB* 70 (1963): 492.

18. E. Puech, "Fragments d'un apocryphe de Lévi et le personnage eschatologique: 4QTest Levi^c-d et 4QAJa," in *The Madrid Qumran Congress: Proceedings of the International Congress on the Dead Sea Scrolls* (Madrid, March 18–21, 1991; ed. J. Trebolle Barrera and L. Vegas Montaner; Leiden: Brill, 1992), 449–501.

19. Ibid., 496.

20. Note however E. M. Cook, *Solving the Mysteries of the Dead Sea Scrolls* (Grand Rapids: Zondervan, 1994), 164, who suggests that the priest in question is not the eschatological priest but perhaps the priest of the fourth jubilee.

21. J. Jeremias, "*Pais Theou* in Later Judaism in the Period after the LXX," *TDNT* 5 (1968): 682: "First, it should be noted that the modern isolation of the Servant Songs . . . was completely unknown in that day."

22. Puech, "Fragments d'un apocryphe de Lévi," 477–78.

23. Pace Puech, ibid., 499. Puech makes a rather tortured suggestion that there is an allusion "en négatif."

24. See further J. J. Collins, "Asking for the Meaning of a Fragmentary Qumran Text: The Referential Background of 4QAaronA," in *Text and Contexts, Biblical Texts in Their Textual and Situational Contexts: Essays in Honor of Lars Hartman* (ed. T. Fornberg and D. Hellholm; Oslo: Scandinavian University Press, 1995), 579–90.

25. *New York Times,* November 8, 1991; *Times* (London), November 8, 1991. This interpretation was attributed to M. O. Wise and R. Eisenman.

26. G. Vermes, "The Oxford Forum for Qumran Research Seminar on the Rule of War from Cave 4 (4Q285)," *JJS* 43 (1992): 85–90.

27. U. B. Müller, *Messias und Menschensohn in jüdischen Apokalypsen und in der Offenbarung des Johannes* (Gütersloh: Mohn, 1972).

28. See J. C. VanderKam, "Righteous One, Messiah, Chosen One, and Son of Man," in Charlesworth, ed., *The Messiah,* 169–91.

29. J. J. Collins, "The Son of Man in First Century Judaism," *NTS* 38 (1992), 459–64.

30. On the textual evidence for the reading "son," see M. E. Stone, *Fourth Ezra* (Hermeneia; Minneapolis: Fortress Press, 1990), 207–8. Stone concludes that the Greek was probably in all cases *pais* and the Hebrew probably *ebed*. The context of ch. 13, however, clearly evokes Psalm 2, which refers to the messiah as son, not servant.

31. J. J. Collins, *Daniel* (Hermeneia; Minneapolis: Fortress Press, 1993), 72–79.

32. E. Puech, "Fragment d'une Apocalypse en Araméen (4Q246 = pseudo-Dan^d) et le 'Royaume de Dieu,'" *RB* 99 (1992): 98–131.

33. To the best of my knowledge, the messianic interpretation was first proposed orally by Frank M. Cross. For a defense, see J. J. Collins, "The 'Son of God' Text from Qumran," in *From Jesus to John: Essays on Jesus and New Testament Christology in Honour of Marinus de Jonge* (ed. M. de Boer; Sheffield: JSOT, 1993), 65–82. J. A. Fitzmyer, "4Q246: The 'Son of God' Document from Qumran," *Bib* 74 (1994): 153–75, also sees the figure as positive, a Jewish king in an apocalyptic context, but insists that he is not messianic.

34. This view was originally proposed by J. T. Milik, in a lecture at Harvard University in 1972. Milik proposed that the figure in question was Alexander Balas. Cf. Cook, *Solving the Mysteries,* 168–70; K. Berger, *Jesus and the Dead Sea Scrolls* (Louisville: Westminster John Knox, 1995), 77–79.

35. Puech, "Fragment d'une Apocalypse"; E. Puech, "Notes sur le Fragment d'Apocalypse 4Q246—'Le Fils de Dieu,'" *RB* 101, no. 4 (1994): 533–57.

36. J. J. Collins, "The 'Son of God' Text," 70–71; J. J. Collins, *The Scepter and the Star,* 158.

37. Puech, "Notes sur le Fragment d'Apocalypse 4Q246," 549–50.

38. Neither Puech nor any of the proponents of the "negative" interpretation addresses this objection.

39. Pace Puech, ibid., 555. His attempt to exclude parallels from the first century C.E. is unjustified by any cultural watershed.

40. Ibid, author's translation. It is also difficult to imagine that Luke would have adapted his messianic titles from supposedly pagan propaganda.

41. For the full range of meanings of the title "Son of God," see M. Hengel, *The Son of God: The Origin of Christology and the History of Jewish-Hellenistic Religion* (Philadelphia: Fortress Press, 1976).

42. J. J. Collins, "The 'Son of God' Text," 71–72.

43. Pace Puech, "Notes sur le Fragment d'Apocalypse 4Q246," 555–56. The accusation that this suggestion arises from a desire to find a Jewish background for the messianic titles of the NT is unfounded.

44. A. Schweitzer, *The Quest of the Historical Jesus* (New York: Macmillan, 1969), 337.

45. M. Hengel, *Was Jesus a Revolutionist?* (Philadelphia: Fortress Press, 1971).

46. Hengel, "Jesus, der Messias Israels," 164.

47. E. Puech, "Une Apocalypse Messianique (4Q521)," *RevQ* 15 (1992): 475–519; E. Puech, *La Croyance des Esséniens en la Vie Future: Immortalité, Résurrection, Vie Éternelle?* (Paris: Gabalda, 1993), 627–92.

48. Pace P. Grelot, "Sur Isaie lxi: la première consécration du grand-prêtre," *RB* 97 (1990): 414–31, who argues that the speaker is a High Priest. Grelot is followed by E. Puech, "Messianism, Resurrection, and Eschatology," 243.

49. See however 1 Kgs 19:6, where Elijah is told to anoint Elisha.

50. CD 2:12; cf. 6:1; 1QM 11:7.

51. 11QMelch 2:18. P. J. Kobelski, *Melchidezek and Melchireśac* (Washington, D.C.: Catholic Biblical Association, 1981), 9.

52. For fuller argumentation, see J. J. Collins, "The Works of the Messiah," *DSD* 1 (1994): 98–112. Puech also allows for the role of an agent: "In 4Q521, God himself accomplishes these signs (probably in the days of the Messiah and through his messenger)" ("Messianism, Resurrection, and Eschatology," 245).

53. Puech, "Une Apocalypse messianique," 497. He claims support in 4Q521 frag. 2 iii line 6, where he reads the word *šbt* as meaning scepter rather than "tribe." See J. J. Collins, "The Works of the Messiah," 103.

54. M. Soṭah 9, end; y. Sheqalim 3:3; Pesiqta de R. Kahana 76a; Puech, "Une Apocalypse messianique," 492.

55. Puech recognizes allusions to Elijah in other fragments of 4Q521, but he argues that Elijah is the precursor of the royal messiah and tries to harmonize this text with the dual messianism found elsewhere in the Scrolls (*La Croyance des Esséniens*, 669–81).

56. There is a very fragmentary reference to the return of Elijah in 4Q558 (4QarP). See Puech, *La Croyance des Esséniens*, 676–71.

57. Puech, "Messianism, Resurrection, and Eschatology," 245.

58. Cf. K. Berger, "Zum Problem der Messianität Jesu," *ZTK* 71 (1974): 1–30; K. Berger, "Die königlichen Messiastraditionen des Neuen Testaments," *NTS* 20 (1973–1974): 1–44; A. E. Harvey, *Jesus and the Constraints of History* (Philadelphia: Westminster, 1982), 120–53.

59. Hengel, "Jesus, der Messias Israels," 165, tries to build a cumulative argument. Jesus might be called messiah if he were a prophetic teacher, referred to himself as the apocalyptic "son of man," and was descended from David. But the last two propositions are extremely doubtful.

60. M. de Jonge suggests that "Jesus may have understood himself as a prophetic son of David" (*Jesus the Servant Messiah* [New Haven: Yale University Press, 1991], 72). See the criticism of this position by H. J. de Jonge, "The Historical Jesus' View of Himself and His Mission," in *From Jesus to John: Essays on Jesus and the New Testament Christology in Honour of Marinus de Jonge*, 21–37.

61. D. H. Juel, "The Origin of Mark's Christology," in *The Messiah* (ed. J. H. Charlesworth; Minneapolis: Fortress Press, 1992), 453.

62. The best account of these movements is that of R. Horsley and J. Hanson, *Bandits, Prophets and Messiahs* (Minneapolis: Winston, 1985). On the prophetic figures, see also R. Gray, *Prophetic Figures in Late Second Temple Jewish Palestine* (New York: Oxford University Press, 1993), 112–44.

63. Josephus, *J. W.* 2.258–60.

64. Gray, *Prophetic Figures*, 139–40.

65. Josephus, *J. W.* 2.261–62; Josephus, *Ant.* 20.169–71.

66. Compare the case of Theudas in *Ant.* 20.97–98, who promised that the Jordan River would be divided at his command. For the distinction between sign prophets and practical revolutionaries, see Gray, *Prophetic Figures*, 138.

67. Matt 21:1-11; Mark 11:1-10; Luke 19:29-38; John 12:12-16. In favor of the authenticity of the passage is the fact that Zech 9:9 is never cited as a messianic prophecy in Jewish texts from the period between the Bible and the Mishnah. See Harvey, *Jesus and the Constraints of History*, 122.

68. M. Specter, "The Oracle of Crown Heights," *New York Times Magazine*, March 15, 1992, 34; J. L. Sheler, "A Movement Goes On without Its Leader," *U.S. News & World Report*, December 26, 1994, 94.

69. *New York Times*, August 29, 1993.

70. See A. Yarbro Collins, "The Origin of the Designation of Jesus as Son of Man," *HTR* 80 (1987): 391–407; A. Yarbro Collins, "Daniel 7 and Jesus," in J. J. Collins, *Daniel*, 92–96.

71. The similarity between Christ in Revelation 19 and the messiah in *4 Ezra* is noted by A. Yarbro Collins, "Eschatology in the Book of Revelation," *ExAud* 6 (1990): 70.

15. JEWISH MONOTHEISM AND CHRISTIAN THEOLOGY

1. J. D. G. Dunn, *The Partings of the Ways between Christianity and Judaism and Their Significance for the Character of Christianity* (Philadelphia: Trinity Press International, 1991), 19–21.

2. P. M. Casey, *From Jewish Prophet to Gentile God: The Origins and Development of New Testament Christology* (Louisville: Westminster John Knox, 1991), 159.

3. Compare the review of this material by L. W. Hurtado, *One God, One Lord: Early Christian Devotion and Ancient Jewish Monotheism* (Philadelphia: Fortress Press, 1988). Hurtado distinguishes "personified divine attributes" (including Wisdom), exalted patriarchs, and principal angels. See also Casey, *From Jewish Prophet*, 78–96; J. D. G. Dunn, *Christology in the Making* (Philadelphia: Westminster, 1980); M. Hengel, *The Son of God* (Philadelphia: Fortress Press, 1976).

4. E.g., Dunn, *Christology in the Making*, 74; P. M. Casey, *Son of Man: The Interpretation and Influence of Daniel* (London: SPCK, 1979), 7–50.

5. For full discussion, see J. J. Collins, *Daniel* (Hermenia; Minneapolis: Fortress Press, 1993), 304–10.

6. Some ancient interpreters read this text so that the "Ancient One" and "the one like a son of man" are one and the same. This reading is found in some manuscripts of the Greek Bible, but it is incompatible with the Masoretic text.

7. On the continuity between the angels and the pagan gods, see further P. Hayman, "Monotheism—A Misused Word in Jewish Studies?" *JJS* 42 (1991): 1–15.

8. A. F. Segal, *Two Powers in Heaven* (Leiden: Brill, 1977), 36.

9. C. Rowland, *The Open Heaven* (New York: Crossroad, 1982), 94–113.

10. See P. J. Kobelski, *Melchizedek and Melchireša* (Washington, D.C.: Catholic Biblical Association, 1981), 3–23.

11. Ibid., 24–36.

12. Y. Yadin, *The Scrolls of the War of the Sons of Light against the Sons of Darkness* (Oxford: Oxford University Press, 1962), 230.

13. C. A. Newsom, *Songs of the Sabbath Sacrifice: A Critical Edition* (Atlanta: Scholars Press, 1985), 23.

14. J. J. Collins, "The Son of Man in First Century Judaism," *NTS* 38 (1992): 448–66.

15. Chs. 37–71 of *1 Enoch* are called the Similitudes or "parables" of Enoch.

16. See P. Alexander, "3 (Hebrew Apocalypse of) Enoch," in *The Old Testament Pseudepigrapha* (ed. J. H. Charlesworth; New York: Doubleday, 1983), 1:223–315.

17. P. W. van der Horst, *The Sentences of Pseudo-Phocylides* (Leiden: Brill, 1978), 185.

18. C. R. Holladay, *Poets* (vol. 2 of *Fragments from Hellenistic-Jewish Authors*; Atlanta: Scholars Press, 1989), 363–65.

19. Philo, *Life of Moses* 1:55–58; W. A. Meeks, "Moses as God and King," in *Religions in Antiquity* (ed. J. Neusner; Leiden: Brill, 1968), 354–71.

20. C. R. Holladay, *Theios Aner in Hellenistic Judaism* (Missoula, Mont.: Scholars Press, 1977), 125.

21. See J. J. Collins, *The Scepter and the Star* (New York: Doubleday, 1995), 154–72.

22. b. Ḥagiga 14a; b. Sanhedrin 38b.

23. Collins, *The Scepter and the Star*, 136–53.

24. The Teacher of Righteousness is believed by many scholars to have been the leader of the Qumran community that produced the Dead Sea Scrolls.

25. D. Winston, *Logos and Mystical Theology in Philo and Alexandria* (Cincinnati: Hebrew Union College Press, 1985).

26. Philo, *On the Cherubim* 36; Philo, *Who Is the Heir?* 2–5.

27. Cf. *On Dreams* 1.230–33; Segal, *Two Powers in Heaven*, 163.

28. Segal, *Two Powers in Heaven*, 159. The Hebrew text has "I am the god Bethel" (usually translated "the god of Bethel").

29. F. H. Colson, in the Loeb Classical Library, translates the phrase *en katachrēsei* as improper, but the reference is clearly to analogical usage.

30. Hurtado, *One God, One Lord,* 28–34; Hayman, "Monotheism—A Misused Word in Jewish Studies?" 6–7.

31. The significance of eschatological figures in this context is noted by P. A. Rainbow, "Jewish Monotheism as the Matrix for New Testament Christology: A Review Article," *NovT* 33 (1991): 88. The failure to note the new context created by eschatology is a flaw in Hurtado's otherwise excellent book.

32. The conclusion of M. de Jonge, "Monotheism and Christology," in *Early Christian Thought in Its Jewish Context* (ed. J. Barclay and J. Sweet; Cambridge: Cambridge University Press, 1996), that Jesus' relationship to the Father in the Gospel of John "did not in any way lead to his deification" is difficult to justify.

33. See A. Yarbro Collins, "The 'Son of Man' Tradition in the Book of Revelation," in *The Messiah* (ed. J. H. Charlesworth; Minneapolis: Fortress Press, 1992), 536–68.

34. In Rev 14:14, in contrast, "one like a Son of Man" appears as one in a series of angels. Whether the "Son of Man" in this passage should be identified as Christ is unclear.

35. For a fuller account see Dunn, *The Parting of the Ways,* 183–229.

36. See A. Yarbro Collins, *The Combat Myth in the Book of Revelation* (Missoula, Mont.: Scholars Press, 1976), 101–14.

37. Since both the Logos and the Danielic son of man were thought to be preexistent by first-century c.e. Jews (that is, to have been created before the rest of the world), Jesus was believed to be preexistent, too. In the Gospel of John, the Logos is not said to have been created: It simply was in the beginning. Eventually Christian doctrine would settle on the claim that Jesus was "begotten, not made."

38. R. Bauckham, *The Climax of Prophecy: Studies on the Book of Revelation* (Edinburgh: Clark, 1993), 118–49 ("The Worship of Jesus").

39. Christ appears as a seventh figure with six angels in Hermas, *Similitudes* 13:6–9 (mid-second century c.e.), in such a way as to suggest that he is the principal of the seven archangels.

40. H. Chadwick, *The Early Church* (Harmondsworth: Penguin, 1967), 85–86.

41. This position became known as "Patripassianism" (the doctrine that the Father suffers) because it implied that God the Father died on the cross, and as "Modalism" because it viewed the Father, Son, and Spirit as modes of the same being.

42. For a summary of the controversies and illustrative texts, see W. G. Rusch, *The Trinitarian Controversy* (Philadelphia: Fortress Press, 1980); and R. A. Norris, *The Christological Controversy* (Philadelphia: Fortress Press, 1980).

43. E. R. Goodenough, *By Light, Light: The Mystical Gospel of Hellenistic Judaism* (New Haven: Yale, 1935), 121–234.

ACKNOWLEDGMENTS

The author and publisher gratefully acknowledge the following publications and publishers for their permission to employ specific articles in this volume:

1. "Is a Critical Biblical Theology Possible?" in William H. Propp et al., eds., *The Hebrew Bible and Its Interpreters* (Winona Lake, Ind.: Eisenbrauns, 1990), 1–17. Used by permission.
2. "Biblical Theology and the History of Israelite Religion," in Kevin J. Cathcart and John F. Healey, eds., *Back to the Sources, Biblical and Near Eastern Studies in Honour of Dermot Ryan* (Dublin: Glendale, 1989), 16–32.
3. "The Politics of Biblical Interpretation," in Carmel McCarthy and John F. Healey, eds., *Biblical and Near Eastern Essays in Honour of Kevin J. Cathcart* (London and New York: T&T Clark International, 2004), 195–211. Reprinted by permission of The Continuum International Publishing Group.
4. "Faith without Works: Biblical Ethics and the Sacrifice of Isaac," in S. Beyerle, G. Mayer, and H. Strauss, *Recht und Ethos im Alten Testament, Gestalt und Wirkung, Festschrift für Horst Seebass zum 65. Geburtstag* (Neukirchen-Vluyn: Neukirchener Verlag, 1999), 115–31.
5. "The Development of the Exodus Tradition," in J. W. van Henten and A. Houtepen, eds., *Religious Identity and the Invention of Tradition* (STAR 3; Assen: van Gorcum, 2001), 144–55. Used by permission.
6. "The Exodus and Biblical Theology," *BTB* 25 (1995): 152–60. Used by permission.
7. "The Biblical Vision of the Common Good," in O. F. Williams and J. W. Houck, eds., *The Common Good and U.S. Capitalism* (Lanham, Md.: University Press of America, 1987), 50–69.
8. "The Biblical Precedent for Natural Theology," *JAARSup* 15/1 (1977) Supplement, B:35–67. Used by permission of the American Academy of Religion.
9. "Proverbial Wisdom and the Yahwist Vision," *Semeia* 17 (1980): 1–18. Reprinted by permission of the Society of Biblical Literature.

10. "Natural Theology and Biblical Tradition: The Case of Hellenistic Judaism," *CBQ* 60 (1998): 1–15. Used by permission of the Catholic Biblical Association.

11. "Temporality and Politics in Jewish Apocalyptic Literature," in C. Rowland and J. Barton, eds., *Apocalyptic in History and Tradition* (JSPSup 43; Sheffield: Sheffield Academic Press, 2003), 26–43.

12. "The Book of Truth: Daniel as Reliable Witness to Past and Future in the United States of America," with Adela Yarbro Collins, in Mariano Delgado, Klaus Koch, and Edgar Marsch, eds., *Europa, Tausendjähriges Reich und neue Welt: Zwei Jahrtausende Geschichte und Utopie in der Rezeption des Danielbuches* (Freiburg: Universitätsverlag, 2003), 385–404. Used by permission.

13. "The Legacy of Apocalypticism," adapted from "Apocalyptic Literature," in Leo Perdue, ed., *The Blackwell Companion to the Hebrew Bible* (Oxford: Blackwell, 2001), 432–47. Used by permission.

14. "Jesus and the Messiahs of Israel," in H. Lichtenberger, ed., *Geschichte-Tradition-Reflexion: Festschrift für Martin Hengel* (Tübingen: Mohr, 1996), 3.287–302. Used by permission.

15. "Jewish Monotheism and Christian Theology," in H. Shanks and J. Meinhardt, *Aspects of Monotheism* (Washington, D.C.: Biblical Archaeology Society, 1997), 81–105.

INDEX OF MODERN AUTHORS

Aberle, D. F., 219
Adam, A. K. M., 37, 57, 198
Ahlstrom, S. E., 223
Aichele, G., 198
Albertz, R., 60, 61, 62, 63, 65, 204, 205
Albright, W. F., 38, 39, 40, 41, 43, 151, 198, 199, 224
Alexander, P., 229
Allis, O. T., 150
Alt, A., 38, 199, 208
Alter, R., 19, 194, 203
Anderson, B. W., 208
Armstrong, A. H., 217
Assmann, J., 61, 204
Ateek, N. S., 199
Attridge, H. W., 218
Auerbach, E., 57, 194, 203
Aune, D. E., 221
Austin, J. D., 144

Bacon, F., 149
Barclay, J. M. G., 218
Barr, J., 2, 6, 18, 20, 25, 35, 91, 117, 191, 192, 193, 194, 195, 196,

198, 206, 207, 209, 214, 216, 217, 224
Barth, K., 20, 21, 57, 117, 216
Barton, J., 193, 194, 196, 207
Batson, D., 216
Batto, B. F., 206
Bauckham, R., 230
Bauer-Kayatz, C., 211
Baum, G. 210
Baumgarten, A., 131, 133, 219
Beardslee W. A., 196, 214
Begg, C. T., 220
Beker, C., 216
Benjamin, W., 140, 221
Berger, K., 208, 228
Berger, P. L., 195, 213, 214
Berrigan, D., 140, 153, 154, 221, 224
Betz, H. D., 197
Black, M., 215
Blenkinsopp, J., 208, 209
Bliss, S., 222, 223
Bloom, H., 130, 219
Blum, E., 60, 61, 200, 201, 203, 206

Borgen, P., 226
Borris, B. von, 218
Bovon, F., 201
Boyancé, P., 217
Boyer, P., 223, 225
Brekus, C., 221
Briggs, C. A., 150
Bright, J., 198
Brooten, B. J., 217
Brueggemann, W., 5, 6, 70, 71, 91, 192, 206, 207, 210, 214
Brunner, E , 216
Brunner, H., 211, 216
Buber, M., 162, 225
Bull, M., 221
Bultmann, R. K., 3, 14, 15, 30, 31, 164, 191, 197, 225
Burkert, W., 201
Burridge, K., 130, 219

Caird, B. G., 194
Campbell, A., 145, 199
Cancik, H., 133, 220, 225
Carroll, R. P., 198
Casey, P. M., 229
Chadwick, H., 217, 230

Charles, R. H., 152, 224
Charlesworth, J. H., 221, 225
Childs, B., 4, 15–16, 17, 25, 26, 27, 28, 31, 32, 33, 48, 50, 56, 65, 71, 72, 73, 91, 152, 192, 193, 195, 196, 197, 200, 201, 203, 205, 207, 208, 209, 211, 224
Chilton, B. D., 202
Clark, M. W., 105, 215, 216
Coats, G. W., 49, 200, 201
Cobb, J. B., 92, 210, 214
Collingwood, R. G., 35, 198
Collins, J. J., 192, 194, 196, 197, 209, 215, 216, 217, 219, 220, 221, 223, 224, 225, 226, 227, 229
Colson, F. H., 230
Cook, E. M., 226
Cook, S., 130, 131, 219
Coote, R., 207, 209
Cox, H., 91
Crenshaw, J., 91, 103, 191, 209, 211, 212, 213, 214, 215, 216
Croatto, J. S., 70, 206
Cross, F. M., 205, 211, 227
Crossan, J. D., 98, 105, 112, 155, 212, 215

Daly, R. J., 202, 203
Davies, P. R., 38, 197, 202
Day, J., 196, 206, 225
Delcor, M., 197
Delgado, M., 220
Denzinger, H., 216
DeRoche, M., 207
Dever, W., 43, 199, 203, 204, 206
Dewart, L., 210
Dillon, J., 120, 217
Doan, R. A., 142, 148, 221, 222, 223
Donahue, J. R., 209
Dozeman, T., 69, 206
Dunn, J. D. G., 228, 229, 230
Durkheim, E., 148

Eddy, S. K., 220
Eden, C., 199
Edwards, J., 144
Eichrodt, W., 11, 13, 24, 25, 193, 195
Eisenman, R., 226
Eissfeldt, O., 51, 201, 215
Eldredge, L., 193, 195
Epstein, L., 208
Erdman, C., 150
Evans, C. A., 202
Evans, R. J., 200

Feldman, L. H., 218
Fensham, F. C., 216
Festinger, L., 159, 225
Fewell, D. N., 198
Fichtner, J., 213
Fierro, A., 206
Finkelstein, I., 41, 42, 44, 199, 203
Fish, S., 37, 198
Fishbane, M., 72, 207, 208
Fitzmyer, J. A., 217, 227
Flanagan, J. W., 210
Flusser, D., 169, 220
Fohrer, G., 213
Fox, M., 191
Frei, H., 203
Frerichs, E. S., 225
Fretheim, T. E., 196, 197
Friedman, R. E., 204
Fuchs, H., 221
Fuks, A., 218
Funk, R., 155

Gabler, J. P., 11, 13, 24
Gadamer, H. G., 16, 193, 195, 198
Gager, J. G., 219
Geertz, C., 157, 206
Gemser, B., 211
Georgi, D., 213
Gese, H., 93, 98, 113, 197, 210, 212, 213, 214, 216

Gilkey, L., 25, 193, 195, 210
Gnuse, R., 207, 209
Goedicke, H., 204
Goldingay, J., 152, 197, 224
Goodenough, E. R., 230
Görg, M., 218
Gottwald, N., 21, 26, 27, 40, 41, 43, 69, 80, 194, 195, 196, 199, 208
Gowan, D. E., 212
Grabbe, L. L., 224
Gray, R., 228
Green, W. S., 225
Greenberg, M., 52, 202
Grelot, P. P., 227
Griffin, L., 208
Griffiths, J. G., 204
Gruen, E., 204
Gunkel, H., 18, 48, 49, 53, 194, 200
Gunn, D. M., 198
Gustafson, J., 208
Gutiérrez, G., 69, 70, 73, 206, 207

Halpern, B., 62, 204
Hals, R. M., 202
Hanson, J. S., 209, 228
Hanson, P., 130, 196, 207, 211, 219
Harrelson, W., 208
Harvey, A. E., 228
Harvey, V. A., 13, 35, 92, 193, 194, 195, 198, 210
Hasel, G., 152, 207
Hauerwas, S., 192
Hayes, J. H., 193
Hayman, P., 229

Hayward, C. T. R., 202
Heidegger, M., 96, 164, 211, 212, 213
Heider, G. C., 202
Heinisch, P., 217
Hendel, R., 204
Hengel, M., 169, 171, 175, 213, 225, 226, 227, 228
Hermisson, H. J., 211, 215, 216
Hodge, A. A., 149, 223
Hodge, C., 149
Höffken, P., 220
Holladay, C. R., 229
Horsley, R. A., 209, 228
Horst, P. W. van der, 229
Houck, J. W., 208
Hultgård, A., 220, 221
Hume, D., 117, 149
Hurtado, L. W., 229, 230
Huxley, T. H., 43

Iersel, B. van, 69

Jacobson, D., 199
Jaeger, W., 210, 211, 216, 217
Jaspers, K., 212
Jefferson, T., 165
Jeremias, J., 226
Jolles, A., 107, 108, 109, 215
Jonge, M. de, 228, 230
Joyce, R., 224
Juel, D., 176, 228

Kant, I., 35, 56, 57, 198, 203
Kaufman, G., 210
Kaufman, S. A., 220
Kayatz, C., 213
Kelsey, D., 20, 57, 194, 203
Kierkegaard, S., 49, 54, 56, 201
Kilian, R., 200
King, M. L. Jr., 71, 153

Kitchen, K. A., 67, 152
Knauf, E. A., 204, 205
Knierim, R., 196
Knight, D. A., 206, 207, 208
Knohl, I., 205
Knox, J., 117
Kobelski, P. J., 227, 229
Koch, K., 99, 151, 155, 213, 220, 224
Kolakowski, L., 202
Kraus, H. J., 205
Krentz, E., 198
Kugel, J. L., 202
Kuhn, T., 43, 200

Lambert, W. G., 216
Lang, B., 209
Larcher, C., 217
Lawrence, D. H., 139, 221
Leach, E., 212
Lemche, N. P., 206
Lerch, D., 201
Levenson, J., 3, 4, 13, 50, 66, 68, 70, 71, 73, 191, 192, 193, 195, 198, 200, 201, 202, 205, 206, 207, 209, 219
Liberg, G., 217
Licht, J., 221
Lindbeck, G. A., 16, 194, 219
Lindsey, H., 148, 156, 223, 225
Locke, J., 149
Loewenstamm, S. E., 208
Lohfink, N., 206
Long, A. A., 217
Lull, D. J., 194, 196
Luther, M., 49, 201

Machen, J. G., 150
Mack, B. L., 208, 214
MacMullen, R., 221
Malamat, A., 204
Malinowski, B., 212
Mannheim, K., 130, 136,

219
Marböck, J., 213
Marsch, E. 220
Marsden, G. M., 223, 224
Martin, D. B., 198
Martin, W. J., 224
Marty, M. E., 224
Mason, S., 220
Mathews, S., 150
McCarthy, D. J., 206
McGinn, B., 222
McIntyre, A., 198, 203
McKane, W., 96, 109, 212, 215
McKenzie, J. L., 214, 216
Meland, B. E., 215
Mendelson, A., 218, 219
Mendenhall, G., 40, 41, 68, 69, 199, 209, 210
Metzger, B. M., 197
Meyers, C. L., 224
Middendorp, T., 213
Miles, J. A., 194
Milik, J. T., 203, 227
Miller, W., 145, 146, 147
Mitchell, T. C., 224
Moberly, W., 56, 57, 203
Modrzejewski, J. M., 218
Montgomery, J. A., 151, 224
Moor, J. C. de, 204, 205
Moore, G. F., 53, 202
Moorhead, J., 222
Müller, H. P., 201
Müller, U. B., 226
Murphy, N., 192
Murphy, R., 95, 210, 211

Nation, M., 192
Neusner, J., 194, 225
Newsom, C. A., 229
Nicholson, E. W., 68, 205
Nickelsburg, G. W. E., 197
Nilsson, M. P., 218
Norris, R. A., 230
Noth, M., 64, 205
Novak, M. 210

Ochs, P., 192
O'Connor, F., 141, 221
O'Connor, M. P., 224
Oden, R. A., 26, 195
Ogden, S. M., 194, 196
O'Leary, S., 148, 222, 223
Ollenburger, B. C., 195
Otto, R., 98

Pannenberg, W., 191
Parente, F., 220
Parker, T., 142, 143, 144, 145, 146, 221, 222
Patrick, D., 196, 208
Patton, F. L., 149
Paul, S., 207, 209
Paz, O., 211
Pelikan, J., 217, 218
Pépin, J., 210, 217
Perdue, L., 191, 192, 205, 206, 207
Perlitt, L., 207
Perrin, N., 156, 157, 225
Pfeifer, G., 213
Philonenko, M., 221
Pixley, G., 70, 71, 206
Pleins, D. J., 199
Pomykala, K. E., 225, 226
Preuss, H. D., 93, 94, 105, 113, 210, 211, 213, 214, 215, 216
Prissner, F., 193
Pritchard, J. B., 209, 216
Propp, W. H., 64, 205
Puech, E., 171, 173, 174, 225, 226, 227, 228
Pusey, E. B., 28, 176, 196

Rad, G. von, 4, 11, 14, 24, 47, 48, 50, 64, 68, 69, 71, 96, 97, 98, 100, 108, 110, 111, 112, 113, 114, 192, 193, 195, 200, 201, 202, 205, 206, 207, 211, 212, 213, 214, 215, 216
Rainbow, P. A., 230

Ramsey, I., 110, 215
Rankin, O. S., 213
Reid, T., 149
Reider, J., 218
Rendtorff, R., 64, 200, 203, 205
Reventlow, H. G., 48, 200, 201
Ricoeur, P., 16, 20, 21, 158, 194, 195, 197, 225
Riecken, W., 225
Rinngren, H., 213
Rist, J. M., 217
Robinson, A. W., 210
Robinson, J. A. T., 156
Rorty, R., 4, 192
Roth, W. M. W., 215
Rouiller, G., 201
Rowe, D. L., 148, 222, 223
Rowland, C., 136, 197, 221, 229
Rusch, W. G., 230
Russell, D. S., 197
Ryan, D., 24, 32, 195
Rylaarsdam, J. C., 95, 96, 211, 212, 213

Sandeen, E. R., 223, 224
Sanders, J. A., 27, 31, 72, 76, 196, 207, 208
Sandys-Wunsch, J., 193, 195
Sarna, N., 49, 51, 201, 202
Satran, D., 220
Schachter, S., 225
Schäfer, P., 219
Schiffman, L., 170, 225
Schleiermacher, F., 98
Schmid, H. H., 204, 211, 212
Schmidt, J., 215
Schneerson, M., 177
Schneidau, H., 105, 112, 113, 115, 214, 215, 216
Scholes, R., 108, 215
Schönmetzer, A., 216

Schürer, E., 225
Schüssler Fiorenza, E., 221
Schweitzer, A., 43, 164, 175, 200, 227
Scott, R. B. Y., 211, 213
Sedley, D. N., 217
Seebass, H., 49, 200, 201, 203
Segal, A. F., 229
Seters, J. van, 200, 204
Sevenster, J. N., 219
Shea, W., 152
Sheler, J. L., 228
Sheppard, G., 73, 207
Shulman, D., 201, 203
Sievers, J., 220
Silberman, N. A., 39, 199
Skladny, U., 212
Smith, M., 170, 225
Smith-Christopher, D., 134, 153, 220, 224
Smolinski, R., 144, 222
Snell, B., 109, 215
Snow, S. S., 147
Soggin, J. A., 205
Specter, M., 228
Spiegel, S., 202
Stager, L. E., 201
Starcky, J., 226
Stein, S. J., 222, 223
Stendahl, K., 3, 191, 194, 208
Stern, M., 218
Sternberg, M., 19, 21, 57, 194, 195, 203
Stone, M. E., 226
Stuhlmacher, P., 194, 195
Sturm, R., 224
Sullivan, W. M., 192
Swain, J. W., 136, 220
Swetnam, J., 202, 203

Talmon, S., 202
Tcherikover, A., 218
Thiel, J. E., 192
Thompson, B. P., 224
Thompson, J. M., 215, 216
Thompson, T. L., 38, 197

Thrupp, S., 219
Tiller, P. A., 221
Tillich, P., 100
Tobin, T. H., 217
Tracy, D., 92, 98, 194, 206, 208, 210, 212
Troeltsch, E., 12, 14, 15, 16, 17, 18, 26, 193, 194, 195, 198
Toorn, K. van der, 60, 61, 63, 204, 205
Trible, P., 202
Tucker, G. M., 206
Turner, V., 115, 214, 216

VanderKam, J. C., 202, 203, 225, 226
Vaux, R. de, 202, 209
Vawter, B., 197, 212
Veijola, T., 56, 200, 203
Vermes, G., 202, 203, 226
Voegelin, E., 106

Waltzer, M., 207

Warfield, B. B., 149, 205, 223
Weber, M., 130, 219
Weiler, A., 69
Weinfeld, M., 202, 206, 213
Weiss, J., 164
Wellhausen, J., 68, 69, 206
Westermann, C., 48, 49, 52, 56, 200, 201, 202, 203, 206
Whitelam, K. W., 34, 38, 39, 41, 42, 43, 44, 197, 198, 199, 209
Whybray, R. N., 213, 215
Widengren, G., 221
Wiesehöfer, J., 220
Wilken, R. L., 214
Williams, O. F., 208
Wilson, R. D., 150, 151, 152, 224
Winston, D., 124, 217, 229
Wise, M. O., 226

Wiseman, D., 152, 224
Wismer, P. L., 195
Wolff, H. W., 207, 214
Wolff, S. R., 201
Wolfson, H. A., 214
Woude, A. van der, 220
Wrede, W., 12, 13, 14, 15, 23, 25, 193, 194, 195
Wright, G. E., 13, 14, 17, 20, 25, 91, 105, 193, 195, 196, 214, 216
Wright, M. R., 217

Yadin, Y., 229
Yarbro Collins, A., 142, 209, 221, 225, 228, 230
Yoder, J. H., 206
Young, E. J., 152, 224

Zenger, E., 205
Zimmerli, W., 52, 94, 95, 200, 202, 211

INDEX OF ANCIENT LITERATURE

HEBREW BIBLE

Genesis

5:24	182
22	47, 51, 54
22:1-4	47, 48
22:1-3	49
22:1-2	48
22:3-10	48
22:4-10	49
22:9-14	49
22:11-12	48
22:11, 14	48
22:13	48
22:15-19	48
22:15-18	48, 50, 53
22:19	47, 48
31:13	185
49	226
49:9	170

Exodus

1–15	19
1–5	60
2:11	61
3:7-8	65, 70–71
4:22-23	124
7:1	183
15:22—18:27	68
17:1-7	68
20:11	81
20:22—23:33	82
21:2-6	83
21:12-13	79
22:24	83
22:28-29	52
23:10-11	82
23:12	81
23:13	62
34:18	61
34:19-20	52

Leviticus

18:21	51
19:5	87
20:2-5	51
25	82
25:20-21	82
25:23	81
25:25	209
25:35-37	83
25:39-46	82
25:42	82
25:55	65, 70

Numbers

24	170
24:7	171
25	32

Deuteronomy

4:6	102
5:2-3	207
5:13-14	82
6:4	81
6:24	70
8:17-18	81
12:31	51
15	82
15:4	82
15:7	82
15:9	83
15:11, 12	82
15:12-18	83
18:10	51
23:20	83
24:10-13	83
24:19-22	82
26	63
27:21	83
29:14-15	73
33	63

Joshua

3–5	61
24	61, 63

Judges

5	63
6:13	204
11	63
11:13	204
11:31	53
19:25	80

1 Samuel

4:28	204

2 Samuel

7	173, 174, 226
7:6-23	204
7:12-14	174
7:14	183

1 Kings

11:28	61
12	60
17	176
19:6	227
21	85
22	55
22:23	55

2 Kings

3:21-27	54
16:3	51
21:6	51
23:10	51

Ezra

7:7	144
7:14, 25	102

Nehemiah

10:31	82

Job

8:8	114
28	102
28:13	100

28:25-27	100
42:3	98

Psalms

2	173, 174, 226
2:7	183
2:9	171
19:1	120
37:25	114
45	173
68	63
110	173
110:1	184
110:4	188

Proverbs

1–9	96, 99, 100, 107
1:20	96
1:26-27	100
3:7	97, 101, 216
3:16	101
3:19	100
4:5-6	101
8	99
8:2-3	96
8:22	184
8:27, 30, 31	100
9:1	106
10:15	107
10:30	99
11:28	115
14:4	107
16:1	97, 112
16:2, 9	215
19:14, 21	215
19:31	97
20:24	215
21:30	97, 113
21:30-31	112
22:2	115
24:30-34	114
25:25	109
26:4-5	108
26:6	107
26:11	109
26:12	113
26:17	107

27:1	97, 99, 113
27:7	107
27:8	109
27:10, 23-24	107
28:13	213
28:26	216
29:13	115
30:4	95
30:18-19	110, 111
30:20	111
30:24-28	110

Qoheleth

3:1-8	114
3:19-22	32
6:1-3	115
9:13-16	114
12	111

Isaiah

5:8	85, 87
7:23	87
10:5	86
11	170
11:2	170
11:4	170, 171, 172
11:5	170
26:19	31
26, 66	32
27:1	157
31:1-3	86
40:3-5	19
42:1-4	172
42:6	172
43:16-20	106
43:16	75
43:18-19	75
44:25	113
49:1-7	172
49:6	172
50:4-9	172
51:9-11	19, 75
52:13—53:12	172
53	153, 172
53:7, 8	172
57:5	51
61:1	175

Jeremiah
9:23   113
19:4-6   51
23   226
23:18   95
23:28   203
33   226

Ezekiel
20:25-26   52
28:2   97
37   31

Daniel
1–6   29, 31, 151
2   131, 144
2:38   134
4:16   135
4:31   174
7–12   28, 31
7   132, 134, 136, 142,
     156, 172, 173, 174, 187
7:8   143
7:9   180, 184
7:13-14   180
7:14   174, 186
7:27   132, 138
8   144
8:9   143
8:14   143,144
9   143,144, 158
9:25   144
10–12   137
10:13   180
11   151, 162
11:2-39   32
11:35   137
11:40-45   32
12   31, 154, 182
12:1   173
12:7   143
12:12   144

Hosea
11   30

Amos
2:6-8   85

2:7   74
2:10   74
3:1-2   74
3:1   74
3:6   74
5:25   74
6:1-6   86
7   30
8:5   81
9   226
9:7   74

Micah
4:4   87
6   74
6:6-8   52
6:8   75

Habakkuk
3   63

Zechariah
1–8   130
9:9   228

———————————————

NEW TESTAMENT

Matthew
11:2-5   176
11:2   176
11:10   176
21:1-11   228
22:34-40   75
25   209
25:31   187

Mark
1:1-10   228
6:4   176
6:14-15   176
8:27   176
12:28-34   75
12:35-37   184

Luke
1:32, 35   174

4:17-19   175
7:22   176
7:27   176
10:15-28   75
12:16-20   115
19:29-38   228
24:19   186

John
1:1   179
5:18   179
6:14   176
10:30   188
12:12-16   228
19:7   187

Acts
2:34-36   184

Romans
1:4   187
1:19-20   121
2:28-29   125
11   144

1 Corinthians
15:19   164

Philippians
2:10-11   188

Hebrews
1:5   188
5:6   188
11:17-19   49
11:32-34   53

James
2:21-23   47
2:26   58

Revelation
1:13-14   187
3:15-16   160
4:1-2   129
5:13   188
10   160

11	176	18:13	124	*3 Enoch*	
12	188	18:24	125	4:1	182
12:11	187	19:13	125	10:1	182
13	163			12:5	182
14:14	230	*Ben Sira*		16:3	182
19	129	1:26	102		
19:15	178	22:14	111	*4 Ezra*	
19:18	139	24:2-5	184	12	136
19:20	188	24:23	101, 102	12:11-12	134, 158
20	129	33:2	102	12:32-33	135
20:6	164	33:8	114	13	172, 173, 174, 178
21	130	44–50	101	13:35	173
21:24	138	44:8-9	102		
22:9	188	48:3	176	*Jubilees*	
				17:16	54
		1 Maccabees		31:12-20	226

APOCRYPHA

		1:54	159	*Psalms of Solomon*	
		2:26	32	17:21-25	171
Wisdom of Solomon		4:54	159		
1–5	122	6:49, 53	82	*Sibylline Oracles*	
1:6	124			3:765-66	53, 202
1:7	106	*2 Maccabees*		5:252	138
1:7	119	2:18	131		
2:13-20	124			*Testament of Judah*	
2:13, 16	187			21	226
7–9	122	**PSEUDEPIGRAPHA**			
7:22—8:1	119			*Testament of Levi*	
7:23	124	*Baruch*		18	226
7:25-26	119	3:9-37	102		
8:1	106	4:1	102	*Testament (Assumption)*	
9	120	4:3-4	102	*of Moses*	
9:14-17	121			9:7	137
9:14-16	120	*1 Enoch*			
10–19	122, 123	10	138		
10:5, 6, 10	102	22	32	**DEAD SEA SCROLLS**	
10:15-18	76	46:1	181		
10:15	124	48:5	186	*1QM*	
11:17	119	48:10	172	11:6-7	171
11:24—12:1	124	52:4	172	11:7	227
12:10-11	125	60–62	181		
12:19	124	71:14	182	*1QS*	
13–15	122	91:12	137	9:11	169
13:1-9	120	91:13	138		
16:2, 3, 5	124	94:7	139	*1Qsa*	170
16:10, 21, 26	124	104	32, 139, 182		
18:4	124			*1QpIs*	170
18:6	124				
18:9	124				

1Qsb   170

11QMelchizedek   175
2:18   176, 227

4Q174   170, 183

4Q175   170

4Q225   54, 55

4Q246   173, 183

4Q285   170, 172

4Q491   184

4Q521   175, 176
12   175

4Q541/4QAaronA 171, 172
12   175

CD
2:12   227
6:1   227
7:19   171

HELLENISTIC JEWISH
AUTHORS

Josephus
Against Apion
1.228–50   204

Antiquities
10:195–210   135
10:210   135
10:276   135
20.169–71   228

Jewish war
2.258–60   177, 228
2.261–62   228

Philo
On the Cherubim
36   229

Decalogue
12§§52–54   121, 219
66   218

On Dreams
1.227–229   185
1.230–33   229

Qu. in Genesis
2.60   124, 218

Qu. in Exodus
2.2   219

De Opificio Mundi
1.3(1)   102, 118–19, 214
1§3   217

On the Special Laws
1.12–17§§66–97   219
1.3§§13–20   217
2.29§163   219
2:282   208

Life of Moses
1.7§35   123, 218
1.55–58   229
2.7§44   219

De Virtutibus
51–174   125

Pseudo-Philo
Biblical Antiquities
32:2–3   55

CLASSICAL SOURCES

Herodotus
1.30, 1.95   220

Cicero
De natura deorum
2.5§15   217
2.61§153   217
2.47§154   218

Dionysius of Halicarnassus
1.2.1–4   220

Diodorus Siculus
40.3.4   125, 218
34/35.1.1   125, 219

Plato
Laws
10   121, 217

Republic
382C, 414B, 459   29, 197

Polybius
29:21   133, 220, 225

Plutarch
Moralia
1.6(329A–B)   218

Seneca
De otio
4.1   218

Suetonius
Augustus
31.1   221

Tacitus
Historiae
5.8–8   220

Velleius Paterculus
(Aemilius Sura)
1.6.6   132, 220

Virgil
Aeneid
1.278–79   133

RABBINIC
LITERATURE

MISHNAH AND TALMUD
y. Sheqalim
3:3   228
y. Ta'anit
68d   171
b. Sanhedrin
38b   229
89b   54
m. Sotah
9   228
B. Hagiga
14a   229
Baba Batra
3b–4a   135, 220

GENESIS RABBAH
56:4   201

TAN. MISHPATIM
4   220

PESIQTA DE R. KAHANA
76a   228

───────────────

CHRISTIAN SOURCES

Augustine
City of God
6–8   118
6.5, 6, 12   216
8.6   217

Eusebius
Praeparatio evangelica
13.12.1   217

Diogenes Laertius
Lives and Opinions of
Eminent Philosophers
7.1§148   217
7.1§33   218

Hermas
Similitudes
13:6–9   230

───────────────

EGYPTIAN SOURCES

Amen-em-opet
19:16   113
19:13   113